THE COPPER & LEAD MINES
around the
MANIFOLD VALLEY
North Staffordshire

Lindsey Porter & John Robey

'There is a point, called the Great Opening, where if a good stone thrower was to stand in its centre it would be impossible for him to hit the sides or roof of this artificial cavern with a stone, the distance being too great.' – a reference to the Ecton Mine by W Niness, a mining engineer, in the *Mining Journal* of November 24th, 1883

Ecton Copper Mine Dressing Floor in the mid 1880s. The photograph is taken above the tips

'In the large open we have landed upon a heap of loose stuff, but a considerable extent of water exists to the north and west and we can see no side in either direction' – from the report of the unwatering of the Clayton Mine, by William Bowman, Managing Director, in the *Mining Journal* of Oct 27th, 1884

Depths were usually referred to in fathoms; one fathom equalling six feet. This traditional notation has been used throughout this book and has not been converted to either yards or metric.

[See page 4 for a conversion table]

Contents

1	Introduction	5
2	Geology and Mineralogy of the North-East Staffordshire Mines	16
3	Ecton Mines	27
	3.1 Introduction	27
	3.2 The Early History to 1760	38
	3.3 The Duke's Mine, 1760-1818	50
	3.4 The Burgoyne Mineral Field, 1648-1818	67
	3.5 Exploration and Expectation	72
	3.6 Social Conditions	98
	3.7 Ore Production	104
4	The Dale and Other Mines, Warslow	110
5	The Mines of the Upper Elkstones Area	135
6	Mixon Mines	151
7	Butterton & Grindon	173
8	Wetton Alstonfield, Ilam & Newton Grange	179
	8.1 Bincliff Mine	179
	8.2 Mining at Ilam	188
	8.3 Newton Grange	193
9	Mines South of the River Manifold	196
	9.1 Mines at Blore, Calton, Swinscoe & Waterfall	196
	9.2 Ribden & Thorswood Mines	199
	9.3 Oakamoor & Stanton Mining Company	215
10	Richard Niness of Warslow	218
11	Ore Dressing in the Manifold Valley	222
12	Smelting	236
	12.1 Smelting of Ecton Ore Prior to 1764	236
	12.2 The Whiston Copper Works	237
	12.3 Greenlowfield Smelting Mill, Alstonfield	242
	12.4 Mill Dale Calamine Mill	245
	12.5 Ellastone	246
	12.6 Packhorse Routes to Whiston	247
13	The Ellastone Smelter Survey	249
14	North Staffordshire Copper and Lead Mining Terms	252
15	Bibliography of papers on North Staffordshire Mines	262
	Subscribers List	264
	Index	267

Landmark Collector's Library

The Copper and Lead Mines Around the Manifold Valley, North Staffordshire

Published by
Landmark Publishing Ltd,
Waterloo House, 12 Compton, Ashbourne, Derbyshire DE6 1DA England
Tel: (01335) 347349 Fax: (01335) 347303 e-mail: landmark@clara.net

ISBN 1 901 522 77 6

© **Lindsey Porter and John Robey 2000**

The rights of the authors of this work
has been asserted by him in accordance with the Copyright,
Design and Patents Act, 1993.

All rights reserved. No part of this publication may be reproduced, stored in a retrieval system or transmitted in any form or by any means, electronic, mechanical, photocopying, recording or otherwise without the prior permission of Landmark Publishing Ltd.

British Library Cataloguing in Publication Data: a catalogue record for this book is available from the British Library.

Print: MPG Ltd, Bodmin, Cornwall
Editor: Dr T. D. Ford
Design: Mark Titterton

Front cover: Ecton in 1884 showing the double-track incline from Clayton to the dressing floor
Back cover: The 160 fathoms deep engine shaft in Clayton Mine, Ecton

CONVERSION TABLE

1 Fathom = 6 Feet
Feet to Metres x 0.305
Yards to Metres x 0.914
Metres to Yards x 1.094

DISCLAIMER
The publishers and authors accept no responsibility for any loss, injury or inconvenience sustained by anyone entering or approaching old mine workings. They should be regarded as dangerous and avoided.

1 Introduction

This is the story of local history around the Manifold Valley. It is woven around the fortunes of the copper and lead mines of the area. In the 18th Century, wealthy people invested money in the mines, hoping that the 'boat would come in'. For forty years at Ecton, the proverbial boat 'docked'. In the 19th Century, fortunes were spent trying to repeat the Duke of Devonshire's good fortune. Some of these ventures were well capitalised, others mere trials. Some involved people who appear to have been less than fair, if not downright dishonest.

The Upper Hamps Valley saw five law suits in fifteen years and another perhaps more serious case which nearly went to law over £1,000 'misappropriated' money. At Mixon Mine in 1840, a widow even had to resort to law to recover the wages of her recently deceased husband, as if the loss of the breadwinner and presumably hungry mouths to feed was not enough.

This is not just the story of an ancient and defunct industry, it is the story of a hard way of life that was taken for granted and is now not even a memory. Care has been taken to try and show glimpses of this way of life, so that we can appreciate how our forefathers and mothers lived.

Mines of copper, lead and zinc are scattered throughout the Carboniferous Limestone areas of North Staffordshire, with occasional workings in the neighbouring Triassic Sandstones, such as the copper mine at Snelston, south of Ashbourne. Standing head and shoulders above the rest of the mines in terms of size, output and historical significance are those on Ecton Hill. Here the Ecton Mine became, for a short time, the richest and deepest mine in the country.

This book looks at the activities of these non-ferrous mines in North Staffordshire. In many cases, it is known that a lease to extract minerals was granted but other subsequent records as to the production or even the exact location of the mines are completely lacking especially where a lease covered a whole estate. Elsewhere, mineral workings may be found, but with no historical details as to when they were worked or who was involved. The recent discovery of prehistoric hammer stones and an antler pick on Ecton Hill would seem to indicate workings here which are amongst the oldest in the country, but nothing else is known about mining activity in this period.

In many cases, the nature of the documentation is very incomplete. Account books, which can be informative and which are the most important source of material for the Ecton Mines in the eighteenth century are virtually non-existent for the remaining mines. However this is, to some extent, compensated by the reports which appeared in the *Mining Journal*. Also, being outside the area of jurisdiction of the Derbyshire Barmasters and the Barmoot Courts, there are not many records from that source.

Nevertheless, in many instances, a fairly complete picture can be pieced together of the mine's history.

From time to time the picture may be found to vary as new records are found. The chance discovery of some early mining records at the Derbyshire Record Office amongst uncatalogued domestic records of the Harpur family came as a surprise, especially as those on the Ecton Mine have a particularly important historical significance. Equally, some 400 documents came up for sale recently which also helped our understanding of early activity at mines other than Ecton and also highlighted the extraordinary deceit which brought about the closure of the Dale Mine near Warslow.

Other struggles, against difficulties both man made and natural, make a story that more than compensates the reader for the lack of ore output which characterised most of the mines.

1 Introduction

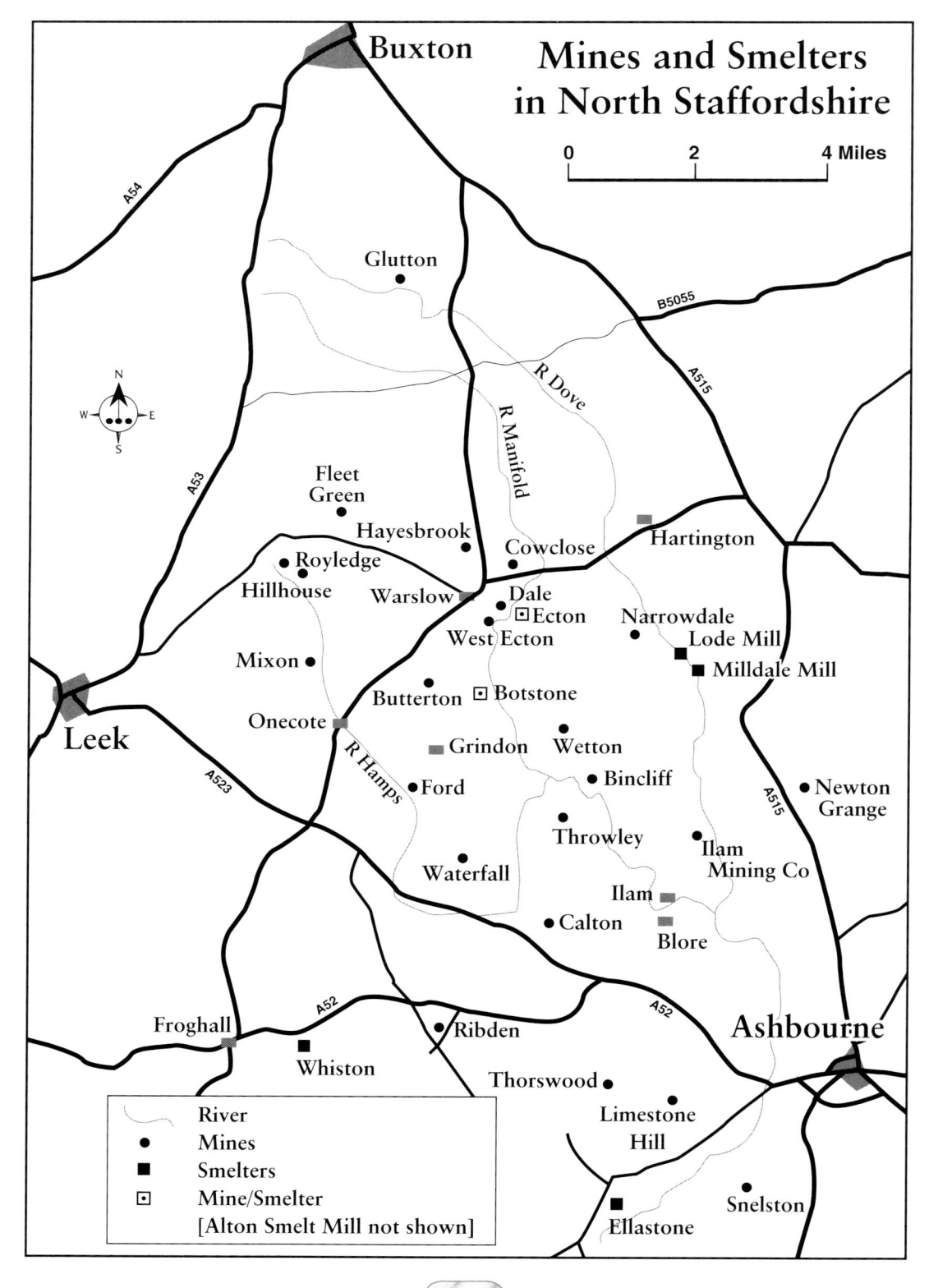

Mines and Smelters in North Staffordshire

1 Introduction

One feature of this history, which is of particular interest, is the social conditions of the workers. Although much more of this is known at Ecton, very little is known elsewhere. The complete disregard for the pollution the miners caused in the River Manifold is dealt with but equally important was the complete lack of concern this had on the people who depended upon the river for domestic water. Standards of welfare and concern for the wellbeing of others, especially employees, was far below the standards we expect today. Where information is available on the lives of people connected with the mines it is given. It helps us to improve our understanding of how our predecessors lived not too many decades ago.

Being outside the Derbyshire 'free' mining area (where anyone still has the right to mine lead ore by-and-large unrestricted, except by planning restraints, beyond the developed areas), the mineral rights belonged to private individuals (usually the owner of the land), so any mining of the land by other people was usually under a mineral lease. The ancient rights and customs in the 'Kings Field' of Derbyshire encouraged the establishment of many small mines employing little capital and few people. In North Staffordshire, the mines were worked by partnerships or Companies, initially on the cost-book principle and later by Limited Liability Companies. In a few instances, the mines were worked by the mineral owner (such as at Ecton where the mine was worked during its richest period by the Duke of Devonshire).

The working of mines by the mineral owner was the exception rather than the rule: generally the owner was quite happy to take his royalty and kept out of the management and control of the mines on his land. For instance, the Marquis of Bath had a royalty income from the Snailsbeach Mine in Shropshire of £3,000 a year for a long period. Also the Duke of Bedford, who at one stage was receiving over £10,000 a year from Devon Great Consols in the Tamar Valley, a fabulously rich mine which produced 742,400 tons of copper ore during 1845-1902, all with no financial risk to the owner.

In the years after the Restoration, the Earl of Shrewsbury worked the Ribden Mine, but nothing came of the venture and therefore he leased out his mines (1).

After the 17th Century, the Devonshire family at Ecton and Wetton, the Sneyds at Mixon provide the other examples in the area of a mine worked by its mineral owner. It would seem that the Mixon mine had been worked by John Sneyd since 1770 when he purchased an estate at Onecote (either for the mine or for shooting rights). His sons worked the mine in the early years of the 19th Century, investing in steam engines, waterwheels as well as purchasing the Duke of Devonshire's copper smelting works at Whiston, near Froghall. Unlike Ecton, the costs of keeping the mine free of water and the lack of good sized deposits of ore meant that the mine probably lost a fortune rather than made one.

After the abortive venture in the 17th Century, the Earls of Shrewbury seems to have kept out of mining speculation on their land and from what is known, this might have been a shrewd move. Unfortunately, very little is known of the history of the mines on their land.

The 18th Century mining activities in the area were largely dominated by the activities of the Gilbert brothers from Cotton near Oakamoor. They were engaged in mining at Mixon, Ribden, Thorswood, and Ecton as well as lead smelting at Lode Mill in Dovedale and at Dimmingsdale, near to Alton, in the Churnet Valley. Limestone quarrying at Cauldon Low, collieries, at Cheadle, Staffs, and canals were some of their other Staffordshire interests.

Until 1852, when the *Limited Liability Act* was passed, all companies worked on the cost book principle unless a special Act of Parliament was passed to enable them to be of limited liability. Basically, the cost-book system meant that the shareholders were personally liable to the full extent of the debts of the company, whilst the limited liability shareholders were limited to the extent of their shareholding in the company.

Consequently, all the companies and adventurers, as they were called, working the mines operated on the cost-book system until the mid-1850s. In the 18th Century, the losses which were likely to be incurred were generally not very great, for as the mine became deeper or wetter it was abandoned in favour of another vein or another part of the same vein.

An exception was the working of Ecton in 1723 when the adventurers are said to have

1 Introduction

Above: Ecton Engine House and the structure built for the counter balancing weight shaft in 1924. The base of the chimney can be seen to the right of the roof   **Below:** The formation of the last major Company to work non-ferrous metal mines in North Staffordshire

---

Nov. 3, 1883.]　　　　　　　THE MINING JOURNAL.　　　　　　　1259

THE ECTON COMPANY (LIMITED).

The SHARE LIST will **CLOSE** on MONDAY, NOV. 5TH, at Four o'clock in the afternoon.

THE ECTON COMPANY, LIMITED.

CAPITAL £50,000, IN 50,000 SHARES OF £1 EACH.

Deposit 1s. per share; upon allotment 2s. 6d. per share; three months after allotment 2s. 6d. per share; six months later 2s. 6d. per share. The Company is registered under the Companies Acts. The liability is strictly limited to the sum of £1 per share.

LOCAL DIRECTOR—WILLIAM BOWMAN, Esq., Alport, near Bakewell.
BANKERS—THE ALLIANCE BANK (LIMITED), Bartholomew Lane, E.C.
SOLICITOR—ALEX. WM. KERLY, Esq., 14, Great Winchester Street, E.C.
TEMPORARY OFFICES—80, CORNHILL, LONDON, E.C.
SECRETARY (pro tem.)—MR. F. STANDRING.

There is situated in the parish of Wetton, near the village of Warnslow, on the borders of Staffordshire and Derbyshire, one of the most remarkable groups of copper mines—known as the Ecton Mines—ever discovered in the United Kingdom.

For more than 50 years they are stated to have yielded a profit exceeding £70,000 per annum.

The Ecton Company has been formed to purchase leases of these marvellously rich mines, and to resume the working of them.

The Ecton Mine stands on a hill about 600 ft. above the River Manifold, and comprises about 1000 acres, partly on the property of his Grace the Duke of Devonshire and partly on the land of an adjoining proprietor. From very limited workings on the Duke's property, profits of about Two Millions are believed to have been realised. From a small part of the adjoining property, about 20 fathoms long and 140 fathoms deep, a profit of £20,000 per annum was paid for eight years.

The facilities for rapid and economic development are very great; there is a powerful stream of water available for all purposes; coals are procurable at low rates; an excellent road skirts the boundary of the property leading to a railway station within a few miles.

The Articles of Association, together with all deeds and documents in the possession of the Company, are open to public inspection at the offices of the Solicitor.

Applications for Shares can be sent to the Bankers, accompanied by a cheque for the deposit of 1s. per share on the number of shares applied for. All cheques should be crossed "Alliance Bank (Limited)."

Full prospectuses, together with form of application, section of the mine and reports, specially made for the directors by Wm. Sowerby, Esq., C.E. and F.G.S., W. Eddy, Esq., M.E., and J. Kitto, Esq., can be obtained from the Bankers, or from the Secretary, at the offices of the Company.

expended £13,000 in driving a drainage level, the Ecton Sough. However, there is a general pattern of adventurers such as the Gilberts taking out leases to work mines (chiefly lead) which were later abandoned in favour of fresh localities when output declined.

The increase in private partnerships and joint stock companies went hand in hand with more efficient and economic transport facilities. This not only enabled raw materials and ore to be moved more easily, but also enabled the production of newspapers for distribution on a national scale via the railways, including the *Mining Journal* founded in 1836.

The Industrial Revolution had given rise to a new middle class which enjoyed a wave of prosperity from industrial activities. Weekly mine reports and shareholders advice freely given in the paper's columns aroused a tremendous desire to speculate in mining operations. With the introduction of the *Limited Liability Act*, the poorer classes could also invest some of their savings in a few mine shares in the hope that they would provide useful income by way of dividends.

As a result, the surge of interest in the 1850s was tremendous; naturally, the risks were high, but the possible returns were correspondingly great. Prudent speculators could diversify their portfolio amongst the 'blue chip' companies such as the big Cornish mines on the one hand and those with a greater element of risk – such as the North Staffordshire mineral mines – on the other.

As an example, in 1855-56, Devon Great Consols on the banks of the River Tamar, declared a dividend of £57,344 and £59,392 respectively. By comparison, the best mine at the time in the Peak District was the Peak United mine at Calver. The dividends for 1855-56 were £2,100 and £4,200 respectively. In 1857, Eyam Mining Company had a particularly good year and declared several dividends amounting to £9,800. It sold 326 tons of lead ore in the three months ending 5 November 1857 alone (*Mining Journal*, 1857, p772).

The greater risk shares may be compared to today's flutter on the football pools or the lottery. The shares were usually cheaper than the safer shares, which increased the attraction.

In order to satisfy the demand for mine shares, companies sprung up in profusion and North Staffordshire was no exception, with every copper and lead mine of any value (and in some cases of no value) being worked. Previous successes at Ecton were not overlooked and conveniently exaggerated. It was quite common for the *Mining Journal* to print letters stating the favourable prospects of a particular mine and that the Ecton Mine nearby had produced an income of two million pounds. In actual fact the Duke of Devonshire's profit had been a third of a million pounds from ore worth about £850,000! (2) Nonetheless, this risk capital did help ventures which were worth exploring. Clayton and Waterbank mines at Ecton and the Dale Mine fall into this category and probably the New York shaft at Royledge.

In the Derbyshire orefield, this reference to a neighbouring mine followed the success of the Eyam Mining Company, which in the late 1850s was the only mine in the Derbyshire/Staffordshire orefield which was yielding a reasonable dividend. Numerous companies were formed, some of which enjoyed a certain degree of success, such as the North Derbyshire Mining Company at Calver Sough and Wren Park Mines; Mill Dam Mining Company at Great Hucklow; and the Mill Town Mining Company at Ashover. Other companies had little hope of success, such as the Robin Hood Mining Company at Matlock, formed in 1858, and described in the *Mining Journal* as being managed by a Board of Directors 'including a superintendent of police, a doctor, and a regular medley of professors etc'!

In this kind of market, it was easy for the shareholders to be misled and the paper gave repeated warnings of this. The Robin Hood Company is a good example and it was not an isolated one in this area. A letter in the Journal in 1860 regarding the Dale Mine was pointedly typical of many mines when it was stated that the management

> 'affords another illustration of parties entering into mining without previous knowledge and little business tact'.

At Mill Dam Mine, twice the shareholders had to threaten legal action in order to obtain a general meeting (in 1860 and 1862). It was however at Mixon Mine where matters finally came to a head, indicating how careful investors had to be, in *Re Mixon Copper Mining Company*,

1 Introduction

Above: The mine manager's house. Notice the extent of the tips in former times
Opposite: A 19th Century map showing the extent of the Dale Mine Adit Level

Edwards' Case. The Mixon Great Consols Mining Company had been formed in 1852 on the cost book principle. It was to join a small group of mines that hit national headlines because of sharp practices that were bound to follow such a boom of companies. With shareholders scattered over a very wide area and still relatively poor communications, in practice the directors wielded considerable power and their actions were not easily checked or accountable. When the Mixon Company went into liquidation, the liquidator was so alarmed that he referred the practices of the mine to the Court of Chancery.

The Hamps Valley includes other mines upstream of Mixon which also saw a series of mining lawsuits, chiefly between the Royledge and New York Mining Companies, but also concerning the activities of a John Williams who also involved one of the Ecton Companies in contractual problems.

Another good example of manipulation of the truth concerned the Bincliff Mines below Beeston Tor. A new company set up in 1853 to invite investment in these mines stated that there was no shortage of water in the River Manifold to work waterwheels, yet the river bed is dry for most of the year, all the water disappearing underground!

The history of this ore field will be seen as the development of the very rich deposits at Ecton in the 18th Century and the boost it gave to exploration elsewhere. By contrast, in the 19th Century, despite the many attempts to find fresh deposits like that at Ecton, none were found that were as important. This occurred against a background of a willingness to invest in new ventures despite falling metal prices and increased competition from abroad. By the end of the 19th Century, all the mines had closed, bringing to an end an industry which had been established for perhaps 500 years. It was a way of life completely unlike anything that exists today. Not only the working conditions in the mines, but in the dressing of the ore, a job often left to the women and often out of doors except at the bigger mines.

Drainage

Being relatively few in number and small in size, the mines in the area were not especially noted for their technical achievements. The Ecton Mines were a special case having drainage problems that could readily be solved by short adits (or levels) or simple hydraulic engines (and later small steam engines) for drainage below adit level. The main technical problem here was winding from a great depth (nearly 1,400 ft), but this was effectively solved with the use of one of James Watt's rotative engines in 1788. This was one of the earliest rotative winding engines ever built, only four or five others predating it, out of about thirty-six built before the end of the century. Other mines in the area had problems that were more typical of metal mines elsewhere. The mines were not as deep an Ecton so horse gins or whims sufficed for haulage.

Drainage was a greater problem than haulage, however. Tunnels, (known as soughs, adits or levels) driven horizontally from a valley bottom or other convenient low point were a well established method of providing drainage for mines situated at a higher elevation. Such levels were driven at Ecton, Dale, Hayesbrook, Mixon, Royledge, Thorswood, Bincliff, Fleet Green, Hillhouse and Ford mines, but apart from those at Ecton (particularly the Dale and Clayton Levels) these adits were small affairs, being of no great length and not providing drainage to any great depth. In Derbyshire the techniques of sough driving became perfected so that once the effectiveness of short, shallow soughs had been exploited then longer low-level soughs were driven. The expenditure of these soughs was such that their construction was not undertaken by the mining companies themselves, but the task was let to specialist companies of 'soughers' who claimed an agreed 'composition' or proportion of the ore obtained by the drainage of the mines. Such practices generally did not spread to the

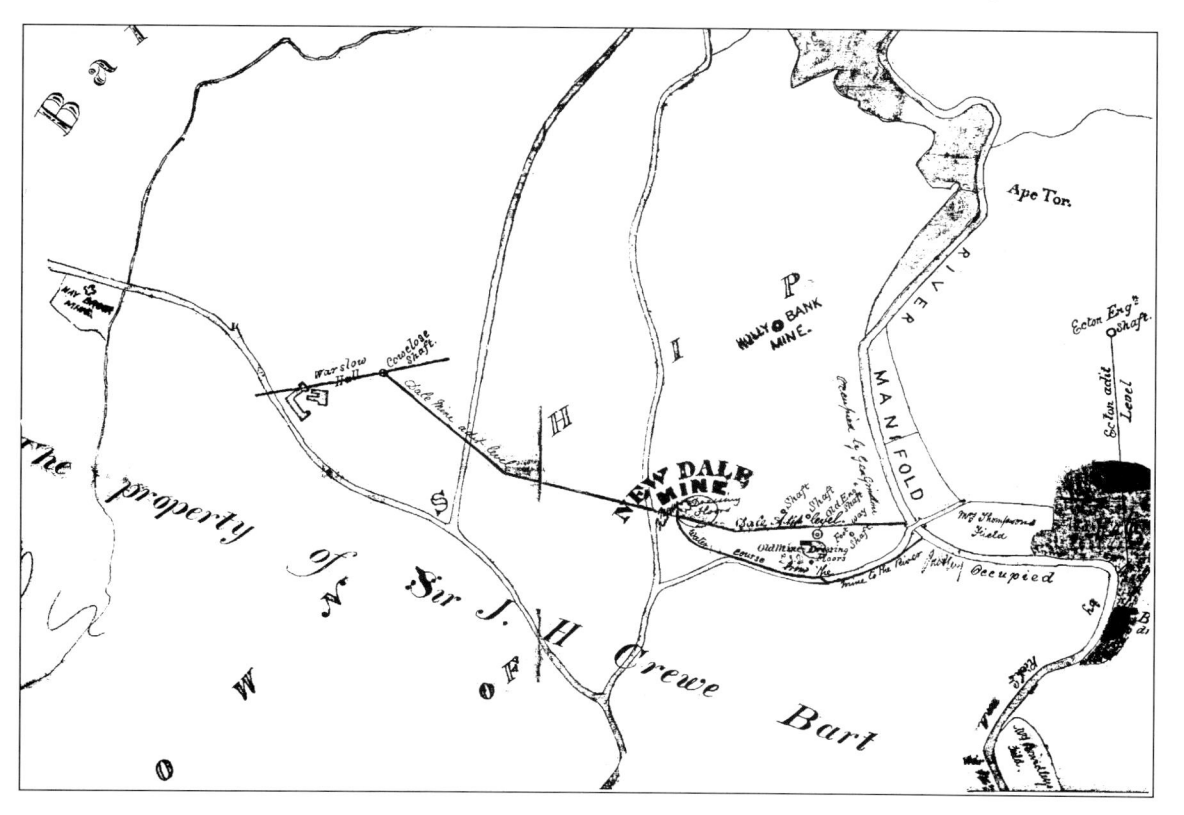

In 1924, Ecton Creamery installed this pump on Clayton Engine Shaft to provide water for the creamery during a drought. They had previously used water from Ecton Deep Adit

neighbouring Staffordshire mines. An exception may well have been the Clayton Sough, which was specifically driven in 1755 to unwater 'Clayton's Mine' which may have been leased to a separate partnership. Only one drainage adit over a mile in length is known to have been considered in the area: from the River Churnet to the Ribden Mine which was a distance of 1,421 fathoms (1.6 miles) at an estimated cost of over £8,000 in 1825 and even this was never driven.

Below adit level, drainage could be effected by pumps operated manually, by horses, hydraulic power or steam engines. At Ecton hand pumps were superseded by 80 gallon water barrels lifted by horse-whim, later, by an hydraulic 'bucket' engine which was itself replaced by a waterwheel. Elsewhere drainage was by waterwheel (as at Mixon and Botstone) or by steam power (as at Mixon, New York, Ribden, Dale and Hayesbrook) or by an hydraulic engine as at the Dale mine. This latter engine was similar to the one preserved at the Peak District Mining Museum at Matlock Bath and was probably of similar age.

With no long tradition of extensive soughs, when capital was available for the drainage of mines in the 19th Century, the choice was usually a steam engine. Both soughs and steam engines had their advantages and disadvantages. Soughs were expensive to drive and took a very long time to reach their destination but once finished required little maintenance and consequently were not a large burden on the mine accounts. Steam engines on the other hand required less capital (although a large engine was still the major item of expenditure of a mine) and would produce an almost immediate effect.

Furthermore, if the mine proved to be less productive than originally envisaged (as usually was the case) then the engine could be sold off to recoup some of the expended capital, but a sough was valueless to another mine in another district. However large steam pumping engines were costly to run and maintain due to their large consumption of fuel.

On collieries, the cost of fuel was of little account as the otherwise waste slack could be burnt in the boilers. Here many hundreds of Newcomen engines were employed to drain the coalfields and the improved efficiencies produced by James Watt and the Cornish engineers were of little consequence. Metal mines, usually remote from a cheap source of coal, could have all their potential profits swallowed up by a coal-hungry Newcomen engine. Watt's improved engines were warmly welcomed by the Cornish copper mines until it was realised that much of their savings in fuel costs were going into the 'premiums' charged by Boulton and Watt.

After the expiry of Watt's patent in 1800, the Cornish engineers developed the steam pumping engine to a very high state of efficiency and the tall empty shells of the engine houses to be found in mining areas throughout the world are a testimony to their widespread use. But as the shallower veins became exhausted, the mines were sunk deeper, thus adding considerably to the drainage problems and throughout the centuries the success of many a mine has depended upon the ease with which the water could be removed. Ecton was an exception; if there had been more serious drainage problems then the story there would have had quite a different outcome.

Not many Staffordshire mines were as dry as Ecton; the Mixon Mine is a classic example of a mine whose success was dependent upon efficient drainage. Two 40ft diameter waterwheels and a Watt – type steam engine were insufficient to unwater the workings and even a Cornish steam engine was to fare little better. At the Dale Mine the steeply inclined nature of the workings meant a very tortuous path for the pump rods until a new shaft was completed. At the Ribden Mine the erection of the engine on what was effectively the wrong shaft did not help the success of the venture, although here lack of an economic quantity of copper ore was the most serious problem.

The method of drainage also had an important bearing on the management of the mine. Once committed to a long sough, there was little that could be done if the mine ran into a bad spell apart from complete closure, whereas a steam engine could be dismantled and erected elsewhere. For the limited liability companies, with their objectives of quick profits, the steam engine was the ideal answer and this helps to explain its use in North Staffordshire to the almost complete exclusion of long drainage soughs.

1 Introduction

Above: Lindsey Porter in Clayton Adit Level, originally driven in 1755 to unwater John Clayton's workings. This photo was taken nearly 1,600 feet from the entrance

The Research For This Book

The majority of the text in this book has been contributed by Lindsey Porter. In the early 1970's, several papers together with John Robey were written on the mines together with the previous history of Ecton, which was published in book form in 1972. These tended to be divided with the former contributing the 19th Century material and the later that of the 18th Century. In the case of Ecton, John provided much of the writing to 1825 and the chapter on smelting. Since then, further studies have been made, including detailed work on the geology by Martin Critchley. The discovery of more recent material resulted in two articles by John Robey on copper smelting in Derbyshire and Jim Rieuwerts has unravelled more of the 17th

1 Introduction

Century activity at Ecton and at Newton Grange. Lindsey Porter has added more on the 19th Century Companies working at Ecton.

A list of these papers is given together with others, which may be of additional interest on related topics. More recently, the discovery of some 400 documents on mining in the area by Lindsey Porter and Len Kirkham has enabled a greater understanding of the late 18th and early 19th Century activity at mines other than at Ecton. Pat Bromfield has written a thesis based on the reckoning accounts for the Duke's mine at Ecton in the late 18th Century. Its title is *Industrial workers in a peasant community: Manifold Valley parishes in the eighteenth century with special reference to workers at Ecton copper mine, c.1760-1820*, unpublished PhD thesis, Keele University (1998).

This has brought about a reappraisal of what had been written previously. The amendments to the Porter/Robey papers have been made by Lindsey Porter and additional material written by him on other mines not previously covered (both with assistance from Len Kirkham). Dr Trevor Ford kindly wrote Chapter 2 and edited the book. To date there has been no comprehensive publication of the geology of the Staffordshire mineral deposits. The section on the 17th Century activity at Ecton was chiefly based on the work of Jim Rieuwerts, and John Barnatt, building on John Robey's earlier work. Len Kirkham contributed the descriptions of Fleet Green and Waterfall. Phil Mottram wrote much of the Ilam section. Chapter 13 was written by Robert Vernon. Mrs B Williams agreed to the use of the extract on packhorse routes to Whiston. Photos were provided by the authors, Paul Deakin, Adrian Henstock, Harry Parker and from the Ferguson Collection.

Further work on the area, from the point of exploration for historical purposes has been made by Len Kirkham and his team, consisting of Peter Thompson, Lindsey Porter, Wes Taylor and with contributions by Steve Mills, Dave Noble, Alan Rollinson and others. Further work at Ecton is being co-ordinated by John Barnatt. A big thank you to all those mentioned and others whose work is unrecorded here.

As a result of the work undertaken by the Kirkham team, our knowledge of some of the Ecton workings, Fleet Green Mine, Royledge, New York, Ford, Waterfall and other mines has been enhanced. However all the mines covered in this book should be considered to be dangerous and also on private property.

Access is not available generally although the Ecton Education Centre, established by the Ecton mineral owner, Geoff Cox, has enabled thousands of students over the years to visit the mine in a controlled and safe way. Also, concerns have been raised about radon gas, which are still being assessed, from a practical point of view relating to how this affects levels and workings which are currently accessible. **On no account should old mine workings be approached or entered without permission or supervision.** Even to those with expert knowledge, the mines are inherently dangerous and the unexpected can, and sometimes does, occur.

Acknowledgements

The authors which to thank in particularly the following. However, they do not overlook all those who were acknowledged in the original papers and the Ecton book of 1972 on which much of this book is based: (in alphabetical order), John Barnatt; Pat Bromfield; Tom Buxton; Martin Critchley; Paul Deakin; Trevor Ford; Len Kirkham; Phil Mottram; Jim Rieuwerts; David Swinscoe; Wes Taylor; Peter Thompson; Rob Vernon; David Williams. Thanks are also due to the various source libraries quoted in the chapter references but in particular, the Trustees of the Chatsworth Settlement; and both Derbyshire and Staffordshire Record Offices.

References

1. Lead P, 1989, *Agents of Revolution: John and Thomas Gilbert – Entrepreneurs*, p18 (privately published by the author at Stafford).

2. Amanda Foreman in *Georgiana, Duchess of Devonshire*, Harper Collins, 1998, p4, states that 18th Century values should be multiplied by 60 to convert to equivalent current values.

2 Geology and Mineralogy of The North-East Staffordshire Mines

To understand the nature of the rocks hosting the mineral deposits of north-east Staffordshire it is necessary to go back to Carboniferous times, some 300 million years ago, when the limestones were deposited as sediments on the floor of a tropical sea. This part of Britain then lay more or less astride the Equator and has been moving slowly northwards ever since. The Peak District of Derbyshire lay to the east and its limestone massif represents a shallow lagoon bordered by reef-like mounds, of which fine examples occur in Dovedale. Staffordshire was, however, in a deeper water basin which received fine-grained lime sediments interspersed with sheets of almost lime-free muddy deposits, giving us the alternation of thin dark limestone beds and shale partings seen in many old mine levels. Within these thin limestone sequences occasional build-ups of lime mud resulted in mud-mounds, commonly but incorrectly called reefs or reef knolls. The boundary between massif and basin lay roughly along the line of Dovedale, but its position fluctuated during early Carboniferous times and some more massive limestones are to be found in places, for example within the core of Ecton Hill. A fragment of a separate limestone lagoon is exposed in the Weaver Hills, far to the south of the Manifold Valley. In later Carboniferous times the limestones were covered by the sandstones (often known as gritstones) and shales of a massive series of deltas but these rocks are rarely hosts to mineral deposits.

Stratigraphy

Geologists divide the sequence of limestone beds into formations which accumulated during sub-divisions of Carboniferous time. The lower half of Carboniferous time (the Dinantian, 354-310 million years ago), was the period of limestone formation, whilst the overlying Millstone Grit Series was deposited during middle Carboniferous times (the Namurian, 310-300 million years ago). The Dinantian shallow-water limestones of the Derbyshire massif are better known and have a different set of formation names. An approximate correlation is shown in the table below, together with sub-divisions or Stages of Dinantian time. The distribution of the various strata is shown on the British Geological Survey 1:50000 maps Sheet 111 (Buxton, Leek and Bakewell) and 124 (Ashbourne and Cheadle) and descriptions are presented in the accompanying Memoirs (Aitkenhead et al. 1985; Chisholm et al. 1988).

Beneath the last-named are the Rue Hill Dolomites and Red House Sandstones, but they are nowhere exposed and are known only from deep boreholes and need not concern us further.

The **Milldale Limestones** are generally fine-grained, with numerous mud-mounds. They outcrop along much of the Manifold Valley south of Ecton and form the core of the Ecton anticline near Wetton and extend beneath Ecton Hill at depth. Individual mud-mounds are present at Beeston Tor and the Thors Cave hill. Similar mounds are also present in central Dovedale. The total thickness of the Milldale Limestones is uncertain, but at least 2,265ft (700m).

Brigantian – Mixon Limestones with Shales = Monsal Dale Limestones
Asbian – Ecton Limestones = Bee Low Limestones
Holkerian and older – Milldale Limestones = Woo Dale Limestones

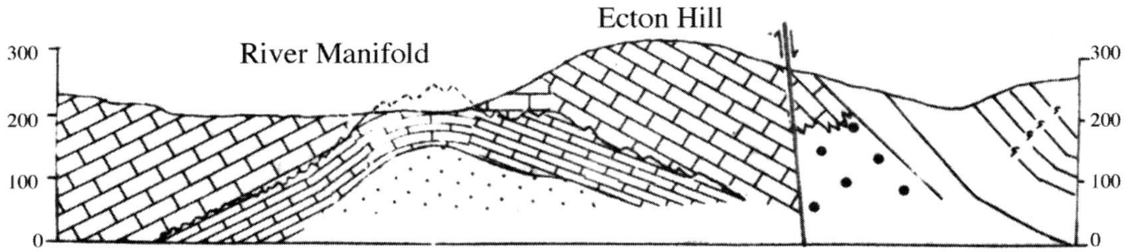
Ecton Hill
River Manifold
300
200
100
0

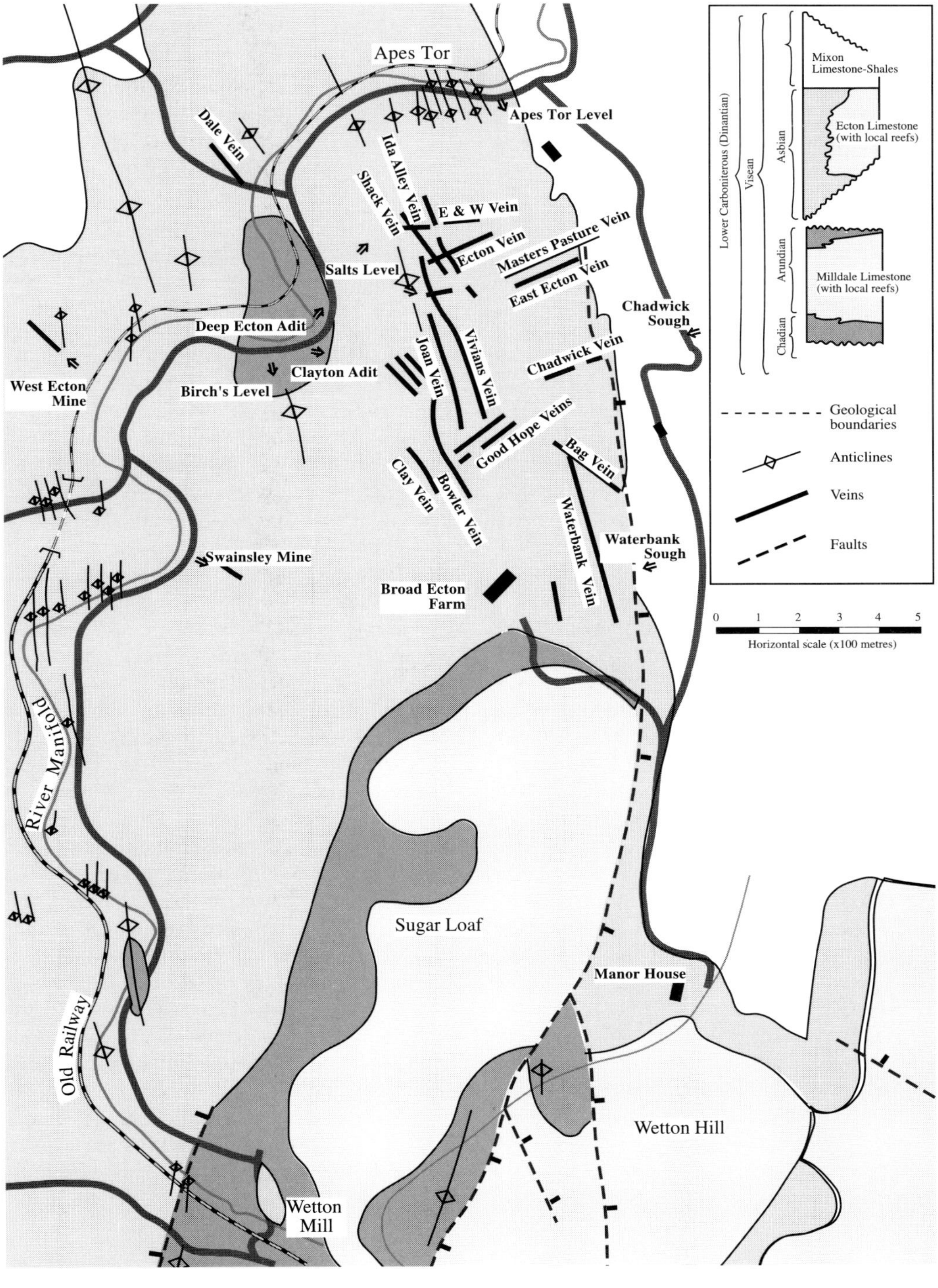
Apes Tor
Apes Tor Level
Dale Vein
Ida Alley Vein
Shack Vein
E & W Vein
Ecton Vein
Masters Pasture Vein
East Ecton Vein
Salts Level
Deep Ecton Adit
Clayton Adit
Birch's Level
West Ecton Mine
Chadwick Sough
Chadwick Vein
Joan Vein
Vivians Vein
Good Hope Veins
Bag Vein
Clay Vein
Bowler Vein
Waterbank Vein
Waterbank Sough
Swainsley Mine
Broad Ecton Farm
River Manifold
Old Railway
Sugar Loaf
Manor House
Wetton Hill
Wetton Mill
Lower Carboniterous (Dinantian)
Visean
Asbian
Arundian
Chadian
Mixon Limestone-Shales
Ecton Limestone (with local reefs)
Milldale Limestone (with local reefs)
Geological boundaries
Anticlines
Veins
Faults
0 1 2 3 4 5
Horizontal scale (x100 metres)

Overlying the Milldale Limestones are the generally thinner-bedded **Ecton Limestones,** usually equated with the **Hopedale Limestones** around Waterhouses to the south, and with the massive shallow-water Kevin Limestones of the Weaver Hills. The Ecton Limestones, well exposed at Apes Tor at the north end of Ecton Hill, are composed of alternations of fine-grained limestone and thin shales, with the proportion of limestone generally dominant. Occasionally more massive limestones are developed within the Ecton Limestones. The thickness of the Ecton Limestones is variable, at least 750ft (225m) at Ecton itself.

Above the Ecton Limestones are the Mixon Limestones-with-Shales. They differ from the Ecton Limestones in having much more mudstone (shale) and outcrop over a wide area west of the Manifold Valley. Within the Mixon Shales is the Onecote sandstone, a forerunner of the Millstone Grit deltaic sediments which followed much later. Further east, to the south of the Peak District massif the Mixon Limestones-with-Shales appear to be equated with the Widmerpool Formation. The total thickness is again variable, probably not exceeding 650ft (200m).

The **Millstone Grit** of north-east Staffordshire consists of an alternation of massive sandstones and thick shales of Namurian age. The sequence represents repeated building out of deltas into a muddy sea, with the deltaic lobes deriving their load of sands from rivers draining either from the Scottish Highlands or from an ancient Midland landmass. The lowest unit of thick shales is similar to the more shaley part of the Mixon Limestones-with-Shales, making demarkation and mapping difficult. At least part of these shales can be equated with the Edale Shales further north. The individual sandstone sheets are variably developed in N.E. Staffordshire, and include the Minn, Hurdlow, Lum Edge, Blackstone Edge and Longnor Sandstones. The earliest of these are strictly quartzites derived from the Midland landmass but the later gritstones contain substantial amounts of feldspar and some mica derived from metamorphic rocks in the Scottish Highlands.

Both limestones and Millstone Grit were eventually covered by the thickly vegetated delta-swamps of the Coal Measures (of Westphalian age, 300-290 million years ago). Most of the Coal Measures have long since been eroded away but their continuation is preserved in the North Staffordshire coalfield around Stoke-on-Trent. Their former presence is significant, however, in providing the conditions necessary for the formation of mineral deposits.

Structure

The Carboniferous strata have been folded by earth pressures as is well seen in the crumpled limestones at Apes Tor, along the northern flank of Ecton Hill. The limestone beds in the main mine adits also show complex folding. This contrasts with the Derbyshire massif, which forms a stable block with its thick limestones resistant to earth pressures and only warped into gentle arch-like folds. The thin limestones and shales of the Staffordshire basin were not resistant and crumpled like a concertina. The folds were well-known to the miners who referred to the upfolds (anticlines) as 'saddles or huckle saddles', and to the down folds (synclines) as 'trough saddles' (Watson, 1860). The stresses induced by folding also caused breakage of the limestone beds by joints and faults often along the axes of the folds. Joints are where no relative movement has occurred whilst faults involve displacement of the strata. Numerous examples are to be found in mine levels, though it is not always easy to determine whether there has been displacement or not. The old miners noted 'saddle joints' where vertical fractures bisected the crests of anticlines and, less commonly, synclines. Both joints and faults were significant in the mineralization process. Occasionally two sets of anticlines intersect yielding 'double saddles', which were culminations broken by complicated more or less vertical fracture systems. Double saddles are known to have been recognized at the 34 and 110 fathom (204 and 660 feet below adit) levels in Ecton Mine.

The sudden change from limestones to shales along the east flank of Ecton Hill suggests that there may be a major fault here. Other strong faults probably lie beneath the main anticlines but no direct evidence is available.

The folding noted above was a complex process occurring in episodes over a considerable period of time. Some folding took place during Dinantian times, i.e. whilst the limestone beds were being deposited, resulting in discordances between some of the stratigraphic formations. These are difficult to determine and need not concern us further. Major folding took place later reaching a climax during late Westphalian times (late Coal Measures, about 290 million years ago), resulting in the downwarping of the Staffordshire Coalfield and the progressive uplift of the Derbyshire 'stable block'. Large faults occurred at this time, with major displacements of strata.

The folds represent changing stress fields affecting the Earth's crust during upheavals affecting much of Europe, known to geologists as the Variscan orogeny. Whilst the main pressures were from the south (with complex structures well known in south-west England), Staffordshire was in effect trapped between the Derbyshire block and North Wales and the resultant pressures were directed east-west yielding north-south-trending folds.

The Triassic and Later Cover Rocks

Following the folding of the Carboniferous strata, the higher parts of the South Pennines were deeply eroded during Permian times (290-250 million years ago). This erosion removed much of the cover of Coal Measure and Millstone Grit and exposed the limestones. The detritus from the eroded rocks accumulated in adjacent basins in Cheshire and the Midlands and by Triassic times (250-206 million years ago) it was spilling over onto the South Pennines. Once the gravels and sands of the Triassic Sherwood Sandstone Group (lying beneath much of Sherwood Forest) covered the whole area and they were followed by the Mercia Mudstones, with interlayered gypsum and salt deposits, widespread in the Midlands and in Cheshire respectively.

The Triassic strata too have now been eroded and the Sherwood Sandstones are now seen forming an escarpment lying along the northern flanks of the Trent Valley. In places the basal beds of the Sherwood Sandstones, together with immediately underlying strata, have been mineralized, as at Limestone Hill.

A limited cover of Jurassic and Cretaceous strata once lay above the Triassic strata but they were subsequently removed by erosion.

Still later a sheet of sands and clays of Neogene (Miocene Pliocene) age once lay over the area but the only relics are the silica-sand 'pocket deposits' best known in solution-collapse hollows around Brassington in the Peak District. The silica-rich sands have been worked for refractory brick-making. The sands together with the associated clays are now known as the Brassington Formation. A few comparable pockets are present around Ribden in the Weaver Hills and at least one was intersected by mining in the surrounding limestone there.

Mineral Deposits

The concept of the four different types of mineral vein so well known in the Peak District lead-mining field is not easy to apply in Staffordshire. The Peak District has rakes and scrins as simple fissure fillings, large and small, and more or less vertical. Stratiform deposits include flats and pipes along the nearly horizontal bedding, flats being simple layers of minerals, whilst pipes are generally void-fillings. By contrast Staffordshire has a scatter of nearly vertical veins, usually called lodes, e.g. Vivian's Lode in Clayton Mine, or the ore lies in 'saddles' with the minerals dispersed along bedding planes across the folds, either anticlines (locally called huckle saddles) or synclines (locally trough saddles). The deposition of ores along the bedding in saddles may be because there was void space available, or it may be due to replacement of the unresistant shale being washed out. Replacement ores in the usual sense of direct replacement of rock by ore minerals has not been recognized in Staffordshire.

The bulk of the ores mined came from the great Ecton and Clayton pipes, in which the term pipe is used in a completely different sense from that in Derbyshire. The Staffordshire pipes are more or less cylindrical ore bodies orientated vertically or steeply inclined and penetrating to a great depth. The pipes in Ecton Hill are usually said to be at the intersection of north-south and east west veins but this is not clear in presently accessible sections. Neither are they on the crestal line of the Ecton anticline, as the pipes lie within its steeply-dipping eastern flanking limestones. It has also been said that the pipes lie at the culminations of large double saddles but this cannot be proved in present sections. Indeed several small saddles with little or no ore are visible in the walls of Clayton engine chamber. Rather the pipes seem to be irregular zones of crushed limestone riddled with veinlets of ore and gangue minerals. They may have suffered some karstic cavern development by hydrothermal fluids (see below) dissolving out cavities but those parts of the pipes are under water and cannot be examined today. Some parts of the Ecton pipes were totally extracted leaving large stopes (= artificial caverns). References to these 'caverns' in old documents give a misleading impression that they were natural caves full of loose blocks of ore and limestone. The Clayton Pipe is said to split downwards, but with most of it being under water this is difficult to prove today. Some pipes are not vertical, as in Dale Mine and at Mixon. The reasons for the presence and distribution of the Staffordshire pipes are not fully understood as yet and more research is needed.

Old accounts refer to lums or lumbs in Ecton Hill, Dale, Royledge and Mixon Mines. However, it is not clear what this term means. The miners appear to have meant a zone of broken and loose rock with much clay and some ore, usually situated between steeply-dipping beds of limestone, but how such lums arose is not certain. Like the pipes, more research is needed.

Minerals

The principal ore mineral of copper at Ecton and other North Staffordshire mines is chalcopyrite ($CuFeS_2$) but several other copper minerals are present in lesser amounts. These include Native Copper (Cu), cuprite (Cu_2O), tenorite (CuO), covellite (CuS), chalcocite (Cu_2S) and bornite (Cu_5FeS_4). The chief lead ore is galena (PbS) and the ore of zinc is sphalerite (Blende, ZnS). Other rare sulphides include the nickel mineral millerite (NiS) (Starkey, 1983) and arsenopyrite (FeAsS).

Oxidation products include malachite ($Cu_2CO_3(OH)_2$) and azurite ($Cu_3(CO_3)_2(OH)_2$). Galena is some times coated with its oxiaation product cerussite ($PbCO_3$). The oxidation product smithsonite ($ZnCO_3$; sometimes called calamine) sometimes replaces sphalerite but the combined carbonates of copper and zinc aurichalcite (($Zn,Cu)5(CO_3)_2(OH)_6$) and rosasite (($Cu,Zn)_2CO_3(OH)_2$) are more common (Braithwaite 1983, 1991; Braithwaite et al. 1963). The rare serpierite ($Ca(Cu,Zn)_4(SO_4)_2(OH)_6 3H_2O$) and linarite ($PbCuSO_4(OH)_2$) have also been found (Braithwaite, 1983).

'Black stuff' recorded in the lowest levels in some old accounts seems to have been shale heavily impregnated with either sulphides or manganese oxides. Elsewhere in the higher levels of the mines 'black stuff' seems to refer to unspecified hydrocarbons, which are present in many Peak District mineral deposits.

The gangue minerals (those which are not metallic ores) are dominated by calcite ($CaCO_3$), both in its massive opaque form and as clear to amber-coloured dog-tooth crystals (scalenohedra). Minor quantities of cream-coloured dolomite ($CaCO_3)_2$ occur in some veins. Present throughout the ore-field is baryte ($BaSO_4$), commonly known as caulk or cawk, occurring in its creamy yellow, poorly crystalline variety. Fluorite (CaF_2) is often present in small amounts, usually as small colourless, yellow or blue cubic crystals. It was insufficient to be mined on its own and fluorspar had to be imported from Derbyshire for use as a flux in smelting.

Celestine, strontium sulphate ($SrSO_4$), occurs as pale blue tabular crystals scattered in some calcite veins near the Waterbank end of Clayton adit (Braithwaite et al. 1963).

Mineralization

The geological processes which resulted in the formation of Staffordshire's ore deposits are complex and depend on three factors -- the source of the ions, their transport to their final destination, and the means of precipitation. All of these are controversial matters, and many factors are involved, some not fully understood as yet, so only an outline can be given. Briefly the source is thought to be in the rocks of surrounding basins, mainly in the shales, the transport is by hydrothermal fluids (i.e. hot waters), and precipitation is by reactions with other fluids in the receiving rocks and with the rocks themselves. The whole system is a variant of the type of orefield well-known in the Mississippi Valley of the central United States, and is hence known as the MVT process (see Quirk, 1993). Another variant of the same process was also responsible for the lead-zinc-fluorspar-baryte orefield of the Peak District but the two orefields east and west of the South Pennines differ in the much higher proportion of copper in Staffordshire perhaps because the ore minerals may have been derived from different sedimentary basins with different metal contents lying on either side of the Pennines.

The source of most of the ions is thought to have been in the clay minerals of the shales of early to middle Carboniferous age deeply buried beneath the Cheshire basin. Though these clay minerals are mostly hydrated alumino-silicates, they contain trace proportions of Cu, Pb, Zn, Fe, Mg, F and Ba and these are released into pore-waters during the deep burial which converts sea-floor mud into shale. Na and Cl were also released from the sea-water trapped in the muds as they were deposited so that the transporting fluids were metal-rich brines, often enriched in potassium (K) and calcium (Ca) derived from feldspathic grains in the sediments. Deep burial also raises the temperature and pressure and squeezes the pore-waters out into adjacent more permeable strata.

The pore-waters, generally known as hydrothermal fluids, are the transporting medium. They move through any permeable rocks, such as limestones or sandstones, particularly via bedding planes and joints, and further chemical change may take place. The varying rock pressures caused by folding effectively act as pumps, pushing the hydrothermal fluids through the rocks. The chief source rocks are thought to be the thick Edale and Mixon Shales at the base of the Millstone Grit rocks. These are present beneath the Cheshire basin to the west, but nearer at hand they may be in a thrust-faulted relationship to the limestones beneath both the Ecton and Mixon anticlines.

The processes discussed so far are very similar to the generation of hydrocarbons (crude oil and gas) from buried organic matter in the shales of the World's oilfields, but a somewhat higher temperatures are involved. Quantification of these is not easy but burial depths of at least 2 km are envisaged, and temperatures range around 75-110^{0}C. Even these are barely enough to move the mineral ions and catalysts are required. The fluids expelled from the shale are highly saline, with up to ten times the amount of salt in sea water, and they contain small amounts of hydrocarbons; both salt and hydrocarbons increase the solubility of the mineral ions. So the hydrothermal fluids carrying minerals to Staffordshire were hot, salty and oily. Even then they did not often have more than 1% mineral ions in solution. Traces of the salt water and the hydrocarbons can be found in microscopic inclusions trapped within some crystals of calcite and fluorite.

There have been few studies of the fluids involved in Staffordshire but a small number of calcite and fluorite crystals at Ecton have fluid inclusions containing Ca:Na:K brines in which K is in a higher proportion than the main South Pennine Orefield (Masheder & Rankin, 1988). Homogenization temperatures ranging from 72 to 97^{0}C may need some upward correction according to the thickness of overlying sediments which is difficult to assess. Anywhere from 10 to 27^{0}C may have to be added to the homogenization temperatures for a realistic assessment of the temperature of crystallization to be made.

The final stage in the mineralization process is precipitation. The fluids carrying the ions penetrate any available space in the host rocks and the minerals crystallize therein. The reasons for precipitation involve complex chemistry, but in broad terms the causes are changes in the fluids. Firstly, the mineral-bearing hydrothermal fluids mixed with different fluids within the host rocks and reacted with their ions; excess calcium carbonate from limestones neutralizes any acids; percolating rainwater dilutes the saline fluid; and reducing pressures and temperatures lower the solubilities. These factors cause the precipitation of the minerals we see today, chalcopyrite, galena, sphalerite, baryte, fluorite and calcite.

The mineral veins and pipes show coatings or layers of alternating gangue and ore minerals. Each layer consists of one of the assemblage of minerals, and this is the result of yet more complex chemistry. As each mineral crystallizes the remaining fluid becomes enriched in the others and there comes a point where the next mineral in line precipitates until that is too dilute, when a third mineral may precipitate. However, renewed flushes of fluid entering the system may swing the balance back and the sequence starts again. The proportions of Cu, Fe, S and O at any one site, the state of the wall-rocks, their temperature, pH and other factors together influence which copper mineral crystallizes.

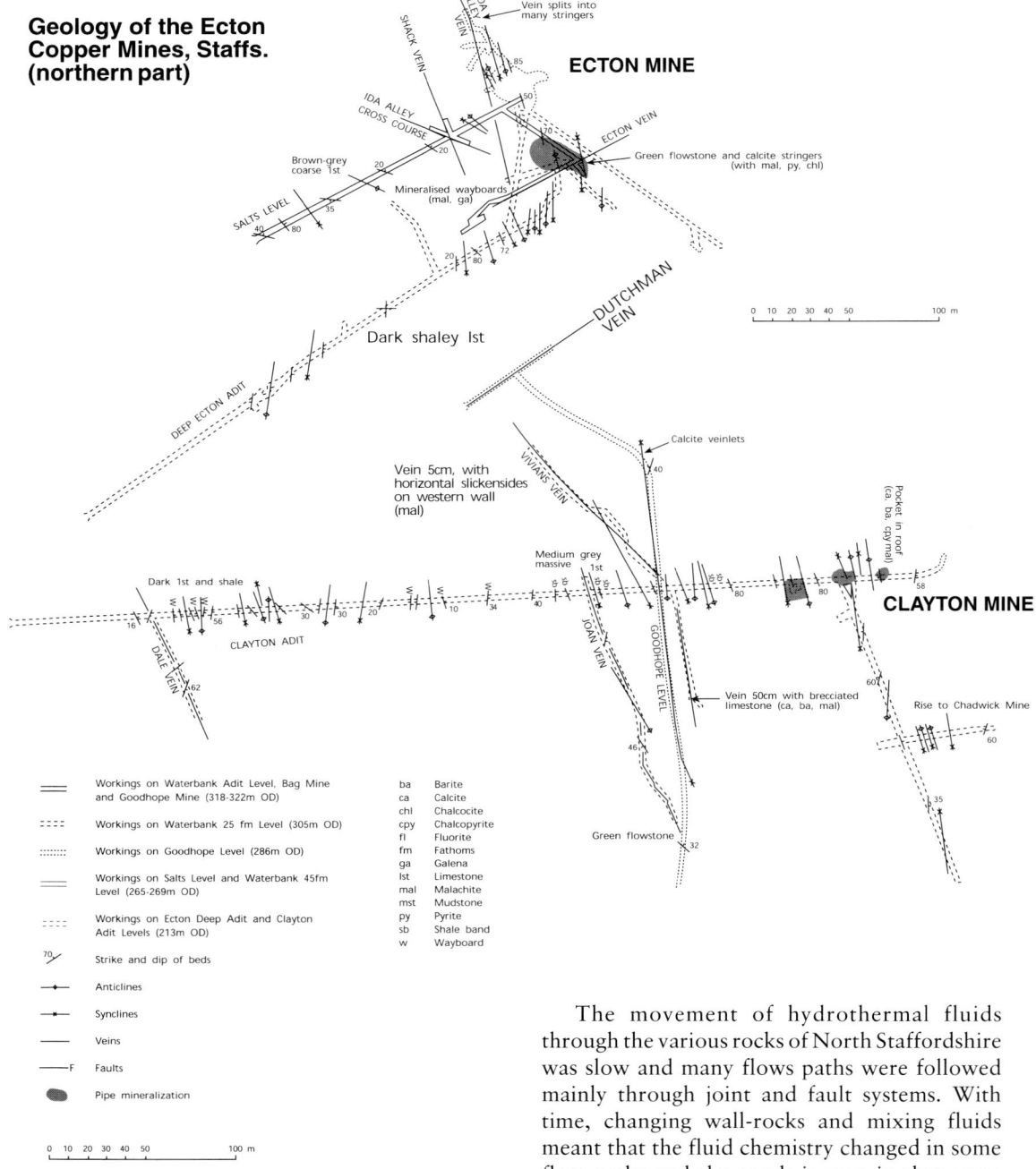

2 Geology and Mineralogy of the North-East Staffordshire Mines

Geology of the Ecton Copper Mines, Staffs. (northern part)

The movement of hydrothermal fluids through the various rocks of North Staffordshire was slow and many flows paths were followed mainly through joint and fault systems. With time, changing wall-rocks and mixing fluids meant that the fluid chemistry changed in some flow paths and the result is seen in that some mineral deposits are dominated by copper and others by lead or zinc sulphides.

As the hydrothermal fluids lose their ions there is excess water to be removed from the

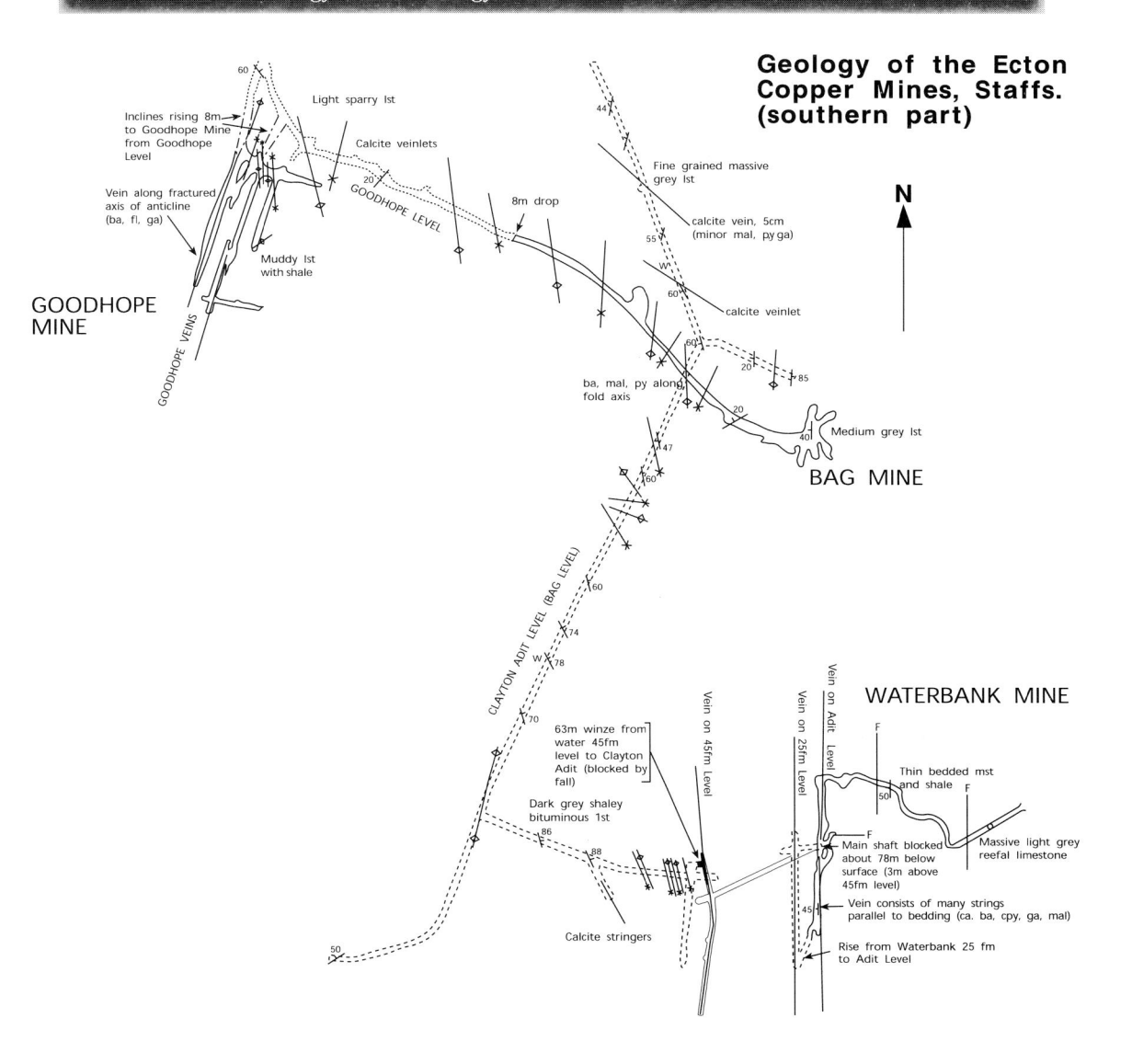

Geology of the Ecton Copper Mines, Staffs. (southern part)

system. Whilst some may be recirculated to transport more ions, most will be lost by percolating either into adjacent shallower rocks or even rising to the surface as hot springs, perhaps similar to those still flowing at Buxton and Matlock Bath.

The timing of mineralization is generally thought to be around the time of maximum folding pressures, i.e. very late Carboniferous, around 290 million years ago. But it was probably somewhat drawn out in a series of episodes over several million years as folding reached a climax and as unroofing by erosion began. The mineral deposits only became accessible to the miners as a result of the erosional removal of some 2km of covering strata. Other mineral deposits, even Ecton-type pipes, may still be hidden beneath the Millstone Grit country but only a determined exploration programme will ever find them – if it is economically worth doing so.

The mineral deposits fall into two groups, those with copper dominant and those with lead ore dominant. This may indicate that two separate mineralizing phases were involved, with fluids depleted in copper arriving later and yielding the galena veins.

In today's situation the copper carbonates are largely present in the highest veins and pipes where oxidation reactions have taken place above the water-table as the overlying strata were removed by erosion. Weathering reactions could take place as soon as the host limestones were exposed, perhaps in late Tertiary times, the last two or three million years. This weathered zone (sometimes referred to as gossan elsewhere) is dominated by malachite, cerussite, calamine and minor cuprite.

Immediately below the water-table is the zone of secondary enrichment where some copper was redeposited in local concentrations of bornite, chalcocite and cuprite. The lowering of the water-table by drainage adits appears to have brought much of the enrichment and primary ores above today's water-table and weathering reactions are giving rise to green (malachitic) stalactite formations. Below the enrichment zone is primary ore, mainly chalcopyrite, galena and sphalerite, revealed by pumping in the deeper parts of the mines.

Geology of Individual Mines

No detailed study of the geological relationship of all the mines of North Staffordshire has been traced. Neither has any study of the distribution of the different copper minerals been carried out. Only the above-water parts of the Ecton mines have been available for research since mining finished in 1889, so the following comments are incomplete. Martin Critchley (1979) provided a useful account of the strata and structures in Ecton and Clayton adits, with notes on the other mines of Ecton Hill, whilst Robey & Porter have given historical descriptions of most of the other mines in a series of articles in the Bulletin of the Peak District Mines Historical Society 1969-1973.

Ecton Pipe lies on the east flank of the Ecton anticline with access from both Salt's Level and the Ecton Deep Level. Salt's Level shows increasingly steep dips to the east in a fairly massive facies of the Ecton Limestones. The beds are crossed by at least two small fissure veins. The pipe lies close to but not exactly on the intersection of Ida Alley and Ecton veins. The Ecton Deep Adit below is in more shaley beds with numerous small folds near the pipe.

Clayton Mine lies further south. The adit starts in the topmost Milldale Limestones but they rapidly disappear below adit level. They reappear on the crest of the Ecton anticline halfway along the adit before plunging below water again but the greater part of the pipe is in the Milldale Limestones. The adit is cut by three fissure veins, Dale Vein, Joan Vein and Vivian's Lode; the last seems to be the same vein as in Dutchman Mine higher up the hill. All have been followed by the miners but the quantities of ore were small. The Clayton Pipe appears to split somewhat above adit level and it is seen both in the 'chimney' workings and just beyond the Engine Chamber. The splits may reconverge below water. It appears to split again in the deepest parts of the mine. The long southerly adit to Waterbank is almost along the strike of the minor folds though the final section where it turns eastwards is in more massive limestones. The branch level to Chadwick Mine leads into a steeply inclined pipe much smaller than Clayton. Workings below water are said to have linked the two so Chadwick may in fact be a split off Clayton Pipe which it rejoins at depth.

Both Deep Ecton and Clayton pipes were worked to a depth of around 1,000ft (300m) so the rich parts must clearly be in the Milldale Limestones, perhaps where the thicker limestones of the mud-mounds provided a better host rock for mineralization.

The Bag, Good Hope and Dutchman Mines are all linked by the long high level crosscut, much of which appears to be in the more massive part of the Ecton Limestones. The higher workings above the adit are once more in the thin-bedded limestones. The principal metal ore in Goodhope Mine is galena, but the others have copper dominant.

Waterbank Mine is only partly accessible and has not been fully examined. It appears to be entirely within the thin-bedded Ecton Limestones except for the deeper part near the intersection with the Clayton cross-cut where more massive limestones were met.

Dale Mine lies about a kilometre west of Ecton, on the opposite side of the valley. It's adit is within thin-bedded and shaley Ecton

Limestones with many small folds. Its pipe is inclined at about 25° to the NNW but only a small portion is above water. The pipe was followed to a depth of about 75 fathoms (137m) and yielded mostly lead ore.

At Hayesbrook Mine the vein was only 18-inch wide, but extremely rich, running as far east of the road as it did to the west (Strahen).

Limepits/West Ecton Mine is an adit in the Ecton Limestones high on the west side of the valley opposite the Ecton Mines. The adit goes into a pipe descending steeply downwards. Its ore seems to have been mainly galena. No description has been traced and little is known of this mine.

Mixon Mine lies on the eastern, faulted flank of a separate anticlinal structure some 3 miles (5km) west of Ecton. The orebody seems to be a main E-W vein and a group of N-S veins at least one of which has a ramifying series of workings suggesting a pipe-like character. Workings reached a depth of 85 fathoms (155m).

Royledge Mine lies within the more shaley part of the MixonLimestones with Shales on the same anticlinal structure as Mixon but about 2 miles (3 km) to the north. New York Mine was effectively the southern end of Royledge Mine. The two together consisted of four veins ranging NE-SW cut by a N-S vein. The workings of the last show ore-bodies along the bedding in trough saddles not unlike the 'flats' of the Nenthead area.

Bincliff Mines in the eastern slopes of the Manifold Valley south of Wetton have several adits going in to intersect NE-SW veins. Only lead ores were produced.

Ribden Mines are in the Weaver Hills, some 6 miles (10km) south of Ecton. The host rock is the thickly-bedded Kevin Limestones, shallow-water limestones comparable with the massif facies of the main Peak District orefield. The ore deposits are mainly a series of NW-SE veins but at least one expands into a 'swallow' of unknown nature, which may have been a pipe. Some workings were very close to a silica-sand pocket and sands ran into the stopes.

Thorswood Mine, east of Ribden, has a steeply inclined pipe which was followed to a depth of at least 70 fathoms (130m).

Cauldon Low cement works quarry intersected several veins of calcite with soft hematite.

Ford Mine, west of Grindon, was little more than a trial. The orientation of its veins is unknown.

This book includes references to many other minor mines of which no geological information is known.

References

Aitkenhead, N, Chisholm, J. I. & Stevenson, I. P. 1985. *Geology of the country around Buxton, Leek and Bakewell.* Memoir of the British Geological Survey. 168pp

Braithwaite, R. S. W. 1983. *Minerals of the Derbyshire orefield.* Mineralogical Record, Vol 14, pp15-24

Braithwaite, R. S. W. 1991. The mineralization of Ecton Hill, Staffordshire. pp96-101 in *Geology of the Manchester Area* by R. M. C. Eagar & F. M. Broadhurst, Geologists Association Guide No 7, 118pp

Braitwaite, R. S. W., Greenland, T. B. & Ryback, G. 1963. *Celestine and aurichalcite from Ecton Hill, Wetton, Staffs.* Exhibit, Mineralogical Magazine, vol.33, p.lxxxvi

Braithwaite, R. S. W. & Knight, J. R. 1968. *Serpierite from Ecton, Staffs,* Mineralogical Magazine, Vol 36, p882

Chisholm, J. I., Charsley, T. J. & Aitkenhead, N. 1988. *Geology of the country around Ashbourne and Cheadle.* Memoir of the British Geological Survey, 160pp

Critchley, M. 1979. *A geological outline of the Ecton copper mines, Staffordshire.* Bulletin of the Peak District Mines Historical Society, Vol 7, No 4, pp177-191

Ford, T. D., Sarjeant, W. A. S. & Smith, M. E. 1993. *Minerals of the Peak District.* Bulletin of the Peak District Mines Historical Society, Vol 12, No 1, pp16-55

Masheder, R. & Rankin, A. H. 1988. *Fluid inclusion studies on the Ecton Hill copper deposits, North Staffordshire.* Mineralogical Magazine, Vol 52, pp473-482

Porter, L. & Robey, J. A. 1972. *The Royledge and New York Copper Mines, Upper Elkstones, near Leek, Staffs.* Bulletin of the Peak District Mines Historical Society, Vol 5, No 1, pp1-9

Section along Clayton Adit Level

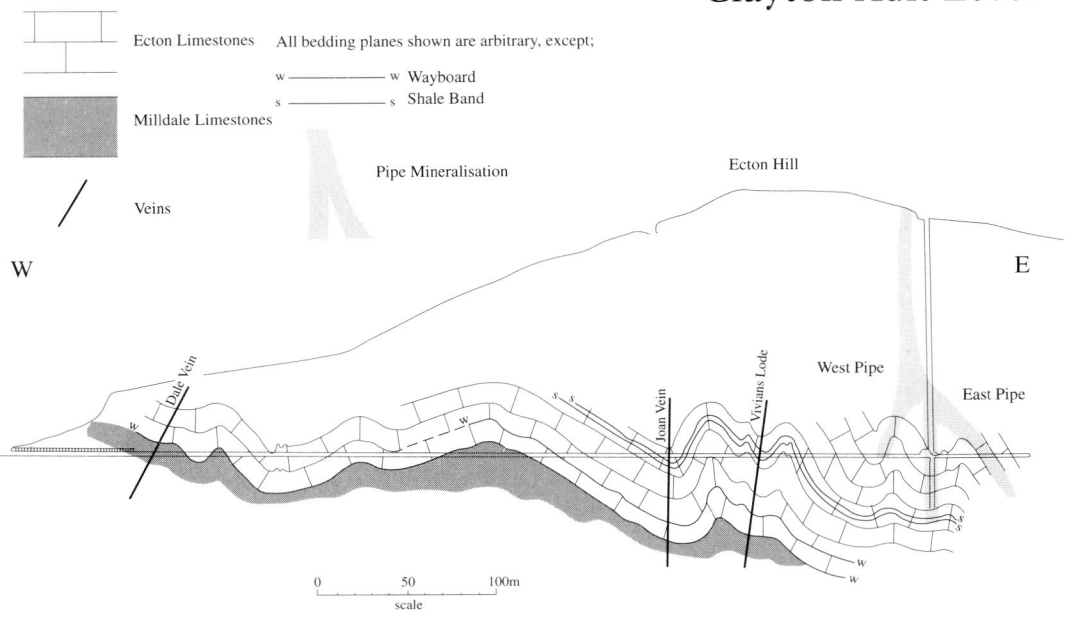

Porter, L. & Robey, J. A. 1973. *The Dale Mine, Manifold Valley,* Bulletin of the Peak District Mines Historical Society, Vol 5, No 2, pp93-106 & No 3, pp161-173

Quirk, D. G. 1993. *Origin of the Peak District Orefield.* Bulletin of the Peak District Mines Historical Society, Vol 12, No 1, pp1-16

Robey, J. A. & Porter, L. 1970. *The copper and lead mines of the Mixon area, Staffordshire.* Bulletin of the Peak District Mines Historical Society, Vol 4, No 4, pp256-280

Robey, J. A. & Porter, L. 1971. *The metalliferous mines of the Weaver Hills, Staffordshire.* Bulletin of the Peak District Mines Historical Society, Vol 4, No 6, pp417-428

Robey, J. A. & Porter, L. 1972. *The copper and lead mines of Ecton Hill, Staffordshire.* Moorland Publishing Co & Peak District Mines Historical Society, Leek & Bakewell. 92pp

Starkey, R. E. 1983. *On the occurrence of millerite at Ecton Hill, Staffoirdshire.* Journal of the Russell Society, Vol 1, pp16-18

Watson, J. J. W. 1860. *Notes on the metalliferous saddles of Derbyshire and Staffordshire.* The Geologist, No 3, pp357-369

Special thanks to Martin Critchley for redrawing the maps in this chapter.

3 Ecton Copper Mines

3.1 Introduction

The copper and lead deposits on Ecton Hill at Wetton in North Staffordshire have been known and worked for at least three centuries, during which time fortunes have been made and lost in the search there for mineral wealth. There are a number of features that make the Ecton Mines worthy of a detailed study, for not only were they important locally but they also made a significant contribution to the national production of minerals. Also the mines were innovators (or at least early users) of several new techniques later to become widespread throughout the industry.

On a local level the Ecton Mine was almost unique in being a rich copper mine on the western edge of the Peak District, an area usually associated with a profusion of lead mines. Although the ore deposits at Ecton were in the same Carboniferous Limestone as the lead mines of Derbyshire the form that the mineral veins took was quite different The geology and mineralogy of the mine has been studied by Critchley, and is covered in Chapter 2 by Dr T. D. Ford.

The impact on the local community was very significant and the mines were the largest single employer of labour in the area outside the traditional industry of agriculture. At one time many hundreds of people were employed at the mines and smelting works as well as many more involved in the carriage of materials by pack horses or carts. It is hard to imagine now that at the height of production, there would have been packhorse trains with perhaps as many as 50 to 70 animals setting off almost daily for Whiston.

One feature of the administration of the Ecton Mines that set them apart from the Derbyshire lead mines was the ownership of the mineral rights. In the Derbyshire Peak, the rights to the lead minerals, (and to these alone) were vested in the Crown. Anyone could (and still can) claim the rights to work a mineral vein for lead, by obeying certain laws and paying duty on the ore produced. Outside these areas the mineral rights belonged to private individuals, at Ecton these being the Duke of Devonshire and the Burgoyne family. Both of these were sold in the 1960s to Geoff Cox who established the Ecton Education Centre. His purchase of the Burgoyne rights included all their mineral rights to the manor of Wetton together with the title of Lord of the Manor.

The Duke of Devonshire

While the mines were originally leased to speculators, or adventurers, once the size of the ore deposits was realised the Duke of Devonshire became deeply involved and became one of the few landed gentry who worked the mines on their own land. Thus he had the responsibility for maintaining a large labour force in an area where many of his workers were also his tenants. This was not done for any great reason of charity, but because it gave him the largest return. It does seem that probably the workers also benefited by this arrangement for the Duke had a vested interest in maintaining both his land and tenants.

He continued to work the mines after they had ceased to be a paying concern, and only reintroduced the leasing of the mines to speculative concerns when it was clear that their economic days were well and truly over. The Duke of Devonshire was also deeply involved in mineral ventures elsewhere, particularly in the neighbouring Derbyshire ore field where he leased the mineral duties from the Crown and he was a shareholder in quite a few mines, not all of which paid their way. Ecton was certainly one his most successful ventures for it gave him a

Clayton Mine's 960 feet deep Engine Shaft

return of over a third of a million pounds in the 18th Century.

Nationally, Ecton was one of the richest individual copper mines in Britain in the 18th Century and received attention from many interested visitors, some of whom, luckily for us today, recorded their impressions of the mine. The mainstay of the copper industry in Britain for most of the 18th and 19th Centuries were the Cornish mines which (apart from the latter part of the 18th Century) produced 80-85% of the country's output. Nearly all this ore, as well as much from elsewhere, was sent to the smelting works of South Wales, the centre of the world's copper industry until the late 19th Century.

Clearly one mine in the North Midlands would find it hard to compete with the scores of mines in Cornwall, yet in spite of this during its period of peak prosperity in the 1780s Ecton was producing 12% of the combined output from all the Cornish mines. Some notable Cornish mines had a greater output than Ecton in the 18th Century; for instance, the

Ecton Hill

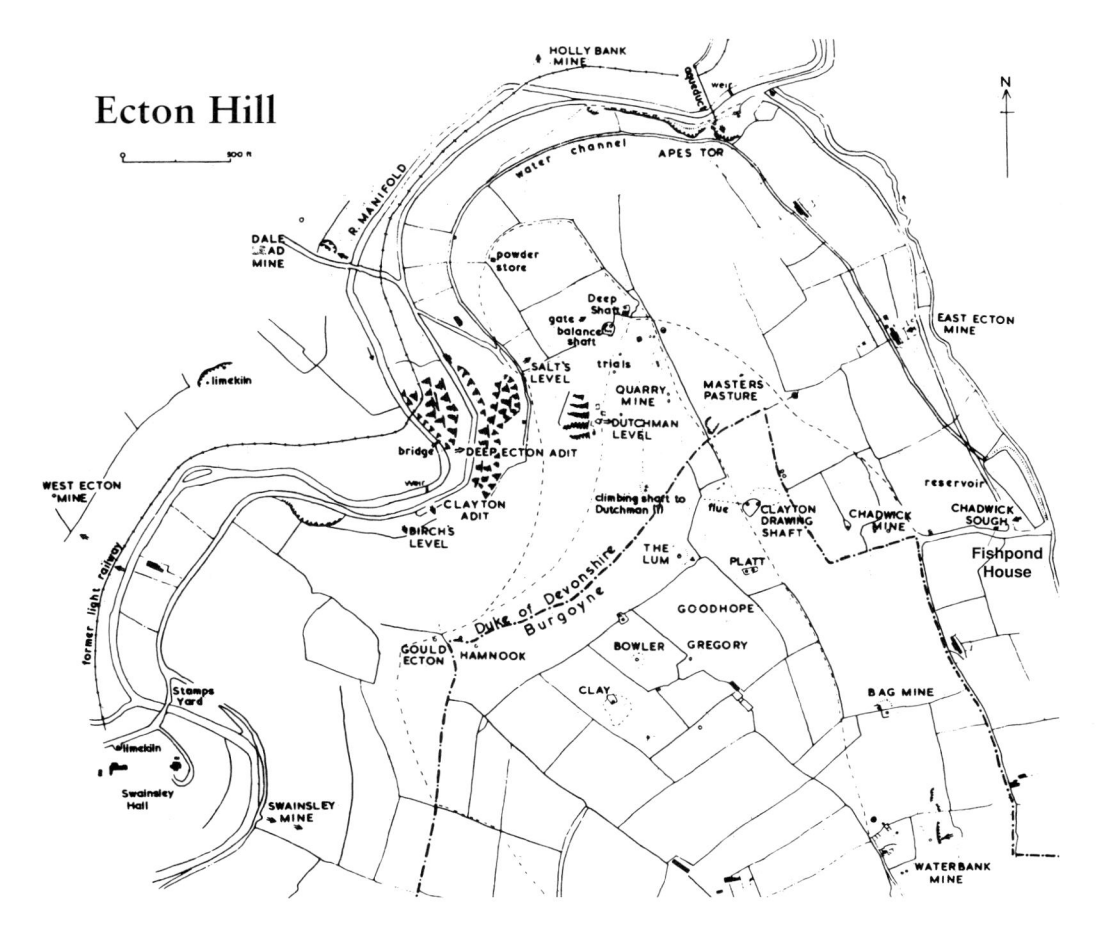

Consolidated Mines at Gwennap had an annual output of four times the Ecton Mine although even this was an amalgamation of five separate mines. During the 19th Century the output from the Cornish mines rose to staggering quantities and at least twenty-six mines produced more than Ecton's estimated total of 100,000 tons of ore concentrates.

The Benefits of a Dry Mine

Notwithstanding all this Ecton was in many ways a very successful mine, for whereas the Cornish mines were inevitably plagued by excessive drainage problems which usually absorbed all potential profits, the mines on Ecton Hill were remarkably free from water. Initially a mine could be drained by an adit (often called a sough in the Midlands) which would remove water down to the level of a valley floor or other low point, while below this a water wheel was often employed to work pumps. If, as often proved to be the case, this was insufficient, recourse had to be made to a steam engine. Until the latter part of the 18th Century steam pumps relied on Thomas Newcomen's 'atmospheric' engines which were used in large number for draining collieries.

They were also widely used in Cornwall (and in the Derbyshire lead mines) but their prodigious fuel consumption in an area remote from a supply of cheap coal made their use extremely uneconomic and many mines were forced to close as a result. The fuel economies, produced as a result of James Watt's improvements to Newcomen's engine, were eagerly taken up by the Cornish miners. Even so the large quantities of water found at depth and the high payment (or 'premium') charged by Watt for the use of his engines took a large slice out of the expected profits. In contrast to this, at Ecton, where the workings were deeper than any other in Britain in the 18th Century, a simple four HP water-operated pumping engine coped with all the drainage problems below adit level. Here a clear 40% profit was averaged over the sixty years the mine was worked by the Duke of Devonshire.

Competition

By the 1770s another competitor appeared on the scene in the form of the Parys Mountain Mines in Anglesey. Here was a great mass of copper ore (albeit of low grade) so close to the surface that it could almost be quarried out. It was also less than a mile from a deep-water anchorage where ships could bring in coal or take ore straight to the smelting works in South Wales or those on the Lancashire coalfield at minimum cost. Very soon the mines were under the control of Thomas Williams, an astute business man who, with an aggressive sales policy and a series of price cuts, soon had virtually the whole of the copper trade under his control.

On top of the strife with Boulton and Watt over the premiums for their pumping engines, the competition with the Anglesey Mines practically bankrupted the Cornish copper industry and Williams soon became the uncrowned 'Copper King'. Mining, smelting and manufacturing combinations (virtually price rings) were formed to counteract the threat from Anglesey, a threat which did not recede until the output dropped in the early 19th Century by which time over 2.25 million tons of ore and a profit of £2,500,000 had been produced. The story of these manoeuvres has been well documented elsewhere (1) and it makes fascinating reading, but further details are unnecessary here.

In general, the Staffordshire mines were not involved in these intrigues, the most serious effect being the overproduction of copper and the consequent drastic reduction in price at the period when Ecton's output was at its peak. Also by smelting his own ore the Duke managed to avoid the price rings of the Swansea smelters and so he had a free choice of market for the finished copper ingots, much of which was sold for brassmaking. In many quarters of the copper industry it was felt that the Ecton Mines offered the only hope of breaking the grip of Thomas Williams on the copper trade. Unfortunately output from Ecton began to drop before it had any real effect on the monopoly of the Anglesey Mines.

Decline

By the third decade of the 19th Century the output of ore from Ecton Hill had become a small fraction of that some fifty years before. Now it was the turn of the speculative mining adventurers, working on a small scale, to probe the hill in an attempt to discover fresh mineral deposits. In this they were unsuccessful and of the many companies that leased the mines very few were to make a profit, while most made a substantial loss. By piecing together the activities of this complex of companies we can see how the attitudes to working the mines changed over the years and how the techniques of mining changed with them.

Technological Innovation

Ecton has a niche of its own in the use of new mining techniques: explosives were traditionally said to have been used here for the first time in Britain for mining purposes (now disputed by Jim Rieuwerts); boats were used underground very shortly after their successful introduction at the Duke of Bridgwater's Worsley Collieries near Manchester; a balance-beam hydraulic pumping engine was used for drainage and was probably the largest of its type ever built; while one of the earliest of James Watt's rotative steam engines was used for raising ore in the 1780s. Not only were the mines deep (over 1,300ft) and rich, but the main mineral deposits were unique vertical 'pipe' veins descending through highly contorted Carboniferous Limestone on the western edge of the Peak District plateau.

Despite the importance of these mines, the previously published accounts rely heavily on a few early descriptions, made mainly by gentry who visited Ecton as part of their Grand Tour, which have been quoted many times since. The most comprehensive previous account is that given by Miss Nellie Kirkham (2), making the best use of the then available published material and mine plans. A valuable second edition included mineralogical data by Dr T D Ford and a series of surveys by the Leicester University Speleological Society of nearly all the underground workings still accessible. Since then a whole series of documents and reports came to light, enabling a comprehensive account of mining activities at Ecton to be written by Robey and Porter in 1972. That book is incorporated here, slightly amended for the better understanding we now have of the mine's history.

In the space available it has not proved possible to give detailed descriptions of the surface

Ecton Ore Sales After 1850

Date	Copper tonnage	value	Lead tonnage	value	Zinc tonnage	value
ECTON MOUNTAIN MINING CO						
1851	96.00.0	777.00.0	01.17.3	11.12.1		
1852	56.19.3	560.00.1	23.04.1	210.14.7		
1853	51.01.1	532.07.8	31.09.0	317.18.3		
1854	42.19.2	506.11.4	15.19.3	141.12.2		
1855	29.00.0	328.04.11	11.19.0	129.13.0		
1856	15.02.0	151.04.0	17.08.0	173.17.7		
1857	9.08.3	115.16.6	5.06.3	44.12.2		
Total	**301**	**1971**	**137**	**1030**		
ECTON CONSOLIDATED MINING CO						
1858	-	-	10.14.0	68.17.0		
1859	3.12.2	38.18.2	0.05.0	2.05.0		
1860	8.16.0	101.12.0	-	-		
1861	10.05.2	63.05.6	7.19.0	74.07.1		
Total	**23**	**204**	**19**	**145**		
NEW ECTON MINING CO						
1862	-	-	-	-		
1863	16.11.0	126.16.2	-	-		
1864	11.06.2	118.06.5	11.14.0	121.02.10		
1865	3.08.1	18.01.10	6.02.2	59.05.6		
1866			1.18.2	19.06.3	4.10.0	18.00.0
Total	**31**	**263**	**20**	**200**		
COLIN MATHER						
1866	4.0.2	16.08.0	1.14.3	17.16.2		
1867	18.04.1	92.01.3	33.08.3	318.11.3		
Total	**22**	**108**	**35**	**336**		
ECTON. CLAYTON & WATERBANK MINING CO						
1868	14.16.3	99.01.5	58.12.3	544.03.9		
1869						
1870	1.15.0*	10.17.8	20.00.0	27.12.6		
1871	-	-	47.00.0	304.11.8		
1872	2.00.0*	13.14.8	52.00.0	382.10.9		
1873	1.05.0*	8.00.10	see 1872	11.08.1		
1874	0.10.0	2.00.4	2.15.0	18.19.3		
Total	**20**	**134**	**180**	**1289**		
ECTON CO LTD						
1883/5						
1886	85.00.0*	265*	25.00.	112.10.0*	150.00.0*	
1887	?	?			120.00.0*	
1888	65. 0.0*	290.0.0*				
Total	**150**	**555**	**25**	**112**	**270**	**1000***
Grand Total	**578**	**3498**	**436**	**3312**	**274**	**1018**

*Approximate
In 1868, some £250 of the lead ore may be attributable to Colin Mather's Company

Dale Mine Ore Sales After 1850

Date	? tonnage	all lead value
1857	27.10.0	348.07.3
1858	25.01.1	371.15.0
1859		798.07.5
1860		3218.14.7
1861	333.15.0	3564.03.10
1862	70. 2.0	524.16.3
1863	nil	nil
1864	567. 4.3	5106.08.11
1865		4357.08.2
1866	401.06.2	2681.14.0
1867	173.03.0	946.06.3
1868	99.04.3	682.16.11
1869	25.17.0	67.04.2
1870	156.14.0	1012.19.1
1871 to October		1314.14.10
Total	**1879.18.1**	**24995.16.8**

Ecton Ore Sales Before 1851

Date	Copper Tonnage	Value	Lead Tonnage	Value	Zinc Tonnage	Value
1826	29.02.1	170.12.10				
1827	237.10.2	1494.14.7				
1828	218.00.0	1299.15.4				
1829	210.07.3	1280.11.8				
1830	211.09.2	1656.16.9				
1831	111.03.3	889.04.10				
1832	93.20.3	831.09.11				
1833	71.13.2	391.05.1				
1834	102.17.0	792.13.11				
1835	71.02.2	658.17.4				
1836	92.06.3	666.18.7				
1837	67.03.0	529.14.4				
1838	68.20.3	461.07.3				
1839			21.13.2	95.11.9		
1840	233.10.0	1022.17.7	14.12.0	102.04.0		
1841	122.20.0	780.12.1	17.19.1	155.00.10	113.13.0	268.09.2
1842	242.18.0	1376.09.6	7.02.0	43.01.4	348.13.0	938.09.10
1843	375.13.1	2094.11.3	-	-	554.04.2	1433.16.3
1844	252.20.1	913.10.4	18.04.1	91.18.3	127.19.2	252.06.2
1845	55.09.3	581.01.8	-	-	1.10.0	2.05.0
1846	56.18.1	525.03.5	11.12.0	63.16.0	41.10.2	72.13.4+
1847	50.18.1	268.15.3	8.00.0	58.00.0		
1848	18.20.1	81.11.10	1.01.0	5.07.7		
1849	21.05.0	164.06.8	6.11.1	37.07.11		
1850	8.02.0	48.18.9	-	-		
1827	22.14.1	57.09.11*	+possibly due to Attwood & 1845 figures			

* mixed Cu & Pb (additional)

1826-38	1608 tons	£11152			
1839-45	1283 tons	£6769	80 tons	£488	1146 tons	£2895
1846-48	115 tons	£810	21 tons	£127	41 tons	£73
1848-50	41 tons	£279	7 tons	£37		

Above: The inner end of Apes Tor level showing the former dam of 1823
Right: Ecton Deep Adit in 1963 when the mine water froze. The dam held water for the former creamery **Below:** The mine sales office, now a dwelling house
Opposite: Apes Tor level near to the entrance

remains, nor the underground workings, but these have been presented elsewhere (3), while it is hoped that the descriptions that follow here are sufficient for the reader to appreciate the general state of the mines when they were in operation.

Ecton Hill, with its large open fields, limestone walls and pasture land is bounded to the west by the River Manifold and on the east by a stream flowing north in a wide shallow valley joining the Manifold at Apes Tor, together with another stream flowing south from near the Manor House through the narrow valley at Wetton-in-the-Hollow to join the Manifold at Redhurst Crossing.

The Mine Workings

About seventy mine workings are scattered over the hill, including forty to fifty vertical shafts, some deep (over 300ft to water), others shallow, some stone-lined, others left rough, while many others are grassed over and show few visible traces today.

The chief mines were Ecton, Clayton, Dutchman, Chadwick and Waterbank, but the principal owner, the Duke of Devonshire, only had royalty over the Ecton, Dutchman and Chadwick mines. The other mines were owned by the Burgoyne family, and, since the main adit to these mines runs through Devonshire land, the private companies of last Century had to pay a token sum (usually £10 per annum) for access through the Clayton Adit, Dutchman Level and Birch's Level.

The position of the main ore body, the Ecton Pipe, is marked on the hilltop by a barn converted from the Boulton and Watt engine house where the main engine shaft, or Deep Shaft, goes down nearly to the base of the mine. Other nearby shafts descend through the workings, while three major adits pierce them. The Apes Tor Level, used to convey water into the mine for pumping purposes, and now filled with mud and water, commences at Apes Tor; the Ecton Deep Adit (the original sough) lies beneath the remains of a creamery and cheese factory built here in the 1920s; Salt's Level also connects with the Ecton Pipe Vein and Deep Shaft some 120ft above the river, although this too was considerably altered in the 1930s and is now only accessible through the Ecton Education Centre. The Clayton Deep Adit, the main entrance to the Clayton Pipe Vein, enters the hill at the side of the road, and this connects with the Waterbank and Chadwick Mines.

The Dressing Floors
The smelting works and dressing floors, which were started in the 1760s and enlarged in the following two decades, were situated between the river and the road along with many other buildings which were clustered on the western slope of the hill overlooking the river. The position of many of these buildings can be determined from old plans (pages 76&91), but the use to which most of them were put is now completely unknown and they have nearly all since disappeared. Early in the 19th Century new dressing floors were built further up the hillside, whilst late last Century, washing and crushing plant, sorting sheds, a two-storey engine house and a great trestled incline from the Clayton Adit entrance to the dressing floors were built. Further up the hillside the isolated tip at Dutchman Mine and remains of ruined buildings can still be seen, now accentuated by the trees growing around the tip.

Ecton Hill Today
Looking south up the hillside from the Ecton engine house several very old workings can be seen, as well as surface workings on a north-south vein. Also from here, looking down into the Manifold Valley towards Butterton, three ridges of disturbed ground are visible, being where some of the rake veins outcropped to the surface. The southerly one is Dale Vein, the middle one is Dutchman Vein and the most northerly either Ecton or Quarry Vein. The principal north-south veins are Waterbank and Vivian's, (see page 31).

At the back of the hill there is further evidence of mining activity, with a number of deep shafts such as Clayton Shaft (449ft to the adit), Bowler (300ft), Chadwick (200ft) and Waterbank Shafts (270ft). Some of the smaller mines shown on the plan (on page 29) connect to the larger systems, such as Bag with Dutchman; Chadwick and Waterbank with Clayton. Waterbank was the only mine on this side of the hill to have its own dressing floor, but this fell into disuse when the mine was joined to the Clayton Adit shortly before all operations finally ceased.

The fishpond at East Ecton and its water course round the hillside still exist. The water was conveyed in a gritstone trough to provide supplies initially to the water wheel of the slag mill and later to the dressing floors. At Apes Tor there are now no remains of the 40ft high wooden raised launder which carried water to the underground waterwheel in the Ecton Mine, while at Swainsley only the name Stamps Yard indicates the position of the ore crushing stamps, erected early in the 19th Century.

Of the buildings now remaining at Ecton, only the manager's house, sales room and offices are left, all now used as dwellings, but the large castle folly is modern, dating from the 1930s.

Copper in North Staffordshire
Ecton was the last of the North Staffordshire copper and lead mines to close, ending an era of metalliferous mining which had seen the development and decline of an important local history unable to compete with the developing orefields overseas. The Mixon Copper Mine, west of Ecton, closed in 1858 followed by New York, Royledge, Ribden, Thorswood, Dale, Bincliff and many more smaller ventures. But mining was only one aspect of the Staffordshire copper industry, originally established in the area on account of the availability of good quality coal from the Cheadle Coalfield and waterpower from the River Churnet. The location was even more advantageous when the Ecton Mines provided a local source of rich ore and the Caldon branch of the Trent and Mersey Canal provided greatly improved communications.

In 1734 Thomas Patten set up a brass works at Cheadle and a brasswire mill at Alton in addition to his works at Warrington in Lancashire, and later he built a brass works and a rolling mill at Oakamoor, as well as a copper works near Cheadle. The Cheadle brass works were later operated by James Keys who afterwards took over the Whiston works, which had originally been established to smelt the Ecton copper ore. The Oakamoor works were sold to Thomas Bolton and Sons in 1851, who still refine copper and manufacture a wide range of copper products for the electrical industry at their works at Froghall, having demolished the Oakamoor works in 1963. Thomas Bolton's factory is the sole survivor today of the North Staffordshire copper industry.

3.1 Introduction

Salts Level in 1924

Bibliography

To avoid overburdening the reader with excessive references the following are the primary sources upon which the bulk of the Ecton chapters have been based. The date and content should identify the sources of information quoted in the text. For the 18th Century the Devonshire Collection at Chatsworth House has provided the bulk of the information, the other account books of this period being duplicates which fill some of the gaps in the Devonshire papers. For the later periods the voluminous pages of the *Mining Journal* have proved to be an invaluable source.

Minor sources, secondary references and additional notes are given overleaf at the end of each chapter.

Accounts, reports, correspondence, plans, leases 1660-1811
Account and day books 1760-1825, 1851-1885
Account book 1783-1792
Account books 1823-31, 1842-4
Account books 1826-1861
Account book 1830-1860
Correspondence, accounts and reports 1811-1846
Whiston account books 1831-1841
Correspondence and drawings
Mining Journal 1847-1891
Prospectuses and reports 1849, 1850, 1861, 1866, 1883
Surveys and plans 1820, 1848, 1858, 1889

Below: Ecton Creamery, occupying former mine buildings, in 1924. Note the Ecton Mine engine house on the skyline and the weir for the Stamps Yard water **Opposite:** The site of the smelters and the creamery today

3.1 Introduction

General abbreviation used in the end of chapter references:
Bull PDMHS – Bulletin of Peak District Mines Historical Society
MH – Mining History (the successor to the above).

References to the Introduction

1. Barton D. B, 1961, *A History of Copper Mining in Cornwall & Devon.* Bradford Barton, Truro

   Dodd A. H, 1933, *The Industrial Revolution in North Wales,* pp152-169 (3rd edn 1971)

   Hamilton H, 1926, *The English Brass and Copper Industries to 1800* (reprinted 1967)

   Harris J. R, 1964, *The Copper King*

   Harris J. R, and Roberts R. O, 1963, *Business History,* V, No 2, pp69-82

   Roberts R. O, 1969, *Development and Decline of Non Ferrous Metal Smelting Industries of South Wales,* In 'Industrial South Wales' ed. by W. E. Minchinton

2. Kirkham N, 1947, Journal Derbyshire Arch Soc, 67. Reprinted 1961 as PDMHS Special Publication No 1

   Kirkham N, and Ford T. D, 1967, *The Ecton Copper Mines,* PDMHS, Spec Pub, No 1, 2nd Edn

3. Porter L, 1969, Bull PDMHS, *Ecton Hill: The Surface Features,* Vol 4, No 2, p156-169 and 1971. *Ecton Hill: The Underground Features,* Vol 4, No 3, pp195-216

3.2 The Early History to 1760

Prehistory

In June 1855, The antiquarian Thomas Bateman entered workings at Ecton and recovered nine stones which he considered to be hammer stones. He reported that they had been found with 'sharpened pieces of stags horns'. However he did not leave any note of the mine he had descended. His stones may be seen in Sheffield City Museum.

Shortly after the end of World War II, the pioneer historian of Derbyshire's lead mines – Nellie Kirkham – published a short history of the Ecton Mines following a series of underground visits. During the exploration of the workings above the Dutchman Adit Level, she observed a piece of bone which looked like an antler tool together with what might have been hammer stones. She left these artefacts in the mine, which became increasingly unstable, the main shaft to the surface collapsing in May 1963. This effectively blocked the workings, sealing the bone in the mine.

During recent exploration in 1994 upwards from the Dutchman Adit in very unstable conditions, a bone was, by chance, found again and brought out. It was discovered by Bob Dearman in association with Garth Thomas. The bone was radiocarbon dated to 1880-1630 BC and may now be seen in the Peak District Mining Museum at Matlock Bath.

Also in 1994 Guilbert reported the discovery of four hammer stones on the large Dutchman tip, which are now also in the Sheffield City Museum and more have been found since. It is a pity that these more recent stones were not deposited in the Peak District Mining Museum at Matlock Bath! These discoveries would seem to indicate the working of ore from prehistoric times but currently one is unable to point to any specific working and say 'this is a prehistoric excavation'. There has been too much reworking to do that and in any case, the most obvious area is exceedingly unstable. It makes exploration, however important, life threatening.

Medieval History

About 1220, William de Wrottesley, Robert Putrel and William, son of William de Buterdon, granted the park and wood of Ekedon to the monks of Tutbury Priory in free alms (1), and the Tutbury Cartulary contains a quit-claim

> 'from William de Wrottesley to the Priory of his rights in the park of Ecton and in the wood lying between the park and the bridge of Warslow, saving his rights of common outside the park and the wood' (2).

The park is said to have been a deer park (3). Upon the dissolution of the Priory, Ecton passed to the Crown which granted 'pastures in Wetton called Ecton and le Halesfield' to Sir John Gifford of Chillington, Staffs, in 1541 (4).

In 1547, John Crymes of London, a clothmaker, purchased from King Henry VIII, through the Court of Augmentations, the manor of Wetton and Butterton; appurtenances in Byncliff; tithes of corn and grain, a tithe barn and rents in Butterton; the tithes of wool and lamb, a watermill, houses and land in Castern and other property in Wetton, Butterton, Castern and Byncliff (Devonshire Collection, Chatsworth House, H/273/1). The manor of Wetton and Butterton plus his property there and in Throwley, Crowfoot (?) and Castern was sold by Henry Crymes to Richard Flyre, a mercer from Uttoxeter, who sold it on to William Cavendish in January 1575 (Dev Coll H/273/6).

By 1575 the Cavendish family (later Earls, and then Dukes of Devonshire) were in possession of Ecton, when William Cavendish established his right against Richard Flyre, Henry Walton and his wife Trewa over 50 dwellings, 20 gardens, 20 orchards, 5,560 acres of land and £4 of rent in Wetton, Butterton, Throwley, Crowfoot and Casturn. Two years later Cavendish was again involved in litigation which showed that his estates in this area had increased considerably (5).

The Burgoyne family also held land at Ecton and in 1580 were involved in litigation to establish their rights to 500 acres of land and various tithes (6). The Burgoynes were originally the Lords of the Manor, although they sold the land (but not the mineral rights) in 1648.

Although none of these early documents mention mining at Ecton, minerals were certainly known in the area at a very early date, for

Above: The remains of buildings at Waterbank Mine. The fence surrounds the engine shaft
Below: Ecton from the Dale Mine in the 1960s. Trees are now masking much of the tips

in 1376 the vicar of Blore along with John and Richard Grendon of Warslow were arrested for taking lead ore to the value of £10 from the land of Henry de Brailesford at Grindon (7).

The Seventeenth Century

This saw the start of serious mining, when Ecton became one of the very few British copper mines at that time and achieved greater fame by traditionally becoming the first mine in this island to use gunpowder, a claim which now appears to be inaccurate (8). In order to understand fully the operations at Ecton it is necessary to review the state of the copper and brass trade at that time.

During the 16th and 17th Centuries the copper and brass industries were under the monopolistic control of the Company of Mines Royal and the Company of Mineral and Battery Works, originally chartered by Elizabeth I in 1568 to encourage the home production of these metals. The Mines Royal had the privilege of mining copper in the counties of Westmoreland, Cumberland, Lancaster, Cornwall, Devon, Gloucester, Worcester and York and in the Principality of Wales, while these rights in the remaining counties of England as well as for the manufacture of brass and other privileges had been granted to the Mineral and Battery Works. During the 16th Century these companies had imported German workers to mine copper and produce brass and iron wire. During the early 17th Century their activities declined and their privileges came under attack, with the formation of brass and copper works in competition to the Mines Royal and the Mineral and Battery Works.

There was also fierce foreign competition, mainly from Sweden, with the result that the importation of brass wire was prohibited in 1638. English copper mining was almost at standstill, so that much Swedish copper had to be imported. In spite of this situation the two companies did little to encourage the production of the metals themselves and the usual answer was to impose further duties on imported copper. As might be expected there was much opposition to the monopolies, which by now were being openly violated. It has been thought that during the Civil War and Protectorate (1642-1660) all the operations of the companies were suspended, no Governors chosen and no meetings held, particularly since most of the shareholders were Royalist (9). This is now known not to have been the case, although both before and after the Restoration in 1660 they were concerned solely with leasing their rights to those wishing to mine copper and make brass (10).

In 1668 Prince Rupert was elected as a Governor of the Mineral and Battery Works and discussions were held between the two companies, but no merger into a United Society took place until the next century. In spite of what has been previously written on the subject, Prince Rupert never played in active role in the copper industry and the sole reason for this election was to influence those in authority to assist the Companies to retain their powers. Eventually these monopolistic rights, which had only stifled the development of the industry were rescinded in two Acts of 1689 and 1694. This, together with the development of the reverberatory furnace for the smelting of copper using coal as a fuel, started a major upsurge in the copper industry, including the Staffordshire mines.

Pre Civil War Mining

The earliest known reference to copper in the area is in 1622, when Gerard Malynes reported that he had seen

> 'excellent copper ore of some mines in Staffordshire, in the hands of Mr Stonewell, which absolutely is the best ore that ever was found in England' (11).

In 1630 the lead mines of Staffordshire were recorded as belonging to Sir Richard Fleetwood of Calwich and Mr Hurt (12).

Nicholas Hurt had leased the lott and cope of lead ore in Wetton manor from the Earl of Devonshire in November 1626. The term was for twenty-one years at a payment of £20 pa and an initial sum of £160. Significantly, all 'copper gotten or to be gotten in any myne' was reserved, which may indicate that this had already been leased to someone else (?Mr Stonewell).

The earliest reference to Ecton occurs in the Alstonfield Parish Register. On 23rd July 1642, one 'Millar of Wessyd being dampt in a groane at Eckton' was buried. In 1652, George Lomas, also of Wessyd, met with the same fate. West Side is just north of Ecton Hill. These are two very early references to gassing in the Peak District.

3.2 The Early History to 1760

The earliest are 1586, at Wirksworth and 1612 at Flagg Moor (13).

The reference to Millar may well have been Mellor, for the family were at West Side a hundred years later. In August 1753, William Mellor of West Side, described as a miller, took a lease with John Fogg of Hartington from the Duke of Devonshire of a water corn mill at Hartington (Dev Coll H/197/17). William Mellor seems to have been a businessman too for in addition to his interests in these two mills, he and his mother, Jane, leased Wetton Mill and its house from the Duke in March 1730 (1731 on the modern calendar). This was renewed to William only in August 1751 (Dev Coll H/26/4 and 27/12). Presumably the Mellors were followed at Wetton Mill by the Redferns who invested in Royledge Mine (see Chapter 5). Wetton Mill dates from 1711, when it was rebuilt. John Smith, a millwright of Youlgreave, contracted with the Duke to pull down the 'water corn mill and kiln house' and rebuild them on the same site or nearby (Dev Coll H/26/26). Clearly a mill existed here in the 17th Century.

There is a reference to the mines being worked before the Civil War for £200 is recorded as having been spent on them. In 1654, 2 loads and 4 dishes of ore (most probably lead ore) were sold by the agent Jeremiah Rhode (14) who had previously worked in the Derbyshire lead mines. He was also known as Jeremy Roades, but this is clearly the same person.

After the Civil War

In 1660 the mines were reopened by the 3rd Earl of Devonshire and were worked continuously for the next five years with Jeremiah Rhodes in charge of the operations, at a salary of £20-£30 per annum. Up to the end of 1664 the not inconsiderable sum of £1,262 had been spent at Ecton and on a smelting mill at Ellastone.

In the 1660s 4 tons 6cwt of copper metal (probably the total produced) was sent to London. A total of 587 kibbles of copper ore (calculated from the wages at the stated rate of 10s per kibble) were mined and 472 kibbles sent for smelting. Also there is the statement that 85 dishes of copper ore (approx 17cwt) were bought at Tissington. This may relate to the mines situated to the west of the Bluebell pub, near Tissington Gates on the A515 or to Newton Grange, although 17th Century records of the latter only refer to lead ore. The quantity of ore produced at Ecton during this period shows a steady decrease:

    1660 180 kibbles
    1661 131
    1662 129
    1663 91
    1664 56

Since $9^{1}/_{2}$ kibbles held about 10cwt this would make a total ore production of about 30 tons, (each of 21cwt, the customary copper measure). The total copper metal production would be just under 5 tons, giving about 15% copper from the ore which is quite comparable with 18th Century values.

Jeremy Rhodes was still in charge of the operations, for which he was paid £20 in 1660, and 1664, £30 in 1661 and 1662, and apparently nothing in 1663. Jeremiah Roades appears in the Hearth Tax returns for 1666 as paying for 3 hearths at Eckton. See Robey, 1969, for more on this period, although some of it has been superceded by Rieuwerts et al (see below).

The Early Use of Gunpowder at Ecton

The material below on the initial use of gunpowder at Ecton is contributed by Jim Rieuwerts and John Barnatt. It is taken from a substantial article on the working of the mines at this period and also discusses the introduction of powder elsewhere in the Peak, plus a description of the likely mines involved at Ecton following on from an exploration of the accessible workings.

Two documents recently discovered by Jim Rieuwerts at the Public Record Office, London (PRO DL 1/427 and DL 1/428) confirm that rock breakage utilising gunpowder blasting was carried out in 1672 in a lead mine belonging to Sir Richard Fleetwood at Hanging Bank (see page 46) within the Burgoyne Liberty on Ecton Hill. Unfortunately, no similar manuscript evidence has yet been located by which similar blasting in the adjacent copper mines in the Devonshire royalty can be dated precisely. These include Stone Quarry Mine and the other nearby workings.

The Published Accounts

The earliest published account relating to gunpowder blasting at Ecton is the oft quoted

Underground Levels

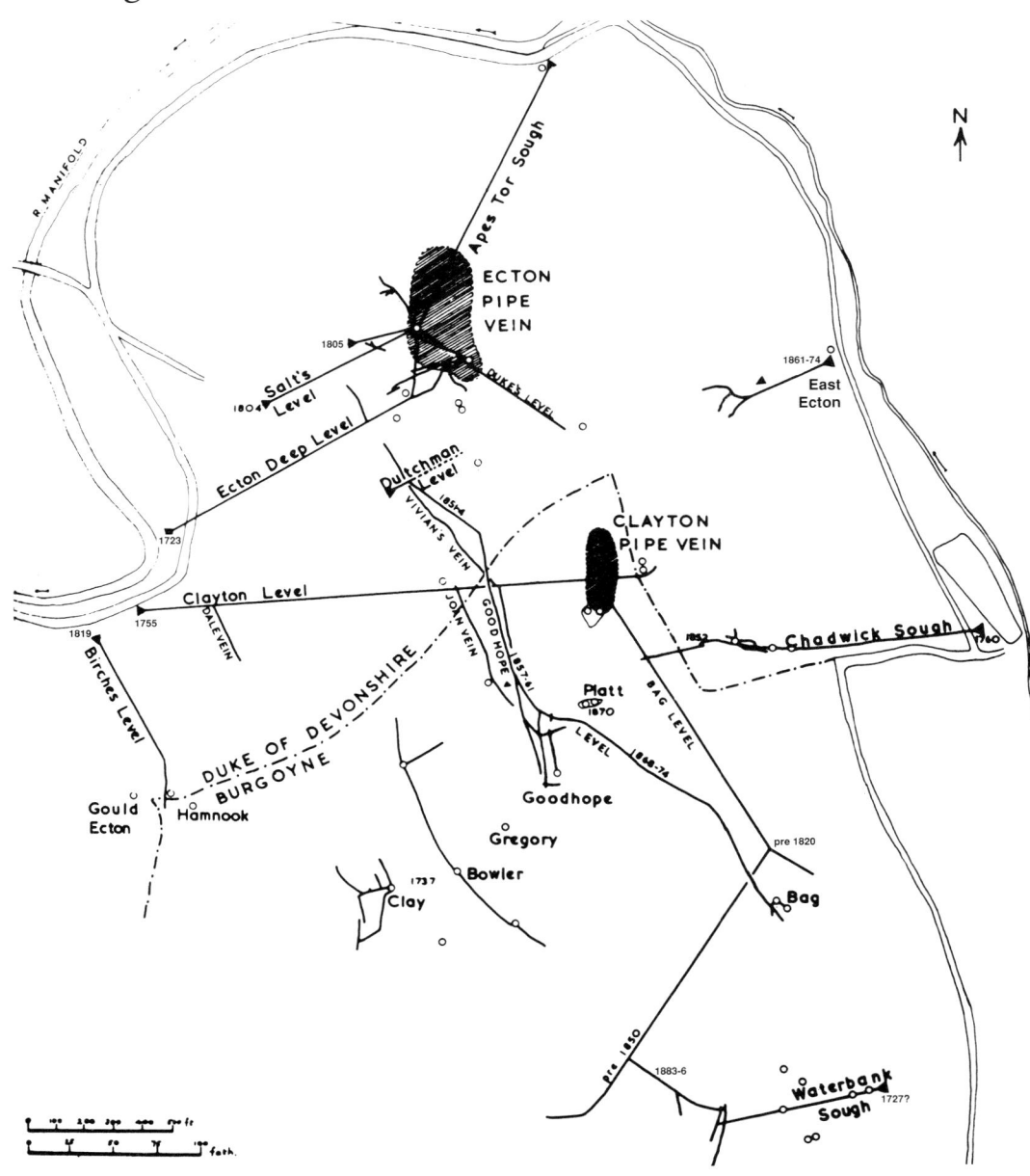

description written by Plot in 1679-80 and published in 1686:

> 'The Mine was workt several years by My Lord of Devon himself Sr. Richard Fleetwood and some Dutch men, but they had all left it off, before I came into the Country as not worth their while; Copper coming cheaper from Sweden than they could make it here; so that the workmen being disperst I could learn little more concerning it, but that the veins lay from eight to fifty yards deep, but all dipt North-Easterly, that they broke the rocks with Gunpowder and got 3 sorts of Ore: 1. a black sort which was best, 2. a yellow sort, the worst, and 3. a mixt sort of both...'

Over sixty years later Hooson (1747) referred to blasting operations at the Ecton

Mines and Watson (1781) also gave useful historical information about the workings. Hooson stated in 1747 that:

> 'About forty Years ago, some workmen came to a place called Ecton in Staffordshire, therefor to venture at an old Work, which was drowned with Water, in hopes to get Copper – but no old People in the Neighbourhood could give any account when it was last wrought, – they got Churn-Pumps, Sweat-Pumps, and Forces and got at length to bare the Soles, and the Water proving very easy, (though they struck it at a very great height) they got great Profit; but in the Work it was admired by all Miners that saw it, what Blast-Holes had been bored, most a Yard or four Foot long, and two Inches or more Diameter, so that in those Days they used not such small holes as we do in these... the report was that they were Dutchmen, others say Germans that was their Workmen'.

Watson, writing in 1781, a little over a hundred years after the introduction of blasting obtained his information from a person who had known the area for more than fifty years, who had:

> 'often seen the smith's shop in which, tradition says, the first boring auger that had ever been used in England was made; and that the first shot that was ever fired in Derbyshire or Staffordshire, was fired in this very copper mine at Ecton. The inhabitants of Wetton (a village adjoining to the mine) tell me the auger was made by some German miners'.

None of these three descriptions give a definite date for the early blasting and it was John Taylor, writing in 1799 in an otherwise sketchy article, who stated that the first use of gunpowder at Ecton had taken place in 1670. The source of his information is not known and the date is argued below to be slightly in error.

In one respect Hooson's 1747 account needs to be interpreted with caution. Many have assumed that the rediscovery of the large shot holes took place in about 1707 based on his statement that it took place about 40 years previously, but it is clear that Hooson's book was compiled over a great length of time. For example, he went to North Wales in 1707 at the request of Mr Thornhill of Stanton. It is therefore perfectly feasible that compilation of that part of his book dealing with the events at Ecton might have been undertaken earlier than 1747. On balance, given that Plot stated the mines had been abandoned for some time by 1679-80, the 'Gentlemen' adventurers could have begun their work anytime between 1680 and 1707. The other possibility, that he was describing unwatering in the 1660s, seems improbable, since the blast holes relating to yet earlier exploitation are unlikely to be of pre-1660s date.

Mining in the Devonshire Liberty 1660-68

Morton and Robey (1985) have discussed the working of copper within the royalty of the Earl of Devonshire by Jacob Mumma who leased mines here between August 1665 and early 1668. Mumma was a Dutchman who previously was a partner in the setting up of a brass wire mill at Esher in Surrey close to one of the main centres of the 17th Century ordnance gunpowder industry. Chancery proceedings dating from 1686 relating to the estate of Jacob Mumma the elder, who died in 1679, indicate that the Ecton mines had been run by his son, also called Jacob. The stated reason the copper mines closed after running at a loss was because they found

> 'the ore rising in very small veins and very small quantities'.

Evidence that the Mumma undertaking was probably responsible for the introduction of gunpowder at the Ecton mines is circumstantial. While the Mummas certainly leased mines at Ecton from the Earl of Devonshire between these dates and they were well placed to know of blasting technology, unfortunately there is no direct evidence to confirm the conclusion. However, the indirect evidence is persuasive. Hooson did not state where on Ecton Hill the mines he described were situated. However, that drill holes matching his description have been found at Stone Quarry Mine and in an adjacent working, both high on the hill above the so-called Dutchman Level, strongly indicates that it was the Devonshire mines on the northern part of the hill that were being described. This is supported by his observation that the work had been carried out by Dutch or German miners. He also noted the holes found were 'blast holes'.

Plot's observation that the veins haded to the north-east is consistent with the workings around Stone Quarry Mine but not the main Ecton Pipe at depth nor the mines from Clayton Pipe southwards. Similarly the stated reason why the mines closed in 1668 is consistent with the nature of the mineralization found at and immediately north of Stone Quarry Mine. The Earl of Devonshire is known to have worked his mines between 1660 and 1665 prior to renting them to Mumma. However, he is unlikely to have used powder blasting as detailed expense accounts survive for this period and these make reference to such items as candles, coal and ropes but not powder (Robey, 1969, pp152-54).

All these observations allow the reasonable conclusion to be drawn that gunpowder blasting took place in the copper workings in the Devonshire Liberty between 1665 and 1668.

Mining in the Burgoyne Liberty – a 1672-4 Dispute

The Burgoyne family had formerly owned the southern portion of Ecton Hill, but when this was sold off in 1648 they retained the mining rights. During April 1672 nineteen articles were drawn up governing the working of lead mines within their royalty (PRO, DL 1/428).

On the 2nd of May 1672, Jeremiah (or Jeremy) Roades (Rhodes) one of Sir Roger Burgoyne's agents, staked out two meers of ground, 30 yards each meer, at Hanging Bank, Ecton, for the use of Thomas Bonsall and William Mayott. The latter lived at Gateham Grange, nearby. They found the charges too great and after only two months work they sold their meers to Sir Richard Fleetwood. He was 'att very great charge' in working the mine, but he continued to do so and it was still at work in June 1673 (PRO DL 1/426).

Sir Richard Fleetwood, Edward Bagshawe and Matthew Redfearne brought a law suit for trespass into the Duchy of Lancaster Court in 1673-4 against John Clayton, Philip Clayton, Gilbert Clayton, John Sleigh, Raphael Bradbury, Richard Goodwin, John Buxton and Thomas Wood. Fleetwood claimed that in 1672, Clayton's miners had worked deeper than his own miners and obtained 500 loads of lead, valued at £700, from the southern end of his meers.

Clayton had been given one meer of ground at the beginning of April 1672 very close to the two meers formerly owned by Bonsall and Mayott. Clayton's meer was described as extending east-west in length and north-south in breadth. In contrast, the other two meers were described as running north-south in a line northwards of Clayton's meer.

Location of the Workings

The exact location of the mines described in this dispute is not explicitly stated. Hanging Bank is a name that appears to apply to the crest of Ecton Hill as a whole. It is a common name for steep sloping ground, such as that to be found where Clayton Shaft exists. It was still current in the 19th Century as illustrated by accounts of the opening of two barrows here. The 1673-4 documentation makes it clear the mines were in the Burgoyne Liberty. A reasonable argument can be made that, as members of the Clayton family are named and that the Clayton meer was probably in a wide but irregular deposit, the mines in question are likely to have been at and near the great Clayton Pipe (cf Robey 1975). The 1755 lease for the construction of Clayton Sough includes a plan and this clearly marks 'Clayton's Mine' as the pipe working.

That the workings in the Devonshire Liberty are described by Plot and Hooson as producing copper, whilst those in the Burgoyne Liberty are noted as lead mines is probably an oversimplification. We know from later mining activity on the hill that while lead became richer in the southern parts of the hill and copper less so, both minerals were present throughout. Both may well have been exploited. Clayton Pipe certainly produced copper in significant quantities in the 18th and 19th Centuries.

Clayton's evidence throws considerable light on the nature of the deposit:

> 'Lead mynes lye in Rakes and pypes inclosed on each side with lime stone sides and do not lie all over the ground like fflots of lead oare or Coales... the Lymestone Rocks by the myners commonly called sides,

Top: The Ecton Mine enginehouse and area of prehistoric working. The fenced shaft descends into the Ecton pipeworking **Above left:** The Ecton Deep Adit level, originally called the Ecton Sough **Above right:** Stone Quarry Mine

Ryders – are the walls and partitions between all mynes they doe not lye perpendicular but sometimes hade or bend – and are forced to be wrought with sumps or turnings – when they are run much out of the perpendicular lyne the miners are forced to set stowes and turne trees underground – the Rake veins and pypes doe runn soe uncertainly under the ground that they would often fall to be out of the length or breadth of the quarter cord – the myners cannot for the hardness of the rock sinke perpendicularly downwards but are forced to worke anyways they can sinke downwards to finde or follow their Rakes, Veynes and Pypes'.

One can imagine the confusion underground at the junction of Fleetwood's two meers with the massive, irregular, near-vertical pipe deposit.

The document includes evidence from Clayton and partners that the miners employed by Fleetwood,

> 'with gunpowder have blowne upp or broken in peeces the hard limestone which were side wall and [partition?] between the defendants said workes and the complainants worke, which they ought not as this defendant conceive to have done, and have endangered this defendants workmens lives thereby'.

Unfortunately the account does not make it clear what type of shot holes were employed and thus whether they were of similar size to those noted by Hooson and found in Stone Quarry Mine. Elsewhere much smaller shot holes were probably being employed in the region in the 17th Century (see Rieuwerts, Barnatt et al, 1997).

Further documents relating to this case exist in the Wolley Collection in the British Museum and the Gell Papers in the Derbyshire Record Office and have been described previously (Robey, 1975); these make no mention of the use of gunpowder. Thus, the quote just given is the only currently known first-hand account of the 17th Century use of gunpowder at Ecton.

When all the available evidence is studied it becomes clear that two separate mining operations were involved that used powder, one on the Earl of Devonshire's property, the other situated within the Burgoyne Liberty. At the latter the blasting work took place in 1672, whilst it is probable, if unproven, that somewhat earlier use of powder took place in the Earl of Devonshire's mines between 1665 and 1668. These may well have included those workings now known as Stone Quarry Mine.

When Plot visited Ecton the works had been abandoned and it appears that what little information he obtained may have been an amalgamation about mining on both Devonshire and Burgoyne Liberties. Thus, as Robey has pointed out, Plot's statement relating to the mines at Ecton being worked by 'My Lord of Devon, Sir Richard Fleetwood and some Dutchmen', was in error in that there may well not have been one partnership, but that at least two separate companies were involved (Robey 1975).

A few years after the cessation of mining operations, Ecton was visited by John Woodward, an early geologist, who collected some fine mineral specimens. His collection, which dates mainly from 1680 to 1690, is the oldest mineral collection in its original state and may still be seen at Cambridge. Many of his fine samples are labelled from 'Ekstone Mine, Staffs,'. Unfortunately, it is not clear whether he was referring to Ecton or Elkstones, copper being worked in both localities.

As indicated above, Ecton is stated to have been reopened about 1707, and after draining the mine the old large blast holes were found, (18). This seems to have been only short-lived venture and no serious mining took place for another sixteen years, until the commencement of the Ecton Sough.

Adventurers at Ecton 1723-1760

In his oft quoted description of the Ecton Mine, Efford (19) gave the romantic story of a Cornish miner stumbling upon a piece of rich ore and so initiating large scale mining at Ecton. This rather fanciful story cannot be substantiated, but other more reliable facts are known. On 1st November 1723, a lease to work the mine for twenty-one years was made between the third Duke of Devonshire and eight adventurers from Staffordshire and Derbyshire. The lessees undertook to 'begin, bring up and perfect a Sough Levell Additt or Watergate to be called Ecton Sough or Levell and to work the same in and through certain lands and Grounds of the Duke of Devonshire'.

The sough was to be commenced at a place then known as Poyser Ecton (Dev Coll H/26/6).

Although they started Ecton Sough (later known as Deep Ecton Adit) and reputedly spent £13,000 on the project with no return, by 1739 the level had been abandoned and the lease surrendered.

A new twenty-one year lease was made on the 12th December 1739, between the Duke of Devonshire and John Gilbert-Cooper of Locko, near Spondon, Derbyshire, with four others: Anne Chaney (the widow of William Chaney, a doctor, who had been one of the 1723 lessees); John Thompson of Ashbourne, an apothecary, Samuel Longford of Leek (a 1723 lessee) and Alexander Taylor of Buxton Hall, described as a 'Gentleman'. This lease contained the usual clauses giving the lessees authority to sink shafts, erect buildings, have right of access and free use of water, provided as little damage as possible was done, all pits and shafts were filled in when finished with and that compensation was paid for cattle falling into the shafts. For this they were to pay the Duke 1/9th of all the lead ore, copper ore and calamine that was raised, with fourpence a load (nine dishes each of five Winchester Quarts) (20) paid as cope (21).

Gilbert-Cooper agreed to a bond of £1,000 to indemnify the Duke from any claims of the previous lessees (Dev Coll H/25/4/II). He also took a lease from the Duke of mines in part of Hartington Common from Michaelmas 1739. The term and the royalty was as at Ecton, for twenty-one years and at 1/9th (Dev Coll H/25/4/I).

The Gilbert family came from Locko, and owned an estate at Denby as well as lands at Birchover, all in Derbyshire. The former contained coal mines, the latter lead mines. They inherited the estates of John Cooper of Thurgarton, Notts and changed their name to Gilbert-Cooper. Their Derbyshire estates were sold in 1746 and they moved to Thurgaton priory. John Gilbert-Cooper (1723-69) achieved some fame as a writer (22) and died at the age of 46 'by one of the most excruciating tortures flesh is heir to'. He was only sixteen when he took control at Ecton.

Of the activities during the next twenty-one years we know very little except that Ecton Sough was completed to intersect the Ecton pipe, and large quantities of ore were mined with a considerable profit. An estimate of the cost of working Ecton made in 1759, together with a section of the mine made about the same date, give us some of the few details that are known of this period of working. An engine shaft had been sunk on the pipe from the top of the hill for a depth of 240ft before much ore had been discovered, but for the next 210ft to the Sough level (23) the vein was very irregular, bearing a large quantity of copper ore. In this part of the pipe there were five sets of staging for the men to work from, as well as a further five in the 210ft below the Sough.

At this depth the pipe began to widen from about 18ft across, so that a heading 45ft high by 24ft wide was driven horizontally for 126ft. Of the 108 men employed at the mine, 24 were working at the forefield at the bottom of the mine, with 20 men 72ft above the Sough. There were also 27 pumpers.

Ecton Sough was to remain the only level access for another fifteen years and was the outlet for all the water raised by the manually operated rag-and-chain pumps and water barrels. At some point Apes Tor Sough was driven probably to convey water into the mine but the exact date is not known.

An inventory of the equipment at the mine in 1760 shows that there had been virtually no mechanisation at Ecton during this period. All the items consisted of the usual mining equipment – augers, borers, hammers, picks, buckers, spades, barrows, churn pumps, kibbles, 'Barrels to Carrey water' and 'Six wagons for ye Sough', the total valued at £94.

A Lot of Cope

As the period of the lease grew to a close, representations were made to the Duke of Devonshire, by now the Fourth Duke (1720-64), for a new lease, but this was refused. Just a few months before the lease finally expired, the Duke realised that although the rental of 1/9th of the ore had been paid, his father had never started to collect the cope of 4d a load.

Since the Duke's mineral agent had never measured the ore by the dish, but by weight, no one knew how much was owing, for although a calculation showed that each dish of five Winchester Quarts contained on an average 22lb of copper ore, the density of the ore varied considerably. Since the weight of ore raised during the previous twenty-one years was known, but unfortunately not quoted, the Duke hoped to calculate the number of dishes on which the 4d cope was owing. Legal advice was obtained with rather differing opinions.

Mr George Perrott of Lincoln's Inn thought that if the non-payment had been due to fraud or collusion between the lessees and the Duke's agent then the money could be recovered by a Bill in Equity. But if the cope had not been collected because of negligence by the Duke, then the money could not be recovered. Mr R Wilbraham also of Lincoln's Inn, thought that the demand was justified, although it had to be decided whose duty it was to measure the ore by the dish, for this was not mentioned in the lease.

It must be remembered that in the neighbouring lead mining area of the King's Field of Derbyshire where the Duke of Devonshire collected much of the duty on lease from the Crown, the ore was always measured by volume not by weight by ancient law and custom. Wilbraham though that the lessees should have measured the ore, and so the non-payment was their fault. He advised that a Bill would stand a good deal of success, but the outcome of the dispute is not known.

References

1. Staffordshire Historical Collections (SHC) 6, pt 2, 1903, p34. Ekedon is erroneously described here as being Elkstones
2. SHC, 4th Series, 4, 1962, p163-4
3. L. M. Cantor, 1964, N. Staffs Journal of Field Studies, 4, p63
4. SHC, 5, 1902, p118
5. SHC, 14, 893, p178, 194
6. SHC, 15, 1894, p131; SRO, D239/M639
7. SHC, 13, 4 892, p119-120
8. Barnatt J. & Rieuwerts J. H, 1997, *The Early Use of Gunpowder in the Peak District etc*, Mining History, Vol 13, No 4, pp24-43
9. Hamilton H, 1926, *English Brass and Copper Industries* (Reprinted 1967)
10. Robey J. A, 1969, Bull PDMHS, 4, No 2, pp145-155
11. Malynes G, 1622, *Lex Mercatoria*, p185
12. France R.S, 1947, Lancs & Ches Record Soc, 102, p84, 95
13. Rieuwerts J. H, 1998, *Glossary of Derbyshire Mining Terms*, p56
14. DRO, 158M/E43
15. Plot R, 1686, *Natural History of Staffordshire*, p165
16. Dev Coll, see J. A.Robey, 1969, op cit
17. Watson R, 1781, *Chemical Essays*, 1, pp341-3
18. Hooson W, 1747, *The Miner's Dictionary*
19. Efford W, 1769, *Gentleman's Magazine*, Reprinted in Bull PDMHS, 1961, 1, No 5, pp37-40
20. The Derbyshire dish contained 14 Winchester pints for the Low Peak
21. Cope was a duty paid so that the miners could sell the ore as they pleased and not only to the owner of the mineral rights
22. Dictionary of National Biography
23. These figures are inaccurate, the true depth being 317ft to river level from the surface. These reports were by a John (or Jonathan) Roose, an experienced Derbyshire miner, who owned shares in Derbyshire and North Wales lead mines. He was the mineral agent for Charles Roe and Co of Macclesfield as well as reputedly discovering the rich copper deposits at Parys Mountain, Anglesey

Above: The top of the Clayton pipeworking. It descends to a depth of 1,439 feet
Below: Ecton in Victorian times. The building second from the left was a cottage

3.3 The Duke's Mine 1760-1818

When John Gilbert-Cooper's lease expired at Michaelmas 1760, the 4th Duke of Devonshire decided to work the mines on his property to his own account, no doubt to pay for the rebuilding of Chatsworth House on which he was busily engaged. This was the start of a period of great expansion and prosperity for the mines.

Early Operations

The new agent appointed to supervise the running of the Ecton Mine was Robert Shore of Snitterton near Matlock, Derbyshire, who also had interests in the Derbyshire lead-mining and smelting industry. The first operations under the new management were to repair, rail and wall the Sough and to do some work in the Dutchman Mine. By September 1761, 36 men were employed for raising water out of the mine in buckets and hand winches, and by June 1765 this had risen to 53. Shortly afterwards horses were introduced for winding water and the number of men employed on this arduous task fell to about 30, with a further reduction to 22 in 1767.

Other early operations were the sinking of a new shaft and the erection of a horse gin or whim to facilitate the raising of ore from the mine. This had previously been raised by hand and trammed out along the Sough. In March 1764 appears the first entry for the Apes Tor Level, almost certainly the lower 34 fathom level, not the Sough. This level was driven from the pipe vein to a drawing shaft at Apes Tor (still visible at the side of the road, although flooded and concreted over), through 'dead stone without a spark of oar'. This enabled water in the mine to be raised to the level and then lifted the final 200ft by a horse gin on the surface at Apes Tor, leaving the Sough to be used solely for hauling out ore and stone.

The main efforts made after the Duke took over were to assess the extent of the ore body. By 1767 the mine had reached 160 fathoms from the top of the hill (1), making the lower parts some 430ft below the River Manifold. The vein started to get very rich at a depth of 96 fathoms, just below the 34 fathom level (34 fathoms below river level), the limit of' the previous adventurers. W Efford in 1769 (2) quoted the mine as being 160 yards below the river. The ore was wound from below by a man at a winch and put into four-wheeled wagons having cast brass wheels running in grooves, and pushed along the Sough by boys aged from 12 to 14 years old. Efford's non-technical eye probably had not observed that the wheels had flanges and ran on rails, but this important feature was not missed by the Swedish visitor Eric Geisler only three years later (3).

A Visitor in 1769

In the mine there was:

> 'such a horrid gloom, such rattling of waggons, noise of workmen boring of rocks under your feet, such explosions in blasting and such a dreadful gulph to descend, present a scene of terror, that few people, not versed in mining, care to pass through. From the platform the descent is about 160 yards, through different lodgments, by ladders, lobs, and cross-pieces of timber let into rock, to the place of action, where a new scene, ten thousand times more astonishing than that above, presents itself; a place as horrible to view, as imagination can conceive.
>
> On the passage down, the constant blasting of the rocks, ten times louder than the loudest thunder, seems to roll and shake the whole body of the mountain. When at the bottom, strangers are obliged to take shelter in a niche cut in the rock, to avoid the effects of blasting the rocks, as the miners generally give a salute of a half dozen blasts, in quick succession, by way of welcome to those diabolical mansions. At the bottom of this amazing work, the monstrous cavern of vacuum above, the glimmering light of candles, and nasty suffocating smell of sulphur and gunpowder all conspire to increase your surprise, and heighten your apprehensions. There is no timber made use of, except for lodgments, or platforms, ladders or steps set into the rocks, for ascending or descending into the mine: neither is there any

3.3 The Duke's Mine 1760-1818

quantity of water to retard the works, notwithstanding it is at least 150 yards below the bed of the river; four horses, six hours each at a common wem (4) or engine, are sufficient to keep the Mine clear.

The timber works about the Mines are very ill contrived and worse executed. In descending from the principle lodgment, you pass thirty ladders, some half broken, others not half staved; in some places by half-cut notches, or steps in the rock, in others you must almost slide on your breech, and often in imminent danger of tumbling topsey-turvey into the Mine; nor are the shores which support the lodgement below in a better condition'.

Ecton was described as the deepest mine in Britain, yet it was to become 480ft deeper by the 1790s. Efford estimated a total workforce of 300 persons in 1769.

The Gilbert Enterprise

Another venture in the 1760s was the driving of Chadwick Sough, also known as the Lead Sough and many years later as 'Messrs Gilbert's Sough', as well as the sinking of an engine shaft at Chadwick Mine. In April 1760 an agreement was made between Thomas and John Gilbert who owned a lead smelting mill at Alton (5) and the Duke of Devonshire, together with eight other persons, all of whom were 'Partners and Proprietors in Certain Lead Mines at Ecton – which are likely to produce large Quantities of Lead Oare' – for the smelting mill to be divided between all concerned in the same ratio as the shares they owned in the Ecton Mines (6).

This is possibly the same group that had previously worked the Burgoyne mines but the interrelationship between the various parties is not clear. What is known is that the Gilberts and the Duke worked the Chadwick Mine and Sough from 1761 to 1773, mainly for lead ore, although only a modest amount was raised. The accounts for these operations are included along with those for the Ecton Mine, so presumably there was a lease or agreement that has not yet come to light.

It is perhaps ironic that the Gilberts were mining Clayton and other mines in the 1740s and before, drove the Clayton Sough with the Duke and worked Chadwick also with the Duke, yet were not part of the Gilbert-Cooper partnership which found the valuable Ecton pipe deposit and thereby made a fortune from it.

Thomas Gilbert (1720-98) was from Cotton Hall, Staffs. He became an MP and a well-known Poor Law and industrial reformer, as well as being the legal agent to the second Earl Gower of Trentham, the brother-in-law of the Duke of Bridgewater. His younger brother John (1724-95) became a distinguished canal and mining engineer, being the instigator of the Duke of Bridgewater's underground canals at Worsley, Manchester. He was apprenticed to the Boulton firm at Birmingham, where he grew up with Matthew Boulton (later to form the famous firm of Boulton & Watt) who remained his lifelong friend. The Gilbert brothers were actively concerned in many North Staffordshire mining and quarrying ventures (7). There is no connection with John Gilbert-Cooper.

The Underground Canal

Rather surprisingly, Efford completely overlooked what was one of the most important early innovations at Ecton, the Boat Level, for by 1767 the 34 fathom Ape Tor Level had been converted to carry boats. Sir Joseph Banks (8) described it thus:

'The workmanship of this mine is as wonderful for its boldness and cleverness as any other part of it particularly a navigable drift much under Level by which the Ore is convey'd with scarce any trouble from the Farfield to a convenient shaft (9) where it is drawn up with horses to the day'.

The labour for making a new boat cost £ 3. 8. 0. (£3.40) in 1769. Although the accounts mention 'widening the sough Levil for a Bote gate' in 1769, it is clear from Bank's Journal and more particularly from James Watt's notes, made when negotiations were taking place for the installation of a steam winding engine in 1788, that the 34 fathom level was the 'Bote Level' mentioned throughout the accounts.

It is highly likely that this Boat Level was constructed at the suggestion of John Gilbert, the

Duke of Bridgewater's canal engineer, who had been responsible for the use of boats underground at the Worsley Collieries near Manchester in 1759, as well as in the Hillcarr Sough, started in 1766, and the Speedwell Level at Castleton in 1771-1781, both in Derbyshire. As already noted, John Gilbert was closely connected with Ecton and no doubt his knowledge and expertise as a mining and canal engineer were used in the construction of the Ecton Boat Level. This level was enlarged in 1780, possibly to take larger boats, and was in continuous use until 1788, when the Boulton and Watt winding engine came into operation.

The successful use of boats underground at Ecton for twenty years seems to have impressed Cornelius Flint, who was to succeed Robert Shore as agent in 1779, for in 1796 a level for boating and drainage was started at the Grassington Lead Mines, in Yorkshire by 'Mr Flint, the Mineral Agent of His Grace the Duke of Devonshire' (10). Unfortunately, in this case the cost of building new dressing floors at the level entrance and driving a passage large enough for a boat turned out to be greater than winding the ore to the surface and the project was abandoned.

The Visit of John Harpur

The recent discovery of John Harpur's 'Jottings', which date from 1767-1770 give us the only description of the huge ore deposits to have survived. He walked up the Ecton Sough, (he conveniently also made a sketch which proves conclusively that the current Ecton Deep Adit was the original Ecton Sough). The sough was 'a boarded passageway', i.e. the water ran out underneath the floor. His description reads:

> 'Then come to a large circular opening vault or chamber abt 30 yards wide. Ye sides and roof of it all stone and spar with holes or places in it from whence ore taken away pretty much alike, from all parts of ye circular vault.
>
> The floor of this opening or chamber is rock. At ye southern end there is an opening or trap door down into another opening vault or chamber abt 80 yards below ye first.
>
> Ye descent down to this and other chambers is by ladders aside the mine (?) rocks and there are a kind of landing places called by ye miners bundings and this 2nd in a circular form below ye 1st. Ye roof of this 2nd chamber appears to be near 30 yards high overhead.
>
> In ye walls or sides of this vault in some parts more, in some fewer, holes or places dug into ye rock than others. Most holes appear to be on ye south side or south east side. [he describes the holes as being as small as cupboards and others as big as a room of 10 or 12 feet].
>
> In all there are 7 of these vaults or chambers including ye first and an eighth now sinking 20 yards and which had a good deal of water in it (being Sunday when seen and pumps not working, for ye miners can only work only as ye water pumped out from some of ye vaults from time to time but some of ye vaults are quite dry – in others springs break in.
>
> The 3d like ye second but some of ye seven vaults are cut more oval and one or two nearly triangular. This 3rd one of ye largest. [Note some of these Vaults are 30, 20 and ye lower ones not above 15 yards high. Some appear to be 30 yards wide across – and some much larger near 60 – The 3d appears to be one of ye largest].
>
> To all appearance ye Vaults lie partly near one under another and no great appearance of varying or Hading to any point of ye compass any way equal to one or two hundred feet but of keeping a kind of circular form. Late Duke went down to part of ye 4th Chamber.
>
> From ye 3rd floor a sough or water carriage for boats which goes eastward to ye place where ye engine (horse engine) is worked – which is abt 50 fathom high (abt 300 feet). It is cutted abt 100 yards from ye Sough up to ye engine.
>
> Water in ye carriage abt 2: -3 (sic) and in some places where boats pass near 4 feet. Ye pumps and windlasses with two handles which draw ye water up into troughs'. (Derbys Record

Office, 2375/M No 63-65).

Harpur went on to mention that there was a proposal to drive a level from the Ecton pipe working to the Dale Mine but this was never implemented. The latter mine was 'now working again'. The description of the width of the boat level is surprising. Clearly the mine was not working on a Sunday, but there is a tradition that at one point, men were working on a Sunday and the local vicar went down the mine to preach!

Fraud at the Mine

In 1768 the Duke's attorney, Godfrey Heathcote of Chesterfield, who audited all the Ecton Accounts, discovered certain discrepancies amounting to £1,090 in 1764 at the time of the Fourth Duke's death.

The accounts for this period are rather complicated since at the Duke's death the books were closed and from that time two accounts kept – one with the executors of the late Duke, the other with guardians of the new one, who was only sixteen at the time, until he became of age. It seems that Robert Shore took advantage of this confusion to embezzle the mine accounts by this amount, and in the light of later developments this is almost certain. Shore was required to take out a mortgage on £1,000, and after paying the balance of £90 owing, paying it back at the rate of £100 per year plus 3% interest. His salary as Ecton Mine agent was initially only £70 per annum, although soon increased to £100.

During the first ten years of the Duke's operations at Ecton the quantity of ore had declined, although the quality was improving. Most of the effort had been concentrated on improving the raising of ore and stone out of the mine by the Boat Level, widening the sough, sinking engine shafts, and improving the drainage (although this was still by rag-and-chain pumps and horse engines). Once it became clear that the mine had a rich potential a period of expansion started, the workings on the pipe were sunk much deeper and large smelting works were erected at Whiston.

All this required a considerable amount of capital which the old adventurers were unable to provide. A short report by Robert Shore indicates the state of the mine at the end of 1770:

> 'The Copper Vein at Ecton goes down pritty near in a Perpendicular direction at this time, is now sunk from the Sough or Levil which is taken from the River Manifold, upwards of 70 fathoms and all the conveniencys compleated to that depth and now ready for sinking a fresh. The works upon the Sd. Bothams is not so large a compass as they have been nor able to raise such large quantities as they have heretofore But the Quality much better' (11).

There was a stock of 2,800 tons of ore about the mine at this date. By 1772 there were 260 people employed, 90 people for dressing the ores and surface work, 154 workmen and labourers underground, 12 coal carriers, 4 smelters, as well as 12 engine horses. This does not include the numerous carriers taking the ore to Whiston, many of them part-time from their farming.

The Ecton Sough, or Deep Ecton adit, used to have a keystone at its entrance and the legend RS 1774. This is the date of the current level, but exploration by Geoff Cox, the mineral owner, and the late John Rottenbury found that the current level replaced an earlier level, which runs parallel and which may be observed from the inner end of the walled section of the level.

Further Fraud

In 1779, shortly after he had finished paying off his old debt, it was discovered that Robert Shore was embezzling again. He had failed to pay sums of money owing to various miners, tradesmen and merchants, even though the money had been forwarded by the Duke for that purpose; but this time the amount totalled £5,000. Shore was instantly dismissed from his post as agent and overseer at Ecton and Whiston, all his goods, estates and mineral interests were taken over by trustees appointed by the Duke to be sold off to discharge the debts and any surplus paid back.

Shore's assets at this time included a few farms and cottages in Derbyshire as well as shares in Orchard, Drake & Limekiln, Overpitts and Oxclose Mines, Derbyshire; Mixon Mine, Staffordshire; Pitt Moss and Derbyshire Mines, Grassington Yorkshire. In the 1770s and 1780s he was operating lead mines in Cardiganshire, and was also a partner in a paper mill at Masson in Derbyshire, which was powered by the water from Cromford Sough. This mill was sold to

Arkwright for conversion to a textile mill (12). After his dismissal from Ecton he appears to have been involved in the copper works at Ravenhead near St Helens, Lancashire, owned by the Parys Mine Company.

Cornelius Flint

Shore's successor was Cornelius Flint of Great Longstone in Derbyshire. Flint had been the agent to the Hubberdale Lead Mine at Flagg, Derbyshire, a large horizontal pipe vein that had been very rich in the 1760s (13). Shore and Flint must have met at this period for the former acted as an adjudicator in a dispute over the freeing of veins at Hubberdale in 1767 when Flint was agent. After his appointment to Ecton, Flint moved to live at Hartington, just over two miles from the mine, where he spent the rest of his life. He lived in the house near to the Duck Pond known as 'The Old Vicarage'. Although most of his duties were concentrated at Ecton, he was still concerned with the Hubberdale Mine in 1795, as well as in other local lead mines. We have already seen that he was connected with the Duke of Devonshire's lead mines at Grassington. An anonymous writer in the *Mining Journal* of 1838 implies that he had been the agent for all the Duke's mineral interests, but it is not known if this was so, although he did also become the Devonshire's land agent in the Wetton area.

The Water Engine

Late in 1780, Cornelius Flint and James Newbold, millwright at the mine, went 'to View a Watter Engine upon Lord Ferreas Land'. (? Lord Ferrers. He was operating lead mines at Staunton Harold, Leics, about this time). Shortly afterwards there was much activity at Ecton preparing for new pumping machinery, with one rather intriguing entry reading 'Cutting Room for the Great Wheel 38 yards £14. 12. 6. (£14.62$^{1}/_{2}$)'. It is clear that by 1783 they were installing a hydraulic pumping engine of rather unusual, but elegantly simple design. Prior to this date water had been raised to the Boat Level by large numbers of men labouring at rag-and-chain pumps, and by gin-horses raising water in barrels.

By 1780 the four horses drawing water described by Efford in 1769 had been increased to four horses underground, together with four men each with three horses drawing water at Apes Tor. A later reckoning gives three horses and two drivers at Apes Tor Engine, although, of course, the actual number employed would depend to some extent on the dryness of the season. Throughout the accounts there appear regular entries for rag pumps and cylinders. In 1766, £64 was paid for 'Mettle Pumps' while cast metal pumps cost £53 in 1772 and £120 in 1773.

Considering the great depth of the mine (nearly 1,300ft by 1795), situated beside a sizeable river and sunk entirely in the normally waterlogged Carboniferous Limestone, Ecton was remarkably free from water troubles. Just a few miles away the lead mines of Derbyshire were plagued by severe drainage problems, even though most of them were quite shallow in comparison with Ecton, and their story is a never ending struggle with the water. Yet again, just three miles to the west, the Mixon Copper Mine, less than half the depth of Ecton, had extremely heavy drainage costs that could not be met by the use of a steam engine and two 40ft diameter water wheels. Eventually a Cornish beam engine had to be used here to conquer the water (14).

At Ecton the situation was quite different. Flint estimated that prior to the erection of the pumping engine, 8,800 gallons were raised by horses per six hour shift, in barrels each holding 80 gallons; also nearly 8,000 gallons came from a spring in the vein in the wettest weather. In the 19th Century the water flow was said to be only 20 gallons per minute, and the mine took two years to fill up after it was abandoned below adit level (15). One of the reasons for this small quantity of water was that the mining area was very small with a small catchment area so that there was little chance for the water to travel long distances through worked out veins and other fissures, as for example, in the Alport and Millclose Mines, both very heavily watered ventures in Derbyshire.

The pumping engine eventually installed was a bucket operated balance beam. An untitled, undated diagram at Chatsworth House (see page 55) is almost certainly a representation of the Ecton Water Engine, and makes clear the simple mode of operation. Water from a high level source filled a large bucket attached to one end of a massive beam, slowly tilting the beam to work a pump rod attached to the other end. As

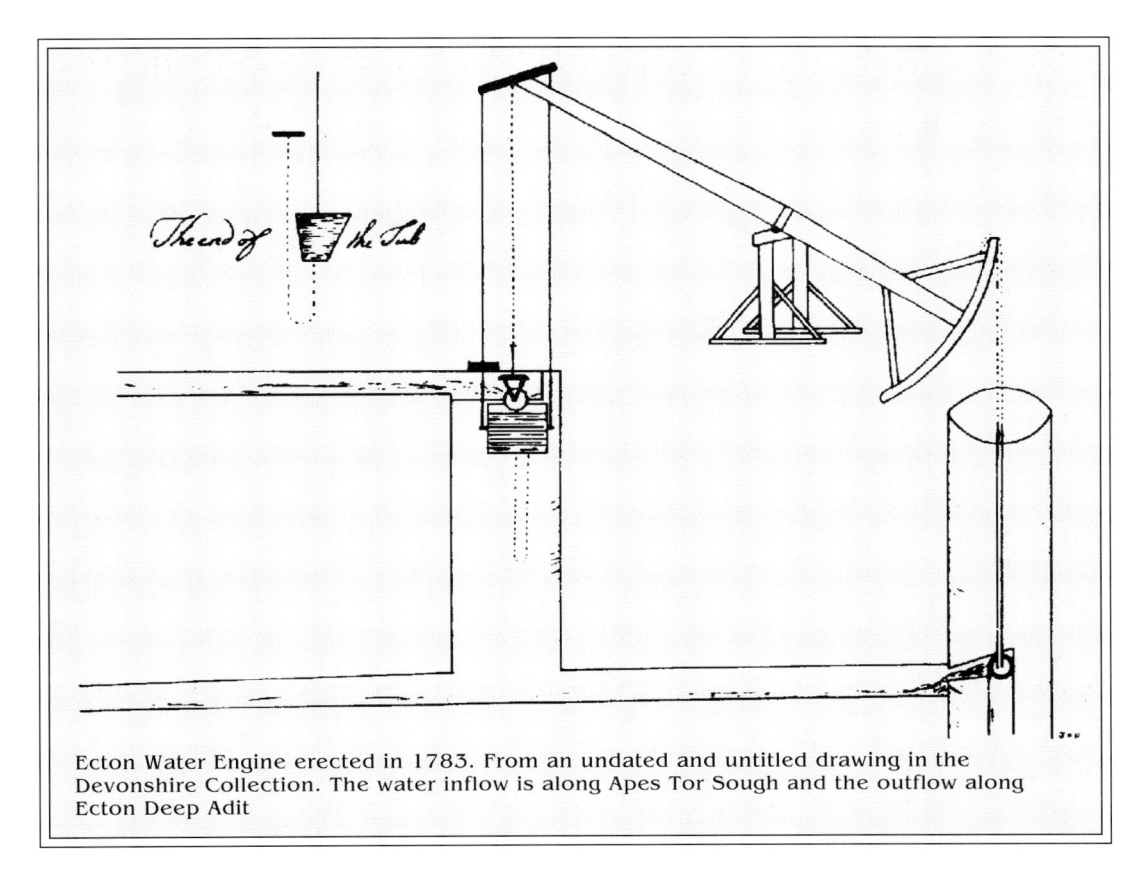

Ecton Water Engine erected in 1783. From an undated and untitled drawing in the Devonshire Collection. The water inflow is along Apes Tor Sough and the outflow along Ecton Deep Adit

the beam tilted, a valve shut off the feed water supply and at the end of its stroke the bucket was automatically inverted, emptying into a lower level. The bucket ascended and the cycle was repeated.

The water supply came from the River Manifold where a weir was built at Apes Tor to divert water along the Sough to the Water Engine. The outflow was along the Ecton Deep Adit Level, in a launder, or fang, beneath the floor level. With such a low head of water – the difference in height between the two levels is only a few feet – and with the need to avoid large quantities of water flowing into the mine so that the levels could still be used for haulage, a waterwheel was clearly impractical. With these conditions imposed this design of engine was far superior. It had a 5ft stroke, working $2^{1}/_{2}$ strokes per minute and pumped with 8-inch diameter pumps from a depth of 550ft below the Manifold up to Ecton Deep Adit.

Water was raised the 150ft from the sole of the mine to the engine pumps by eight men working hand pumps. The engine worked 12 to 16 hours a day or 'even 20 Hours sometimes' (16). Each stroke would raise $10^{1}/_{2}$ gallons, giving 19,000 gallons in every 12 hours, equivalent to just over four horse power. Details of the physical size of the engine are not known, but calculations show that the bucket must have held over 1,100 gallons (i.e. over 6ft cube) assuming the engine to be 100% efficient. Taking into account the inevitable losses the bucket could easily have been twice this capacity and the engine must have been a formidable piece of machinery. Similar devices were used in a few Cornish mines of small depth where they were known as 'flop-jacks' (17), as well as for providing a water supply to large country houses, but these all seem to have been much smaller than the Ecton engine. An engine possibly of comparable size was in use at a colliery in Dumfriesshire in Southern Scotland during the 1790s (18).

When Dr Hatchett visited Ecton in 1796 he described this engine thus (19):

'In this level (Deep Ecton) is a machine or Balance Bob which is worked by a Tub which is filled with water at the top and empties itself by a Valve when it descends this raises the Ore in a

Above: The remains of the Apes Tor weir which provided water to work the balance beam in Ecton Mine **Below:** John Robey by the Water Engine Shaft in Ecton Deep Adit. It is nearly 600 feet deep

— 56 —

barrel. There is a similar machine which works some Pump Rods'.

This is the only reference to the use of such an engine for raising ore although there are many references in the accounts to the pumping engine. John Farey in 1811 (20) listed Ecton Sough with the comment:

> 'conveys water to and from the Hydraulic Pumping-engine of the Mine', and he briefly described the engine: 'large Buckets fixed on the ends of the Beams are applied to work Pumps in the Ecton Mine'.

The mine accounts give us various glimpses of the erection and installation of the engine:

Reckoning ending 10th May 1783
Cutting the Roof over the shaft
for the Pump Rods to Rise 80 shifts   £5. 6. 8
8 men Cutting room for the Rods
142 shifts   £9. 9. 4
Driving and Cutting room for
the Ballance Beam 252 yards   £98.10. 3

Reckoning ending June 31st 1783
Cutting Room for a Cistern 10 yards £4. 0. 0
Cutting the Roof for the Pump Rods
to Rise and for the Capstan   £15. 4. 6
Expenses to the Miners when the
Great Beam was Got into the Mine   £1. 9. 0

It is likely that the 'Great Beam' would be of oak, similar to those of steam engines of the period, yet the above entry implies something more substantial. Brass 'Working Barrels' or pumps, each 10ft long and 8-inch internal diameter, weighing nearly half a ton each, were purchased from the Coalbrookdale Company for £490 who also supplied gudgeons, clacks, buckets and swords for the engine and pumps, as well as a double pinion and wheel with wrought iron spindles. The use of very expensive brass pumps instead of the usual wood or iron ones is an indication of the corrosive nature of the mine water.

The pumping engine evidently functioned satisfactorily for forty years, although in 1814 the beam was replaced by one of cast iron at a cost of £170 with a consequent improvement in its operation:

> 'The Balance Engine employed in raising the water from the Mine was set to work again... and by having a Cast Iron Beam already indicates an improvement to that piece of machinery, the stroke being more complete forces the water more copiously'.

Later it was replaced by an overshot waterwheel, with a special arrangement for the water supply, in 1823. The original engine of 1783 was variously referred to as the Bucket Engine, Tub Engine or more usually the Water Engine. James Watt called it the Cataract Engine, for it was similar to the control gear used on steam pumping engines of the time. Later entries in the account books make it clear that horses were still employed as well to raise water, both underground at the Water Engine Shaft and on the surface at Apes Tor.

Ventilation

Just as drainage was an important, though not insuperable problem at Ecton, a similar situation existed with regard to ventilation. The only information that we can glean is from the scattered references in the account books, but certainly it seems that poor air was not a major difficulty. Wind gates were driven in 1762-3 and 1773, while pipes, almost certainly for air, were put into one level in 1780. A few years later they were sinking a sump for wind to the shaft and driving a gate for the same purpose. In 1782 three boys were employed blowing bellows at Apes Tor, while in 1791 we read 'Assisting to fix the Bellows & the Air Pipes', and three boys were still 'Blowg. Bellows for wind to the Shaft'. In many of these cases as soon as a level made connection with another level or shaft natural ventilation ensued and the forced draught could be discontinued.

By 1786 ore production was at its peak, with over 4,000 tons being raised in that year alone. There were over 400 people (21) employed at Ecton and Whiston, including 144 copers, 34 carriers, 40 refiners at Whiston, 20 copper smelters and 4 lead smelters at Ecton, 12 water drawers below the pumps and three men tending the Water Engine. With such a large quantity of ore being raised from what was by now the deepest mine in Britain (22), not to mention the waste rock that needed removing, improved means of winding were necessary. With the unique geological structure of the workings there was very little opportunity to stack deads in the worked-out ore pockets as was normally done, and so all waste had to be removed along with the ore. The mine was at the maximum depth that could be worked by horse gin, even with the use of several horses, so steam power was the obvious choice. The use of a steam engine had been contemplated over fifteen years before by Robert Shore (23) but at that time the only practical arrangement was for an engine to pump water to an overshot waterwheel connected to the winding drum. This system was widely used in the collieries of the Durham and Northumberland and was not superseded until James Watt perfected his rotary engine in the early 1780s.

In the summer of 1787, Cornelius Flint and James Newbold took a journey to Cornwall to view various mines there, no doubt to see and discuss the latest mining methods in that highly mechanised mineral field. One of the main purposes of the visit was to see the new Boulton and Watt steam whims, of which three had recently been erected in Cornwall. The first of these, an 18-inch diameter cylinder single acting engine, erected at Wheal Maid in Gwennap in 1784, drew ore from 100 fathoms. When this engine was later re-erected at another Cornish mine, it is said to have put 40 stout horses out of work and to cost only £20 to do the work that had previously cost £150 (24).

The Boulton & Watt Engine

Immediately after his visit to the south-west, Flint had discussions with James Watt at Birmingham and a few months later he recommended Watt should visit the mine or at least send some responsible person to discuss the problems involved. By February 1788 the steam engine had been decided upon and the first of the drawings were sent from Birmingham. In these negotiations it is interesting to speculate whether the decision to use a Boulton and Watt engine had been influenced by John Gilbert who had close connections with both the Ecton Mines and Matthew Boulton. The engine was designed to work an eight-hour shift, raising 40 tons of ore a day, to the Ecton Deep Level, although some of it was to go only to the 34 fathom level. An additional task was to raise 7,680 gallons of water a day out of the vein to the Water Engine Lodge, so that it could then be pumped to the surface.

From James Watt's notes and calculations quite a lot of information can be gleaned. Each kibble held 5cwt of copper ore or 6-7cwt of lead ore, this normally requiring three horses at a time by the horse gin. Another note gives an average of 4cwt of copper ore per kibble with 95 kibbles raised a day for the previous four or five years; this is only half the figure allowed for, so considerable expansion of output was expected. Watt finally allowed for 160 kibbles, each of 6cwt. raised 120 fathom per eight hour shift. Each kibble would take 2 minutes 20 seconds to ascend with 40 seconds for stopping and emptying. The final design of engine was a 8 HP sun-and-planet wheel engine with a double acting 16-inch diameter cylinder, 4ft stroke (almost identical to the engine preserved in the Science Museum, London), with Watt's special double spiral balancing drum for winding to compensate for the great weight of the ropes.

The flywheel was 12ft diameter and the winding drum 16ft, 'which is the same that the present Gin in Workmanship now is', although Flint thought that it should be increased to 18 or even 20ft diameter and the design was subsequently altered. The arrangement of the engine is shown on pages 59, 61, & 63, based on drawings in the Boulton and Watt Collection. Being situated on the top of the hill there was no water supply for the boiler and condenser, so this was pumped up 3-inch diameter pipes by 4-inch diameter pumps at or just below Sough level to a small reservoir. These pumps were worked by a secondary beam connected to the main beam.

The Coalbrookdale Company supplied the pumps and pipes at £81, which were transported down the River Severn to Stourport, up the Staffordshire and Worcestershire Canal to join the Trent and Mersey Canal at Great Haywood and then along the Caldon Branch from Etruria to Froghall. From there, horses and carts carried them to the mine. The cylinder and piston, together with the air pump and some of the fittings, were supplied by John Wilkinson of Broseley for £50, while most of the remainder came from the Soho Works at Birmingham, where the precision parts could be accurately machined. Boulton and Watt charged £394 for the parts supplied by them and for their services.

A few iron castings were supplied locally by Walter Bassett of Winkhill Bridge near

3.3 The Duke's Mine 1760-1818

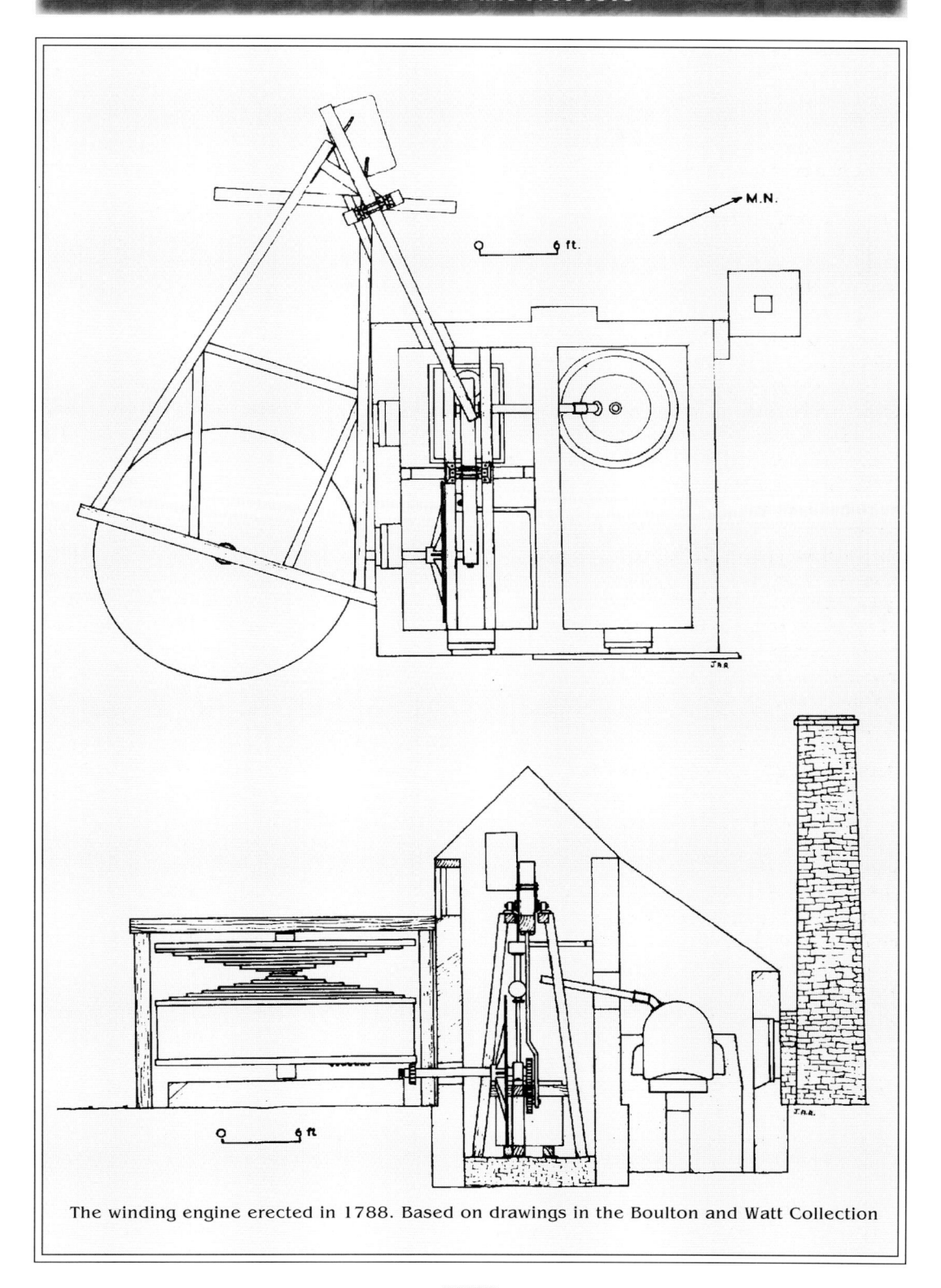

The winding engine erected in 1788. Based on drawings in the Boulton and Watt Collection

Waterhouses (25), who were regular suppliers of iron and brass castings to Ecton and Whiston, particularly cast iron rails. The copper boiler cost £15. 8. 7d (£15.43), while the total cost of the engine, including the building, was at least £750, although no annual premium was paid to Boulton and Watt. The latter evidently was not too satisfied with his patented sun-and-planet wheels, for two sets were supplied at his recommendation and a further two sets had to be provided in 1801.

The engine was nearly completed by the October of 1788, and in anticipation of its successful working, there was 'a Feast to the Workmen on the Memorable 5th of November 1788 £21. 11. 6 (£21.57$^1/_2$)', when all work stopped and the Duke paid the workmen their wages for the day. The engine was first given a fair trial on 29th November 'when every part thereof was put into motion and seems to act in every respect agreeable to the wishes of everyone concerned in it'. Isaac Perrins, Boulton & Watt's engine erector, was in charge of the installation, while his assistant John Varley stayed at Ecton until December 1789 supervising the engine until it could be entrusted to a local engine man. Perrins had a reputation as a pugilist, though there is no hint that the pitted his skill against the Ecton miners.

James Watt's double spiral balancing drum was used to compensate for the weight of the ropes in very deep shafts. The two winding ropes, each 220 fathoms long and weighing nearly a ton, were wound around the cylindrical winding drum, driven by a spur gear from the engine. On the same vertical cast iron shaft were the two spirals of opposite hand. The balance rope with its weight was fixed between the two spirals when the kibbles were at the passing place, where the shaft was widened. With a loaded kibble at the foot of the shaft and an empty one at the top, the balance rope was fully wound onto one of the spirals to provide maximum torque for assisting the engine. As the full kibble ascended, the weight of its rope down the shaft decreased, as well as being increasingly assisted by the extra weight from the descending empty kibble.

Thus less balancing effort was required and this was accomplished by the balance rope unwinding from the spiral. Once past the half way point the weight of the descending rope was greater than the ascending one and the engine acted solely as a brake, assisted by the balance rope which was now wound onto the opposite hand spiral. This system of balancing was in common use only until the power of steam engines was increased by the use of higher steam pressures, although colliery engines in Durham used a simplified form of this system until the present century. The spiral balance was probably based on the idea of the fusee, used to regulate contemporary watches as the spring ran down.

Ropes for Hauling

Engine ropes were a major item of expenditure requiring replacement about every eight months, although by 1811, due to the reduced output of the mine it was estimated that they would last at least two years. They were made from Riga dressed hemp, tapered from seven inches circumference at the top to five inches at the bottom. Originally a John Hall of Leek was to make these special tapered ropes, but he seems to have failed in the task, and they were supplied by Samuel Goodwin of Leek, although in 1797 and 1798 and occasionally afterwards the ropes were supplied by Daniel Hill of Chesterfield. A pair of ropes initially cost £100, but the steadily rising price of hemp, particularly at the beginning of the 19th Century during the Napoleonic troubles, raised the price to £155 in 1807 and no less than £273 in 1809.

In spite of Cornelius Flint's letter of satisfaction to Watt in 1794:

> 'Our Taper Roapes, they answer (past my first expections) indeed as far as I am able to Judge the common shape of A Roap at Ecton, considering the depth we are at, would not have answered'.

He later took the advice of Grimshaw, Webster, Hills and Scarth of the Patent Ropery, Sunderland who wrote in 1804:

> 'Several arguments may be advanced in favour of Tapered Ropes for deep mines especially, and in consequence of this, Men of Science have sometimes from the want of practical knowledge been led away with that opinion. There are however facts within our own observation, sufficient to convince us of the fallacy of this reasoning

3.3 The Duke's Mine 1760-1818

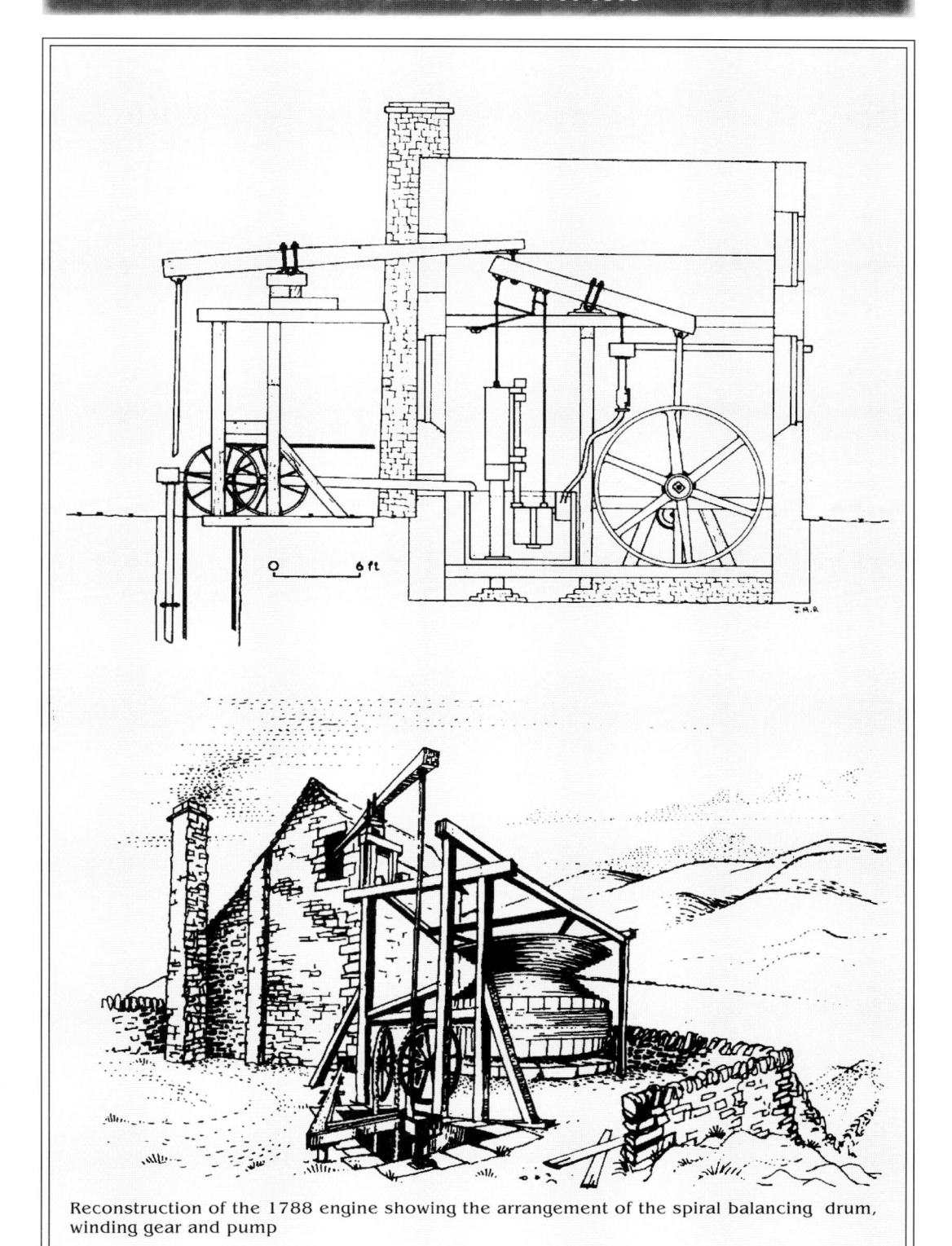

Reconstruction of the 1788 engine showing the arrangement of the spiral balancing drum, winding gear and pump

and we think that the circumstance of your having to splice a new Rope to the Upper part of the Old one, is a strong point in favour of our opinion that Cylindrical Ropes are the most covenient and best calculated for the use of mines'.

After this date most of the ropes came from Grimshaw and Co, (26) the engine ropes, being $5^{3}/_{4}$ inches circumference, weighing 35cwt per pair, while the balance rope was 50 fathom long, $6^{1}/_{2}$ inch circumference and weighed 4cwt. The ropes from Sunderland were sent by sea to Gainsborough, then along the Chesterfield Canal Navigation, and by road from Chesterfield to Ecton. By 1844 wire ropes were in use (27).

The Boulton and Watt engine did not get off to a very good start, for in the first month of operation there were two major breakdowns. During a very cold spell in December 1788, the water froze in the house-water pumps which supplied the boiler, causing the pump rod to break. This was soon repaired and by arranging for warm air to pass up the shaft the chance of a similar occurrence was reduced.

The more serious accident is best described in Cornelius Flint's own words:

'the Ballance Weight which has dropped down the Shaft – the Iron Pin being perfectly wore by the Friction of the Weight that connects the Roap & Chain to the Pin that goes through the Spiral Shaft. We have remedied the matter by a Stronger Pin made of Steel & Iron... For tho we had placed three different Strong Stages of Timber and other Flexible matter of considerable Height betwixt them, to resist anything that might fall down the Pit, to injure the Workmen in Sincking the Pit lower, than whear the Engine is at present employed, Yet such was the length & Force the Weights did fall that one part thereof made its way through every guard we had made, whear three Workmen had (fortunately) 2 or 3 minutes before left the place... I had no doubt in determining to sink a Pit Solely for the purpose of the Ballance to Work in, which is now going on placed exactly upon the opposite side of the Gin to the Present Pit'.

Watt's original plan of having both kibbles, the balance weight as well as the house water pump rods all in the Deep Shaft had been followed, but after this accident a shaft was sunk solely for the balance, well away from the engine shaft. This shaft is still visible today with its large built up mound to bring it level with the winding gear, and is now capped by a substantial stone 'beehive'.

The Engine in operation

Although all the indications are that the engine was an undoubted success it was not without its troubles. In the period up to 1811, hardly a year went by without some repairs having to be made, particularly to the boiler. Much of this was replacement of the moving parts such as the various 'brasses' or bearings and the sun-and-planet wheels. In 1806, major renovations were carried out and two engine erectors were sent from Soho works to supervise the fitting of new nozzles (steam valves), working gear, eduction pipe, piston, piston rod and steam pipe socket. Repairs to the copper boiler appear very frequently, usually involving the re-rivetting of leaky plates, although on one occasion (in 1808) eight sheets of copper, each 4ft by 2ft inches. and weighing 84lb (29) were supplied by Thomas Patten of the Cheadle Brass Wire Company, Oakamoor. This engine was finally scrapped in 1855.

In 1795, Flint wrote to Boulton and Watt describing how they had met a spring of water of 80 gallons per minute at a point 22 fathoms below the Sough. The water was being allowed to fall the remaining 12 fathoms to the 34 fathom level. Flint wanted to know if the steam engine could be modified by fitting pump rods down the Deep Shaft to pump the water up the Water Engine Shaft to Ecton Deep Adit.

He thought that by putting in two iron boilers (which were available locally, one of them new) the power of the engine might be increased. Watt made a number of calculations based on increasing the size of the driving pinion so as to speed up winding, to allow more time to draw water. An alternative was a crank working from the output shaft of the engine to work pump rods down the

3.3 The Duke's Mine 1760-1818

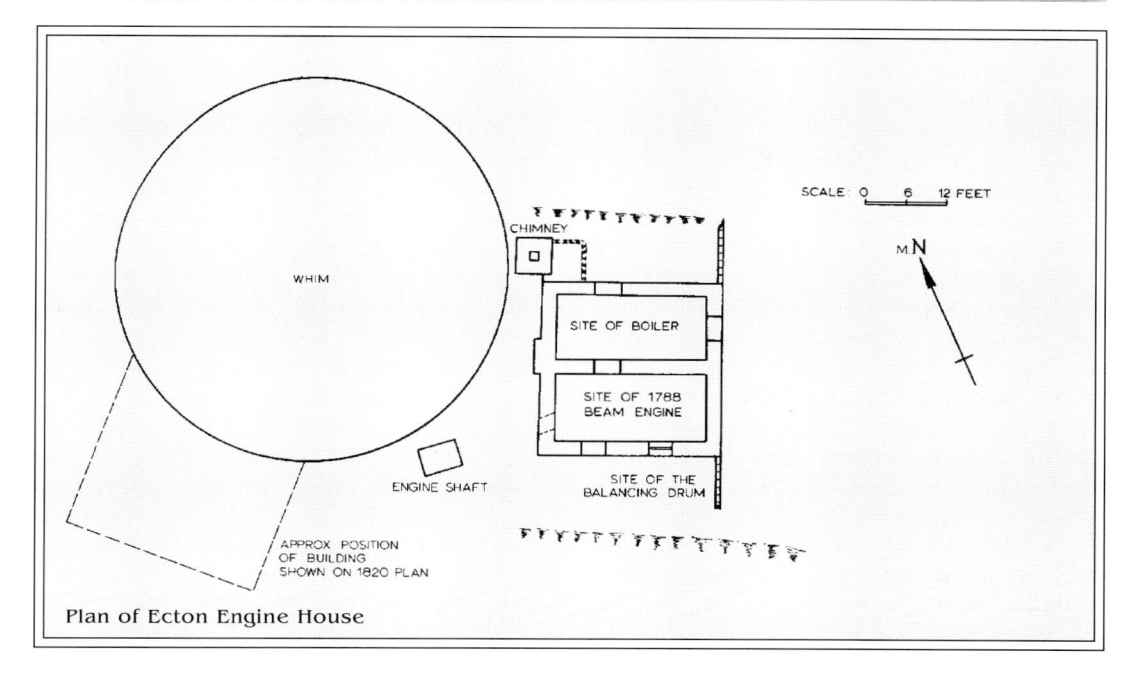

Plan of Ecton Engine House

shaft. It seems from the mine accounts that eventually a more fundamental solution was found – the spring was sealed off where it entered the mine, and no more was heard of the proposed modifications to the engine.

'Mine Failed'

By the time the steam engine was installed, production had passed its peak with output falling sharply, and in the early part of 1790 the great ore-body was found to contract to virtually nothing at depth. Ore output, which had been averaging about 450 tons per six to seven week period, suddenly dropped to half that amount, while a cryptic note pencilled in the account book states simply 'Mine Failed'.

Exploratory shafts were sunk to find a continuation of the pipe vein, but to no avail and the miners had to be content with extracting what had been left in the small side veins and pockets of ore. With output reduced fewer miners were needed so that in 1790 £550 was paid out to people discharged from the mine. As the 18th Century drew to a close the heyday of the Ecton Mine was passed, with the ore output continuing to fall steadily. Several trials were started both at the back of the hill and in the mine, but very little ore seems to have been found. In 1795 an intended watercourse from Hulme End Bridge to Apes Tor Weir was surveyed and set out, but does not seem to have been made. A further group of workers were discharged in 1797, this time 57 men and 21 women who were paid a gratuity of £1. 1. 0d. each to the workmen and 10s. 6d ($52\frac{1}{2}$p) to 5s. 0d (25p) to the ore dressers. Those remaining included fourteen companies of copers and 68 sundry workers.

Salt's Level

In the autumn of 1804, work started on the driving of the New Level to intersect the Deep Shaft and Pipe Vein 120ft above the River Manifold, so that ore could be wound up the shaft and trammed out along this level onto new dressing floors specially built for the purpose. The level continued past the Deep Shaft to the Ecton Pipe, where a climbing way was cut in 1807 in a small parallel pipe working. This level was later known as Salt's Level. Together with the climbing way it is still used to explore those parts of the mine above water.

Over 1320 cast iron rails (each set in stone sleeper blocks which can still be seen) were supplied by Walter Bassett of Winkhill Bridge for installation in the level and along to the dressing floors. We do not know why the New Level and the new dressing floors were constructed at this time, particularly as it was reported that the 'body of Copper Ore seems now nearly or quite exhausted' (30) and they were now only working the small veins and scrins branching from the main pipe.

Perhaps the new dressing floors were needed for the Clayton Mine, which the Duke had taken over in 1804 and which supposedly struck rich in 1812, but even this would not justify the enormous expense of the level, with driving alone costing £8 per fathom. Viewing the situation nearly two centuries after the event, with only the impersonal accounts to quote from, one can only speculate on the original reasons. This is all the more curious when we consider the other major operations that were started at this time.

One of these schemes was the re-opening of Chadwick Sough in 1804-5 at which time it was called 'the Late Messrs. Gilberts Sough'. The level had been filled with deads up to the roof; these had to be removed, new rails laid and new trials were made. At the same time miners were active in a new trial in a vein 'on the Back Side of the Hill', as well as in a new venture for lead that was opened on Wetton Hill Pasture.

In 1805, there are entries for 'Driving in a Gate near to the Head of the deep shaft for the conveyance of the Dutchman Water'. This refers to a short level, 140ft long, at approximately the same altitude as the Dutchman Level, leading straight into the side of the Deep Shaft. Cast iron pipes of 3-inch bore were laid the 600ft from a dam in the Dutchman Level to the gate, or level, most probably to provide house water for the Boulton & Watt engine, so that it would only have to be raised 55ft instead of 320ft as previously.

At this time a new ore pen was built at Onecote, 'together with converting of an old Building into an Habitation for the Man that attends it', confirming that two different routes from Ecton to Whiston were in use. The Onecote ore pen was in the field by the River Hamps behind what is now the Admiral Jervis Inn. A plan of 'land adjoining the new pen' dated 1809 exists in the Devonshire Collection plan press. Most of the country roads in the area were built by the Duke for his mines at Ecton, and they were usually charged to the mine account. An instance of this is the rebuilding and enlarging of the picturesque pack horse bridge over the River Manifold at Wetton Mill at a cost of £84 after it had been destroyed by a severe flood in 1807. The Duke and his agents were also actively concerned with the establishment of the turnpike roads in the area to the obvious benefit of the Ecton Mines and the Whiston Smelter (31).

The continuous series of mine accounts that provide so much information on this period end at the beginning of 1811, so that from that date to 1825 when the Duke of Devonshire ceased working the mines our knowledge is much less complete. This period, together with the explorations in the rest of the 19th Century are considered in Chapter 3.5.

References

For more detailed references to the various papers examining the mine in the 17th Century, see Chapter 15.

1. Joseph Banks' Journal. Cambridge University Library, Ad Mss 6294

2. Efford W, 1769, *Gentlemen's Magazine*, Reprinted in Bull PDMHS, 1961, Vol 1, No 5, pp37-40

3. Althin T, 1971, *Eric Geisler and his journey abroad of 1772-3*, in Med Hammare och Fackla, XXVI. The authors are grateful to L Willies for bringing this account to their notice

4. A whim or horse gin

5. At what is still called 'Smelting Mill', in Dimmings Dale (SK060432), although it is now a dwelling house with no trace of any previous metallurgical use. It must have been to smelt lead ore from the Gilberts' mines at Ribden, Thors-wood and elsewhere in the area, see J A Robey, 1970, Bull PDMHS, Vol 4, No 3, pp217-221

6. Staffordshire Record Office D554/57. A similar lease exists in Sheffield City Library, Bag 734

7. Malet H, 1961, *The Canal Duke*, J R Harris, Victoria County History, Staffs, 2, 1968, p266

8. J Banks, op cit

9. At Apes Tor

3.4 The Burgoyne Mineral Field 1648-1818

10. Raistrick A, 1967, *Old Yorkshire Dales*, pp101-2

11. Devonshire Collection, Chatsworth

12. Nixon F, 1969, *Industrial Archaeology of Derbyshire*

13. Robey J. A, 1965, Proc. British Speliological Assoc, 1, No 3, p3 and Kirkham N, 1964, Bull PDMHS, 2, No 4, p206

14. See Chapter 6

15. Mining Journal, 1860, p810

16. Watt also quotes $9\frac{1}{2}$-inch diameter pumps and a $4\frac{1}{2}$ft stroke in calculations most probably made in 1795

17. Barton D. B, 1968, *Essays in Cornish Mining History*, Vol 1, pp178-9

18. Donnachie I, 1971, *Industrial Archaeology of Galloway*

19. Raistrick J, 1967, op cit, p66

20. Farey J, 1811, *Agriculture and Minerals of Derbyshire*, 1, pp329, 339

21. It is difficult to estimate the exact number from the accounts since many of them worked in teams or 'companies' – the number in each not being stated

22. Althin, 1971, op cit 172 fathom by 1788 and 213 fathoms in 1795. Dolcoath in Cornwall was 160 fathoms by 1778; it was the deepest mine in Cornwall in 1818 at 227 fathoms (Ecton was 230 fathoms by then) and eventually reached 550 fathoms in 1920. Collieries did not reach these depths until well into the 19th Century, when North Staffordshire took the lead with 1,030ft (171 fathoms) at Fenton Park Colliery in 1818, while Apedale Colliery reached 2,177ft (363 fathoms) in 1836. See R L Galloway, 1898, *Annals of Coal and the Coal Trade*, Vol 1, reprinted 1971

23. Althin op cit

24. Barton D. B, 1965, *The Cornish Beam Engine*, p185

25. The firm also had a corn mill and paper mill at Winkhill in 1818

26. This firm was a major supplier of long ropes for collieries in the North of England, and in 1812, Rowland Webster patented his flat rope which was widely used in the deep shafts of the area. See E. Hughes, 1965, *North Country Life in the 18th Century*, Vol 11, pp170 and 204

27. Garner R, 1844, *Natural History of the County of Stafford*, p514

28. Both a rope and a chain were in use at the balance shaft and there are references later to getting the chain 'when the Ballance Chain was Broak', in 1795 and 1797

29. This makes the plates $\frac{1}{6}$ inches thick

30. Farey, op cit, p353. He visited the Peak District in the years 1807-1810

31. Chesterfield Ref. Library, Devonshire Collection

Thanks to Peter Kearney for the drawing on page 61

3 Ecton Copper Mines

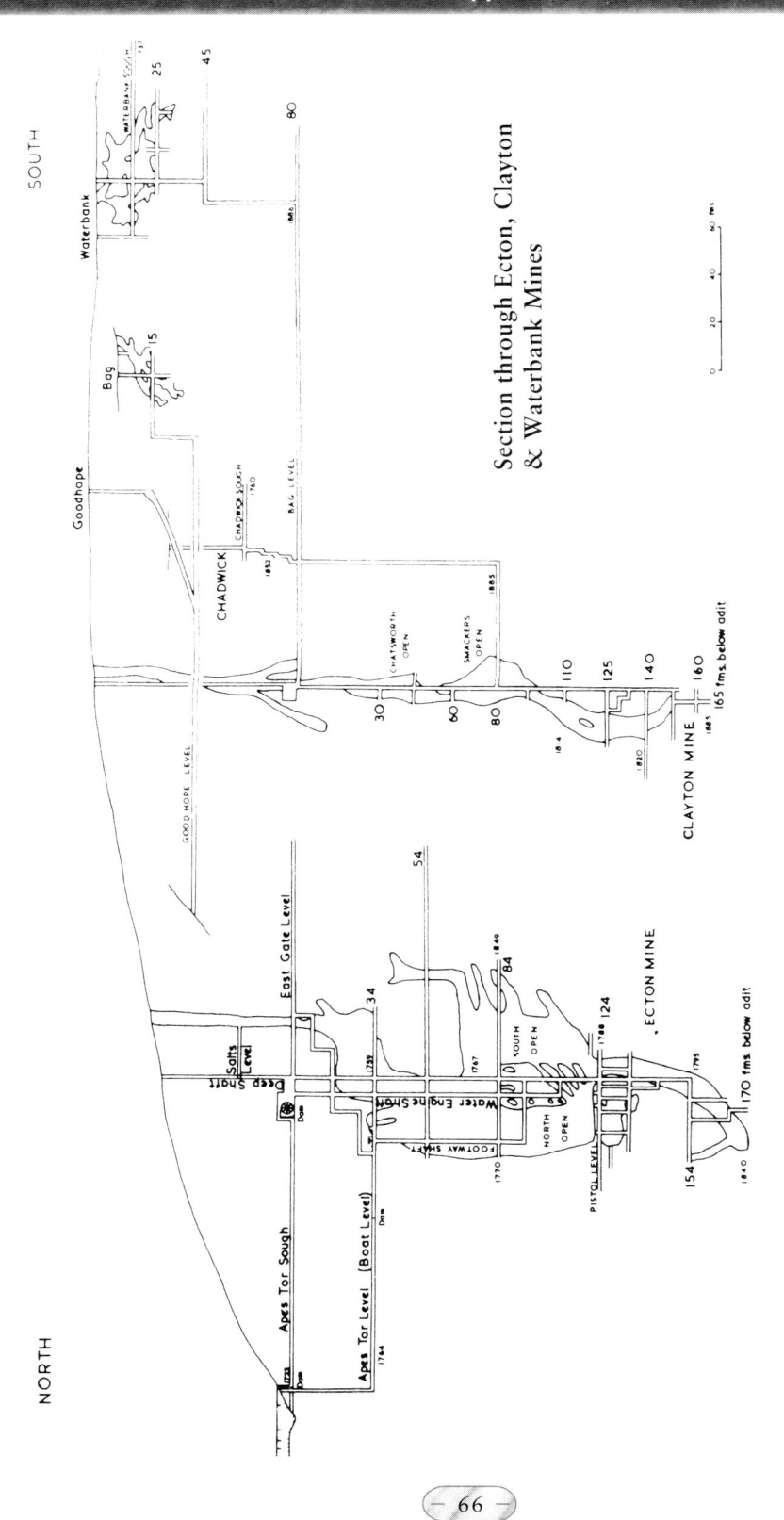

Section through Ecton, Clayton & Waterbank Mines

3.4 The Burgoyne Mineral Field 1648-1818

Compared with the detailed records of the mines on the Duke of Devonshire's land our knowledge of the pre-19th Century operations on the rest of the hill is pitifully small. This is especially unfortunate since the Clayton Pipe Vein, second in importance only to the Ecton Pipe, lies in this property and was evidently a major source of ore. This is due in part to the loss of most of the papers of the Burgoyne family, who held the mineral rights to this area of Ecton Hill, when their house at Mark Hall, Harlow, Essex, was sold to the Arkwrights in 1819. A fire at their family seat at Sutton Park, Bedfordshire, in 1828 destroyed any further records of the mines at Ecton. Owing to this lack of detail some information that is perhaps more properly placed in other sections is presented here for completeness.

Early Leases

In the 16th and early 17th Centuries this mineral field was owned by Sir John Burgoyne and his son Sir Roger of Sutton in Bedfordshire. In 1648 they sold part of the land (1) to James Bulkeley of Bagotts Bromley in Staffordshire for £1,127, with the exception of

> 'all Manner of Myne and Mynes of Lead or Lead Oare or any other Oare',

which were retained by the Burgoynes. They also reserved the tythes on the ore and the right for the workmen to have 'free Liberty power and authority of Ingress, egress and regress... to earth for, dig, open, Make or pursue any New or Old Myne... for the Washing, Clipping, knocking, dressing, cleaning makeing fitt for Sale... And for the Erecting Buildings... or any Coe Houses' (2).

This certainly indicates that lead had been mined previous to this date on Burgoyne land.

At some time prior to 1737, the mines had been leased to a partnership that included Thomas Gilbert and Robert Bill. Thomas Gilbert (1669-1741/2) of Cotton was the father of John and Thomas Gilbert, who were later to become involved in mining at Ecton and elsewhere, while Robert Bill (1684-1751) of Farley was a partner in the Cheadle Brass Wire Company.

The two families were not only neighbours, but were also business partners as well as being related by marriage. From the few business accounts between Gilbert and Bill that have survived we can gather that 'Clayton Grove, Water Work, Clay Work and Bowler Grove' were active from 1737 to 1744 (3). When Gilbert died he left his 1/24th share in these mines to his son John. The Gilberts also owned a 1/24th part of a smelting mill at Greenlow Field, Alstonfield which had been erected by Paul Nightingale, a grocer from Derby.

Nightingale assigned the lease to Thomas Gilbert, Junior, for £200 in January 1741/2, together with 'two Harths... Mill Pools, dams, floodgates, Wheels, Bellows and other Utensils' (4). This is now known to have been Lode Mill, clearly a derivative of Lead Mill. More recently it has been a corn mill, and although now disused, the waterwheel is still intact, but there is no visible evidence of its use for smelting (5). It probably served to smelt the Gilbert's lead ore from the Burgoyne mines as well as from the Chadwick mine, which they later worked in conjunction with the Duke of Devonshire.

An account books (Dev Coll L/91/1) indicate that in 1743, £2.12.6d (£2.62$^1/_2$) was being paid to John Chadwick for 'damages done to his farm by the copper mine'. He had occupied the farm since at least March 1737 (1738 by our calendar) (Dev Coll H/25/14). The damage payment was still being paid in 1759. Another partner was Edward Coyney of Alton in Staffordshire, whose will, dated 23rd April 1772, implied that at that date the mines were still working under the original lease (6).

In 1714, Bulkeley complained that the partnership was working several mines on his premises and they had opened a large stone pit to build their coes and other mine buildings as well as digging turf for roofing. They had spoilt grass and corn with their roads to the mines and had covered much ground with their waste (7). The details of the complaint need not be considered in detail but it is clear that the miners had overstepped their rights as laid down in the original lease, although it is also true that the lease was very loose in defining the miners' powers.

3 Ecton Copper Mines

Inside the Clayton Sough (now Clayton Adit) of 1755

In December 1753, Thomas Gilbert took a thirty year lease from Sir Roger Burgoyne at 1/8th royalty and an annual payment of £3. 'Clayton's Mine' was specifically excluded. Gilbert then entered into an agreement with the Duke of Devonshire in September 1755 to drive a sough through the Duke's land from the River Manifold to Clayton Mine. The Duke took a 1/12th share in the Sough Company, paying 1/12th of the Companys costs.

The above Chatsworth account books indicate that the Duke was in partnership with both the Gilberts for in 1755 and 1756, the payment is recorded of £21, being a 1/12th share, being paid to first Thomas and then John Gilbert for 'a reckoning to Clayton Mine in Ecton'. The term of the lease was twenty-one years, paying 1/8th royalty on any ores obtained in the Duke's lands in driving the sough and 1/10th of the ores obtained in the Duke's lands out of any vein leading from 'Clayton's Mine'. The lease included the right to drive sideways up to a distance of 50 fathoms.

Although it is known that Gilbert was working Clayton Mine, it is unclear if this extension of his activities was with different partners, beyond the arrangement he had with the Duke. It would seem that this might be the case as no other partners were a party to the lease with the Duke. It seems that the driving of Clayton Sough in 1755 could have been in the nature of a separate sough company, similar to those that existed in Derbyshire, earning income from draining another Company's mine, allbeit both concerns involving the Gilberts. This seems the only reason why Clayton Mine was excluded from the lease, rather than surrendering the older Clayton lease and taking out a new, all embracing one (Dev Coll H/25/1).

However what is important about this 1755 lease is that it includes a plan which shows the existence of the Ecton Sough. It proves that the original Ecton Sough predates 1774 (as does the plan in John Harpur's Jottings, discussed above). The supposition, based on the latter date on the Ecton Sough keystone, that the Apes Tor Sough was the original Ecton Sough (Robey and Porter, 1972), is incorrect. A paper on the initial use of Apes Tor Sough is being prepared by John Barnatt for publication in Mining History.

In 1769 lead ore was being produced at Clayton Mine (8) while in 1775 reference to 'ye Sough Levil' at that mine and the Clayton Engine Shaft make it clear that the adit Level had reached the Clayton Pipe by that date. The probability is that it reached the pipe vein in around 1757. Whether the mine had reached the depth of the sough is unknown.

Barker and Wilkinson, the Derbyshire lead smelters, may have taken an interest in the Burgoyne mines for Jim Rieuwerts has found a slip of paper listing the mines in which they 'have ruling shares'. All are in Derbyshire but at the bottom it states 'Copper Mines in Staffordshire'. It is undated, but dates from 1782 by inference from other documents attached (Dev Coll Currey Papers box 55/3).

The Duke and the Burgoyne Royalty

The 18th Century leases by John Gilbert and associates had probably expired by the turn

BURGOYNE MINING COMPANY.

At the ANNUAL GENERAL MEETING of the Company, held this 11th day of June, 1846, at the Crewe and Harpur's Arms Inn, Longnor, pursuant to notice given, agreeable to the Deed of Settlement, PHILIP HEACOCK, Esq. in the Chair:—

The minutes and proceedings of the Directors having been gone through, were approved and sanctioned.

A Report of the Directors, together with a Statement of the Accounts of the concern since the commencement, were then presented and read.

When it was unanimously resolved, That the said Report and Statement of Accounts be received and approved of, and that the same be printed and a copy sent to each Shareholder.

(Signed)   PHILIP HEACOCK, CHAIRMAN.

The DIRECTORS of the BURGOYNE MINING COMPANY, in making a Report of their operations, beg to remind the Shareholders that in consequence of past arrears in providing an engine for Clayton Mine, and other payments, together with the delay with which some have paid their calls, little has been attempted during the last year.

The little which has been done only convinces the Directors that vigorous and well-directed measures would crown their object with success. In extending levels westward in Clayton Mine, copper ore to the value of £295 16s. 5d. has been procured since the last General Meeting; and the prospects give every assurance of an available return to the Shareholders, at a lower depth.

It is therefore the determination of the Directors, taken and adapted by personal inspection, to get out the water from Clayton Mine, to the depth of 120 fathoms, and to direct, for the present, their active attention to this mine, and to the driving of a short level from the Clay Mine, to intersect the Ham Nook vein. It is for this purpose that they have made a call of £1 10s. 0d. on each share, and have only to request that this call will be promptly paid, and that no time may be lost during the season of Summer, to make this trial under as favourable circumstances as may be.

The Directors would respectfully intimate their great reluctance to proceed in any operation without the means; and they have scarcely need to add, being themselves holders of one half of the shares, that they have and will conduct all its affairs according to the best of their judgment, and at the least possible expense *or risk*.

CASH ACCOUNT.—GENERAL STATEMENT.

	£.	s.	D.		£.	s.	D.
To cost of Mine from the commencement to the 27th of April, 1846, including the Duty paid for Royalty	11,080	19	2½	By Cash received for Ores sold and Calls made, to May 18th, 1846	10,488	2	7
				By balance	592	16	7½
					11,080	19	2½

Arrears of Calls on the 18th of May, .. £215 0s. 0d.

W. Hoon, Printer and Bookseller, Ashbourn.

---

of the century for the Duke of Devonshire opened negotiations to work the Burgoyne royalty in association with his own. The result was a lease dated December 26th 1804 between the Duke, Montague Burgoyne as the mineral owner and James Bulkeley as the landowner (Dev Coll L/59/27).

This lease granted to the Duke the right to work the mines for a thirty year term at a yearly rent of £1 and a royalty of 1/10th of the ore. The Duke held the mines with a three-sixteenth share in trust for each of the other two parties. Presumably the Duke hoped to repeat the success at the nearby Clayton Mine that he had enjoyed at Ecton, which by now was producing a greatly reduced revenue. It is difficult to say whether he achieved the objective for the ore figures for this period of Clayton's history are not available, but nearly all the evidence points to the mine having been a disappointment. However if this is the case, was the pipe working exploited by the Gilbert partnership with the Duke under the 1753 lease from Sir Roger Burgoyne and the 1755 partnership agreement?

The manager of this new venture (including both the Ecton and Clayton Mines) was George Cantrell who had been the clerk to the Duke's mines. Although still under Flint, George Cantrell was to play an ever increasing role in the running of the concern. After 1811, Cantrell seems to have been in full command, for Cornelius Flint was by now an old man (9). Cantrell

> 'had full powers to do what is requisite in the Mine & that tho Mr. Flint objected still it was to be done' and 'I every reason to believe that things would go on in a very different way, had you proper authority' (10).

These quotations imply some friction between Flint and Cantrell, but no details are known.

One of the earliest known events of any significance was the transportation of an engine beam (probably of cast iron) from Froghall to the Pepper Inn in 1806 for the use of the Burgoyne Mines. The purpose of this is not known, but it seems to have been destined for Waterbank Mine. Again, no further details are known.

A Derbyshire-built Engine for Waterbank

In 1812 a steam engine was purchased from the Butterley Company of Ripley, Derbyshire, for £600 but no further details are known here, either (11). Since the lower levels of the Clayton Mine would need to be kept dry this engine was probably used for pumping. Some twenty-four years later the water in Clayton was described as 'constantly kept under by a four-horse engine worked two hours per day' (12), implying the Butterley engine of 1812. The very small size of engine again emphasises how little water seeped into the mine workings.

A Steam Winder for Clayton

In 1814 a steam winding engine of eight horsepower was also purchased from the Butterley Company, for £750, and installed underground in the Clayton Adit to wind up the Clayton Engine Shaft. This used flat ropes, each 195 yards long, supplied by John Curr. The flywheel and boiler were made in sections to enable them to be taken up the level, and the smoke was conveyed up the old Clayton Pipe via a wrought-iron chimney to a flue and a stone chimney on the surface. Remains of the flue on the surface and the soot-covered walls underground can still be seen, but the engine beds now visible appear to belong to two smaller steam engines, one for winding and one for pumping, installed late in the 19th Century by the Ecton Company Ltd.

The engineer involved with the erection of the underground engine was William Brunton, a noted engineer who received his early training at the Soho Works of Boulton and Watt. While at the Butterley Company he invented a walking steam locomotive. He later moved to south Wales where his achievements included a colliery ventilating fan and improved valve gear for pumping engines (13). His most widely used inventions were the Brunton calciner for treating copper ores containing arsenic, and his automatic stoker for firing steam boilers.

Operations by the Company

The Butterley Company also supplied a crushing machine for £250, but three years later Cantrell was considering having the rolls 'Hooped with Broad harnesses of wrought Iron' as being cheaper than having them repaired at either Butterley or Birmingham. It has been stated that the Clayton Pipe cut rich in 1812 and a considerable profit made for many years afterwards (14), but from the correspondence between George Cantrell, Montague Burgoyne and Col Bulkeley it seems that Clayton never achieved the expected output. In December 1811 Bulkeley wrote to Cantrell:

> 'I am pleased you continue to think favorable of the mine notwithstanding the disappointment which seems respecting the new vein of copper thought to have been so prosperously discovered'.

But three years later Cantrell wrote:

> 'that part of the Vein which the Workmen are driving through... with an

3.4 The Burgoyne Mineral Field 1648-1818

intent to drive in a Lead work at higher Level turned out unfortunately'.

By 1816 they had lost the pipe (15) and the vein – 'continues divided into different branches... if these branches will meet together at a lower level which is our principal aim then... the Mine will improve'.

But these hopes were not fulfilled and there was a loss of £500 on the Burgoyne Mines during the second half of 1816, with the comment:

'I was in hopes of Clayton Mine would have improved but that is not the case at present'.

Operations were confined to three companies of men working cope bargains in the bottom of the mine, with

'the Small strings (or Ribbs) of ore continue going down in a similar direction to what they have done for sometime which is rather extraordinary being so much below where the strong bodies of ore have previously been raised'.

These ore bodies are probably those found at 40 fathoms below adit level in a large working known as Chatsworth Open, which was followed by a contraction of the pipe and another large ore body below the 80 fathom level, called Smacker's Open (page 66). Trials were also being made at Gould Ecton, Hamnook, Bowler, Dutchman, Chadwick Pasture and Swainsley, as well as driving in a gate 'at old Jone on the South side of Clayton Level leading towards the Lumb'.

A plan dated 1818 gives a good impression of the state of the mines at that time. In Clayton, Bag Level had been driven nearly to Bag Mine from Clayton Pipe at adit level (a connection that was never completed), and Goodhope Level had reached the Lum (or Lumb), where a shaft is shown. The Lum was a local term for a natural fissure filled with rock and minerals in a clay matrix; little is known of the Lum at Ecton but it was an important feature of the Mixon and Dale Mines nearby and several Derbyshire mines including Nether Water Mine near Bradwell. The Dale Mine Lum is discussed in detail in Chapter 4. A tramway ran from the Ecton Deep Adit to the tips to the North of the entrance and the large number of buildings still existed.

References

1. The area concerned contains all the major mines, apart from those of the Duke of Devonshire
2. Staffs Record Office (SRO) D239/M638
3. SRO D554/55
4. J. A. Robey, 1970, Bull PDMHS, 4, No 3, pp217-221
5. See also Chapter 12
6. RO D238/M/850
7. SRO D239/649
8. Sheffield City Library, Bag 593
9. Cornelius Flint died in 1822 aged 84 and is buried at Hartington; George Cantrell died in 1860 aged 80 and his grave may be seen at Wetton
10. Burgoyne to Cantrell, Dec 1811; Pattinson Papers, SRO
11. Derbyshire Record Office, 503B. Butterley Company, Furnace Book B
12. Prospectus of Burgoyne Mining Company, 1836
13. Mining Association of Great Britain, 1924, *Historical Review of Coal Mining*, p144, Dictionary of National Biography
14. Prospectus of Ecton, Clayton and Waterbank, Mining Company, 1868
15. Later reports in the *Mining Journal* state that the pipe was lost at the 110 fathom level below adit

3.5 Exploration and Expectation

The Introduction of Cornish Influences, 1818-1825

Early in 1818, John Taylor the celebrated mining engineer and manager took responsibility for the Duke of Devonshire's mineral affairs and introduced a number of important changes at Ecton. His first action was to appoint a Cornishman, Captain John Goldsworthy, as underground manager. This, not unnaturally, did not please George Cantrell who resented this interference from outsiders. He was also continually criticised by Taylor for not sending regular reports and for not co-operating with Captain Goldsworthy. In April 1819 Taylor claimed that Cantrell had behaved badly towards the underground manager, and Cantrell was dismissed from his post. It seems that there was bitter resentment between Cantrell and Goldsworthy, with the former strongly denying the charges levelled at him.

It was claimed that the mines were being subjected to a considerable loss by Cantrell's 'want of science', since he had not appreciated that the old refuse could now be reworked for copper (see Chapter 11 for the details of ore recovered from the river in 1836 under Goldsworthy's direction). Cantrell countered this by stating that Captain Goldsworthy had let a bargain to a company of workmen whose son and brother in law had exacted a bribe of 10s. from each man, and by not keeping quiet about this and other injustices he was being thrown out of employment. Goldsworthy had offered a hundred guineas reward for anyone detecting Cantrell opening a spring of water to destroy the Ecton mine which Cantrell said,

> 'shows more the wickedness of his imagination than it proves anything against my principles which thank God art well known to many respectable Gentlemen here and also the incessant application I have always given to the interests of the Concerns'.

Despite this defence Cantrell left the mines, but two years later attempted to lease the Ecton Mine at a 1/10th duty, but this was refused. With the passage of time it is not possible to judge the claims and counterclaims in this dispute, but from the papers left by George Cantrell we can gain some insight into his character. He was certainly an educated and very literate person, much more so than Cornelius Flint whose correspondence was always poorly written, with indifferent spelling and punctuation. Cantrell's wide interests included such subjects as history, grammar, mineralogy, assaying, science, geology, accounting, theology and etiquette.

The Stamps Yard

Under Taylor, the ore was raised by tribute instead of cope-bargains and the miners had to contribute towards their own welfare. Large scale reworking of the old tips and waste ores, left as worthless by the previous generation, was commenced. To enable these waste ores (now called for the first time by the Cornish name of halvans) to be dressed economically to produce at least 6% of copper metal, a set of Cornish stamps were erected downstream at Swainsley. The stamps were driven by a waterwheel supplied with water from the River Manifold, with a weir opposite the entrance to Clayton Adit diverting water along a leat to the wheel. A tramway was also constructed to take the ore from the tips to the stamps. Although there are now no traces to indicate its former use, the site of these operations is still known as Stamps Yard and the bridge over the river is called Stamps Bridge.

In 1819-22, a trial level was driven from near the slag mill with the intention of cutting the veins at Hamnook and Gould Ecton but was abandoned before reaching its objective. This trial was known as Slag Level and later as Birch's Level (after John Birch, the original miner). The driving of this level had originally been at the suggestion of Cantrell, but Goldsworthy had claimed the credit for this and other trials, thus deepening the rift between them. Another change was the closure of the Whiston Works and the smelting of the copper ore at Swansea, although smelting and calcining of the waste ores continued at Ecton until 1826. The optimistic naming of one of the smallest mines 'Wheal Swainsley' for a short time is a further example of the Cornish influences during this period.

Staley's 1820 plan of Ecton Hill

The inner end of Apes Tor Sough had a dam across it so that water coming into the mine from the aquaduct rose up to flow onto the top of the 33 feet diameter waterwheel. The dam and wheel were constructed in 1823 and this date stone could be seen on the dam wall. The black image on the photograph is of soot from the fires which were kept burning to prevent the winding ropes from rotting through damp.

The dam was wantonly destroyed by vandals using dynamite and the date stone has never been found.

Work in the 1820s

The statement that after 1820 the operations at the mines consisted solely of tributing for copper and zinc blende in the heaps and shallow workings (1) is not strictly true, for some work was going on at Clayton in the 140 fathom level during 1820-1. However, in general the mines were being cleared of all traces of ore. One puzzling exception to this was the replacement of the old Ecton water engine by a 33ft diameter by 6ft wide overshot waterwheel to keep the mine dry. Perhaps it was realised that if the mines were to be leased to adventurers who would have little capital then the Ecton mine would have to be kept dry at the Duke's expense, with the hope of a return from the ore duties. Whatever the reason this waterwheel was installed in 1823.

The section of the mine (see page 66) shows the arrangements for the water supply, the source of which was quite a distance to the north of Cowlow Farm. The water crossed the River Manifold on raised wooden launders some 30-40ft high, flowed down a shaft at Apes Tor, along the flooded Apes Tor Sough to rise up a shaft constructed behind a gritstone wall near to the water engine shaft, and so onto the top of the wheel.

The Duke of Devonshire finally ceased operating Clayton Mine in 1822 and Ecton Mine at the end of 1825. Unfortunately, a document dated March 1821 which might shed more light on this period is misplaced in the Devonshire Collection. It is a 'release and assignment of a share in Ecton Mines' between the Duke and Col Buckley's executor. Although mining at Ecton continued under the management of a private company, the Clayton Mine was neglected for sixteen years until the formation of the Burgoyne Mining Company.

Captain Goldsworthy continued to work at the mine under the succeeding company. Both a Thomas and a John Goldsworthy were supplying the Whiston Copper Works with scrap copper, brass, slag and slime in the early 1830s. Most of the scrap etc came from Manchester but on one occasion the copper slag came from Ecton. In the 1870s, Thomas Goldsworthy, a grandson, owned the Ecton Emery Works at Hulme, in Manchester. Further, a Mr Goldsworthy is mentioned as receiving payment for services to the Ribden Copper Mine, south of Ecton in 1828.

The Cost-book Companies 1826-1857

The mines lay dormant for only a short period before adventurers were eager to try their luck and see what could still be extracted from what had been such a rich mine a generation before. No doubt they all hoped to cut ore as rich as the Ecton Pipe Vein and so make their fortune, but all were to be disappointed. The more realistic of those who came to Ecton were content to clean out the last scraps of ore from the known veins, or to apply improved dressing techniques to recover from the tips the ore that had been previously thrown away as not worth extracting. On the other hand the more speculative were involved in schemes to drive new levels, sink new shafts and install expensive machinery in the hope of discovering new copper and lead deposits. But the heyday at Ecton had been in the previous century, and it was never to return.

New companies came and went with remarkable regularity (a total of eleven separate enterprises from 1826 to 1890 have been identified) and the events which surround them are still far from clear, particularly before 1850. In the middle of the 19th Century, Government legislation simplified the formation of joint-stock companies, and this had wide spread repercussions on speculative mining.

In the early period the mines were worked by cost-book companies which were small partnerships of mining adventurers who were each liable to the full extent of any debts, or by private individuals willing to contribute their own capital. Compared with this, limited liability companies enabled shareholders to raise capital much more easily because the shareholders were only responsible to the extent of their own shareholding.

Consequently, the outlook on mining activities changed accordingly. Companies came and went with hardly any interruption of work and the objectives and mode of working the mines little changed. It is therefore convenient to consider the events at Ecton before and after the legislation of the 1850s, which gave birth to the limited liability companies.

The Ecton Copper Company

The first of the new companies took out a twenty-one year lease at a 1/10th royalty sometime between late 1826 to early 1827 and was chiefly concerned in getting ore from the bottom of the Ecton pipe-working. Apart from ore production statistics, very little is known of this concern and even its name – the Ecton Copper Company – taken from the Whiston account books, must be regarded with suspicion. Copper ore was raised in moderate quantities along with small quantities of lead obtained from isolated pockets of ore. Small quantities of copper ore were also raised at Swainsley mine in 1829-31.

An interesting account of a trip into Ecton Mine during 1838 (2) makes it clear that conditions had not materially altered since Efford's visit some seventy years previously, with half rotten ladders and poor illumination. The chamber at the bottom of the pipe working is described as being some 50-60ft high, with the engine shaft and waterwheel still in use. A capstan was used for hauling heavy loads up the Water-engine Shaft and fires were maintained underground to prevent the capstan ropes from rotting. Twelve miners were working the lower levels at this time.

The Ecton Mine Company & Melville Attwood

The Ecton Copper Company made its last delivery to Wm. Sneyd and Co at Whiston on December 15th 1838 and assigned its lease to a new company. Entries in the Whiston ledgers referred to the new company as the Ecton Mine Company and this style has been adopted here also. The lease of the mines was assigned to Melville Attwood, a young mining adventurer who had just returned from the gold and diamond fields of Brazil. He was born in 1812 at Prescott Hall, Worcestershire and went to South America before the age of seventeen. See also Chapter 7 for more details of Attwood and his father-in-law, Edward Forbes, at Ford, Grindon, Royledge and Chrome Hill. He was also engaged in metallurgical work and in 1843 gave zinc blende ore an added value by being the first in England to roll zinc successfully. He sailed for California in 1852 because of his wife's failing health and established the first gold mill there. He practiced as a mining engineer and invented many appliances for gold extraction including the 'Attwood Amalgamator' (3).

Melville Attwood, in association with a George Attwood, continued working the side veins and in the bottom of the Ecton pipe-working, making his first delivery to Whiston on December 15th 1840. Ore production during the early 1840 s was at its highest level during the whole of the period 1827-1889, with large quantities of copper ore and zinc blende being produced together with a smaller quantity of galena. Generally speaking throughout the whole of the 19th Century, all the copper ore was sent to Whiston.

The main exception occurred at this period when Attwood sent 500 tons of ore worth £2,650 (as well as at least 330 tons of copper slag, value £460) to Pattens at Cheadle. Although it is possible that the smelter had been brought into use again, it is more likely that Attwood had commenced reworking the tips on a large scale to extract the copper-bearing slags formerly dumped as being uneconomic to merit further treatment. The blende was sold to three main smelters viz:- approximately 500 tons each to Pattens and Messrs Cleaver & Co of Ripley in Derbyshire, and 200 tons to Whiston (4).

Ecton Mining Company

Attwood worked Ecton apparently as a private venture, but from evidence available, it appears that he ceased his activities in 1846 and the duty on the ore was decreased to 1/15th in that year. This may well have been due to representations from his successor, the Ecton Mining Co, although there is unfortunately no proof of this. George Attwood later claimed that work ceased because of pumping difficulties as

> 'the wheel underground had not power to fork the water, our intention was to have let the water in up to Ape Tor Level, the second cavity that would have lightened the weight and the wheel would then have managed the water' (5).

The Duke's agent, John Taylor, had insisted that the mine be kept drained to the bottom whilst obviously the Attwoods had in mind keeping the mine drained only to the 34 fathom level. It is interesting that both Attwood and Harpur, eighty years previously, describe the depth of the mine by reference to its 'cavities'. There were eight of these, arranged vertically and were the result of the removal of large deposits of ore.

ECTON DRESSING FLOOR 1820

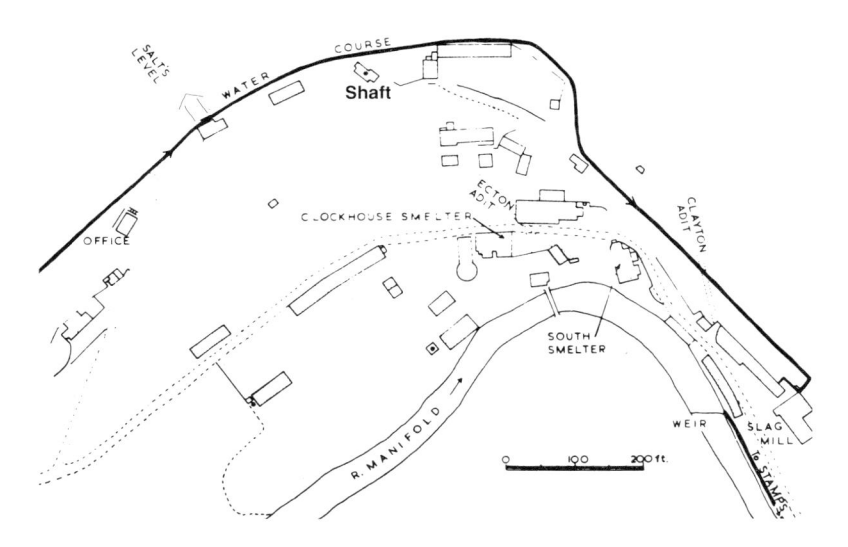

Fortunately, a little more is known of the next concern, the Ecton Mining Co, as a few reports were published in the *Mining Journal*. This new company was established on the cost book system, with 1,024 shares, and took-over the residue of the twenty-one year lease from Attwood. The Chairman was Mr Peter Davey, who also chaired (on occasions) the meetings of Wheal Concord Mining Co and Wheal Walter – two short lived West Country venturers which were also established on the cost book system with 1,024 shares each. The Secretary was Mr James Crofts, a sharebroker of London, who was later to become the secretary of Ecton Mountain Mining Co. It is also worth noting that among the other shareholders were Messrs Niness and Edwards, who were also associated at Dale and Mixon Mines – the former as Mine agent, the latter as a director – a capacity he also held at Ecton.

At the beginning of 1847, Old Ecton mine was being worked, but operations were confined to the 30 and 150 fathom levels. In the former, seven men were raising ore on tribute whilst only two men were employed (on tribute) at the latter. However, the 150 fathom level appears to have been soon abandoned for in February operations were confined to the 30 and 90 fathom levels and possibly at Swainsley Mine,

(see below). The workings were being managed by Capt John Williams, a Cornishman of Lower Town, Gwennap, who appears to have taken a number of mines in the district about this time, including New York Mine where he was involved in expensive litigation.

Problems with John Williams

At the February meeting of the Company, it was agreed to sublease to Williams the Old Ecton Mine in addition to a new adit level which was being driven on a lode recently discovered. (This, by inference from the *Mining Journal* of 12th January, 1889 was at Swainsley). The term was for three years from February 12th 1847. Williams had the right to work the halvans at 13/4d (67p) in the £, with a covenant to employ at least twelve persons on the halvans, eight on the old mine and four on the new lode. Further, at the end of the term, Williams was to have had the option of continuing the contract for a further three years at a reduced tribute of 10s in the pound.

Although the details are not too clear it is evident that it was the intention of Ecton Mining Co and Williams to form a new subsidiary company. A code of rules and regulations were drawn up, again on the cost-book principle, and a finance committee appointed which

3.5 Exploration and Expectation

included Messrs Davy and Edwards. The secretary was James Crofts and the purser Abraham Thompson.

However by April, 1847 it was found that the contract could not be fulfilled on account of the headlease only having eighteen months to run. Either this reflects considerable naivety or lack of good management by the Ecton directors. The prospective terms for a renewal of the lease required by John Taylor, the Duke's steward, were that eighteen men should be employed underground, no tributing of the halvans was to be set for more than twelve months and no underground pitch for over two months.

These terms conflicted with the agreement with Williams, who demanded £600 compensation plus an appointment to be given to him (or his nominee) as superintendent of the mines at £100 per annum plus also 5% of the net profits! Finally, Williams agreed to reduce his demands to just the second condition. By October 1847, Williams was raising ore although operations were confined to the 30 and 150 fathom levels.

However, with the termination of the original twenty-one year lease in 1848 it appears that a new company known as the Ecton Copper Mine Co. was formed, although again, details are far from clear. A report on the state of the mines was made in March 1849. The depth of Ecton is given as 1,272ft, with the ore deposit extending 90-120ft north and 300-360ft south of the Deep Shaft; the North lode was found to be up to 120ft wide. The main points of work were at the 80 fathom level, which had been driven 456ft from the Deep Shaft with the hope of intersecting three east-west veins near Dutchman (including Dutchman lode).

Sinking at the base of the mine was proceeding in unproductive ground in an attempt to reach an inverted saddle thought to exist below the main workings (it must have been a hunch, expecting a ninth deposit to exist below the eight already exploited above). Dutchman Shaft had been cleared down to the adit level '150ft below' and it was hoped to use Dutchman Adit if ore was

Richard Niness outside his home in Warslow. He is the figure in the middle

found on reaching Dutchman lode. Driving in Duke's Level at adit level in Ecton Mine had been undertaken but at the time of the report had been abandoned.

The lessees had covenanted that a minimum of eight men were to be at work, and there were in fact sixteen employees, excluding the agents, eight of them working on tribute. The lease was held on a 1/16th duty. By this date nearly £1,500 had been spent on exploratory work, while the previous company was reported as having spent £2,000 in the previous two or three years. It was appreciated that the future of the mine lay in discovering fresh ore deposits and this was the policy of the company. It was estimated that a total of £1,700 – £1,800 would have to be spent before it could be ascertained whether the mine could be worked profitably.

Abraham Thompson is reported as being the manager, with Samuel Bonsall as the clerk, (6) although Thompson collected the Duke of Devonshire's duty ore from the 1830s onwards.

By early 1850 the Ecton Copper Mine Company had ceased work after failing to find new deposits (ore sales were less than £1,000), resulting in a loss of about £1,000. They were the last company to work the Ecton Mine below adit level and the last to work only the Devonshire royalty.

The Duke returns to Ecton, 1851

After the failure of the Ecton Copper Mine Company the mines on the Duke of Devonshire's property were worked, not by a mining company, but by the Duke. The decision to rework the Ecton Mine was probably taken on the advice of Stephen Eddy, the Duke's mining agent at Grassington, for the balance of the Ecton Account was charged to the Grassington Mines and Eddy regularly visited Ecton during this period.

The insistence of the agent four years previously that the mine be kept free of water is an indication of the Duke's intention to work Ecton below adit level, although it is difficult to visualise why, as the quantity of copper ore extracted was insignificant. However, the tonnage increased almost immediately and in the next four years men were employed on tribute raising copper and lead from below the adit level. 218 tons of copper ore worth £2,124 and 31 tons of lead ore worth £237 were obtained during this period.

Despite the increase in revenue, it is interesting to note that from 1849 to 1861, the Duke sustained a loss of £900 even after deducting the revenue from royalties. This was reduced to £450 by the sale of equipment to the Ecton Mountain Mining Company, who subsequently sold it for scrap. It is interesting to note, however, that during the period 1851-1855, which was the period when the Duke reworked the mines himself, his Ecton account sustained a loss of only £10. The majority of his remaining losses include expenses of estate management and strictly speaking ought to be excluded from the mine accounts.

From at least 1830 to 1861 the Duke kept an agent at Ecton at a salary of £54.12.0d. (£54.60p) a year, this post being occupied by Abraham, John and George Thompson at various times, while from the 1850s, John Wagstaff, the Barmaster, acted as agent from the other royalty.

It is difficult to justify the employment of a full-time agent by the Duke, for most of his duties consisted solely of collecting the royalties from the Ecton and Bincliff Mines although he may have acted as the land agent also. From 1855 the major expense to the Duke was the agent's salary and this consistently exceeded the revenue from royalties. All work below adit level in Ecton was abandoned after 1854 when the mine was allowed to fill up.

Shortly afterwards the raised wooden launders at Apes Tor collapsed probably as a result of age and neglect. In December 1860, Captain Niness of the Dale Mine, who had also been 'an agent at Ecton for two or three years', stated that the Ecton Mine took two years to fill with water after the launders had blown down. As late as March 1858 the Dale Mine Secretary had visited the 30 fathom level but the inference from his letter in the *Mining Journal* was that he did not go any deeper. This would seem to date the collapse of the launders at about 1856.

It was only during the term of the Ecton Company thirty years later that Clayton Mine was unwatered and Ecton Mine has remained flooded to this day.

There is confusing evidence that the Ecton Mountain Mining Company had also worked the Ecton Mine. In March 1858 the *Mining Journal* published a letter from James Crofts (a

London sharebroker) who had been the secretary of the Ecton Mountain Mining Co. He stated that the company, after about three years and having spent some £5,000, found that explorations of Old Ecton were quite useless and it was abandoned. Apart from a note in the company's cash book of £30 received 'per Mr. Moore for Big Open men' – the Big Open being the large excavation in the Ecton Mine – there is little evidence to support Crofts' statement. The account books do record that £5,500 was spent during this period, but not at Old Ecton. Consequently the picture of operations at this time is far from complete and awaits the discovery of further documentary evidence.

The Burgoyne Mining Company 1836-1850

While the Duke's mines had continued working throughout the 1820s and 1830s the Burgoyne mines had been abandoned, until George Cantrell of Wetton, the clerk and later manager to the mines during the Duke of Devonshire's operations, revived interest in the Clayton and Waterbank Mines in 1836. This resulted in the formation of the Burgoyne Mining Company in 1836 on a twenty-one year lease from Mrs Burgoyne. The agent was Captain Samuel Bonsall, the nephew of Sir Thomas Bonsall, an eminent miner of his period who made a sizeable fortune in the lead mines of Wales during the second half of the 18th Century (7), while the majority of the shareholders were local personalities. The Chairman was Joseph Heath and several prominent people from Leek were shareholders, plus Mr Manclark, the Harpur-Crewe estate manager.

All the workings in the Clayton Mine below adit level had been allowed to fill with water and those above adit level were in a dilapidated state, but the usual over-optimistic prospectus promised great riches, at an initial cost of only £2,000-£3,000. The water had previously 'been constantly kept under by a four-horse engine worked two hours per day', referring to one of the Butterley engines, and draining was regarded as no serious problem.

A report on the mines was made in November 1839. Waterbank had been drained to a depth of 16 fathoms and worked for a further 10 fathoms. All the workings below the sough had been choked with stone and water, which had been cleared away to reveal the vein. After some exploratory work the main vein was found to intersect various feeders, which produced 20 tons of lead and six tons of copper ore. The engine shaft previously had been sunk to 45 fathoms and a level driven to intersect the vein.

This had proved to be unrenumerative, causing the mine to be abandoned. Waterbank was proving difficult to drain by horse-power, so operations there were suspended and Bag level in Clayton was driven in an attempt to unwater the mine. Six men had driven about 25 fathoms and a tram road had been laid. Goodhope Mine had been cleared out and good stope of lead ore found at the Northern end leading to the Lum. It was expected that this mine would pay for the whole expense of the company. Joan Level in Clayton was also being driven towards the Lum in an attempt to unwater Goodhope Mine. Bowler Mine had been cleared to reveal several veins of galena, but the shafts were in a very dilapidated state and had needed repairing. Similar work had been done at Clay Mine, although nothing had been done at Clayton.

A further report in 1845 stated that copper, lead and blende ores had been raised, 'principally attributed to the facility with which the water had been got out of the Clayton Mine, since the erection of the Steam Engine'. No details of this engine are known, although in 1853 it was stated that

> 'a 6-inch box is sufficient to drain the mine even at a greater depth than the present... a rotary steam engine is erected in Clayton in a portion of the adit level, where it quietly rests, partly buried in water' (8).

There were only twelve men employed in Clayton, with a company raising lead from Clay Mine, all other trials had been suspended for lack of funds. By this date the mines had cost £10,000, with a return from ores of £3,528. A year later another £1,000 had been spent and efforts were being concentrated on lowering the water in Clayton Mine to 120 fathoms. Although a lode of copper some 4ft in thickness and a lead lode were discovered in Clayton in 1847 and over 10 tons of ore raised within 24 hours, the success was short lived.

It seems that the Burgoyne Mining Company had been responsible for driving the branch towards Bag Mine from the Clayton Adit in 1839, while the continuation of the Clayton Adit towards the Waterbank Mine must have been a later venture by this Company. The 1868 prospectus estimated that this level had taken some five to six years to drive and cost £2,000. It is interesting to note that both the branch to Bag Mine and the level to Waterbank deviate quite markedly from the most direct routes, which indicates that their surveying could have gone seriously wrong.

This is substantiated by the curious bend at the extreme south of the level where it terminates under Broad Ecton Farm, which suggests that they were searching without success for the vein. Although later companies also proposed to link the Bag and Waterbank Mines with the Clayton Level the Bag connection was never made, while the crosscut to Waterbank Mine was almost one of the final projects before the mines eventually closed for ever. Even then the Ecton Company had dialling troubles for it was found that a shaft sunk from Waterbank Mine was a considerable distance from its intended position. It is possible that the shaft is simply out of plumb. This happened at the Dale mine where the new engine shaft is 105 fathoms deep and 38ft out of plumb.

Ecton Mountain Mining Co Ltd 1851-1857

In 1850 a prospectus was issued for the formation of a new company 'under a committee of the Old and New Proprietors'. It was stated that the old proprietors of the Clayton Mine Company, i.e. the Burgoyne Mining Company, had held a lease from Lady Burgoyne at a 1/12th royalty, and had expended £10,000, installing 'tramroads, steam-engine, whimseys, etc.' The old company proposed to give up half the mine or 500 shares at £10 each to lay dry the ores in Waterbank, Chadwick's Pasture, Goodhope and Clayton Mines.

Further particulars were available from Capt Bonsall at the mine or from Michael Blackett, a Manchester solicitor. This is the earliest reference to the mine's connection with the Blacketts and also to the mine's links with Manchester, upon which it became increasingly dependant.

The outcome was the formation of a new Company by the amalgamation of the former Ecton and Burgoyne Companies. The share out of capital was on the basis of 564 shares to 536 shares and the new company commenced operations in November 1851. The secretary was W D Geary and his salary was £25 per annum, which was only paid once, in 1855. The agent was Captain Samuel Bonsall, who was paid £96 per annum. He had been paid this salary in the 1830s and was still only paid this when he died in 1870.

The Duke of Devonshire's agent was Abraham Thompson, whilst the Barmaster, John Wagstaff, acted for the Burgoyne royalty. Whether this was in a private capacity or not is not known. It is most unusual for the Barmaster to be involved in a Staffordshire mine at all. The majority of the work was done by contractors and a summary of their activity is given below. The company had passed its peak in 1855 and the amount of activity steadily declined after that time.

The company's main intention was to search for fresh ore as distinct from trying to find offshoots from the old worked-out deposits. Consequently the efforts of the company were directed towards exploration work, which was quite expensive. In fact, the company only raised 142 tons of lead ore, worth £1,060 but spent £5,033.13.8d. The actual revenue to the company from the lead ore appears to have been only £23, for the men seemed to have received the full value of the ore after deducting the royalty. Even where a tribute bargain was made, the men were receiving 17s.0d to 18s.0d (85p to 90p) in every pound. Presumably the company was forced into this by low ore prices. Later companies were also forced to pay a subsistence to the tribute men when the value of the ore was insufficient to provide a reasonable wage.

Initially, the company commenced operations in Good Hope Level, Clayton, Chadwick and Clay Mines, chiefly on contract work. In Good Hope Level six to eight men were employed driving south eastwards on a cross branch 15 inches wide with the intention of cutting one of the main north-south lodes and unwatering Good Hope mine. It cannot be ascertained if the company commenced work in the Dutchman Level or whether the level had been driven a short distance previously.

Nevertheless, it is known that the majority of the level was driven in 1851. A total length of just over 88 fathoms was driven at a cost of nearly £560. The cost of driving the level varies from £6.10s to £10 per fathom. The company did not do any work in the level after 1854, presumably because of the high expenditure incurred, which included the laying of rails to the end of the level and repairing the steam engine.

Clayton & Chadwick Joined Together

In Clayton Mine all of the work was above the adit level, chiefly in Vivian's Level where 317 feet were driven at a cost of £300. However, work ceased in 1854, similar to Good Hope when the emphasis changed to exploration in other workings – see below. The intention was to intersect the Quarry Lode and although various lead veins were cut, the lode was never reached. The other important activity in Clayton was the rising of the connecting shaft to Chadwick Mine, which was achieved in August 1852. Chadwick is described in the *Mining Journal* 1852 as being 'nearly inaccessibly filled out at all the higher levels with rubble', which was cleared away.

This work in Chadwick adit level was probably responsible for destroying much of the last known 'Coffin Level' work in a North Staffordshire mine. Some of this type of work may still be seen in this level, but it no longer drains to the Fish Pond and this important feature is often flooded to a height of about five feet. 'Coffin Levels' are shaped to the body – hence the name – and have characteristic pick marks which sweep down from shoulder height ahead of you and then from about knee height, they change direction and sweep back behind you. Presumably, this work was executed during the Gilbert era, or before.

In Chadwick itself after initial repairs to the engine shaft, the adit level rail tracks etc, the emphasis was on driving the adit level although stoping was done in 1852 and 1853 when it was described as producing sufficient lead ore to cover the cost of extraction.

As already intimated, about 1854 a change of policy apparently occurred. Up to the early part of that year the contractors had been working on extensions of existing levels with the exception of Clay Mine where in 1852 42 fathoms were driven at a cost of £153. It is interesting to note that the four men employed at this place went onto tribute in July but the income per man was only two guineas for the month and the men promptly went back onto contract work the following month! With the change in policy the contractors commenced work in the 'New Trial' – believed to be Quarry Mine by cross references in different ore accounts – and in Bowler Mine where the men were 'set on' to drive the level.

At the 'New Trial' during 1853 the men were driving and stoping to a considerable extent but appear to have been hindered by water and as many as ten men were drawing water at this one mine in October. During the following year up to thirteen men were employed here and a further difficulty – bad air – was encountered. In 1852 and 1853 there were references to 'Dutchman Shallow Level' which could refer to the shallow trials between the Dutchman entrance and the Boulton & Watt engine house, or the inclined working referred to as 'Fly Mine' by Nellie Kirkham.

At Bowler Mine a new whim was erected in 1854 and a footway put into one of the shafts, presumably the 10 fathom climbing shaft. However the total amount of contract work done was small. All contract work ceased during 1855 and thereafter few people were employed other than a few tributors.

The ore accounts do give some additional indication of what work was done, both before and after the contract labour was terminated. The number of men on tribute was never much above a dozen and indicate that they were working all the mines mentioned above until 1857.

Initially some 80% of the annual outlay was spent on the payment of the men underground (excluding tributors) but this fell to only 30% in 1855 with a corresponding drop in those employed. In 1852 there were 52 employees (excluding S Bonsall) although it is unclear if this included tributors of which 36 were employed underground and a further four were boys. In October 1855 the total was only a maximum of 13 which consisted of 6 men and 3 boys underground and 4 men on the surface. Thereafter generally the tributors were employed and they washed and dressed their own ore, presumably at the Stamps Yard, although this is uncertain.

Apes Tor

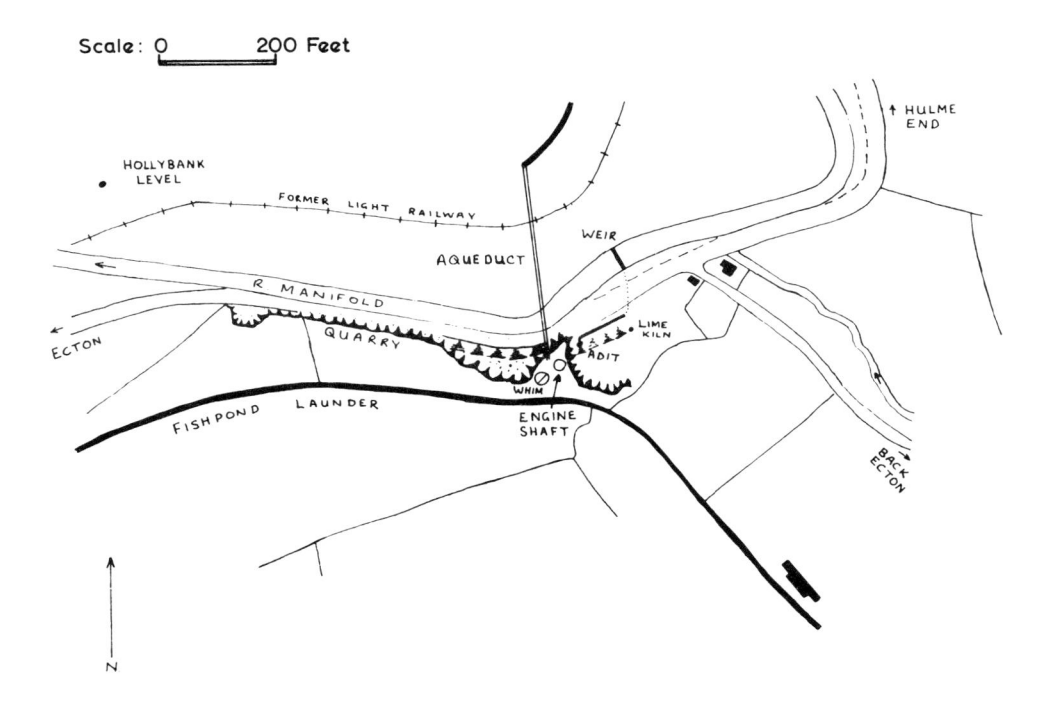

In addition there were also a few men who did general work such as 'waggoning and wheeling' the ore to the surface, dressing ore, moving stone etc. Sometimes their work was of particular significance such as the erection of the ore house and blacksmith's shop in 1853, and repairing and redecorating the office. They also undertook carriage of materials such as plant in 1852 from the Alport Mine sale and coal from the Goldsitch Colliery Co near Leek etc. It is surprising to find that they were also employed in surface trials and in working Nook Close Mine, (location unknown). Although this was a common practice with later companies, it was unusual with this company.

Loss of the Ecton Mine Engine and the Aqueduct

Although the revenue from ore was practically nil, more substantial sums were obtained from the sale of surplus materials, particularly towards the end of the company's life. Of particular interest is the Boulton & Watt engine which had been disused from about 1850 when the Ecton Mine was completely abandoned below river level. The 'engine' (probably the piston to be precise) was sold for £32 and the boiler for £40. Further, 655lb of brass was sold at $9^{1}/_{2}$d per pound, presumably representing the other valuable parts of the engine. Other material was sold, weighing 5 tons 8cwt (to Mollard & Son, probably scrap dealers) plus 4cwt of joint pins and 58 tons of 'old cold blast mettle' for £290. Additional material was sold to the Bincliff, Dale and Mixon Mines. The stamps yard at Swainsley is mentioned in 1855 and remained in use until 1866.

Finally, two independent references may hold the clue to the date the Apes Tor raised launders were blown down. The cost book for the December 1853 reckoning states that James Phillips & Co (six men) were repairing Ecton Launders, indicating their existence, whilst in December 1860 Capt Niness of the Dale Mine stated (Mining Journal, 1860 p810) that it took the Ecton Mine two years to fill with water after

3.5 Exploration and Expectation

the launders had been blown down. He also stated that he had been 'an agent at Ecton for two to three years'.

Perhaps a further clue lies in the sale of the Boulton & Watt engine in 1855. The reason for selling the engine could be related to the decision to allow the mine to flood after the launder collapsed. At the mine meeting on 22 July 1857, with a Mr Moore in the chair, a resolution was passed to discontinue further workings and to wind up the affairs of the company (*Mining Journal*, 25/7/1857, p532). Despite the fact that the machinery was being scrapped and the mines being run down, a new company took over almost immediately. Samuel Bonsall's salary ceased to be paid as from August 1857 and yet by October of the same year another company had been formed. However, the reluctance of the investors to continue working at the base of Ecton Mine could have been an influencing factor. The Duke's agent did try making it a condition of a lease that the bottoms be kept dry. Perhaps this was becoming difficult for the miners to accept and the collapse of the launders sealed the issue.

Ecton Engine house in 1924, before the roof was lowered. It kept losing tiles in high winds

Ecton Consolidated Mining Co 1857-1861

The new company commenced operations in October 1857. In all probability the firm took over the lease of the former company for the terms of the royalty were the same and the annual level rent of £10 was paid to the Duke as previously. The history of the company is very similar to that of its predecessor. Over £2,700 was expended in obtaining a revenue from lead and copper ore of just over 10% of that figure. However it differed for whilst Ecton Mountain Mining Co's expenses quickly diminished, Ecton Consolidated's rapidly rose and continued to do so until it was renamed the New Ecton Mining Co in 1861.

The company's main development was the extension of Good Hope Level towards Good Hope Mine. Six to eight men were continually employed on contract work driving the level until a rise up from the level made contact with the mine in May 1861. Many of the contract parties bear the same names as those working for Ecton Mountain Mining Co.

As the driving of the level progressed clay was brought from neighbouring Narrow Dale. This was laid on the floor of Good Hope Level and rails were fixed on sleepers to carry the

wagons to and from the face to the surface tip. Difficulty with air was experienced and the air pipes in the now abandoned Bowler Mine were transferred to Goodhope level in 1859. An 'air machine' – presumably a hand operated bellows – was made in 1860 and thereafter three boys were employed blowing air. Buildings were erected at the surface but their nature isn't specified.

The company drove at least 135 fathoms at a cost of £600. Having made the connection, between the level and Good Hope Mine, water and ore was removed via the level. This cut the cost of drawing ore and water up Good Hope Shaft although some pumping was still necessary. The horse whim at Good Hope had been removed in November 1858 and presumably the shaft was not used thereafter. Although it is not clear whether the Dutchman lode was ever intersected it is obvious that a minor lead ore deposit was found for men were employed driving and stoping in Good Hope Mine and also sinking below the level. A little lead ore was raised.

Further explanatory work was done in Ecton, chiefly in Salt's Level by Thomas Brindley & Co. This was a contract party of four men driving the level in 1857-1858. During 1859 a party were employed on the footway between Salt's Level and Ecton Deep Adit Level repairing the ladders, blasting and cleaning stone. A little copper ore was raised during 1860 and sent to Whiston.

Samuel Bonsall also employed two men in 'exploring and clearing' Quarry Mine in 1858 but evidently without success for his attention was turned to the eastern side of the hill where a rich deposit of lead ore was cut only 6ft below the surface at East Ecton, in Twigg's Field by Samuel Twigg & Co, during November 1861. The exploration of this new mine was undertaken by the New Ecton Mining Co.

The New Ecton Mining Co Ltd 1861-1866

The company started work with only ten men and a post boy under Samuel Bonsall, the agent. This gradually increased and although the number of employees fluctuated weekly, on average there were around twenty-one employees by 1861, including one woman who was employed to dress ore. The emphasis on ore dressing is indicated in the cost book from 1859 onwards when ore was brought up in increasing quantities.

The water channel from the fishpond was repaired to provide a supply of water for buddling and the dressing floor was also repaired. A hand grinder was made and the Stamps Yard brought into use once again. It cannot be ascertained whether any of the poorer quality ore was refined at Ecton, but a reference to the purchase of larch poles may be significant in this respect.

The Ecton dressing floor was originally near to the Ecton Deep Adit, i.e. between the road and the river at this point, although how it obtained a head of water isn't clear. From 1804 the dressing floor at the Salt's Level horizon was used. The Burgoyne royalty dressing floor was on the flat ground between the entrances to Clayton and Birch's Levels, using the Fishpond water.

These floors remained in use after the construction of the Stamps Yard, which had buddles and fifteen head of stamps worked by a waterwheel. Initial crushing and separation of ore from rock was carried out prior to removal of finer material to the Stamps Yard.

However, the cost of the ore extraction was far in excess of the revenue and by 1861 it was found necessary to obtain fresh capital to continue working. This was done without any disruption of work and the company continued under the name of the New Ecton Mining Co Ltd from December 1861.

The New Ecton Mining Co Ltd purchased the leases of Ecton Consolidated on the terms of distributing paid up shares to the amount of £4,000 among the shareholders of the latter company. The plant and machinery was purchased from the old company but unfortunately no figures are available. The capital of the new company was £10,000 in 1,000 shares of £10 each. The secretary was Mr Herbert Drinkwater of Manchester who may have been the secretary of Ecton Consolidated; the agent was Mr Samuel Bonsall.

Having obtained the injection of fresh capital it was planned to open up Good Hope Mine and sink a shaft from Good Hope to Clayton Adit to unwater the mine completely. There can be no doubt that the management believed that the future of Ecton as a viable concern lay in the

3.5 Exploration and Expectation

A stope in East Ecton Mine

exploitation of fresh deposits and that Good Hope was considered to be sufficiently rich to merit a large capital outlay. One has only to walk around the Good Hope workings to appreciate the amount of work and quantity of rock extracted that caused the high expense. Before the end of 1861, already 27 tons of lead had been sold at about £10.7.6d (£10.37½) per ton which had given much encouragement.

However, the work at East Ecton must have also caused a great deal of interest. Lead ore had been found only six feet below the surface and half a ton of ore had been raised in the short distance of nine feet enabling the initial costs to be covered by the revenue so obtained. The vein had a bearing of east to west and the adit level was driven westwards along the vein. It was intended to sink a shaft to intersect the adit and although this is shown on Wheatcroft's plan of 1873, no such shaft is known to exist. This level must be the one at the rear of East Ecton Farm.

In Good Hope Mine the company employed a large number of men stoping and cross-cutting. In 1862 there were at least twenty-six men on contract work alone and in 1863 there were around two dozen tributors. In 1868 there were two major cross cuts being driven and in particular Good Hope Level was driven some 200ft eastwards, possibly indicating the intentions to link up with the disused Bag Mine, which was achieved by a later company. The proposal to sink a shaft to Clayton Adit was never undertaken and there was not even an attempt to prove the Good Hope vein at that depth.

All contract work in the mines ceased at the end of June 1865 and thereafter the only work done was on tribute, raising a small quantity of lead ore.

At East Ecton the adit level was driven some 750ft. Generally only two or three men were employed on contract work and other men were employed on day work laying rails, walling and arching the level and carting stone from Ecton and Apes Tor to the mine. Further work was, of course, on tribute, raising various quantities of lead ore. Additional work was done at the rear of the cottages above the mine in the shallow adit driven in a rather sandy limestone also found in the main adit. Men were sinking the East Ecton shaft some 80ft deep during 1862 at a cost of 10s.0d (50p) per foot. This shaft is 9ft wide and is the largest diameter shaft on the hill.

The fresh capital also enabled a certain amount of repair and maintenance to be carried out. The gritstone launders from the Fish Pond were cleaned out during 1862, for instance. It is probable that a similar motive was behind the numerous references in the accounts to 'the building of the dressing floor including removing 150 yards of earth to the dressing floor...'. This work was done in the first six months of 1862 but could only have been used to a small amount before 1863 when the first ore sales commence. Furthermore, a smithy was built in 1864, possibly at East Ecton.

Initially the company employed just under fifty people, excluding tributors, of which some 50% were employed underground. In 1863 there were some two dozen tributors. Thereafter the numbers dropped until in the last year less than 10 men were employed plus about six tributors. As may be expected the company followed the pattern of its predecessors, accumulating a total expenditure of £3,990 and earning a revenue from ore of under £500 which showed a remarkable similarity with Ecton Consolidated.

Other than the two main underground centres of activity, namely East Ecton and Good Hope, there was little attempt to turn to possible alternatives. In fact a small amount of work was done in Clayton Deep Adit in 1865 driving 16ft eastwards on a vein and extracting a small amount of copper ore which was sent to Whiston. An unusual entry appears in the account books for March and April of 1863, referring to 'sinking in Vivian's Level' (Clayton), for no shaft can be found. However, it may refer to the shaft in Joan Vein which remains undated. Additionally work was done in Salt's Level in 1863 on contract and a small amount of copper ore was raised. Clay Mine was let on tribute where lead ore was extracted. A single entry for four tons of zinc blende occurs in 1864, raised in the Duke's royalty and therefore in either East Ecton or Salt's Level.

All contract work finished at the end of June 1865 and thereafter the only employees were half a dozen tributors and a handful of men on day work, employed chiefly in arching and walling Clayton Level and at East Ecton. The tributors washed and dressed their own ore and purchased their own powder and candles through the company. Powder was supplied by Messrs Williamson & Co at £2.8.0d (£2.40p) per barrel and candles came from various merchants at between 5/3d (26p) and 6/6d (32p) per dozen.

In 1866 the walling in Clayton Adit was still continuing with a small amount of walling in East Ecton. It is unlikely that much tribute work was being done either.

Waterbank and Ecton Mines 1866-1868

It is clear that activity was on a care and maintenance basis only. The mining rights were taken over by Colin Mather, of Mather & Platt Ltd, who appears to have paid £3,000 for them. Mather & Platt is still in existence today and are internationally known engineers.

Colin Mather was an industrialist and brilliant engineer known as 'Cast-iron Colin'. Mather & Platt Ltd were based at the Salford Iron Works and advertised themselves as 'Engineers, machine-makers, millwrights and iron-founders'. They produced a wide range of goods and designed and made anything which a customer required. It was as a result of the success of the firm which enabled Mather to purchase the assets of the New Ecton Mining Co and finance an expenditure of £2,656 between August 1866 and May 1868. His ability and shrewdness is perhaps well expressed in the fact that he earned a revenue from ore in 1868 which exceeded the combined total revenue of both of the previous two companies.

Although work continued in Good Hope, East Ecton and Salt's Level, Mather staked his capital in Waterbank and later, Bag Mines. Within a month of taking over, a steam engine and boiler were brought from Manchester via the High Peak Railway to Parsley Hay and was started a week later, on 2nd October, 'by Colin Mather Esq of Salford Iron Works and at his sole expense'. Coal for the engine was supplied by Francis Barton from the Parsley Hay Wharf of the Cromford and High Peak Railway Co. Barton commenced supplying coal to the mines in 1857 when supplies from the Goldsitch Colliery near Leek ceased. Mather & Platt Ltd also supplied the following to the mine:-

December 1866	Stone crusher	Value £80
May 1867	Spiral cylinder	Value £25
November 1868	Rotary pump	Value £20

Further, according to Mather & Platt Ltd's records, earth boring equipment was supplied to Mather in January and April 1867, to the value of £635, probably for Mather's exploration of Waterbank Mine (9).

The Ecton accounts indicate that all of the bills were paid by John Mather, an accountant who probably acted as the secretary. Samuel Bonsall, of course, continued in his capacity as agent at his salary of £96 per annum. Mather spent a considerable sum in developing the Waterbank Mine. As well as the engine, a smithy, office, saw pit and reservoir are known to have been built. A road to the mine was constructed and work was started in cleaning out the mine and repairing the engine shaft.

Mather chiefly employed men on day work in the mine and therefore received all the profit from the ore obtained. In 1867 up to twenty men were employed here alone. Work was concentrated in opening up the ground between 15 and 25 fathom levels below adit, in a southwards direction. Further work was done in the 45 fathom level rising on a vein of lead ore.

At East Ecton further contract work was directed at driving the adit level during 1866-1867 but thereafter the mine appears to have been abandoned. Contract work also terminated in Good Hope in 1867 but 13 tributors were still employed thereafter raising lead ore. The contract work had more or less finished in 1866 but a small amount of work was done towards the end of 1867 in driving eastwards towards Bag Mine. The respite was, however, brief for the level regained fresh importance when Bag Mine was developed. Additional contract work was done in 1867 in Salt's Level but the mine was also being worked by tributors who were raising copper ore. The ore was sent to Whiston at a carriage cost of 10s.0d (50p) per ton.

During 1867 Mather turned his attention from Waterbank to Bag Mine possibly because of increased costs at the former. The shaft was cleared out and a footway put in. Further preparatory work was done and an engine erected in April 1868. This was, however, costing Mather a lot of money and it must have been obvious to him that capital would have to be raised to finance future exploratory work, both in Bag and Waterbank Mines.

Ecton, Clayton and Waterbank Mining Co Ltd 1868-1874

The Company was to have a capital of £10,000 in 500 shares of £20 each with Colin Mather holding 150 shares. John Mather was the Secretary.

The prospectus for raising the share capital states that the Steam Engine at Waterbank worked operated both winding and pumping machinery and that there also existed a Blake's Patent Ore Breaker, a large ore crusher and Mather's Patent Improved Revolving Buddle. During 1868 work was concentrated in Bag Mine where twelve men were employed both on contract and day work clearing out refuse, straightening and driving the main tram level and 'stoping for the tramway'. The number employed increased so that by the end of the year there were twenty-two men (including six tributors) and five boys employed underground. During August, pipes (probably for air) were brought out of Waterbank.

At the latter mine there were generally six men working on tribute and raising ore whilst at Good Hope further tribute work was undertaken for a short period as well as contract work in driving the Good Hope Level to meet the Bag Level. The only other underground work was in Ecton Adit where men were driving from March onwards and also on tribute. It is interesting to note that the ore (copper) was drawn up the Ecton Engine Shaft to Salt's Level by a horse whim, the Boulton & Watt engine having been removed.

The use of a whim indicates that the ore was being obtained from the Ecton Adit and not Salt's Level.

After 1868 additional material on the company's activities is limited to the rather sparse information available from the cost book and the day book of 1861. Entries in the cost book cease on 1st July 1874 when presumably the company ceased operations. The company spent a total of £7,334.8.4d (£7,334.42) and raised copper and lead ore to the value of £1,162 which was considerably more productive than Mather's predecessors. It is known that the communication between Bag and Good Hope Level was achieved before the company ceased working for the work was not undertaken by the next, and last company. Expenses remained high until 1874 although ore sales dropped to an insignificant amount in 1873. The only statistics of employees indicate that the compliment in early 1870 had remained fairly static. Presumably Platt Mine dates from this period.

Captain Bonsall died in 1870 after being captain of the mine for 33 years. He was buried at Wetton and a stone bearing the effigy of a hand holding a pick was erected by 178 subscribers as a token of their esteem and respect for his integrity. His obituary states that he had been ill for some time and the vein he had been searching for was found whilst he was ill. The good news was communicated to him and such was it's effect that he suffered a relapse and died. He was succeeded by Joseph Beresford who retained the position until the company ceased operations.

3 Ecton Copper Mines

Above: Ecton in the 1880s, showing the incline to haul tubs from Clayton to the dressing floor
Opposite: The Clockhouse smelter and South smelter, 1883. The machinery was being assembled in Clayton mine

The 1870's also saw the advent of a new era; in 1871 the first steam bus delivered coal into the area from the Cheadle Coalfield. Half of the first load was delivered to Captain Niness of the Dale Mine, not Ecton, but the implication was the same – the days of fetching coal by carts was drawing to a close. Carting costs were as much as 50% of the cost of the coal but the excitement and speculation that arose after the introduction of this cheaper transport did not rebound with a new lease of life for either Ecton or the Dale Mine. The latter ceased working in 1873 after litigation for river pollution although it is said locally that the mine ceased after three men were brought out badly burnt following an explosion.

The Ecton Co Ltd 1883-1891

For the next nine years the mines lay unworked, until William Bowman of Alport, took them in hand to negotiate new terms and form a fresh company. Bowman commenced preparatory work in April 1883, employing three to four men but it was October before the newly formed Ecton Co Ltd. commenced serious operations. On 5th July 1883 Bowman entered into an agreement with Frank Sandring (acting secretary of the Ecton Company) to purchase the leases for £10,500 in cash or in fully paid shares. The latter alternative was adopted by the directors and shares valued at £10,000 (out of a capital of £50,000) were allotted to the Duke of Devonshire and Major E O Blackett (whose family appear to have acquired the Burgoyne mineral rights, through marriage in the 1850s) and £500 to Bowman.

The company was of limited liability and the lease covered most of the hill from Apes Tor to Wetton Mill, for a term of thirty-one years at a

3.5 Exploration and Expectation

royalty of 1/20th for the first ten years and 1/16th thereafter, or a rent of £100 per annum, whichever was the greater. The level rent of £10 per annum was reimposed by the Duke for the use of Clayton, Goodhope and Birch's Levels.

The re-working of the mines coincided with a national copper depression, with supply from abroad outstripping demand, yet there was considerable interest in the new venture.

Initial Activity

The first place to be reworked was Vivian's Lode in Clayton Adit. Six men were employed on contract at £4 per fathom in driving to intersect the Dutchman's Lode. Further work was started in driving eastwards from Clayton Engine Room at £6 per fathom and on Dale Vein, south of the Adit, at £2 per fathom.

On the surface development was commenced with the construction or repairing of buildings at Ecton and Waterbank. In November 1883 the launders from the Fishpond were cleaned and repaired and pipes for conveying the water to the Engine Room were purchased. At Ecton, the south smelthouse was repaired and retiled for use as the blacksmiths' and carpenters' shops and as a changing room for the miners. The Clockhouse Smelter (it had a stone-faced clock on its northerly side) was also repaired and new windows, doors etc added.

Between the two smelters the sawpit, toilets etc were erected. Although the miners had only Christmas Day off in 1883 the surface hands were less regular in attendance and held up delivery of a boiler and steam pump from Hartington Station. However, delivery was made by the end of the year. Shortly after the beginning of the new year the powder store was erected away from the other buildings.

The Clayton pumping engine was started in January 1884 and by May 1884 £4,500 had been spent in clearing out the levels into the property, fencing the shafts and plant and laying miles of tramway. Four or five engines had been

3 Ecton Copper Mines

Ecton dressing floor in the 1880s. On the left is the jig tub building where sieves in water filled troughs separated ore from waste. Ahead is the engine house for the incline winch, the tubs coming down the ramp. The buddles are on the right and the crusher was probably in the building behind

purchased along with three or four boilers. These would have included the haulage and pumping engines at Clayton and possibly an engine for Waterbank. There do not appear to have been two engines at that mine.

An engine was bought to haul wagons up the incline to the dressing floor, but that may have been purchased later. The use of the other engines is not clear. The Company was already employing some forty people in May 1884. The two chief objectives of the Company were said to be the unwatering of the old mines and the connection of other smaller mines to the more extensive ones. The latter was, in effect, an adaptation of Mather's policy of over a decade earlier.

Ore Dressing Plant Purchased

The increased development of the works necessitated more and more equipment and in July second hand rock drills were purchased from the Mold Foundry at half the price of new ones. At the same time an air-compressing engine and its associated equipment (pipes etc) was purchased from Talargoch for Clayton as well as two new boilers and a second hand four horse power engine and boiler for driving the tools in the fitting shop.

In October, a new type of rock drill was ordered from Taylors of the Sandycroft Foundry, for use in Clayton. On 20th October 1884 the Manager was offered a complete Cornish crushing mill, jigger and two round buddles, with attachments, to be delivered by rail for £160. The Manager accepted the offer as they were now beginning to amass ore of sufficient quality and quantity for dressing. By the end of November, the machinery for the crushing mill, weighing twenty tons and occupying nine railway trucks in transit, had been delivered to the mine.

3.5 Exploration and Expectation

Most of the ore for dressing was dumped in the levels and literally under the miners feet awaiting the completion of the dressing plant. Coal was also stockpiled as the winter approached so they would have sufficient supplies during the winter when the mine would be snowbound. Fortunately the machinery worked with only a small consumption of coal.

The Annual General Meeting, held on 15th October 1884 showed that since operations commenced in November of the previous year, £3,146 had been spent on plant and machinery worth at least £6,000. The amount of capital held by the Company was £9,135 and 25,003 shares had been taken up, including 10,500 fully paid up shares given to principals. It was also revealed by a Director (Mr W W Urwick) that the Duke's Agent at Ecton (Joseph Beresford who lived in the Manager's Cottage for a time) had told him that because of water problems the previous Company abandoned the mine.

At the end of 1884 heavy storms set in and the influx of water into the shallow workings, particularly Salt's Level and Waterbank, retarded work for a while.

The severe weather conditions prevalent at the end of 1884 continued well into March 1885 when the sun shining on dumped ore began, at last, to thaw it out. During the same month work commenced on the erection of the crushing mill and the trestle incline over the Duke's gravel pit which connected Ecton with the dressing floor. This was used for hauling Clayton, and later Waterbank, ore up from the river level. The incline took just six months to complete and the 'heavy parts of the Cornish crusher' were on their foundations in early May. The crusher was brought into operation at the beginning of November. At the time Mr Bowman said that a number of boys were being trained at the picking table but, he complained, 'progress is slow'. He also said that the classifiers in the crushing mill had had to be altered to catch the copper slimes more firmly. These were breaking off from the granulated zinc blende ore as it passed through revolving screens and were being lost. The

Ecton Dressing Floor 1890

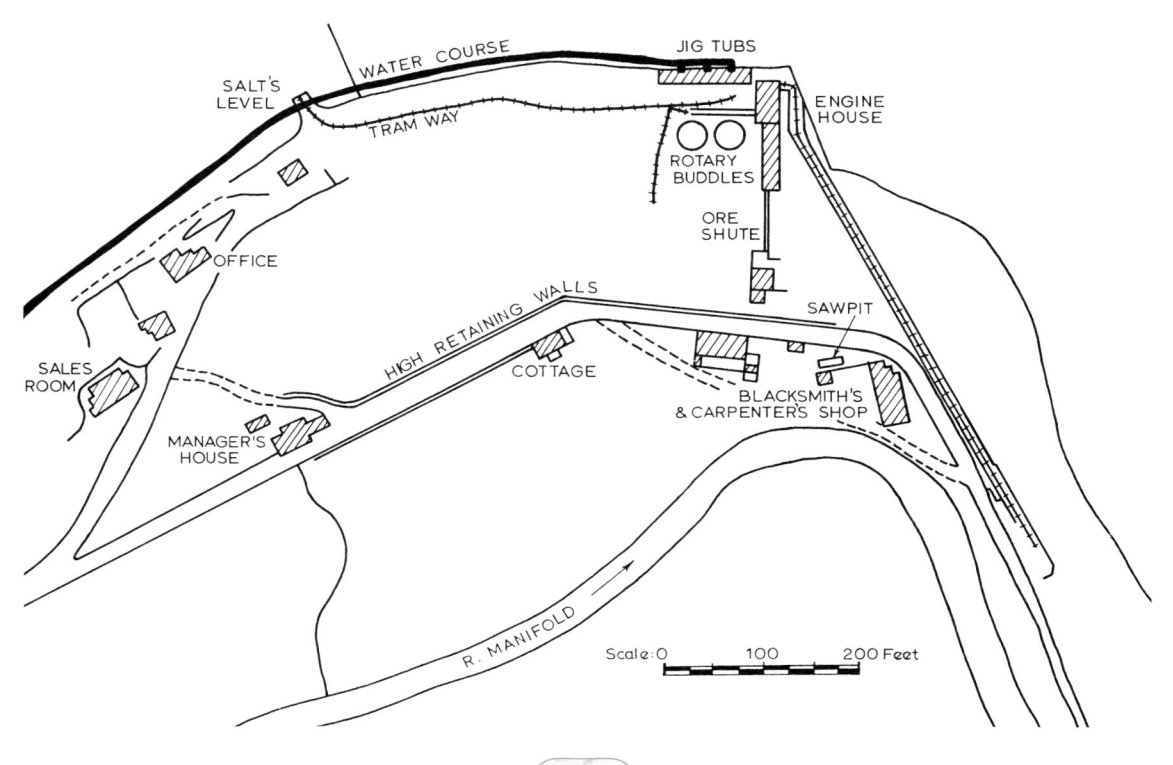

incline is traditionally said to have used one ton of nails in its construction.

The Second AGM

In September the manager spoke of the speculation of the Buxton – Ashbourne railway and the rumour that it was to pass through and have a station at Hulme End, less than 2 miles to the north of the mine. In fact it went to the east of Hartington. A month later, on 12th October 1885, the 2nd Annual General Meeting was held. In his speech to the meeting the Chairman, Mr James Judd, said that more emphasis had been placed on developing the sett than on buying machinery and that labour costs had risen over £1,000 to £3,084 in the last year. The 25,000 reserved shares had been issued to the shareholders, pro rata, and they had all been taken up. The company now had £30,000 at its disposal.

Drainage of the mines was a main topic discussed. The Directors stated their intention to unwater the old Ecton Mine. They estimated that it would take fifteen to eighteen months and cost about £3,000. It was hoped that large quantities of zinc ore would be found, as in Clayton, dumped by previous miners who did not know how to reduce it. It was anticipated that the zinc (and copper) ores would realise about £1 per ton profit. The Clayton Mine was pumped clear to the bottom by the end of August. About two feet of water per day was collecting at the bottom but was giving no trouble. The engine shaft was dry and what little water entered from above was collected at the 30 fathom level and removed in a one inch pipe.

This state of affairs was most fortunate for at the time a lot of exploratory work had been done at the base of the mine where the ore was getting richer the lower they descended. It is worthy of note that during the year 182 fathoms had been driven and 26 fathoms had been sunk throughout the sett.

The Kitto Report

A lively description of the work done in the mines affairs in March 1885 is given in a report to the Directors by Mr T C Kitto, published in the *Mining Journal* June 1885. Parts of the account are given below.

The first mine he inspected was East Ecton, 'where a circular shaft 9ft in diameter has been sunk to a depth of 120ft to where a good lode of lead has been struck'. This seems to be contrary to what was previously said regarding the 1873 plan showing a shaft here. Could the shaft have been widened to accommodate the pumping and lifting gear it contained? Such was the influx of water at the bottom of the shaft and the price of lead so low that he suggested operations to be suspended here. East Ecton adit was being driven westwards towards the Dutchman Vein.

The next mine he visited was Waterbank where he found zinc ore in favourable quantities scattered over a lode 7ft wide. Nine men were sinking towards Clayton. The machinery here consisted of a winding engine (working the cage or bucket used by the miners and for bringing ore and rock out), an air compressor and a direct action steam pump.

Kitto recommended that Bag Mine should be developed and united with Clayton as soon as was economically possible. In Salt's Level the (copper) carbonate pipe he had recommended twelve months previously was being worked. He thought it was just a feeder to the worked out ore body in Old Ecton and suggested that it be abandoned. He went on to say:

> 'from Salt's Level, I descended about 120 feet through the footway vein; the long dark caverns stretching on either side of the ladders… the ancients have left nothing here which will pay to remove'.

In Ecton Deep Adit Level four men were driving Northwards to intersect the Ecton Vein, coming down from Salt's Level above. This, he said, was money being well spent.

In Clayton the winding and pumping engines were in good order and the mine drained to a depth of 800 ft below adit level. The engine shaft was in hard rock a little distance from the ore body with which it was connected at intervals of 60-80 feet. Here one could be lowered to the bottom in a bucket but, fortunately, he chose the ancient workings –

> 'sometimes down ladders which were fastened to the side of extensive excavations, at other times dragging one self through a mere crevice to emerge on the top of a dark yawning cavern almost as large as a church, into which

3.5 Exploration and Expectation

he descended by means of chain ladders'.

From the 45 to the 100 fathom levels the whole of the main lode had been excavated, in some places to a breadth of 120ft. He forecast (rightly) that the 110 fathom level would open out into a rich deposit. He added that the ancient miners had contented themselves in working out the main lode and had not made any exploratory work. The smithy and carpenters shop, fitting shop and 'commodious storeroom as well a convenient offices and changing room' were completed on the dressing floors.

An appendix to the article states that Kitto had revisited the mines in the previous few days and had some ore blasted from the side of the 100 fathom level which assayed at 23% pure copper, (i.e. metal in the ore). He also discovered a rich ore pipe at the 125 fathom level (to be called the 'Kitto ore pipe'). He estimated that £8,130, well spent, would place the mine in first rate condition.

> 'In order to check some old reports', the report continues, 'Kitto carefully measured some of the ancient excavations and he found that one enormous chamber, known as "Chatsworth Open", in the Clayton Mine must have produced 180,000 tons of copper ore which at £10 per ton, a conservative estimate, produced £1,800,000.'

'Dream on', you may say.

In Clayton, the second half of the year saw the equipping of the main shaft and the removal of loose ore and rock accumulated from exploratory work and which had been left by the previous workers. In Waterbank, exploratory work and the sinking of the shaft towards Clayton was the main source of activity throughout the year.

During 1886 the majority of work was confined to the 140-150 fathom levels in Clayton and the 45 fathom level below adit level in Waterbank. In the former copper and zinc were the chief minerals being wrought and the dressing floors were well employed dressing the ore. In Waterbank, the connecting shaft between Clayton and Waterbank was finally finished during April.

It was then used for taking both ore and water out of the mine, i.e. into Clayton and out via Clayton Adit, which was quicker and less expensive. The chief ore in Waterbank was galena and it was being wrought in stopes at the 45 fathom level. The stope was very rich and maintained its yield and quality for a considerable time. Elsewhere a little work was done in Old Ecton, Ecton Deep Adit Level, and Chadwick Shafts. Preparations were made for unwatering the shafts at Ecton but whether this was done or not is doubtful.

Problems on the Horizon

In 1887 the Clayton 140-150 fathom levels ore was being worked at various ends and the Waterbank stope was also being worked. However before the end of the year work had begun in the development of Clayton 110 fathom level which gradually took precedence over the lower workings. In Waterbank a number of shafts and cross-cuts were driven in the search for more ore but the quantity of ore gained decreased considerably and most of the men were transferred to Clayton 110 fathom level where they proved more useful.

The *Mining Journal* reports make no mention of a stoppage of work at the mines. Indeed, the manager (William Bowman) created a picture of increased development and output. Yet the edition of the *Leek Times* for March 5th states that on the previous Saturday, February 26th, all hands received a week's notice that they should discontinue work on the following Saturday, March 5th.

Alfred Ludlam (Superintendent) spoke about the situation at a meeting called at Warslow on Saturday March 5th to discuss the proposed Ashbourne to Buxton Railway. He stressed that the stopping was not a permanent closure. It seemed that the difficulties were of a financial nature. Referring to the carriage of ore, Ludlam said that he was in favour of having it transported by rail for he states that in the previous week the mines had

> 'sent off a considerable amount of mineral and in one case, zinc blende to the English Crown Smelter Co, the cost of carriage from the mine to the smelter was 100%, i.e. £1 worth of ore cost £1 to transport'.

He states further that the smelter was 23 miles away and therefore a 46-mile round trip

Refurbishing Clayton Mine, 1883

was involved which was 'ruinous for any concern'. The desire was expressed that if the railway was constructed, Ecton would continue on a larger scale with many more men employed. However, on the 14th March, only about thirty of the original one hundred hands were re-employed. It is a pity that their dreams were not to be realised. The smelter referred to as being 23 miles away must be the one at Lea, near Cromford in Derbyshire, and therefore the ore sold would be lead.

The Third Annual General Meeting

This was held in the spring and the report was for the previous eighteen months. No dividend was paid because the work in hand was taking longer to complete than had been anticipated. Nevertheless, the shareholders were urged by the Directors to continue their faith in the venture. In the interest of economy, work had been discontinued to a large extent in certain parts of the mine which did not appear to be worthy of special attention.

Waterbank Mine had been developed to a certain extent, for this was the part of the sett which was proving to be remunerative. The need for economy had reflected on the Directors also, for they had reduced by one third the fees to which they were entitled under the Articles of Association. On the expenses side of the accounts, the following items were shown: £558 for Agency and Superintendents and £476 for cartage. The auditor, Mr Pannell, said the Agency and Superintendent's charges consisted entirely of wages at the mine, for Mr Bowman and the Superintendent there. The item for freight and cartage was for expenses at the mine, the cartage for the various machines etc.

Mr Bowman told the meeting that the lead ore found in Waterbank was found as pockets and it was difficult to say whether the pockets

3.5 Exploration and Expectation

were off-shoots to new or worked out ore bodies. A body of ore at the end of Waterbank Adit Level had the appearances of opening out into a large deposit, but further work had proved nothing of interest. In the south, and also at the bottom of Clayton Mine, appearances were better that they had been for a long time, particularly to the west of Clayton Shaft.

He therefore had no hesitation in telling the shareholders that they would be well advised in sticking to the mine in spite of the fact that approximately £21,250 of the £25,000 share capital had been spent, i.e. approx 17/6d (98.5p) of every £1 share. Mr Urwick, one of the Directors, then gave a description of work in hand and its possibilities.

'They had in Waterbank a width of 10 fathoms of ground and something like 20 fathoms in length, mixed up with strings of ore. These things were always considered a indications of an ore body being near and the implications had warranted them persevering with the development of the property. Where they were driving south they were expecting, in the next 12 months, to find veins that were going in other directions. For example, there was Dale Vein which had been a rich vein on the other side of the hill and which was going right through their property. They might, therefore, look forward to the time when they could intersect that, and when that was done there was generally a productive body of ore to be found.

There was another vein going south in the Waterbank and wherever a pond was sunk or a road made, lead was discovered, and in some cases copper, so they felt convinced that there must be a very large body of mineral in the property.

As to the indications at the Clayton, the pipe or great body of ore was lost somewhere about the 110 fathoms (below adit level). Many years gone by the mine came under the management of a particular firm of miners and they discontinued this work. These people had sunk the engine shaft and it was supposed that this shaft took away the water, and they lost the body of that pipe, which had never since been found again. [The water was considered to give an indication to the whereabouts of the ore. This is why the miners were so anxious to follow this water course when it was refound and this was what they were doing now at the 140 fathom level. A consulting engineer had visited the property and had placed that pipe as likely to be fifteen fathoms in advance of where they were now driving].

The old miners had gone through a large black body of limestone which they could never hope to find copper in. He was happy to say that the Company were now driving at the bottom of the Clayton in grey limestone (Ecton thick beds) and since the ore body of blende was commenced, which was a body above 3 inches wide, and of better character than they had had before. This was going in the direction where it was pointed out as probable that a large body of ore would be met within Clayton. Where they were driving they had indications of rich ore somewhere in the neighbourhood, and this would justify them in doing all they could to develop the mine and find the body of ore which they felt must be present...'.

It is interesting to know that the Directors only held between three and four thousand of the shares and that the Company had been approached with an offer of approximately £16,000 if sold with free possession, which had been turned down.

After the spring, the work was chiefly confined to Clayton at the 110 fathom level where a short cross-cut to the east was started. After driving five fathoms, high quality copper ore was reached. This same ore-body was worked in consequence at the 125 fathom level as well. The ore was associated, as in Waterbank, with a black substance. It was likened to a lead/silver and copper mine in California, known as Falstaff, where the ore occurred in limestone and was also associated with the black substance. A director of this Company had told an Ecton Director 'wherever you get the black stuff, follow it... it is almost certain to lead to a large amount of mineral sooner or later'.

All the 'ends' working in ore in Clayton (even down at 140, 150 and 160 fathom levels) and in Waterbank were found to be in association with the black substance. It is described as being a black shale containing manganese, copper, blende etc. The copper ore being worked in Clayton was yielding an average of 20% (metal) and was found with blende, side by side and surrounded by black shale. Mr Bowman said he believed that the 110-120 fathom ore body was a continuation of the ore pipe which was so rich above, and which the old miners had lost about the 90-100 fathom level. He hoped to get £10 per ton for the 100 fathom copper ore.

The final year

1888 was the last full working year, for active operations ceased in December and only a little work was done elsewhere. During the year, the main work was done at the Clayton 110 fathom level, little work was being done in Waterbank or anywhere else. Swainsley received special attention and Ludlam fortunately mentions a little of its history.

> 'Some fifty years ago, an old miner with his son-in-law worked some copper outcropping on the surface from which it is reported that he made enough to buy his freehold farm. It possibly closed because of water, for two weeks ago there was a rush equal to 5,000 gallons an hour. As there were two men and two girls working, pumping machinery was out of the question.
>
> Their shaft does not appear to be more than 3 to 4 fathoms deep and from it they worked the course of the ore into the hillside. Captain Williams, who was there afterwards, commenced an adit lower down to drain the water, but left before much was done and before the lode was cut. I am now driving to get under the shaft and let down the water. I expect to cut the lode after about 5 fathoms.' (*Mining Journal* 1889).

This mine is high on the hillside and provides a supply of water to Swainsley Hall. It has done so since at least 1873.

After active working ceased in December, Clayton shaft was put on care and maintenance and little work was done in Waterbank.

Voluntary Liquidation

The fifth Annual General Meeting was held on 3rd May 1889. After reading the report and passing the accounts, the meeting was made Special to consider five resolutions. The first was simply 'The Company be wound up Voluntary'. The other four provided for the transfer of the assets of the Company to a new Company.

The new Company was to be of Limited Liability, having a capital of £40,000 in £1 shares, credited as having 17/6d paid per share. (This was the amount spent of each of the shares of the Ecton Co Ltd).

The Chairman, in moving the voluntary liquidation resolution, said the Directors had tried various means of raising the necessary capital to continue. Their first idea had been debentures and preference shares but only half of the £5,000 thought necessary to justify continuation was subscribed.

> 'The idea of trying to reconstruct the Company', the Chairman (Alexander Kerby in the absence of Mr Urwick) said 'was because there is a clause in both leases that the plant must first be offered to the landlord at a valuation and we were not in a position to offer it to the landlord in that way. We could only put an end to the leases by giving one years notice next Christmas and during the whole of that time we should have to take care of the plant. Then we were morally certain that the landlord would not have purchased it and if we had sold it, after expenses, we should have got next to nothing for it'.

Unfortunately it appears that this is what happened. The Company was wound up and the other resolutions were passed. The Directors were, however, unable to raise the required capital and no new company was formed. The Company gave twelve months notice to the landlords that they wished to terminate the leases at Christmas 1889 and the leases formally

3.5 Exploration and Expectation

terminated on January 1st 1891. (*Catalogue of Abandoned Mines*, 1929, HMSO).

On 5th February 1890 the following was reported in the *Mining Journal*:

'The liquidator of the Ecton Co Ltd, Mr Newman Goldman (the Company Secretary), has issued his report to the shareholders and in doing so he has given them a few facts concerning the Company in it's more hopeful days. "The property", he states, "was held under two leases, one granted by the Duke of Devonshire and the other by Captain E. U. Blackett, reserving a dead rent of £100 per annum upon each lease, merging in a royalty of an extra £10 per annum to the Duke for a way-leave (through Clayton Adit) making a total of £210 per annum. The mines, which were full of water, were got in fork on the Company taking possession, i.e.drained, but hopes of finding anything good as a result were not justified and it was resolved to develop further. The lessors, however, were not so liberal as they might have been for after some correspondence, the only concessions that could be obtained were £5 from the Duke and another £10 from Captain Blackett.

Nothing daunted by the want of encouragement on the part of these gentlemen, the Directors resolved to try and get further capital, but failed". The harsh and arbitrary conduct of the lessors is blamed for the collapse of the Company and the circular speaks in rather severe tones of their "meanness".'

Despite these reasons, clearly there was another reason for the Company's decline. This was the downward spiral of metal ore prices. To make any great profit, it was stated that the ores should be rich and abundant enough to be raised, dressed and marketed for less than £40 per ton of metal (*Mining Journal* 1884).

In 1883, copper metal was fetching £65 per ton while in 1887 the Company Report indicated that the price had dropped to £40 per ton. It was the same in 1889 after rising in 1888. Lead had realised £15 per ton in 1883 and was down to £13 per ton in 1887 after a low of £10 per ton in 1887. Zinc ore also fell to half it's value when the mine had been taken over in 1883.

Willies states that the price of lead per ton on the London market in 1883-1889 varied between £11.30 and £13.24. In 1883 it was £12.90 and in 1889 £13.04. This differs from the comments above. If these prices were obtainable as an average, it makes one wonder why the Ecton Co Ltd was not taking advantage of it unless the yield was poorer than the shareholders were being told (10).

Another difficulty was that while the mine had a good dressing floor by Derbyshire standards, the copper ore had a tendency to reduce to fine slime easily and it was not difficult for the wastage factor to increase. The company had to be very diligent over this factor and the sieves had to be watched to ensure that the slimes did not end up on the hillside waste heap.

So, Ecton's last operative Company came to an end. In 1892/3 the Whiston smelter also ceased operations. The last load of ore was lead, taken from Ecton to Lea, near Cromford, by Mr Orlando Bonsall. On the occasions that ore was taken to Lea, coal, which had been brought along the Cromford Canal, was often collected from Cromford Wharf and brought to Ecton on the return journey. The price paid for the last load of lead ore was £4.10s.0d (£4.50p) per ton. (Pers comm, the late John Bonsall). Mr Jessie Bonsall, Orlando's brother, was also a carrier and was responsible for bringing machinery to Ecton from Masson Hill Mine, but the date is unknown (Pers/comm the late Messrs R & W H Bonsall).

The Ecton Company lost nearly all its expended capital of £45,500, more than the combined losses of all the previous companies. As far as can be ascertained all these companies were genuine attempts to rework the mines with nothing to suggest that the proprietors were promoting 'share' mines on the scale of the Welsh and Shropshire lead and zinc mines, or Cornwall's copper and tin mines. A common malpractice was for the promoter to buy the mining rights for a nominal sum and put the mine on the London stock market for the public to invest in, often with a capital of over £100,000. A sizeable proportion of this would be spent on mining and ore dressing equipment, which would impress the non-technical shareholders and force up share prices, but an even larger proportion would be paid to the proprietor for the mining rights. After the promoter had quietly sold his shares at the right time and the mine shown to be worthless, the equipment would be sold off at a great loss to the shareholders.

Although many of the Ecton Company's reports were certainly written in the over-optimistic style of the period to placate the shareholders, and it is certainly true that the mine was endowed with unnecessary equipment, William Bowman only received £500 worth of shares, which after a short time were practically worthless. He may have been misguided, but not dishonest. The failure of the Ecton Company emphasises that the prime requirement for a successful mining venture is an abundance of economically workable ore. This they did not have, and in mining, past history is no guide for the future.

The Leek & Manifold Valley Light Railway, opened in 1904, increased speculation that the mines would be re-opened, but the railway itself was short lived, closing in 1934. The vast tips were used as ballast on the railway and later as road metal. In the 1920s a creamery and cheese factory was built at Ecton using both Ecton and Clayton Mines as a source of water. The whey was initially dumped in the river and later in Birch's Level after complaints about river pollution from Swainsley Hall (for a second time, see Chapter 11). The demolition of the factory and the dressing floor has resulted in an air of dereliction in a beautiful valley and serves as a constant reminder of the price mankind sometimes has to pay for industrialisation.

References

1. Strahan A, 1887. *Geology of North Derbyshire,* (Memoir Geol Survey) pp156-8
2. Anon. *Ashbourne and the Valley of the Dove,* 1839, pp152-5
3. Proc Geol Soc, May 1899, Vol 55, p.lix and Geol Mag, Decade IV, 1898, Vol 5, pp335-6, obituary by George Attwood
4. Garlic Papers
5. *Mining Journal,* 1883, p1335
6. White, 1851. *Directory of Staffordshire,* 2nd edn
7. *Mining Journal,* 1851 and Lewis, W. J, 1967, *Lead Mining in Wales*
8. *Mining Journal,* 1853, p304
9. Colin Mather was an early pioneer of deep boring
10. Willies L. *A Note On The Price Of Lead,* Bull PDMHS, Vol 4, No 2, pp179-191

3.6 Social Conditions

Much of the surviving material on the social conditions at the various mines centres on Ecton. Therefore the Ecton material is given here augmented by the small amout that can be added on other mines.

In 1769, Efford provided a vivid account of working conditions at the time that Ecton Mine was expanding rapidly. He described the raising of ore by men at hand winches who generally worked half-naked, and the pushing of wagons along Ecton Sough by boys of twelve to fourteen years of age. His description of the miners may seem very condescending in this more enlightened age, but were their conditions any worse than miners elsewhere at that time, or even this?

'Figure to yourself the sooty complexions of the miners, their labour and miserable way of living in these subterraneous regions, and you will be apt to fancy yourself in another world. Yet these inhabitants, being trained in darkness and slavery, are not perhaps less happy, or less contented than those who possess the more flattering enjoyments of light and liberty... Above sixty stout, well-made fellows, work here night and day, six hours at a time, for one shilling each man and although the major part work naked (a pair of coarse canvas drawers excepted) they are as merry and jovial a set of mortals, as ever inhabited such infernal abodes'.

Compared with the gentlemanly existence of the writer of that piece, the miners at Ecton certainly worked hard, but such was the lot of any of the working classes in the 18th Century. We must not compare their conditions with those of the present day Welfare State, but must put them in perspective and compare them with other manual workers at that time.

Efford also described how little boys wheeled small hand barrows on the dressing floors, while girls from eight to twelve years old sorted the ores, which had been previously crushed by women using flat hammers (known as buckers). Wages were stated as 2d per hour, six hours at a time for the men (i.e. 30p per week), the women earning from 4d to 8d per day (10p to 20p per week) and the children 2d to 4d (5p to 10p per week). The age span was from five to sixty years of age.

From the Ecton account books these figures can be compared with the actual money earned by the workers, and we can see how the wages changed over a period of 150 years. The work done at the mine was divided into three categories; wage men who were involved in non-productive operations such as winding ore, pumping water and general labouring; dead-work or contract men who bargained to drive a level or sink a shaft at an agreed rate per fathom; and copers who bargained to raise an agreed quantity of ore at a fixed rate per ton.

Wages at the Mine

Dressing the ore and reworking the hillocks was usually by bargain, although some was paid by wage. A good deal of the wage work was on a part-time basis, this adding to the variability of the number of workers employed at any one task. There were eight accounting periods per year, four of seven weeks and four of six weeks, when all wages and bills were settled. The normal working week was six days of six hours each, although pumping was sometimes carried on round the clock and the men raising water by hand usually worked a seven-day week.

The actual wages paid were in general somewhat greater than those quoted by Efford, even before the Duke took over wages were estimated at 5s (25p) to 8s (40p) per week. In 1760, labourers and pumpers earned 5s (25p) per week, rising to 12s (60p) a week for the more skilled craftsmen such as smiths and carpenters. By 1768 the majority of unskilled workers earned 7s (35p) per week, and the boys 3s (15p) to 4s (20p). In 1779 the average wage at the Whiston smelting works was 9s (45p) per week, while in 1786 workmen at Ecton were getting 10s (50p) and lads 4s (20p) per week, so wages seem to have risen as profits from the mine increased.

Joseph Bonsall and Richard Naylor, two overseers at the mine were earning 18s (90p) each per week in the 1790s, as also was the overseer at Whiston. In 1798 the smelters at Ecton as well as those working the Water Engine and drawing water received 9s (45p) per week, the black slag smelter earned 14s (70p), the fire engine man 15s (75p) and his assistant 12s (60p). Those weighing ore received 1s (5p) per day (30p per week). At Whiston the refiners earned 12s (60p) a week plus 1s 6d (7^1/$_2$p) a ton dressing copper cakes, while calciners and furnace builders received 10s (50p) and copper smelters 9s (45p) a week.

The wage men had to be prepared to work overtime in an emergency, particularly when a strong flow of water needed stopping up, or the Water Engine or Steam Engine were being repaired. In these cases work continued virtually non-stop until it was finished. Although the rate of pay was not increased, generous refreshments and food were provided, a typical entry being in 1802:

> 'Refreshments to the workmen Putting the New Tub in at the Water Engine & Confined Night and Day till Finished, £3.4.3d (£3.21)'.

During the 19th Century men and boys provided underground labour, mainly for waggoning and wheeling. The men were paid about 2s to 2s 6d (10p to 12^1/$_2$p) per day and the boys 1s to 1s 2d (5p to 6p). Boys were also employed in blowing air at 10d (4p) per day. Under Mather, men were employed on day work in Bag and Waterbank mines doing the work of tributors at 2s to 2s 6d (10p to 12^1/$_2$p) per day. A similar wage was paid during this period to surface workers with a few exceptions: the smith and carpenter earned 3s 4d to 3s 6d (16^1/$_2$p to

17½p) per day each; the horse driver at the whim 4s (20p) per day and the carters 4s 6d (22½p) per day. As far as is known, no women were employed in the 19th Century, with only one exception in the 1850s.

The rate per fathom for those driving on contract in dead ground, known as tutwork, would depend upon the nature of the level or shaft and the hardness of the rock. For instance at the commencement of the replacement Ecton Deep Level in 1774, driving cost 12s (60p) per fathom and walling the level cost the same amount, but once the soft ground at the entrance had been passed the rate for driving rose sharply. In the massive limestone £7-£8 per fathom was an average rate for sinking and driving, this rate being paid for both sinking the Deep Shaft in the 1780s and for driving the New Level (Salt's Level) in the 1800s. This amount was paid to a partnership, which for driving might consist of two, four or more men.

The copers were the skilled productive miners upon whom the success of the mine depended. Not unnaturally they commanded the highest wages. The Ecton account books give the amount of ore raised and the money paid to each partnership in great detail, but unfortunately we do not know the number of men in each group. Just one loose sheet from a cope-bargain book for 1779 has survived, and a quotation from this will given an indication of the system used

> 'Geo. Hervey & 7 pts. to rase 24 tons at 32s. 6d. pr ton, all above at 15 shillings pr ton and to get 50 wagons of stone and to work According to their last markes: ye forfits as before'.

Working from Hammocks

This system allowed the copers to earn 15s to 16s (75p to 80p) per week, and clearly efforts were made to limit their wages to reasonable proportions. During the extraction of 'Smackers Open', it is traditionally said that the copers were limited to working only three days per week and worked suspended in hammocks. With the ore being so easy to mine considerable gains could have been possible for a determined partnership and this could have led to friction with the wage men. Unfortunately these particular cope-bargains are for a period for which the accounts are missing, so we cannot tell how their predicted output compared with the ore actually raised.

What we do know is that at its zenith nearly one half of the total ore raised was by one company of copers led by a Samuel Carrington, consisting of twenty-eight men. The rest of the ore was named by up to thirty smaller partnerships (of unknown composition) each raising small parcels of ore. At one time these twenty-eight men were regularly producing up to 320 tons of ore per six or seven week period and earning very much more than anyone else at Ecton, Whiston or the Duke's collieries, apart from Cornelius Flint.

For instance in 1786 each man in Carrington's company earned an average of 25s (£1.25) a week, with a maximum and minimum of 33s (£1.65) and 18s (90p) respectively. Like most other miners, both in metal mines and collieries, the workers of Ecton enjoyed higher wages and shorter hours than their counterparts in agriculture or industry, and when discussing social conditions a clear distinction has to be drawn between working conditions and living conditions (1).

Later, in the early 19th Century, the system of tribute (which was widely used in Cornwall) was introduced by John Taylor. Here the miners were paid a certain percentage of the value of the ore raised. By this means a poor mine could be kept going through bad times with very little expense to the owners. If no ore was raised the miners got nothing, but the owners lost nothing either. A typical tribute bargain for the Ecton Mine reads:

> 'Joseph Barker Senr. late pitch. This pitch extends 14 fathoms South from the Engine Shaft and from the back of the 84 Fathom level to as high as bottom of the 74 Fathom Level on the South Side of the Load by two men and no more until 29th Day of May next 1819. Let to Joseph Barker Senr. at 15s. from 20s.'

Each pitch was worked by a company of up to eight men. Reworking the old tips for ore was also let out to tribute in a similar manner, the ore dressers being allowed the use of the stamps provided that they did not drive the wheel more than a regular course 'and to keep the tongues and Caps well greased every day... and to have a carpenter sent from the Mine to repair the Stamps when needed... and to put all the Stamps deads in the Manifold'.

The monies received by the miners on tribute in the early 1820s varied considerably, although the weekly average was about 14s to 16s (70p to 80p). See Chapter 11 for further discussion on the dumping of waste in the river.

Tribute working continued throughout the 19th Century, examples being 13s 9d in 20s (69p in £1) in 1849, rising to 16s (80p) in the 1850s and up to 18s (90p) in some cases for extracting ore from the hillocks as well as from underground. A change of policy occurred under Colin Mather in 1868, for the men were paid a tribute of 6s (30p) in the £1 plus a daily subsistence of 1s 8d (8$^{1}/_{2}$p) and instances occur where Mather was even paying the subsistence to the contractors. Generally, there is no reference to the tributers having to dress their own ore, but they were charged for this by Mather at the rate of 15s (75p) per ton. However, they must have dressed their own ore when the various companies were running down, for in some cases, there were no other people employed to do it.

In all cases (for both wage and bargain work) the miners had to purchase their tools, candles and gunpowder from the agent. An analysis of the accounts shows that up to £900 a year was spent on powder and candles at Ecton Mine alone in the 1780s. The Duke of Devonshire's agent did not take advantage of this system to charge extortionate prices; candles and powder were sold to the men at cost price plus about 5%, just sufficient to cover the administrative expenses. In the 1860s Colin Mather charged up to 1s (5p) per man per month for the depreciation of tools, while candles and powder were charged at the rate of 6d (2$^{1}/_{2}$p) and 8d (3$^{1}/_{2}$p) per lb respectively.

The Manager's Salary

The agent's salary was of course much greater than anything the miners could earn. Robert Shore commenced at £70 per annum in 1760, this being increased to £100 in 1763. Cornelius Flint took over in 1779 at the same salary, but this was increased to £150 per annum three years later and remain at this figure for the next thirty years. Previous to joining the Ecton Mine he had been earning 15s (75p) per week as overseer to the Hubberdale Mine.

George Cantrell, the manager, earned 21s. (£1.05) per week early in the 19th Century. The 19th Century wage books are missing for most of the first half of the century, but it is known that after 1851 Samuel Bonsall, who was the agent until 1871 and Joseph Beresford the agent from 1871-74, earned £96 a year each. Finally, in both the 18th and 19th Century the wages were fetched from Chesterfield, the agent being accompanied by 'two stalwart miners' to avoid being robbed.

Transport Costs

The Ecton mines certainly provided a much needed source of extra income to the inhabitants of this essentially agricultural area. In particular vast numbers of horses and mules were needed to convey the ore to Whiston, coal to Ecton and Whiston, as well as copper and other materials to and from the various canal wharfs. The great expansion at Ecton coincided with, and was dependent on, the improvements in transport provided by the new turnpike roads and canal navigations.

Here we have an interesting example of transport to a remote area in North Staffordshire from as far afield as London, Swansea and Sunderland, and in some cases the cost of transport was much greater than the cost of the goods. Analysis of the land carriage costs show that about 9 1/2d (4p) per ton per mile was charged in the 18th Century, rising to 1s (5p) per ton per mile by the 1820s. The cost of canal transport varied with the distance, the canal company, and the amount of loading and unloading, charges ranging from 1d ($^{1}/_{2}$p) to 4d (1$^{1}/_{2}$p) per ton per mile.

An analysis of the accounts at the peak of production shows that by far the greatest expense at Ecton was for wages, being 70% of the total costs; 20% was spent on carriage of ore and materials while only 10% was spent on the purchase of materials. During the period 1851-66, 83% of the total expenditure was for wages (including Bonsall's salary), the greater proportion of this being for underground work.

Although the work was hard and living conditions primitive by modern standards, there was no attempt by the Duke to over-exploit his employees. He gave them fair wages, provided for their health, housing and education (he provided a teacher for seventy children and built a school at Ecton, and in return expected a good day's work. By working the mines himself not only did he make much greater profits but he was able to treat his employees, many of whom would also be his tenants, much more charitably than might have been the case had he continued to lease the mines to speculators.

In this way the worst of the conditions suffered by the 19th Century Cornish miners were avoided. Most of the miners had their own garden or small farm which provided much of their food and at least it ensured that they did not starve when times were hard.

The truck system, whereby the workers were obliged to buy their goods from their employers at inflated prices was not used in the metalliferous mining areas of the Midlands as it was in Cornwall. There is certainly no evidence that such a system was ever used to exploit the workers at Ecton or Whiston, nor were conditions as degrading as in the colliery districts of the north.

Accidents

Mining was, and perhaps always will be, a dangerous occupation, with accidents and injuries commonplace, though of course metal mines rarely suffered the disasters of explosion, common in collieries. Ecton was no exception, and by and large the mine had relatively few serious accidents with the unfortunate sufferers being treated charitably by the Duke and his agents. From 1760 to 1811 only four fatalities are recorded with about fourteen serious accidents.

One miner was 'Disabled by a Misfortune by a Shot in the Mine, eleven weeks', another 'Maimed by a Fall of Stuff in the Mine, six weeks', while another had to have a leg amputated at the thigh. After any accident a doctor was fetched, usually from Leek, although in 1769 they sent for a doctor from Coventry. One unfortunate miner was paid his

> 'Expenses to Sheffield to be fitted with a pair of Glasses – His sight being wounded by a shot in the Mine – £1. 4. 2 (£1.21)'.

Weekly Allowances & Funeral Costs

In general those off work for any length of time due to injuries received at the works were paid a weekly allowance of 8s (40p) rising to 10s (50p) in 1805. One miner who had been injured in 1796 died in 1808 and his widow was allowed 3s 6d (17$\frac{1}{2}$p) per week, even though we cannot be certain that he was killed in the mine. When another miner was killed in 1802 all his funeral expenses were paid and his widow and her children were paid an allowance of 10s 6d (52$\frac{1}{2}$p) per week until 1808, after which 5s (25p) a week was paid to two of the younger children. An old workman who had previously been injured underground in 1795 was allowed 6s (20p) a week in 1809 on the order of the Duke's attorney, although he was last recorded as receiving any wages, as a hillocker, over two years previously.

Pensions

Also 10s 6d (52$\frac{1}{2}$p) a week was paid to a Calciner 'who is incapable of doing his business'. During the 1830s and 1840s the Duke paid pensions of 1s 6d to 10s (7$\frac{1}{2}$p to 50p) a week to those put out of work by the rundown of the mines and who were unable to find fresh employment due to their age. As the number of pensioners gradually dwindled their funeral expenses were provided for.

There is no record of the many minor accidents that almost certainly occurred, except for the 'Surgeons for their attendance &c on people who Have Got Misfortunes at the Mine'. Even the overseers were not immune to these accidents, for Cornelius Flint wrote to James Watt in 1788:

> 'I am sorry to inform you that Poor Newbold who was lately with you has had part of 2 Fingers of his left hand totally severed by the coggs of a Wheel at the Ecton'.

James Newbold was a millwright, who had been particularly concerned with the installation of the Water Engine and Steam Winding Engine. Further misfortune was to strike the family when his son became totally blind and had to plead for charity. As well as these minor accidents we are told nothing of those suffering from the cold and wet conditions underground, where the air was filled with the fumes of gunpowder. Dampness in the mines necessitated the maintenance of fires underground to help prevent the ropes from rotting and evidence of this can still be seen.

Likewise on the surface, the smelters both at Ecton and Whiston would be badly affected by the sulphurous fumes. At Whiston those farming adjacent to the works were paid annually for damage done to their land by the smoke. Amongst the changes made during John Taylor's reorganisation in 1818 was the deduction of money from the tributer's pay for 'Club & Doctor', amounting to 4s to 8s (20p to 40p) every two months for a partnership of four men.

All in a Day's Work

The accidents with gunpowder in the mine can perhaps be readily appreciated. However, there are two recorded cases of a barrel of gunpowder exploding (see Chapter 5 for the details). It was not without good reason that the Ecton gunpowder store was out of the way behind a belt of trees! For a miner-related incident, involving the use of mine gelatine cartridges at home in Butterton, see Chapter 7.

An Unusual Task

In this category fell the task of clearing blockages in the Apes Tor Aqueduct, or Launder, at Ecton. It was common for ice to form in the water channel and men were sent across the top with long narrow-bladed spades to free the flow. On one occasion a man slipped and fell off (the height was some 30 to 40ft). He had the presence of mind to twist the spade and the blade, between the haft and the outer edge, held until he could be hauled back up again. Stories like this must have been numerous and its a pity that more have not survived.

Death in the Mines

Reference to occasional fatalities at Ecton have been made above. There is an unconfirmed report that seven men were drowned at Hayesbrook Gate Mine and were sealed in (see Chapter 4). See also about the four people sealed in a mine at Butterton in Chapter 7, although in this case the mine was out of work at the time.

Cockfighting and Other Pursuits

In their leisure time cockfighting was actively pursued by the Ecton miners. As might be expected there is little documentary information on this cruel past-time, though a note in the back of one of the Ecton account books records that two birds, both two years olds, were fought at Pike Hall in Derbyshire in 1778. It is said locally that the Pepper Inn at the Back of Ecton was one of the last strongholds of cockfighting in North Staffordshire, lookouts being posted to warn of any interference by the law.

Other pursuits at Ecton included football. There used to be a bridge from the mine to the far side of the river so that the men could use the field for playing football. However the amount of rubbish thrown into the river meant that the men could often walk across without getting their feet wet (see Chapter 11). The Dutchman carpenter's shop/smithy building was also used by the local band, although they must have been pretty poor players to be banished to a shed halfway up a hill in which to practice! Either that or a friendly smith stoked up his fire before going home to fetch his instrument, perhaps.

Miners-cum-Farmers

Many of the men seem to have had a smallholding as well as a job at the mine. In the 1880s, the manager complained of absenteeism as the men were away haymaking. Some people kept cattle even though they had no fields, turning the cows out into the lanes to eat the grass at the side of the road. There was a bad cattle plague in the area in 1866 which may well have had some impact on the miners who had an interest in farming. It reached national proportions, the first outbreak in the locality being at the Charles Cotton Hotel, Hartington, which was the first of several outbreaks in that village alone.

During the problems at Mixon Mine in 1839, Rupert Bullock was continually having to ask for money to pay bills. In one instance, he wrote, the hardship of the men meant that they could not buy the cow they had expected to. In assessing what was due in wages once the mine had ceased working, one miner, Benjamin Goldstraw, commented that he had lost a little time in August 'during the hay'. No doubt he was not alone. Often the wife would be left to do what work she could whilst her man was at the mine. What work was left would be done by him in the evening or before work commenced the next day. It was, by our standards, a hard life.

Employment of Children in the 19th Century

During the 19th Century, the Ecton Mine seems to have not employed boys underground (see Chapter 11 for the Report of the Children's Employment Commission in 1842). However shortly after this date, boys were employed underground at Cow Close Mine, near to Warslow Hall. However as the Dale Mine dressing floor opened at 7am, this may have been a personal arrangement amongst the men who had taken the contract to work the mine from the Dale Mine Company, for the men and boys were also working around the clock.

Round-the-clock working was happening at Mixon Mine too, in 1839. In a heading near the bottom of the mine, Rupert Bullock reported that four men were working for six hours and sixteen men were therefore being employed each day. This would only happen if the mine was in productive ground, or the costs were being met by a mine, or an investor, with plenty of working capital.

At the bottom of the Cow Close Shaft were two levels, one heading west and the other going east. These headings were worked by a man and a boy on an eight hour shift, so a total of six boys were involved. It is likely that the boy would be holding the drill while the miner swung the sledgehammer. An eight hour shift was not the normal; six hours being more compatible with agricultural interests (1).

The names of the hands in the eastern heading at Cow Close survives: they were Robert Greenhough, working with his brother William (Robert had gone to Nenthead in the Northern Pennines to work for Melville Attwood in 1845, returning in 1847; his father Isaac working with Charles Brindley; and Joseph Sutton working with William Barker. The latter was employed here for two years, from 1848-50.

Boys continued to be employed by the mine: in August 1870, about a dozen men and boys were employed in puddling the wall the mine was building at the side of the River Manifold. This was a short distance below Dale Bridge and was done in order to keep the river from entering the mine. It was not unknown for miners to catch fish in the Dale Mine adit after the river had been swollen and started to flow up the level into the mine. 1870 was an exceptionally dry summer, so the mine was obviously taking advantage of the low level of the river.

Boys were also used at Mixon Mine. Rupert Bullock reported in 1839 that there were three boys at the mine. It is probable, however, that they were used on the dressing floor rather than underground.

The only reference to girls working underground was in the 1830s at Swainsley. Here was 'an old miner', his son-in-law and two girls.

References
1. Willies L, *John Taylor in Derbyshire 1839-1851*, Bull PDMHS Vol 6, No 5, p228

3.7 Ore Production

Many estimates have been made of the richness of the Ecton mines, but many of them so wildly exaggerated as to be completely unreliable. Now that manuscript sources are available, reliable production figures can be given for much of the working life of the mines, although there are several notable gaps in the records particularly for the Burgoyne Mines. Throughout this chapter the contemporary term 'ore' will be used for the concentrated material sent to the smelter.

The 17th Century

The known 17th Century production consists of 2 loads and 4 dishes of lead ore sold in 1654 at 1. 8s. 6d. ($92\frac{1}{2}$p) per load, and 587 kibbles of copper ore (about 30 tons) mined from 1660 to 1664. This copper ore gave just under 5 tons of copper metal (a production of 15% metal, quite comparable with 18th Century values), which was sent to London, but probably did not pay for the expenses of the operation to that date (£1,262).

The Eighteenth Century

During the period that John Gilbert-Cooper worked Ecton, there is a great paucity of production figures, although we do know that from 1752 – 1759, 4,784 tons of copper ore, worth £39,395 were raised. An estimate of the expenses of

3.7 Ore Production

Annual Ore Production at Ecton

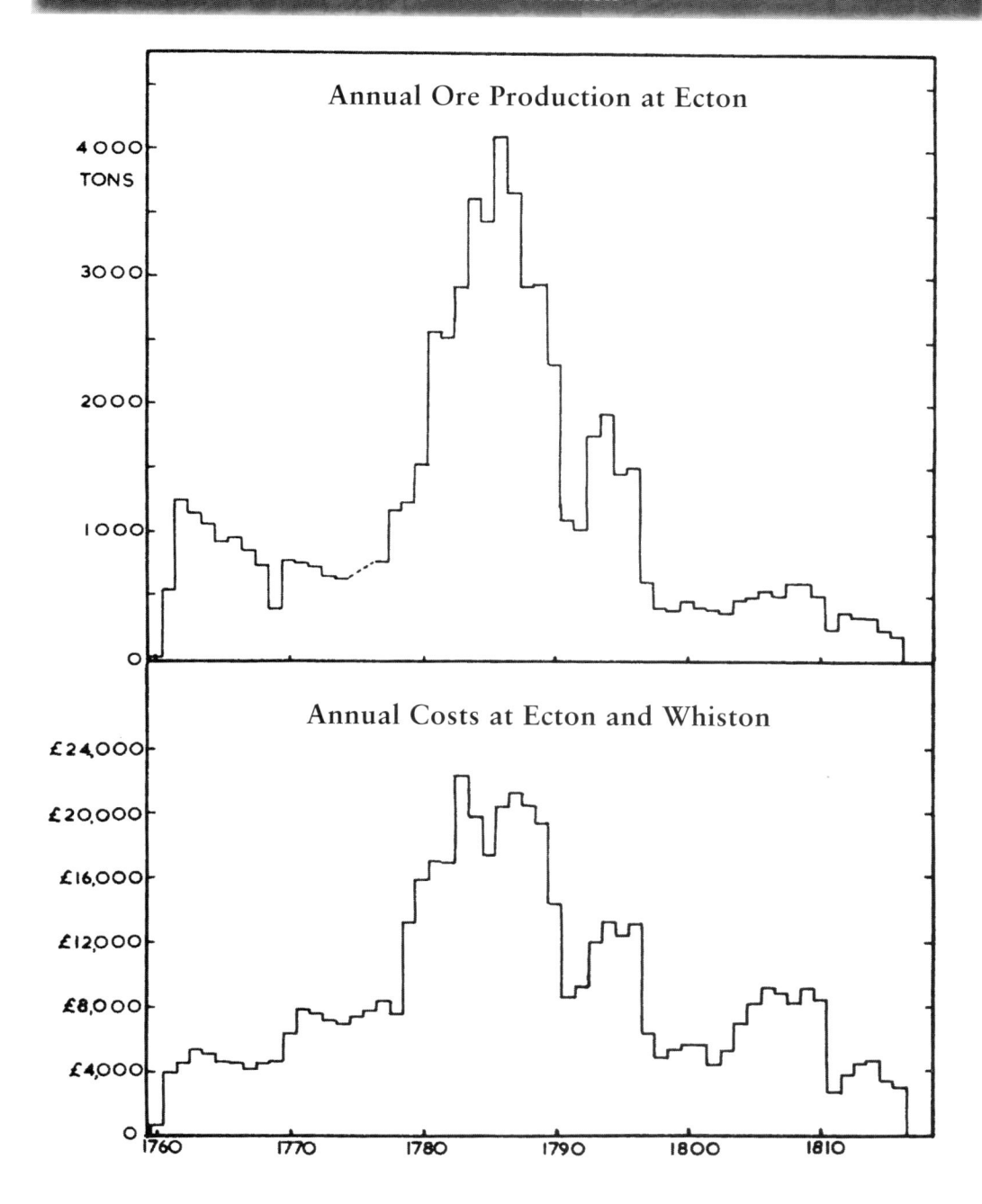

Annual Costs at Ecton and Whiston

working Ecton made in 1759 as John Gilbert-Cooper's lease was running out showed that 45 tons of ore a month were raised at a cost of £223 giving £137 profit, i.e. 580 tons worth £4,320 with £1,640 profit per annum. At the time of the non-payment of the 4d a lode cope it was stated that shortly after 1739 the adventurers 'began to get great quantities of copper ore and the said Mines have ever since continued very rich and prosperous mines and produced 7 or 8,000 £ per ann'.

From 1744 to 1751 the Duke of Devonshire's Wetton duty ore amounted to 414 loads

3 Ecton Copper Mines

of lead ore (equivalent to about 110 tons), which was sold to the Barkers' lead smelters at Rowsley and Shacklow in Derbyshire (1). Since the duty was 1/9th, the total lead ore production was about 1,000 tons, although this probably includes an unknown amount from the other mines on the Duke's land at Wetton.

From 1760 to 1816, which covers the main period of working for the Ecton Mine, there are nearly complete ore and cost accounts, although less is known about the profits made. See across for details from the accounts for this period, during which time a total of 65,700 tons of copper ore were sold, the total costs being £512,000 (including the Foxtwood and Hazlecross Collieries).

From 1760 to 1774 copper and ore worth £163,000 was sold at a profit of £82,000, an average of nearly £6,000 profit a year. The production graph illustrates the highly peaked nature of the output which rose to over 4,000 tons in 1786. This is quite typical of a pipe-vein where a large mass of easily won ore was suddenly discovered and once removed the production falls rapidly to a low level.

This situation was also common in the Derbyshire lead mines where a thin rake vein would suddenly belly out into a large mass of ore and just as suddenly contract again. Clearly this is not a situation suited for a stable long-term development with a high capital expenditure.

Sales of Copper Metal

Before the Whiston Works were in full operation the copper ore was sold by ticketing to Charles Roe of the Macclesfield Copper Company, Cooper and Rotton at Denby and Thomas Patten of the Warrington Copper Company. In 1767

A pre-1883 photo. The middle building is believed to be the Ecton school. See also the photo on page 49, taken later

3.7 Ore Production

the Governor of the Company of Copper Miners in England, who had works in South Wales, became interested in purchasing Ecton ore, but apparently nothing came of this (2). In 1772 samples of Ecton copper were sent to a Mr John White, a copper smith of Houndsditch, London, to see if there was a market in London. White could not use it himself as it was

> 'a Sort of mettling to Mack Brass or Outher Compounds', and London was 'crowded with Large Quantity of Copper at This Time'.

A market for Ecton copper was evidently found in London for 126 tons were sent there in 1775 and 181 tons in 1776. In 1777 and 1778, 172 tons and 164 tons respectively were sent to Derby, but this could have been for rolling there before dispatch to London.

Later Birmingham became a major market and the Duke also had naval contracts for the copper sheathing of wooden ships (3), the introduction of copper sheathing to protect the wooden hulls of fighting vessels from the ravages of the boring worm being a major factor in the superiority of the English fleet and the growth of the copper industry (4). In 1780 12 tons of copper metal were sold to Messrs. Thoyts and Co. (of Marton Abbey, Surrey), 12 tons to Messrs Cazalet and Cooke, and 150 tons to Messrs. Lilley and Robarts, a total of 174 tons at £12,690.

The following year 234 tons went to Cazalet and Cooke, 68 tons to Thoyts and 221 tons to the East India Company, with small quantities to the Gnoll Copper Company, Nairne and Blunt and Mr Joseph Barton (of London), a total of 530 tons worth £44,585. Cake copper cost about £80 per ton, and each block was marked with one of the letters HARDWICK or ECTON, most probably to identify the period of manufacture. At the turn of the Century copper was also sold to the Cheadle Brass Wire Company. Copper sold in sheet form was rolled at the copper mills of Mr Thomas Evans on the Derwent at Derby, and by Smith and Knifton, who had a tin plate works at Oakamoor which was converted to a copper and brass rolling and wire drawing mill by the Cheadle Brass Wire Company in 1790.

The only reliable estimate of the profits made at this time is in 1781 when the sale of copper gave nearly £27,500 profit, and since the peak output in 1786 was to reach 50% more than this a peak profit of £40,000 per annum is likely.

It is ironic that Ecton production reached its maximum when copper prices were at their lowest. Copper fetched only £65 per ton in 1786, although the price had been £100 per ton in the 1760s and reached over £130 per ton at the turn of the century. This slump was due to the opening of the Anglesey copper mines with their vast quantities of easily won, although poor quality ore, which completely dominated world copper prices and had a drastic effect on the Cornish mines for nearly twenty years.

Phillips (5) quotes that from 1776 to 1817, 53,857 tons of copper ore were produced worth £677,112 yielding a profit of £244,734. These ore figures compare closely with those from the Ecton account books, so that together with figures quoted previously we can say that from 1760 to 1817, which covers all but the final few years of the Duke's working, the Ecton Mine produced 66,000 tons of very high grade copper ore worth £852,000 with a profit of £335,000, an average profit of £6,000 per annum. Popular legend has it that the Crescent at Buxton, (mostly built by the 5th Duke of Devonshire during 1780-4) was built from one year's profit from the Ecton Mine. Pevsner's *Building of England* quotes the cost as being £38,600, so the tradition is correct.

The Yield or Richness of the Ore

Most references give the copper percentage as about 15%, a high value which is borne out by documentary evidence. The ore was certainly not often below 10% until the mine became worked out late in the 19th Century, when it varied between 7% and 14%. Mawe's (6) value of 40-60% probably refers to the percentage of chalcopyrite in the material brought out of the mine, and as pure chalcopyrite yields 34.5% copper metal this gives 14-21% copper in the ore. This takes no account however of the efficiency (or lack of it) of concentration during processing.

Ore from the reworked tips in the early 1820s was to be dressed to produce not less than 6% metal. Even in 1818, well past the peak production, John Taylor wrote that Ecton copper was 'of very excellent quality, & worth more than the Common Copper... The sample you gave me is very rich & would now in Cornwall be worth £19. 10. 0d per ton',

and the ores did in fact sell at a price higher than the Cornish Standard.

Sales of Lead Ore

Some lead was also raised from the Duke's mines. During 1760-1774, lead ore worth about £320 was raised, probably from Chadwick Mine, and sold to Barker and Wilkinson in Derbyshire, while some 200 tons of galena were raised during 1781-1784. After the lead cupola was built at Ecton, the lead produced was sent by road to Derby, via Newhaven, but later it was all carried to Cromford Wharf for transport along the Cromford and Erewash Canals and River Trent to Gainsborough for the Hull lead market. From 1792 to 1810, 1132 tons of lead were sent this way, including at least 144 tons from the Burgoyne mines during the latter part of this period.

Burgoyne Figures

Our information on the Burgoyne mines is very sparse indeed, but it can be estimated that at least £726 profit was made during 1737-44 when the Gilberts worked the mines (7). The only other 18th Century production figure available is in 1769 when 14 tons of galena from Clayton Mine was sent to John Barker's cupola at Wash Green near Wirksworth, Derbyshire (8). The Clayton Pipe is reputed to have been struck rich in August 1812 after an outlay of £9,000 to give a profit of £9,000 before the end of the year, followed by profits of upwards of £20,000 per annum for many years afterwards (9).

These figures can be shown to be highly exaggerated, for it is known that during 1813-22 Clayton Mine only produced about 3,400 tons of copper ore plus a very much smaller quantity of lead ore, while the Burgoyne mines are known to have made a loss of £500 during the second half of 1816.

Later 19th Century Operations

During 1819, the Staffordshire copper metal production was 180 tons dropping to 38 tons in 1827 (10), the greatest proportion coming from Ecton Hill. After the Duke sold the Whiston Works, copper ore was sent to Swansea for smelting, with 2,542 tons from Ecton and 622 tons from Clayton sold there from 1819 to about 1826 (11). Ore sent to Swansea was transported by canal to Runcorn (about 16 tons per boat) and then by ship (50-70 tons per ship).

When the main ore deposit was exploited in Clayton remains unresolved. If it was as big as the plans show – and descriptions state – either there are records which have been lost, or the ore was not as concentrated, and therefore not as rich as in the Ecton Mine.

The failure of the private companies to discover fresh deposits is shown clearly in the Table on page 105. Prior to the 1850s ore was being extracted from the side veins of the Ecton and Clayton Pipes, but after this period the mines were allowed to fill up to river level and all efforts were concentrated on finding new deposits. Their complete lack of success is reflected in the pathetically small output.

Although table on page 105 summarises the known production figures from 1826 to 1890, they are incomplete in several details. No accounts are available for the Ecton Company (1883-89) and the figures quoted are deduced from the *Mining Journal* reports. Slight discrepancies also exist between the mine account books and the Duke's royalty account books which are also at variance with the *Annual Statistics* which have been regarded with caution, but the figures quoted are thought to be reasonable estimates.

Nearly all the copper ore produced during the 19th Century was sold to the Whiston Works at £3-£11 per ton, while some ore and the copper slag was sold to Patten & Co of Cheadle in the 1840s. Lead ore increased in significance during this period, being sold in the 1830s chiefly to Messrs Barker & Co of Chester and Mr George Twigg of Derbyshire at £6-£16 per ton.

Sales of Lead Ore

Later, galena was sold to Milnes & Co during 1846-60 and almost exclusively to Wass & Co at their Lea works at Cromford during 1860-74. By the 1880s the depression had brought the price down to £4. 10. 0d (£4.50p) per ton. The galena was very poor in silver, as was most of the Derbyshire lead, although the nearby Dale Mine produced 475oz during 1860-1 (12).

The amount of galena involved to do this in unknown.

Sales of Zinc Ore

Apart from Attwood of the Ecton Mine Company very little attention had been paid to zinc blende, but in the 1840s he sold 500 tons to the Cheadle Brassworks, 450 tons to John Cleaver and Co of Ripley, Derbyshire, (who patented an improved zinc smelting furnace in 1843), and 195 tons to Whiston. In 1843 the zinc tonnage exceeded that of copper, itself a peak during that year. Later, Mather found that large quantities had been dumped in Waterbank Mine and more was found there and at the bottom of Clayton Pipe in the 1880s (at least 270 tons). Blende appear to have fetched £3-£4 per ton throughout the century.

Looking Back

An estimated maximum total ore production from these mines is about 100,000 tons, the greater proportion being high quality copper ore obtained in the 18th Century, This does not include Burgoyne ore prior to 1813, about which virtually nothing is known. The great success at Ecton lay in the very small overheads incurred in the running of the mines, for not only were the pumping costs almost non-existent, but long expensive adits were not necessary and apart from the Boulton and Watt engine little was spent on expensive capital equipment. This was a sharp contrast to many of the Cornish mines whose potential profits were entirely absorbed in prohibitive pumping costs.

It may be asked whether Ecton Hill could provide any more ore, and the simple answer is almost certainly 'yes'. The old miners had no way of exploring the ore-content of a vein other than driving an adit along it. They had no way of forecasting the presence of other ore-pipes or of favourable ore-zones at the contacts of different strata, as modern analysis might reveal. Such testing could be carried out today by the routine method of diamond drilling, i.e. drilling a narrow borehole with a diamond studded drill-bit.

Who knows what such drilling might reveal? For one thing, we have no idea what rocks lie beneath the limestone of this region, or how deep they are. One drill-hole could tell us very easily. There might even be rich copper ores! But for the diamond drill to find ores is one thing; it is a very different matter for there to be enough ore to making mining a profitable venture today.

Even if new ore bodies as large as the Ecton and Clayton Pipes were discovered, they would probably be too small to work economically at the present, for modern mining needs large guaranteed reserves (and richness is of little consequence for extremely poor ores of less than $1/_2$% copper are economically viable if in sufficient quantity) which can be extracted by mechanised means.

Consequently the mines at Ecton may be regarded as having reached the end of their economic usefulness, but which remain as an interesting example of mining history and the exploitation of an unusual geological feature.

References

1. Sheffield City Library, Bag 484
2. Chesterfield Library, Devonshire Collection
3. Harris J. R, 1968, in Victoria County History, Staffordshire, 1968, Vol 2, p267
4. Harris J. R, 1966, *Economic History Review*, 19, pp550-568
5. Phillips J, 1881, op cit, p195, these figures do not include the Burgoyne Mines as suggested by Ford
6. Mawe J, 1802, *Mineralogy of Derbyshire*, p109
7. Staffs Record Office D554/55
8. Sheffield City Library, Bag 593
9. 1868 Prospectus
10. Barton D. B, 1961, *Copper Mining in Cornwall*, p57, and Ure A, 1839, *Dictionary of Arts, Manufacture and Mines*, p827
11. Phillips J, op cit
12. Annual Mineral Statistics

4 The Dale and Other Mines, Warslow

Introduction

The Dale Mine, was situated on the Harpur-Crewe Estate on the western bank of the River Manifold and although it is opposite the Ecton Mine, it lacked the attention which visitors and authors gave to its more famous neighbour.

Associated with the Dale Mine were the smaller mines of Hayesbrook and other mines and trials which were worked by the various Dale Mine Companies from time to time. Historical data on these smaller mines is far from being complete. All of these mines were worked intermittently and consequently material on even the Dale mine is sparse in places. In complete contrast, the activities of the Dale Mining Co Ltd, and the New Dale Mining Company, between 1857 and 1873 are well documented. The lead ore was found in an inclined pipe working which descended to the west away from the Manifold Valley. Although the ore was found in reasonably good quantities, the inclined workings were expensive to operate and water was a problem.

A number of statements (Deposition Papers) were taken by the Mine's Solicitors to defend a law case and these are referred to as DP.

Description of the Mines

The surface features of the Dale Mine are situated above and to the north of the old turnpike road which runs down from Warslow to Ecton. Although the position of several buildings can be traced none are still standing and identification would be difficult without a plan in hand. The dressing floor was situated, at different times, in two distinct places. The earlier one was situated on the hillside overlooking the Ecton Mine on the western side of the Footway Shaft, which can be clearly seen with its surrounding circular stone wall. This shaft gave access to the old pipe vein above the adit level, but the top is now sealed with stone.

To the north of this shaft, in the field at the base of a cinder heap from the old smithy, the ground appears to be rather disturbed and the plans of the Dale Mining Co, mark shafts at this point. These were the Engine, Footway, [one unknown], and the Sawpit Shafts. The latter dropped onto the Sawpit Vein and a level was driven off it fairly close to the top. It was filled in 1853 and the site used as a coal yard behind the boiler house. The engine house built in 1854 was blown up with gunpowder following the removal of the engine to the New Engine Shaft in 1862.

To the north west of these shafts, the site of the old whim can be clearly distinguished. The whim served the No 1 Engine Shaft which is marked only by a few stones over the shaft collar. No doubt this is the site of the whim mentioned in the 1823 valuation of plant and machinery, and its function would be for hauling, the engine being used for pumping.

A further engine was erected on this shaft in 1855 and this served first the No 1 Shaft as a pumping engine until May, 1859 when the 40-inch engine from New York Mine was started. Thereafter, the old engine was used for hauling and crushing and the new engine for pumping purposes. In January 1861, a new pumping shaft was started near to Dale Farm and this was kept dry by a long line of flat rods from the engine on the No 1 Shaft. This system was used until late 1862 when the pumping engine was moved up to the new shaft.

Both the two engine houses and the smithy have been demolished and only a few overgrown foundation stones remain. Close to the site of these buildings are the remains of filter beds or possibly early dressing buddles. At the side of the new engine shaft a new engine house, smithy and carpenter's shop plus ore pen were built in 1862 but only a few insignificant remains can be traced and even the shaft can only be sited approximately. A lime kiln also existed here, owned by the later companies and no traces of this can be seen either although its location is known. In fact, the only item which is clearly visible is the site of the dressing floor, where grass still refuses to grow.

Water for an earlier hydraulic engine erected in 1837 and for dressing came along a very long leat from a small reservoir at SK086 594; both pond, called the Lum Pool, and leat can still be seen. The pond is to the north of the Dale mine, between it and the Hayesbrook mine. At the latter, several shafts remain plus the entrance to a shallow sough. A total of seven shafts seem to have been sunk, all but one of which are in

Below left: The launder laid across the Dale mine lum in the adit level **Below right:** The broken nature of the ground in the lum **Opposite:** Hayesbrook Mine in the 1960s. More trees occupy the site now and some levelling has taken place. It was sometimes known as Hayesbrook Gate mine and is the last resting place of seven drowned miners

4 The Dale and Other Mines, Warslow

the site of the steam engine is unknown.

Seven Fatalities

It is held locally that the Hayesbrook mine which was worked through shale and shaley limestone, suffered a disastrous flood, possibly by water held under pressure beneath the shale capping. The miners had to evacuate the mine immediately and seven of them failed to reach the surface. No documentary proof of this has yet been found however but early problems with water are indicated by the presence of a steam engine before 1823. (But see 'Old Drowned Work in Derbyshire' by Nellie Kirkham, Derbys Arch Journal, 1950, p1). A level was driven from the Dale Mine towards Hayesbrook in an attempt to unwater it, but the operation was unsuccessful, although it is said locally that the level reached to below the gates of Warslow Hall and this appears to be confirmed from a plan in the Niness Collection at the Derbyshire Record Office (see page 11).

This level, like the majority of the workings, is no longer accessible and it is only possible to examine a short length of the Dale Mine adit. The latter contains a good flow of water towards the entrance, and geologically it is rather interesting. The strata are very contorted in places and it is the only mine where it is possible to inspect a 'lum' which is a clay-filled fissure associated with mineral wealth, both at this mine and also at Ecton, Mixon etc. The Dale Mine lum (or lumb) was also a handicap for it allowed water to sink quickly to the base of the mine, where floods held up work and put an undue strain on the engine, already working

The current end of the adit level, blocked following a fall. It was nearly a mile in length, stretching to beneath the gates of Warslow Hall

various stages of collapse. The exception is in a line of shafts probably sunk on a vein and understood to be connected with the other shafts by a shale gate (a level driven through shale) at sough level. The shaft is full of water to the sough which is approximately 30ft below the surface. Other than a few hillocks, no other remains can be traced of any significance and consequently

Mines of the Warslow District

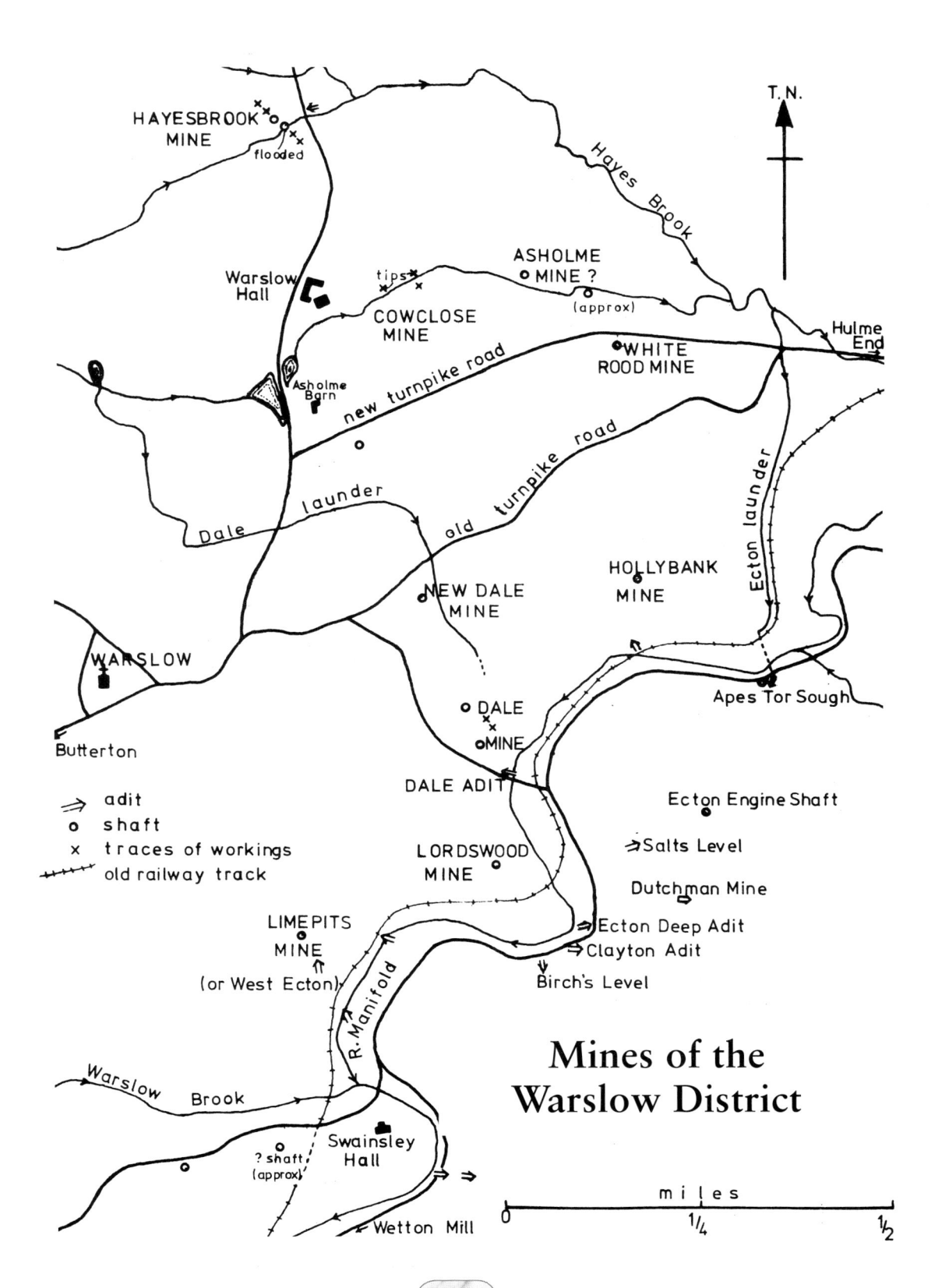

inefficiently on account of the many angles the pump rod had to be turned to reach the bottom of the pipe vein. This difficulty was overcome by installing water troughs (incorrectly thought by Rieuwerts, (1960) to be part of a sledge-run) to carry the water across the lum. These are still intact in places, acting as a useful marker of its position.

Other features of interest can be seen in the Dale Adit. There are rises on a calcite vein and on a fault, and the level opens into the engine shaft which is now flooded to just below the sole or floor of the level. It should be noted, however, that the roof of the level is partially packed with deads (lumps of broken rock) in the lum and that particular care should be taken at this point. The end of the adit appears to have collapsed. At the fall, the roof was supported by iron pegs driven into the rock, in association with a long length of iron bar supporting one end of stone stemples (roof supports) – see photo on page 112.

Early History

No specific records of 18th Century mining exploration naming the Dale Mine exist, although leases of mines in the parish of Alstonefield and also in the manors of Alstonefield, Longnor and Warslow (where the Dale mine is situated) were granted. In 1717, John Harpur licensed three Derbyshire miners to dig in Warslow and at Fleet Green, in Fawfieldhead. The licence was for eleven years, at a royalty of 1/7th of the lead ore produced. In 1723, Henry Harpur leased to four other Derbyshire men the right to dig for lead and copper in Alstonfield Parish for 18 years, paying him 1/9th of ore. However, this may just relate to the civil parish and therefore exclude the Warslow mines. In 1741, he agreed to a new lease, to John Wall of Wensley and Thomas Fisher of Repton, Derbyshire. They were stewards of the Harpur estate. The lease was for twenty-one years at a 1/9th royalty and was assigned in December 1762 to a consortium of local and other people including themselves, with John Wall remaining the largest shareholder. No details of the success or otherwise of this venture are known (Derbyshire Record Office, D2375/7/190/2, D2375/103/1). The accounts of Thomas Barker's Callamine works at Bonsall include the purchase of 13 cast metal bars for the furnace in 1754 from the Dale Company at £1.12.8d. Was this from the mine?

A rich vein of lead ore was found at the Dale Mine in 1766 and the vein was still producing lead ore three years later.

Sir John Harpur's Jottings for 1776-77 survive in the Derbyshire Record Office (1). They include a description of the Ecton Mine, with a comment that

> 'a lead mine beyond ye copper mine [Ecton], near it but a little further up ye river, now working again'.

This must refer to the Dale Mine.

In December 1795, when Warslow Mill, a five storey cotton mill and brewhouse on the north side of the Warslow Brook, near Brownlow Bridge, was offered for sale (2), it was stated that the mill was situated near to a mine shortly to be started by Sir Henry Harpur. The Hayesbrook Mine must also have been started about the same time, and presumably by the same company, for White Watson in his *Delineation of the Strata of Derbyshire* states:

> 'A singular rake vein was worked in this stratum (shale) at Haybrook Gate Mine, near Warslow, Staffs; composed of Sulphuret of Lead, accompanied with Sulphate of Zinc, Carbonate of Baryte, Sulphate of Baryte etc, the vein 30in wide was very productive in 1804'.

It is now clear that a group of twenty-five local men headed by John and Peter Dakeyne, of Gradbach Mill, Quarnford, took a twenty-one year lease of mines in Warslow, Elkstones and Fawfieldhead. The partnership included Sir Henry Harpur and operated under the name of the Dale Mine Company. Clearly Fleet Green Mine was included too, and the reference to Elkstones presumably relates to the trial driven from the Warslow Brook (see Chapter 5) (DRO, 2375M/189/13).

Into the 19th Century

A statement in November 1871 (DP) by George Beresford stated that he could remember the mine working about eighty years previously (i.e. around 1791). Amusingly, he could remember this because as a boy, (aged about nine) he had been to Warslow from Archford Moor, to the east of Ecton Hill, to do some shopping with his brother. On returning, they called at the Dale

Mine and while there, a 'tipsey man' named Charles Birch, who lived at Hulme End, came up and asked the engine man (Richard Johnson) for something to drink. He was given the oil bottle out of which he drank freely! Similarly, another statement, by Samuel Fynney, states that he could remember the mine working in 1812.

John Farey, Snr, recorded in 1811 (3) that the lead ore from the Warslow Mines was sent to Derbyshire for smelting (the lead cupola just across the river at Ecton was apparently used exclusively for the ore from the Duke of Devonshire's mines), and was particularly difficult to smelt 'on account of the extraneous matters which the shale seems to communicate to it'.

The mines of the Warslow area had certainly been worked in the early years of the 19th Century and these early ventures were extensive enough to require the use of steam power in addition to a drainage level. John Farey, Snr described the Dale Level as 'Now Driving' in 1811 (but it should be remembered that he visited the Peak District in the Summer of 1807) and he also stated that

> 'the Mine Engines at any time used in the district were at Dale and Haybrook-Gate Mine, in Warslow, Staffordshire'

but they were presumably not at work in 1810 for he continues 'In 1810, the only Lead-Mine Pumping Engine going in the district, was the newly erected one at Ladygate Vein, at Matlock Bridge'.

In addition to the Dale and Hayesbrook Mines, Farey also mentioned Cowclose or Asholme mine 'in shale and shale limestone'. Virtually nothing is known about this mine at this date although it was probably worked by the same concern. It appears that the manager was Richard Gould, who lived at Brownhill, Warslow. He was the manager for about eight years and raised a lot of lead ore and zinc blende, although the value of the latter was then unknown. Sam Fynney noted in his deposition that the Dale Mine was at work when he came to live in Warslow in 1812. Another man recalled that Cantrell tried to unwater the mine with horses and failed in around 1816-17. The first part of this statement is correct but the date is wrong. However the date could be correct for the closure of the pre-Cantrell operations.

George Cantrell Managing Again

The mines then apparently closed for some time until 1823 when George Cantrell of Wetton took out a lease from Sir George Crewe (4). Cantrell was granted the right to work the mines on the Crewe Estate in the 'Parish of Alstonfield, Warslow, Elkstone and Butterton' for a term of twenty-one years at a 1/20th for the first five years and 1/12th for the remainder of the term. He was formerly the manager at the Ecton mine from 1811 to 1819, when he was dismissed after friction had arisen between himself and John Taylor, the Cornish mining engineer who had been appointed overseer of all the Duke of Devonshire's mines in 1818.

The dismissal was, however, a result of a clash of personalities rather than Cantrell's lack of competence and he was later to form a partnership to work the Burgoyne mines at Ecton in 1836. It is interesting to note that the Cantrell family had other industrial interests and Thomas Cantrell established a cotton mill at Hartington in 1776 and another at Brund on the River Manifold in 1790 (see 2), as well as a textile mill at Wetton (5).

George Cantrell's lease was taken out on the behalf of the Warslow Mineral Company at the beginning of September 1823 and valuations were made of the plant and materials remaining on the mines. The items were primarily at the Hayesbrook Gate and the Dale mines although a reference to a horse-gin or whim at White Road mine (also known as White Roods) indicates that this particular mine had also been worked by the previous Dale Company. Farey, however, makes no mention of this in his list of mines.

A Newcomen-type Engine

At Hayesbrook, there was a steam engine described as:

> '38 inches diameter with a seven feet stroke, built upon Messrs Boulton and Watt's principle with air pump and condenser compleat and one boiler of twelve feet diameter'

valued at £500, although another almost identical valuation quotes a 48 inches cylinder. In addition, at the Dale mine there was:

> 'one small cylinder, 18 inches diameter with cylinder and cylinder bottom and collums, counter and steps of

beams and old arch heads with chains and one boiler, $5^{1}/_{2}$ feet diameter, in bad repare and a few old pipes'.

This was valued at £35.15.6d (£35.77$^{1}/_{2}$p) which would not be much above the scrap value, while the description of the beam with its arch heads and chains shows that it was most likely a simple atmospheric engine of the Newcomen type and possibly quite old. The remainder of the machinery included 480ft of 11-inch pump trees, 108ft of 6-inch pump trees, four working barrels and three old gins in poor condition situated at White Road, Hayesbrook and 'in the field', which could refer to Cow Close. The whole of the machinery was valued at £720 with a further £50 attributed to items in the smithy, tools, buckets and numerous sundry items including thirty-five miners' chests which could be indicative of the number of miners working for the old company.

The Warslow Mineral Company

This Company's activities are obscure, but it is known that the company was divided into twenty-four shares held by eighteen partners. The principal shareholder was Richard Gaunt, who was also connected with the North Staffordshire Mining Company which worked the Dale Mine in the 1830s. The deposition papers also indicate that Richard Johnson (see above) was the engine man under Gaunt. See the end of Chapter Seven for a further reference to Richard Gaunt, described in the 1840s as living in Leek. The family owned land on the west side of Leek and a Gaunt Street survives there where the fields used to be.

Further shareholders were Joshua Brittlebank who was appointed underground manager at the Mixon Mine in 1827 and Charles Flint, son of Cornelius Flint, the agent at Ecton during its great prosperity. Each share, according to a copy of the Rules and Regulations of the company (in Cantrell's hand writing) was worth £100, payable in two £50 calls on July 1st and September 1st 1823. Consequently, the paid up share capital was only £2,400 which appears to be very low.

An undated inventory of mining materials belonging to the Warslow Mining Company shows that they were working the Limepits, White Roads, Hayesbrook Gate and Dale Mines, while the complete exclusion of all mention of the steam engines and pumps indicate that these had been sold off. In fact, drainage was now by water barrels raised by horse gins at each of the above mines,, and since ore dressing equipment was included only for the Hayesbrook Gate mine, this probably dressed all the ore from the others as well. Lime Pits Mine is situated to the south of the Dale Mine and was worked in 1860 as a private venture by Richard Niness (of the Dale Mining Company) under the name of the West Ecton Mining Company.

An affidavit by Samuel Fynney stated that Cantrell had tried to drain the mine by horse power but had failed. Other statements made at the time indicate that several people could remember a round boiler from the old engine being removed in about 1830. A 'round boiler' (with a concave bottom) would seem to suggest a 'haystack' boiler commonly used with Newcomen type atmospheric engines. The Hayesbrook engine was finally removed at the same time, both on the orders of Sir George Crewe of Warslow Hall. Presumably this was after the Warslow Mineral Company had closed down. Clearly, either because the engine was incapable of being used, or because of cost, Cantrell was using horse-power to work the pumps and eventually failed.

Several of the sworn depositions in the pollution case refer to recalling the boiler to the old engine when the person concerned was a child. They were Warslow children who attended the Duke's school at Ecton in the early part of the 19th Century, and they used to throw stones at the boiler. It must have been close to the road in The Dale.

The work of the Warslow Mineral Company did not last for very long, however and the Dale Mine had definitely been abandoned by 1832. The Wyatt papers in Derby Library contain several letters between William Wyatt, of Foolow, and Thomas Sneyd-Kynnersley, of Loxley Park, Staffs, chiefly relating to the Mixon Mine, where Wyatt was the agent. The Mixon Mine was being worked by Sneyd-Kynnersley at a loss, with his two brothers Clement and William and in a letter of 1832, Wyatt suggested that they might like to form a company to work 'a piece of mineral ground adjoining Ecton mine' (6).

By the end of the year Sir George Crewe had stated his willingness to grant a lease to Richard

Surface Plan of Dale Lead Mine

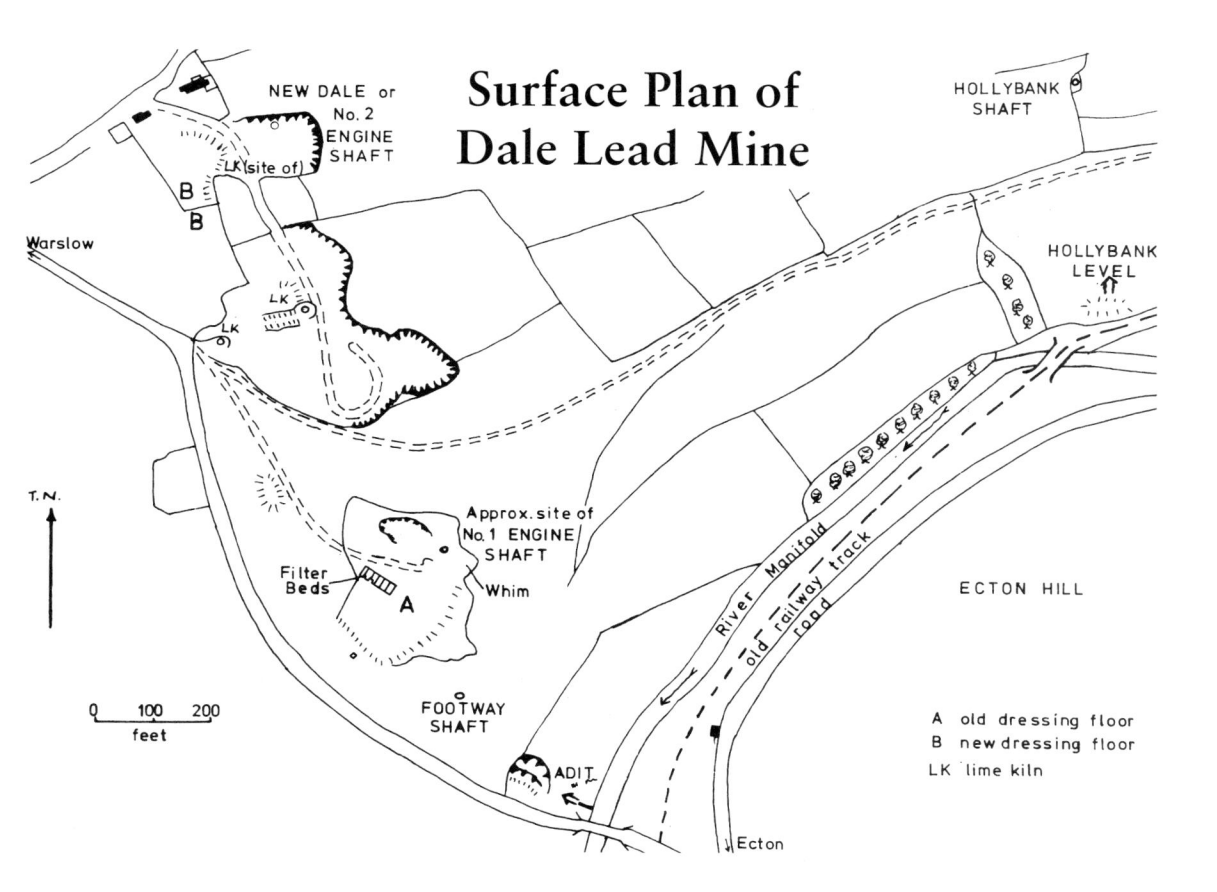

Map labels: NEW DALE or No. 2 ENGINE SHAFT; HOLLYBANK SHAFT; HOLLYBANK LEVEL; Warslow; LK (site of); B B; LK; T.N.; Approx. site of No. 1 ENGINE SHAFT; Filter Beds; A; Whim; River Manifold; old railway track; road; ECTON HILL; 0 100 200 feet; FOOTWAY SHAFT; ADIT; Ecton; A old dressing floor; B new dressing floor; LK lime kiln

Gaunt. There was some speculation as to whether the mine would be predominantly for lead or copper and the agent of the Crewe estate stated that the royalty would be 1/15th if a lead mine and 1/12th if copper. He also said that Sir George would take a few shares and Jesse Watts-Russell of Ilam Hall also indicated his willingness to be a shareholder. Despite the greater royalty, copper was preferred to lead, particularly by Sneyd-Kynnersley who complained of the difficulty of obtaining ore for his copper smelting works at Whiston.

Whether this proposal came to anything is not clear. Probably not, as a prospectus was issued in 1836 for the North Staffordshire Lead and Copper Mining Company. However a list of proposed Rules and Regulations was in the name of George Cantrell, so presumably it had taken him until this date to find sufficient backers.

The Hydraulic Pumping Engine

The mine was reopened in 1836 under George Buckley of Ashover, Derbyshire. The foundations of the Newcomen-type engine was dug out to build an ore house. The adit was cleared and sinking commenced on a new shaft near to the old engine shaft, only to be abandoned later through excessive water. Whilst water problems had overwhelmed Cantrell, Buckley installed an hydraulic pumping engine in the adit level. One of these engines may be seen at the Peak District Mining Museum at Matlock Bath. Instead of using steam power, which depended upon expensive coal, the piston worked by the pressure of a falling column of water.

The water came from the Lum Pool referred to above. This engine worked until 1843. It had a 12-inch piston, the beam had a six feet stroke and worked at the rate of five to six strokes per minute. It generally discharged 150 gallons of water per minute into the adit, where it drained to the River Manifold.

This engine was being erected at the time of Queen Victoria's Coronation (28 June, 1838). The engineer responsible for its erection was called Joseph North and he assisted in erecting arches decorated with evergreens across the road in front of the school in Warslow (DP in November 1871 of Isaac Birch, innkeeper of the Grouse Inn, Warslow, which he had kept since October 1853). North lodged with John Millward, the Parish Clerk.

Buckley sunk the Engine Shaft another 13 fathoms deeper and put down a new lift of pumps. A year later, he drove from the foot of the sinking for about 70 fathoms (the 26 fathom level). He worked the vein about 40 fathoms in length as it dipped down. The ore and waste rock was all drawn up by a horse whim, the site of which still remains. The ore was washed and dressed on the site of the earlier dressing floor, using water from the same leat that served the hydraulic engine. The blacksmith at this time was Sampson Kidd.

There were no catchpits for the finely ground waste spar and rock which was taken away through a culvert and under the road to join a gutter from where it went down to the river. Large quantities of ore are understood to have been raised according to the pollution statements.

The mine was visited by Samuel Scriven in 1842, who was collecting evidence for the Children's Employment Commission and the evidence of George Buckley the mine agent, was short but informative (7). Buckley, aged 60 years, had been the agent for $4^{1}/_{2}$ years. Twenty men were being employed including two boys under 18 years of age who dressed the ore. The boys, who were described as occasional labourers and could neither read or write, were paid 8d a day, considerably less than the boys at the nearby Ecton Mine who earned 6-7s per week. The dressing floor superintendent was Abraham Thompson, who worked all his life at various mines in the area and lived at Ecton.

It was reported in the *Mining Journal* (December 1853) that Buckley's operations had ended 'through a disagreement amongst the proprietors'. James Roland's 1871 DP – he was a mine surveyor – states that he had been the last man to work the hydraulic engine. On the final day, he had kept it working for about six hours longer than his orders allowed 'merely to oblige some men who were working in the mine to get all the ore out which they had broke'. The engine was dismantled by a man called Frost from Fritchley in Derbyshire, although the pump column was left in the mine. Buckley seems to have considered sinking a new engine shaft to the north-east of the old engine shaft for a plan of the early 1870s marks the site of 'Buckley's intended new engine shaft'.

Finally, the first edition of the OS map (of 1840) shows the Onecote road still entering the village of Warslow down the road from Leek. The current road from the village direct to Brownlow Bridge over the Warslow Brook was probably cut shortly afterwards and the 1871 deposition statements reveal that it was built with stone from the Dale Mine tips.

Cornish Miners take out a lease

The mine was to remain idle for nearly five years, when a lease was exchanged between Sir John Crewe and John Williams and others, dated 5th April 1848. In actual fact, Williams had arrived in the area a little earlier and had worked at Ecton with Richard Niness (see Chapter 3.5). Both were Cornishmen and several Cornishmen were set on to clear the adit level. This use of Cornish miners rather than local miners indicates that they probably came north with Williams and Niness, or at their behest.

Niness was letting contract bargains (payments to do so much work for an agreed sum) in November 1847 and James Rowland and Andrew Barker were involved in this work. Both of these men had been the engine men minding (or tenting) the hydraulic engine from 1838, working twelve hour shifts. Another early job was given to John Grindon. It was to fetch an old boiler end from New York Mine with his horse and cart. It was set into the ground to catch a small stream of water running from the Dale road to slack lime and for mixing the mortar to be used in the building of the engine and boiler house. His father is mentioned below, for he was employed years previously in bringing coal, and doubtless countless other jobs with his team of horses. John had had a similar living as he had carted away the stone from the Dale tips to build the new road from Warslow to Brownlow Bridge in the 1840s. By 1853, he was underground, working at the bottom of the Engine Shaft in the 26 fathom level.

During the years 1854-1856, considerable quantities of zinc blende were recovered from the mine tips and sold. Even as late as the operations under Mr Buckley, the blende had been thrown away. However technological breakthrough had resulted in it becoming easier to smelt and in the 1840s, Melville Attwood recovered considerable amounts of blende from the Ecton tips, making a lot of money in the process. It seems strange that Buckley was discarding blende ore at this time, but James Roland, whose DP statement seems to be one of the most plausible, does state this.

Cow Close Mine

Work also commenced at Limepits Mine above Ecton Lea. There was some work done in sinking the shaft and in driving a level out of it. Work at Cow Close Mine, situated in a field called Guttery Meadow, started about this time too and work went on here for a considerable time. There were the 'ends' here, one working westwards and the other driving in the opposite direction. The latter had three eight-hour shifts, with a man and a boy working each shift. The western end worked similarly.

The men working the adit reached Cow Close which would have improved the ventilation, especially in the adit. The adit men then cleared out the 24 fathoms deep shaft and cased and divided it (a Cornish term), into two, one side for hauling and the other becoming a ladderway. A horse whim or winder was erected at the shaft for the benefit of the men at each end of the level below, who would be hauled up and down in a large bucket or kibble. By the beginning of 1849, it had a new use – raising good quantities of lead ore.

The work at these various mines was undertaken by a partnership held in 300 shares, for whom the men worked. The partners included John Williams, Thomas Field, Sidney Jessop, Harry and John Smith Richmond, and a Mr Gillispie. Richard Niness joined this partnership in 1848. The 1848 lease was to Williams, Field and a Mr Hobson. It was on behalf of this partnership and was for 21 years.

A Valuable Speculation

In December 1851, a report in the *Mining Journal* stated that the mine:

> 'holds out great promise to the adventurers and... it is anticipated to erect sufficient machinery to prove this valuable speculation'.

However in 1852, some of he partners retired, presumably despairing of success and not wishing to contribute more to the mine costs. A new partnership was formed consisting of the former partners, including Richard Niness and others including Thomas Lewis, Charles Hinks, William Johnson and James Pemberton. This partnership lasted until it was converted into a limited liability company with most of the partners becoming shareholders.

The Dale Mining Company Ltd

It was registered as the Dale Mining Company Ltd on 29th October 1857, some ten years after Richard Niness and his Cornish colleagues came to Warslow. It had a capital of £21,000 which was subsequently increased until it amounted to £50,000. A resolution to wind up the company was passed on 26 February 1868. However, the consent of the liquidators to register a successor Company was soon obtained and the New Dale Mine Ltd was registered on 4 May 1868. This Company purchased the lease, plant and machinery of the former company.

The capital initially was £5,000 but this was subsequently increased to £20,000. the last increase being registered on 3rd May 1871. The inference from this is that the capital was increased by £5,000 each May. Work continued without a break while the mine was in liquidation.

As the 1848 lease had been forfeited, a new lease was granted on 29th May 1855 to Messrs Lewis and Hinks. The New Dale Mine Ltd held an underlease dated 30th November 1858, the mesne landlords being Messrs Pemberton and Johnson who had taken an assignment of the 1855 lease from Messrs Hinks and Lewis. For more details on some of these personalities, see Chapter 10.

The Dale Mining Company Ltd appears to have taken over responsibility of several mines at this period, for in addition to New York Mine, the Company worked 'Ecton, Dale, Limepits, Narrow Dale, and Hope Dale' (letter from Niness of December 1871). The workings at Hope Dale and Narrow Dale were for ironstone. See Chapter 8 for detail on Hope Dale and below for Narrow Dale.

The Mine Operations

From late 1855, there were numerous reports on the Dale Mine in the *Mining Journal* and these

4 The Dale and Other Mines, Warslow

The Dale Mine may be seen in the top left corner of this photograph from the top of Ecton Hill

enable a fairly comprehensive picture to be obtained of the mine operations at this time. Although the reports are verbose and written in a typically optimistic style, they are nevertheless a valuable guide.

In 1854, the mine erected a 19-inch steam engine on the No 1 Engine Shaft which was started at the beginning of October 1855. This came from the colliery at Hazelbarrow in Staffordshire. This was situated at the southern end of the Goldsitch Moss coalfield, between the Roaches and Ramshaw Rocks, North of Leek. The engine was a steam winder but was converted to a pumping engine at Dale.

The early work of the Company was spent in exploration of two lodes – the north-south 'old pipe vein' and Johnson's Lode, The former was where the principal operations were undertaken, at the 20, 26 and 32 fathom levels. The 20 fathom level was driven north during 1857, but no further details are known. In the 26 fathom level, a trial was driven westwards on a 10-inch leader (small vein) of lead ore and blende. Operations were, however, hindered by poor ventilation and a gate was driven from the level to the pipe to ease this and prove the ore-ground in between the level and the pipe working.

The main workings at this time were at the 32 fathom level on No 3 lode, which was started at the beginning of October 1855. During the following year, the mine purchased several items from the Ecton Mine including three waterwheel arms, although it is not certain that the mine had a waterwheel at this time. What is of greater interest is that the boiler from the Ecton Boulton and Watt engine, of 1788, was sold to a Mr Richmond for £40 (8). This is likely to be J S Richmond, a wine merchant of Liverpool who was a director of the Dale Mine (see above).

The early work of the Company was in the 32 fathom level south which was driven south to meet a winze (a shaft between two levels) being sunk from the 26 fathom level on a 'good bunch of lead' some eight inches wide. The union of the winze and the 32 fathom level south enabled the lode to be opened up and stoped (i.e. the rock and ore between the two horizons was being removed) but already water problems which were to prove critical to the Dale Mining Co., were beginning to manifest themselves. Before the winze could be sunk below the floor of the 32 fathom level, a dam had to be installed north of the winze to hold back the water and the pump rod had to be adjusted to cope with the extra water.

Despite the problems however, sinking commenced in September 1857 and by the end of the year the pipe vein was being stoped below the 32 fathom level, yielding a 4ft wide vein where ore was raised on tribute. In addition, at the end of the year further ore was being raised on tribute in the 32 fathom level south. Elsewhere, the Company turned its attention to Johnson's Lode, where exploratory work was undertaken at the 20 fathom level east, and also in the 37 and in the 13 fathom levels where stoping was carried out in the back of the level.

The ore which was being raised obviously gave rise to optimism but the revenue was insufficient to meet the expenses of extraction and further exploratory work, consequently the private company had to consider further measures of raising capital. This was done by interesting further speculators into forming a public company with sufficient capital to buy out the interests of the old company as indicated above. From 1857 to 1873 the mine had a chequered career, running out of capital and being reconstituted again once more.

A Good Start

The ore, which had been raised in 1856, consisted of 98 tons of lead worth £1,190 which had clearly given encouragement to the new speculators for although the Company raised £21,000, the prospectus had been launched seeking only £13,000 (in £1 shares).

The prospectus of 1856 stated that it was intended to erect a 35ft diameter by 6ft breast waterwheel, with which it was hoped the mine would be drained. The partners had spent £6,000 in developing the mine and took £6,000 in fully paid up shares to compensate for this. There is no reference to the waterwheel ever being built and in any case, a second pumping engine and buildings were erected in 1858. However a wheel 'for the purpose of supplying an extra quantity of air in the [75 fathoms] level' was being made (*Mining Journal*, 28 May 1870, p466).

A possible further reference appears to be also in the same paper (1878, p186), in a letter from Mr E S Darwin. He was requesting information on a wheel purchased by the Buxton Local Board and which had been erected at the Dale or some other local mine. After working for a short time, it had been taken down and deposited on the premises of Sir John Crewe's agent at Warslow.

The wheel was described as being of 18ft diameter and 5ft wide – obviously not the intended wheel of 1856. It had cast iron shrouds, flanges and arms with a wrought iron shaft, along with a 17ft segment with a three feet spur nut. The buckets, rises and sole plank were all constructed of wood. Presumably this was the 1870 wheel. It is interesting to note that a waterwheel existed at the sewage works on the River Wye at Buxton, said to have come from a corn mill nearby. It was moved after the Great War to Ashwood Dale Quarry by Mr John Melland of Harpur Hill. It is said that the wheel had come initially from Ecton but possibly this could have been the 1870 wheel supplied to the Buxton Local Board.

The delay in establishing the new Company referred to above was not unique to the Dale Mine, for Niness experienced similar difficulty at the Ribden Mine, where it took nearly three years to float a Company and nearly cost him his lease because of the delay.

Over Optimism or Misrepresentation?

The new Company differed from the previous mine concerns at Dale because it was of limited liability. Such a system, without the present day safeguards, lended itself towards unscrupulous dealings and in a few circumstances people were swindled out of a lot of money. The activities of Richard Niness in promoting mines in North Staffordshire has already been mentioned and there is some evidence which indicates that shareholders were possibly deceived at Dale. It would be easy to cast suspicion on the shoulders of Niness in view of his activities in other local mines; the fact that he received $2^1/_2$% of all the profits at Dale; and his connection with John Williams at Ecton in the 1840s and later at New York mine, where the mine was in continuous litigation with the Royledge Mine and then with a supplier.

However, because the mine is flooded and physical observation impossible, plus the fact that the documentary evidence is chiefly from

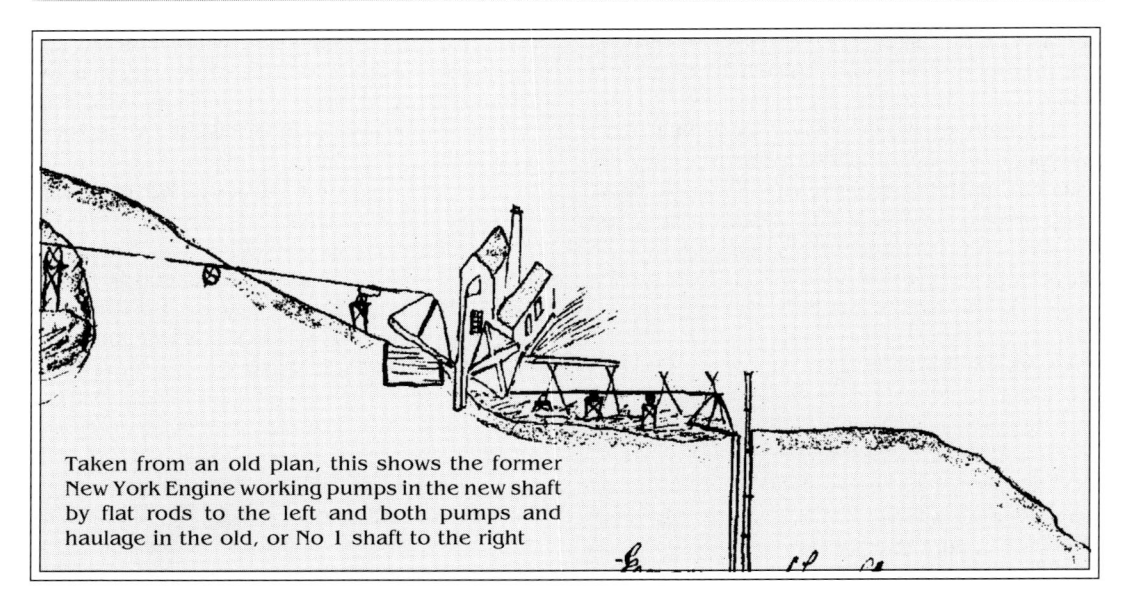

Taken from an old plan, this shows the former New York Engine working pumps in the new shaft by flat rods to the left and both pumps and haulage in the old, or No 1 shaft to the right

reports written by Niness it is difficult to draw strong conclusions. Some shareholders certainly made allegations of deceit in the *Mining Journal*.

The allegations come from two distinct items – ore discoveries in the 37 fathom level and concerning the New York engine to be referred to later). The Dale Mining Company Ltd, was registered on 29th October 1857, as noted above.

In February 1858, a 'rich' ore deposit was found in the 37 fathom level. Full details are given below but its significance is of importance here. It appears that the discovery was a deliberate attempt to increase interest in the mine and thereby help to sell the necessary number of shares needed to raise sufficient capital. The 'discovery' was given maximum publicity. Niness wrote to the press *(Mining Journal*, 1858, p170) that the oldest miners in the area said that the find was the best that they had seen for fifty years. He said that he had visited East Wheal Rose, the richest lead mine in Cornwall 'where the shares are at their top price and I saw no course of lead equal to this'. This was obviously share promoting and at p186, Niness, reported that he considered that 'the lodes are larger than Ecton and in all probability will outrival Ecton'!

James Crofts, a London sharebroker who also acted as secretary to numerous mining companies (including the Ecton Mountain Mining Co) stated that the Ecton Company had spent £5,000 before finding that exploration of the Old Ecton Mine was 'useless' and the work abandoned. He continued on from his pessimistic overtones to add that Dale was causing a sensation (on the Liverpool and Manchester Stock Exchanges) and speculated as to whether another massive lode had been found. The desired effect was achieved and by the middle of 1858 the £1 shares were selling at 32/6d (£1.62$^{1}/_{2}$p) and the Company declared that no further shares would be allotted below 30/- (£1.50). As the Company had at least 2,500 unallotted shares at this date it meant that a good profit could be made by the Company if they were sold.

Shareholder's Suspicions

However, the Company's activities were soon questioned by several shareholders. One quoted Niness as saying that 400-500 tons of ore were in sight and yet no ore was being brought up in tonnages befitting such a deposit. A further shareholder (*Mining Journal* 1858, p369), was more specific, criticising Niness's management and wondering why the 'rich deposit' had been abandoned in favour of proving its width and then this abandoned in favour of sinking deeper. He suggested a greater control over Niness, particularly as the secretary resided in London and the directors in Birmingham.

At a General Meeting held in May 1858, Niness said, cautiously, that he was 'most anxious not to overstate the prospects' and care was taken to emphasise that two of the original proprietors (of the old partnership) had not sold a single share. Unfortunately, it was found that the meeting was illegal under the rules of the Company. The first meeting should not have been held until November 11th 1858. By coincidence perhaps, some of the directors had been involved with illegal meetings previously for Lewis, Pemberton and Johnson had been accused of doing similar things at Mixon.

Shares Slump

The outcome of this was that a few weeks later it was decided to alter some of the rules of the Company, some being 'so stringent as to materially interfere with the Company's operations'. The anticipated output of ore did not of course materialise, and so shareholders soon began to sell out, as must the investors hoping for a quick rise in the share price. This soon brought a glut of shares onto the market and by mid-June 1858, the share price was down to 14/- (£0.70p) for fully paid shares. By the end of the year, they had dropped to around 10/- (50p) and fluctuated around that figure at least until mid 1859.

Unless the intention was to lift the price of the shares so that a quick killing could be made, it is difficult to understand what Niness and the directors in general were up to. One thing is for certain, wild allegations of ore deposits being found was bound to have only one profound conclusion.

The New York Engine

The second allegation of deceit concerned the New York Mine engine. This engine had been the centre of an agreement, the interpretation of which had been the cause of much aggravation and litigation between New York and Royledge Mines. The agent at the former mine was Richard Niness but the Dale directors do not appear to have been involved until after the New York Mining Co had failed. The latter Company advertised its plant and machinery for sale in 1853 and again in 1854, after being withdrawn at auction at £2,500.

Presumably the machinery lay unused at the mine until about 1855 when the Dale Mine partners started work. The machinery and lease of New York Mine was purchased, the machinery apparently costing £2,000 (see below). Whether it was their initial intention to work New York is unknown. It is also possible of course, that the directors, being concerned with Mixon, cast their eyes on New York and subsequently, possibly through Niness's influence, turned their attention to the Dale Mine. Unfortunately, the records do not make this point clear.

Under the Agreement with the old Company, the new Company agreed to pay 10,500 fully paid shares. In addition, it was also agreed to pay £2,000 in cash for the purchase of the mine and £1,000 for the purchase of the New York machinery, The allegations of deceit concerned the payment of the £1,000 for it appears that the inclusion of this item had been masked. The annoyance of the shareholders appears to have been aggravated by the Company appropriating a certain number of shares in order to pay Brunton, the secretary, 1,000 shares for raising the initial capital of the mine or in paying Mr Richmond for the New York machinery (see *Mining Journal*, 1858, p.449).

The purchase of the interest in the mine cost the new Company £8,500 which was divided into the 21,000 shares. In addition to this cost, it is reasonable to assume that the shares paid to Brunton were fully paid up. Consequently, the new Company paid rather heavily to get off the ground.

Shareholder Dissatisfaction

Shareholders and the *Mining Journal* (1858, p401) thought that the £2,000 paid for plant and machinery was for the purchase of the Dale Mine plant at £500 and £1,500 for the New York plant which the shareholders thought included the engine. It is difficult not to see the logic of this for there could have been little at New York apart from the engine, although it should be remembered that the plant had been withdrawn at auction, in 1854 at £2,500 (if the bid was genuine). It was also difficult to interpret the published accounts and a shareholder complained that the auditor had a reputation at other mines for his complicated presentation of the accounts.

Thus the mine found itself saddled with an extra debt of £1,000, which was resisted and Counsel's opinion reinforced this by determining that the sum was not a liability. Earlier it was stated that the shares fluctuated at around 10/- per share until mid 1859. There was a notable exception, however, which occurred at the beginning of 1859 – at the time of this dispute. The shares became very dull, as the details of the 'finds' in the 37 fathom level became obscure and the troubles better known. However in February, a 'new' discovery in the 43 fathoms was conveniently made by Niness and a revival of interest took place again. The man certainly seemed to be good at marketing.

An Impasse

In February 1859, there also occurred a meeting of the Company and one of the most militant shareholders (Lieut R N Watson) suggested a Bill in Chancery in order to determine the dispute. In addition to the £2,000 claimed by the original partners (presumably for the plant at Dale and at New York) and the £1,000 for the New York engine, a further sum was also claimed. It appears that after an agreement had been reached between the two parties (the partners and the Company) in June 1857, the company did not become come operative until March 1858. During this period, the mine had expended a further £2,295 and this was also being claimed. The meeting refused to pass the accounts and obviously concessions had to be made to break the impasse.

The concessions came a month later at a further meeting. It was agreed that the New York engine was to be paid for out of the profits only. In consideration of the accounts being passed, Pemberton (both he and Johnson had retired as directors the previous December) agreed to make a £500 reduction in the £2,000 cash purchase money and also agreed not to press for either the principal or the interest money until the mine was making a profit.

There was however, a further factor which must have contributed substantially towards resolving the dispute. For some time it had been obvious that the mine had been working at a distinct disadvantage. As the workings became deeper, they became further away from the No 1 Engine shaft and the removal costs of water became excessive. On top of this, the existing engine was obviously incapable of coping with the work and was continually breaking down when heavy rain increased the workload of the pumps. This resulted in the more profitable parts of the mine being quite often inundated with surface water. Niness had stated that he could not sink another foot without a new engine and the obvious choice was the one lying idle at New York. It was therefore in the Company's interests to obtain the engine as soon as possible. Whilst the shareholders obviously knew this, they were holding out as long as possible.

A New Engine is Needed

However in March 1859, the month that agreement was reached, the engine must have been found to be in a particularly poor condition. It had broken down just prior to the February meeting and shortly after agreement was reached, the engine was connected by a 7-inch lift between the newly opened 43 fathom level and the 37 fathom level. The extra weight caused the crank to break, straining the engine and it had to be stopped altogether until the New York engine was erected.

In mid March 1859, New York Mine was put to work for the last time. The shaft was drained to the bottom and the pitwork (pumps) removed. By the first week in April, the machinery was ready for removal. It had possibly been altered or broken during removal for new castings, which were late in arriving, held up the starting date. The whole operation only took a few months, in complete contrast to the Ribden Mine. Niness started to remove the Mixon engine in May 1859 and it was twelve months before it started once more at Ribden. At Dale, the water pumped up the shaft was used for ore dressing, which had the advantage of being warm and never frozen in the winter months. Niness was to deny that the water was ever warm in the pollution dispute in the 1870s.

'Ore by the Barrowsfull'

Shortly after the engine was started – ten days later, to be precise, the Niness publicity drive was informing the quarterly mine meeting that

'rich ore in barrowsfull was coming up from the 37 and 43 fathom levels in lumps the size of walnuts to 3-4cwt masses'.

The ore was brought up by the old engine which was used for winding and crushing.

By the end of 1859, the mine was in quite a healthy state: in the previous three months, the lead ore which had been raised, was sold for £1,029 whilst the costs had been £850. This was particularly fortunate in that there was a debit balance in March 1859 of £247, which had slowly been turned into the black.

In fact by the turn of the year, the mine was making a profit of £100 per month. The mine's costs were averaging around £250 per month, which was not much different than the Ribden mine costs, where the mine was nearly twice as deep. This was possibly because of the inclined nature of the pipe vein which increased extraction costs at Dale.

A New Shaft

The obvious answer was a new shaft and this was proposed at the June meeting in 1860. It was to be at the northern end of the workings. The depth was to be 88 fathoms, costing approximately £1,000 and taking nine to twelve months to sink, using four pairs of men on it at once. In order to finance the costs, it was decided to issue the remaining 2,865 unallotted shares. The shareholders were to be allotted one third pro rata, at par, with an option to claim twice the number, also at par within six months. It was considered that the new shaft would halve the costs of raising the ore. The system of removing the ore up the pipe working involved tramming and windlass winding up to the 26 fathom level and then haulage up the No 1 Engine Shaft, employing about fifty men. It was anticipated that with the new shaft, only nine men would be needed. This same meeting also decided to surrender the New York Mine lease.

Dark Clouds

Despite the fact that the mine was raising ore in greater quantities than before, (161 tons worth £1,913 was raised in the second half of the year), dark clouds were amassing and a further storm broke before the end of the year. Criticism of the accounts occurred in the *Mining Journal* and this was not helped by further criticism directed at the Secretary, Brunton. He was Secretary at several mines, including Ribden and its sister Company, the Oakamoor and Stanton Mining Company. He was replaced in September 1860 at Ribden and possibly also at West Snailbeach and West Tolvadden in Shropshire where some of the Ribden directors were also directors. However, Dale kept Brunton on until March 1861. However, further letters appeared in the *Mining Journal*. It was stated that having the management of the mine in the hands of Brunton
'affords another illustration of parties entering into mining without previous knowledge and little business tact'.

Messrs Brunton & Co had regular adverts in the *Journal*, describing themselves as:

'Engineers and mineral surveyors, undertake the management and working of mines, quarries etc and conduct the London agency [their offices were at 5, Waterloo Place, Pall Mall] of all mineral properties in their offices with system economy and regularity.

Messrs Brunton & Co beg to inform proprietors of mines etc that the business of these properties is carried on in their office upon the following principles, viz: Accounts systematically and closely made up. Statements in detail and clear summaries of finance and expenditure. Entire and impartial openness of books, reports and documents to all shareholders, for perusal or extract. Immediate communication of any important occurrence to the shareholders. Mineral properties surveyed and estimates of machinery, plant and costs of working furnished.'

Clearly expectation did not live up to reality. It was also reported that several shareholders had sold out because of the whole affair.

As if this wasn't bad enough, the speculation over the accounts was followed by further letters from shareholders on the flooding problems. The Apes Tor launder, which brought water to the wheel which drained the Ecton Mine had fallen down, and it was queried whether Ecton would flood the Dale Mine. Niness eventually quelled the fears in his characteristic way: he felt that Dale was as likely to be troubled with water from the Thames as with water from Ecton!

Activities in the Various Parts of the Mine

The detailed nature of the *Mining Journal* reports are important in that they give a fairly good picture of the work that was carried on by the Company in the various parts of the mine. Because of the material which is available, it is possible to go into far greater depth in describing

Dale Lead Mine North - South Section Principal Workings 1857-1860

1 Top of the big bye lift underlay on the pipe
2 Top of 7 lift underlay on the pipe
3 Top of the bottom 7 underlay on the pipe (installed 1859)
4 Winze at the 44 fathom level (used as a sump)

the history of the mine. The Dale mine is unique amongst North Staffordshire metalliferous mines in this respect, for even the reports for Ecton are sketchy and although Niness wrote the reports for Ribden Mine, the life span of the mine was relatively short. A fuller report of the work undertaken during this period may be obtained elsewhere (1).

It was mentioned above that the fundamental problem at the mine was the excessive cost of raising ore and water (and also the difficulties of providing adequate ventilation on account of the inclined nature of the pipe vein). An article in the *Mining and Smelting Magazine* in 1862 indicated that the ore had to be drawn through half a dozen inclined winzes by hand tackle before engine power from the 19-inch steam engine could be used. The provision of a new shaft was the obvious answer and work commenced at the very beginning of 1861. At the June meeting in 1860 It had been estimated that it would be 88 fathoms deep and take nine to twelve months to sink. In actual fact 88 fathoms took over two and a half years to sink and the final depth was 105 fathoms which communicated with the pipe during mid November 1863, having taken nearly three years to sink.

The decision to sink to at least 100 fathoms had been made by March 1861 and it in probable that the site of the shaft had been altered. It was situated north of the lum, which it would cut at a depth of 50 fathoms. In actual fact, no mention of cutting the lum was made in the *Mining Journal* and it is doubtful if it was cut at any depth. The shaft initially was being sunk at the rate of one fathom per week and was 10ft by 6ft in cross-section, making it the largest shaft in the North Staffordshire orefield. By the end of 1861, the shaft was between 35 and 50 fathoms deep and in 'disturbed' ground requiring timber shoring. Why it needed to be so large is far from clear.

An interesting reference to a shallow level was made at the March 1862 meeting. Although little information is given, it appears a level was being driven to take off the surface water which was draining into the shaft. Presumably this was driven from the surface but although it is reasonably easy to determine where it must be (to the south of the shaft) owing to the topography of the area no trace of a level can be seen.

The shaft was cased and divided (i.e. sealed at the sides and split into two) as the sinking progressed and a ladderway was put in. By April 1862, a new road to the shaft was being made from the old shaft to convey stone from the

4 The Dale and Other Mines, Warslow

quarry at the mine to build a new engine house, dressing floor etc as well as convey machinery.

Re-siting the Engine

The dressing floor and engine house was situated on the south side of the shaft so that the crusher and jigging frames could be worked by the 19-inch engine. The engine was started at its new site in June 1862 and shortly afterwards, a 'large piston machine' was installed. This would be an air compressor and was worked by the engine to supply air to the shaftmen. Although the transportation of the engine to its new site was not mentioned in the *Mining Journal*, it must have been quite a task. During 1973, Mr Tom Wooliscroft of the School House, Warslow died.

He was in his nineties and could remember David Martin, the Cornish engineer who worked under Capt Niness, and whose grave can be seen by the road at Warslow Church. Martin had apparently recalled the transfer of the engine to Mr Wooliscroft. Apparently it took a great team of horses to move it to the new shaft – presumably up the newly constructed road, which can still be seen crossing the fields between the two shafts – and was regarded locally as quite a feat in itself.

It is also held locally that Martin wished to be buried as near to his native county as possible and when he died he was buried in the south-western corner of the church yard in respect of his wishes!

Work in the New Shaft

The sinking of the shaft was kept clear of water by buckets, but by the beginning of 1863 the shaft was down some 70 fathoms and the amount of water was becoming too great to handle by a horse whim. It was therefore decided to pump the water clear by the 40-inch engine still situated at the No 1 Shaft. This was done by flat rods 130 fathoms long carried on pulley wheel frames. The rods were of two-inch iron connecting rods. Fifty fathoms of limestone had to be cut away on the surface in order to make room for the rods between the two shafts.

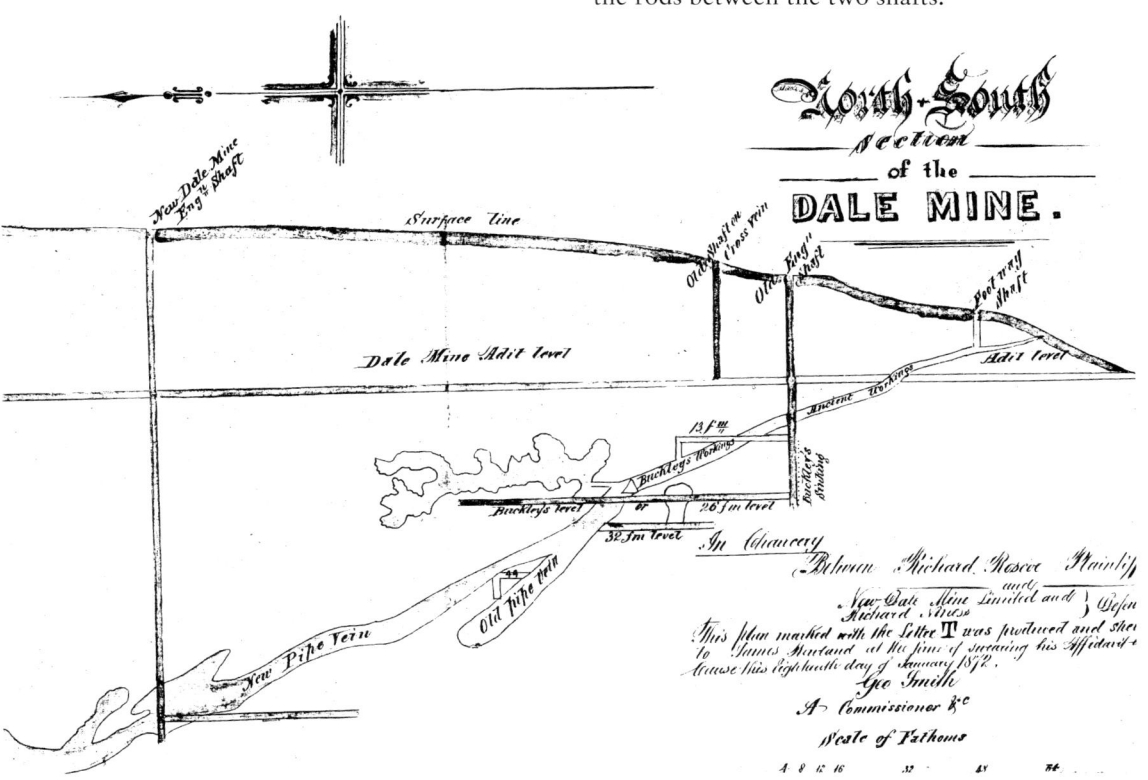

An old plan showing the new shaft

4 The Dale and Other Mines, Warslow

By the end of March 1863, two plunger lifts 33 fathoms each were fixed together with a final section to the bottom – a 'sinking lift' as it was known – and sinking recommenced.

A new smithy had also been built to replace the old one at the No 1 Shaft. Sinking was proceeding rather slowly because the shaft was in compact limestone mixed with chert which had to be blasted away. Chert consists of silica (similar to flint in composition and hardness) and was difficult to drive through. Miners did not like it because it sometimes exploded causing injury. It is also worth remembering that because of the size of the shaft, every fathom of ground was yielding over 40 tons of rock.

At the next Quarterly meeting it was stated that the shaft was down 81 fathoms and ore was expected. The dressing floor was being made ready and a crusher house was being built to house a double-rolled crusher 'to be worked the rotary engine'. Chert was still hindering work, but by mid-July the shaftmen were in a 'trough saddle' (see Chapter 14) indicating a geological change.

Since early 1862, there had been no income. All work had been concentrated on the shaft and surface work with the old pipe working being allowed to fill up with water to the 26 fathom level, i.e. the base of the No 1 shaft. This was now being pumped clear and by mid-September 1863, the men doing this work were down to the 43 fathom level and could hear the shaftmen from the pipeworkings, On the surface above, the men were up to the roof of the crusher and

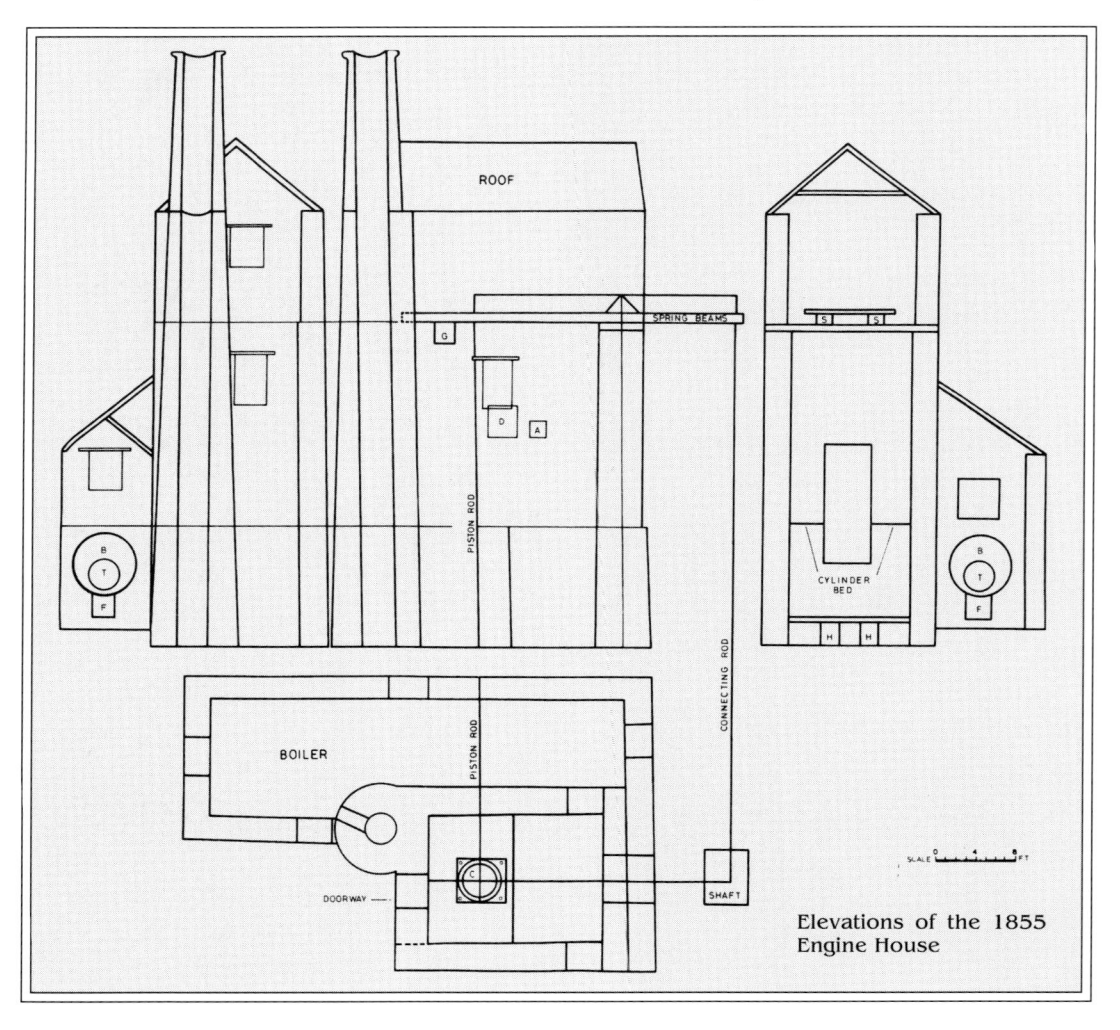

Elevations of the 1855 Engine House

chipping house. Two hundred yards of flags for the dressing floors had been laid and two large passages had been completed to convey the ore through from the landing stage of the shaft to the dressing floors.

Heavy rain hampered work in late September-October and over powered the engine. A further breakage occurred and pumping had to be suspended for a month. Water was, however, draining into the new No 2 Shaft where it could be drawn off. The 40-inch engine from New York had been working at a maximum, giving 10 to $10^{1}/_{2}$ strokes per minute. The load on the engine was 18,000lbs, drawn by a length of connections of nearly half a mile and through sixteen independent lifts and 'over angles of every degree' causing excessive friction which obviously led to the breakages. The sooner pumping could be done via a simple, vertical shaft the better.

The Shaft Reaches the Pipeworking

The breakthrough into the pipe happened at 8pm on Saturday, November 21st at a depth of 101 fathoms. Niness reported that they would start squaring down the shaft and make a dam to prevent flooding from the old mine. It in interesting to note that a plan in the Niness Collection dated 20th November 1870 carries the comment that the No 2 shaft was out of plumb by 38ft. A sump of 4 fathoms was sunk to give a final depth of 105 fathoms. Ore was found close to the shaft and at a depth of 50 fathoms in the old pipe working which was raised and dressed with as little delay as possible. During the sinking of the No 2 Shaft, activity had virtually ceased in other parts of the mine. Ore had been raised at the beginning of 1861 from the pipe; a heading 8ft high and 6ft wide had yielded 10 tons of ore and the pipe was worth £120 per fathom. It was said that good ore was being left at the sides to be worked when the new shaft was down.

More Shareholder Dissatisfaction

Despite the concentration of effort on the shaft, Dale still managed to attract attention in the – even to the point of editorial comment. Brunton was replaced by a Mr Dunsford as secretary after

> 'great irregularities had been understood to have been found in the books'

The directors had issued a circular stating that certain shares, for which the shareholders held the usual certificates, were 'informal' and could not be recognised by the directors. The *Mining Journal* advised that the Company and directors were liable for the certificates. The solicitor for the Ribden mine, Mr Edward Daniel, pointed out that under the Company's articles, every shareholder was entitled to a certificate under the Company's seal upon payment of less than one shilling.

Unfortunately no greater detail is mentioned but the report of the next Quarterly Meeting (March 1861) is intriguing. It was stated that there were 900 shares which would be entitled to dividends, none of which had paid anything into the capital account. The directors wanted an outlay of less than £180 to purchase 600 shares (separate from above). Against this outlay, there was a bill of exchange

> 'which was considered good and against the 900 shares there was an assignment of patent rights, some portion of which had been sold for a considerable some of money'.

From occasional comments in later reports it is possible that of the 2,865 shares offered to finance the shaft Brunton used, some, possibly 865 or 900 shares, to buy the patent rights of machinery from a Mr Crease. The machine appears to have been concerned with rock drills but as Crease wanted the mine to finance the construction of the machine, it was not used. There had been talk of using it in the No 2 Shaft but it was found that the shaft would be down before the machine would be ready.

Possibly Brunton was receiving a 'backhander' and committed the Company to purchase the patent rights in the hope of using the machine in the shaft to advantage and therefore gaining publicity and appreciation from the shareholders. It is a pity the full position isn't clear. Whether this had anything to do with Brunton's dismissal regrettably one cannot be sure. Shares were still in demand, however, and were selling at 13/- to 14/- (65p to 70p). Further, an advert appeared in the *Mining Journal* in May 1861 seeking 1,000 shares. Prospects improved with the discovery of a further ore deposit (see below) and by June the shares were at £1 having risen from 10/- (50p) since early February.

More Sudden 'Discoveries'

The reason for the demand for shares was the discovery of a new deposit of ore beneath where ore was being extracted in the pipe at the bottom of the mine. The Company therefore had two deposits of ore in close proximity. The two deposits are clearly shown on the sections of the mine. In order to keep the bottom of the pipe clear of water, a new lift of pumps was installed and was a 'great saving to the Company'. The lift was over 33 fathoms which would mean a big saving on manpower in the inclined workings. In addition 60 fathoms of railway was laid to convey the ore – presumably underground.

The mine cost for February – March 1861 was £1,074, just over £500 per month, which was twice as much as the cost two years before. This was obviously due to increased costs as the pipe became deeper and of course, the sinking of the No 2 Shaft. All the unallotted shares which had been offered to finance the shaft had been taken up and there was obvious confidence in the mine. It was even suggested that the stone from the shaft be used in the neighbouring limekiln but although this question was raised again, there is no note whether or not this occurred. This was not unusual and the Ribden Company sold lime in the 1820s to cut down expenditure. With the shaft yielding 40 tons of rock per fathom, 4,200 tons of rock had been dumped on the hillside from this shaft alone.

The confidence in the financial side of the mine was reinforced by the fact that by August 1861, the pipe was worth £180 per fathom. The 'old' and 'new' carriages (deposits) were coming together and shortly afterwards, a third one was located.

Water problems were still causing concern and severe influxes of water occurred in September and again in December 1861. On the latter occasion, a further breakage occurred to the engine and water rose up to the adit level [see Porter & Robey for further discussion on this for those interested in the technical detail].

In the second half of 1861, despite ore sales of £1,556, the costs had caused a total loss over the six months of £411. This included £100 paid to terminate an annual payment of £25 for a water course, presumably the one coming across the fields from the Lum Pool, the mine using its own water pumped up the shaft since 1854.

During the beginning of 1862, the mine was allowed to fill with water to the 26 fathom level. This had been prompted by a drop in ore prices which were down nearly 50%.

The annual meeting of June 1862 showed a credit balance of £150 but a balance of liabilities over assets of £400 on the capital account over the year. The actual state of the mine at that time was different of course, for there was no income from ore sales. In view of the fact that there was no capital reserve, additional finance had to be found. This was done by issuing a further 9,000 shares and applications for approximately half had been received by the date of the meeting. The shares were issued at 7/6d (37$\frac{1}{2}$p) which would raise £3,375 if fully subscribed. Matters were not helped by a bad debt of £960 of which details were not given.

Even More Working Capital Needed

Over the next twelve months the money was used up and the capital-holding was increased from £30,000 to £35,000; the 5,000 shares being issued at a discount of 10/- (50p) per share. By the end of 1863 ore was being raised again and share prices were up to 17/6d (87$\frac{1}{2}$p) despite the new issues. The first sale of ore since completion of the new shaft was in March, 1864. It consisted of 68 tons (probably lead ore) and was purchased by Messrs Wass & Sons of Lea near Cromford. James Barker, the head dresser at the mine, received a sovereign (£1) from Mr Wass in recognition of the fine job the men had made of their work.

This was probably due to the catchpits or buddles which caught all the fine particles of ore, separating them from the useless spar or rock. Clearly there was less rubbish mixed with the ore than Mr Wass was used to buying. From this date onwards, for five to six years, the dressers broke 40-60 tons of lead ore per month and 40-50 tons of zinc blende per month.

Extraction costs following completion of the new shaft diminished and at the annual meeting of July 1864 it was stated that the mine was making a profit.

Both lead and zinc ore (blende) was being raised. Despite this it was decided to raise fresh capital by increasing the capital from £35,000 to £40,000 by issuing 5,000 £1 shares at a discount of 12/6d (62½p) per share. This was, however, not implemented and it was decided not to call up any further capital during the following month due to increased ore sales.

By the end of 1864, prospects were much better. Returns were being doubled despite the fact that the pipe still occupied two separate courses. An interesting development was the building of an underground dam which was used to create a water blast. A finely divided stream of water was allowed to fall into the No 2 Shaft which caused a downdraught, which aided ventilation of the workings.

The use of a water blast is uncommon in the North Staffordshire orefield. In fact this is the only recorded example.

At the quarterly meeting, held at the end of the year it was stated that 132 tons of lead ore and 100 tons of blende had been raised. The quantity would have been more but eight men were being employed in sinking the shaft a further 10ft to install a 'trip plat' (platform) to enable the men to discharge the ore from the wagons more easily. The railway, or tramway, which had been installed was being mechanised so that the wagons could be hauled by the means of the winding engine rather than by men. A winze was being sunk from the old top deposit on the pipe vein to the bottom one to aid ventilation so the water blast had not been a complete success. A further addition to the mine at the end of 1864 was another boiler.

A Mr W Ward was elected secretary for Mr Dunsford had died. The profit for the last six months was £350. In the years 1864-66 inclusive, the Company employed about a hundred men in the mine alone. As production fell after this date, the number fell to be only around fifty in total. Along with Warslow Hall, where presumably a good number of people, women particularly, may have been employed as servants, gamekeepers etc, the mine must have been the biggest employer in Warslow.

Hereafter, the reports are fewer and follow a pattern of good times and bad as the ore deposit became larger and then contracted. The demand for shares gradually fell and by November 1866 £1 shares were down 2/- to 4/- (10p-20p). During 1865, the directors had paid £750 to discharge the debt of £1,500 (plus interest) which was still owing for the New York machinery. In return, the Company had received 7,700 shares.

Voluntary Liquidation

These shares increased the number held by the Company to 10,396 and in October 1866 these were offered to the shareholders. It was stated that unless 6,000 were taken up, the question of winding up the concern would have to be considered. No royalty had been paid since January 1865 and at the October 1866 meeting it was stated that half of this would be waived if paid within twelve months and henceforth no royalty would be payable until the mine was making a profit.

Unfortunately matters did not get any better and in February 1868 it was resolved that the Company be voluntarily wound up.

In May 1868 however, amongst a list of prospective companies listed in the *Mining Journal* (p360) was the New Dale Mining Company. It was being formed with a capital of 5,000 shares of £1 each.

A New Beginning

The object of the Company was to purchase the lease and machinery of the Dale Mining Co Ltd, and the memorandum is signed by various people with addresses in the London area – presumably underwriters or possibly speculators.

Hereafter, the reports are far more infrequent, particularly having regard to the general operations of the company, which has been discussed above. The records which do occur are chiefly concerned with information of the various parts of the mine which were being worked and will be referred to later. Up to June 1870, the firm was not quoted in the share list. In that month, two men were put to work on Hollybank Mine but labour was scarce no doubt influenced by the fact that lead ore mining was by now virtually over in North Staffordshire as well as in Derbyshire, for although Ecton was being worked, it was no more important than Dale itself.

An interesting record is that half of the first load of coal (from the Cheadle Coalfield) to be brought into the locality by a steam vehicle came to the Dale Mine in September 1871 (Leek Times). It makes a nice comparison with a comment in the deposition papers by John Grindon. His father had a team of horses and carted the coals for the original engine at the mine.

Operations at the Mine

Following the completion of the No 2 Engine Shaft, operation recommenced in the pipe vein, particularly in the 43 and 44 fathom levels on the pipe working. Whilst cutting out ground to make a dam (to stop mine water overwhelming the engine) some good ore was uncovered in a vein running parallel with the pipe, i.e. east-west, worth £20 per fathom. It was speculated that the vein could have been part of the pipe which was left behind in the 37 fathom level above, where the 'large discovery' which had affected the share price, had been made.

Throughout 1864 work was concentrated on ore extraction in the pipe working, bringing up 100 tons of ore (probably lead ore) by the end of April. The pipe working was deepened to 50 fathoms and ore extraction also started here.

In the last six months of the year, various improvements took place including the provision of a 'railway' worked by the engine referred to above.

During 1865, the bottom of the pipe got progressively poorer during the first half of the year, until part branched off in a north-easterly direction. However, before the end of the year, a change of fortune occurred and the pipe was yielding ore in four different ends. Johnson's Lode was also proving productive and a steady flow of ore was being raised to the dressing floor. During January 1866, the pipe was described as being mixed with zinc ore. A winze (shaft between two levels) in the bottom of the mine was in thin strata, the vein 'mixed with spar and sulphur'. Johnson's Lode was producing 'some very good ore'. A month later, the winze was still in thin dark ground, the vein both contracted and unproductive – described by Niness as being similar to Ecton at the 30 fathom level.

No fundamental change occurred during March and April despite comments that there was another Ecton being discovered, The mine remained 'dull' until the end of May when there was some improvement. Speculation that the pipe might improve as it approached the Millstone Grit came to nothing. Niness had hoped to find copper at Ribden Copper Mine near Cauldon Low at the bottom level which was being driven towards the grit. Unfortunately the intersection in either mine was not, made and any possibility of larger deposits was not revealed. However, the entrance to East Ecton Mine, driven in 1861 started in Millstone Grit shales and a deposit of lead ore was found in the vein 6ft below the surface – presumably at the junction of the two geological series (Carboniferous limestone and the Millstone Grit series), which occurs behind the arching of the entrance.

At the time the Company was wound up the reports are not very plentiful or helpful and little is known of activities except that lead ore was still being raised. A letter from Niness survives which states that the Company was being worked on the old costbook principal, rather than as a limited liability company and as a result he was not obliged to send in the familiar regular reports. The New Dale Company, continued operations in the pipe, developing the connections between the new shaft and the pipe working. By mid-1870, a railroad had been put in, carried on timber over the old workings from the new shaft to the 44 fathoms cross cut. The system incorporated turntables etc to facilitate the transfer of tubs. By the end of 1870, a vein 21ft wide had been opened up but little detail is known.

Throughout 1872 and 1873, operations at Dale were confined to the driving of levels at the 75 fathom level – both south and north, together with the rise up to what became the 65 fathom level. Johnson's Lode at the 44 fathoms cross cut yielded ore in quantities which could well have been quite significant relative to the preceding five years. The last reference to the 26 fathom level was in October 1872. A rather interesting reference at the beginning of 1873 concerned the construction of filter beds and catchpits – obviously relating to the mine water pollution case.

The 75 Fathom levels

In 1868 a cross cut was driven from the south of the new shaft bottom, at a distance of 75 fathoms below the old shaft collar. Some veins of ore were cut but the ventilation was poor and the dam door – the dam built to hold back water in the old workings in bad weather – was removed to increase ventilation to enable more men to be put on the veins. By the end of May, three headings had been commenced, The first one, was driven south being cut through 'blende, chert, whey and everything that can be desired for lead'. Activities continued here until 1871, but no important deposit appears to have been found. Ventilation proved a continual problem and in May 1870, Niness stated that it was hoped to put in a waterwheel in the near future to supply an extra quantity of air. Presumably this would have been built at the entrance of the adit level on the river Manifold. The last references give no hint of a forthcoming closure of the mine.

See Chapter 11 for details of the pollution case between Richard Roscoe, of Swainsley Hall, and the mine. It was as a result of this that the mine seems to have closed, although Mrs Vera Barber, the grand-daughter of Richard Niness, stated that her mother had said that closure occurred after some men had been brought out injured following an explosion.

Hollybank Mine

Within the area of the mine lease were two old mines, one quite close to the Dale Mine, the other, at Narrowdale, some two miles east of the Dale Mine. Hollybank level was started in November 1870 with the intention of unwatering the older Hollybank Shaft higher up the hillside.

By April 1871 it was thought that the shaft and old workings were being drained but little water was actually draining into the level. Some work was done in the old workings above, clearing out the vein and Niness reported that they had 'Opened 22 feet vertical below the $12\frac{1}{2}$ fathom level from the surface'. Because the level, or adit, below was not relieving the mine of water – said to be caused by accumulations of silt, water had to be drawn out of the shaft. By Christmas 1871, the level had been driven to a total length of 68 fathoms 4ft without cutting any ore deposit or unwatering the old mine above. A vein had been cut, however, and at the beginning of 1872 a further level was driven off the adit in a northwesterly direction.

Further attention was given to the old mine and by May 1872 it had been cleared, enlarged and secured to a depth of $8\frac{1}{2}$ fathoms. However the men appear to have been transferred to Dale soon after for a couple of months, together with the men at Narrowdale. The mine was worked until operations of the whole Company ceased. There is an interesting report in October 1873 which stated that Niness had been unable to make any arrangement about 'the ground to tip the stuff on' and he recommended that work be suspended for a short time or a shaft be sunk 'on the flat ground on the top of the hill'.

Narrowdale

The first report is dated December 1870, but it was necessary to repair the shaft before the men would accept the contract for apparently a horse had fallen down it on some occasion and 'cleared everything before it'. A second shaft had not been reopened.

A whim was to be erected in January 1871, but there is no further mention until April 1872, when Niness reported that a new shaft had been commenced on 'the iron vein' as he considered it would be cheaper than opening up the old shaft. The vein, however, was far less productive than it had been at the old shaft, which was 20 fathoms away. The sinking was stopped at a depth of 5 fathoms and the men transferred to Dale Mine the trial presumably being abandoned.

Limepits & Other Mines

To the south of the Dale Mine lies Limepits Mine and several workings, all relatively small and some obviously only trials. The main one is Limepits Mine, known later as West Ecton Mine, the significance of which discussed below. Other than the brief mention of it being worked in the 1820's little is known of it prior to 1860.

It was worked by the Dale Mine in the late 1840s, for Robert Greenhough stated (Deposition in the pollution case) that he first met Richard Niness at Limepits Mine where he (RG) worked for some time in sinking the shaft and in driving a level from the Lime Pits Shaft, the work being let on contract. A shaft exists in the fields above the valley and there are two levels, both of which may not communicate with the shaft. The bottom or deep level is now blocked below the former light railway track. The blockage is substantial to carry the weight of the trains. The upper entrance is now buried.

It is interesting to find that the mine was reworked in 1860 and although a large amount of information is not available, sufficient data exists to illustrate how a mine can be made to look a good prospect in the face of a complete lack of geological evidence.

At the beginning of 1860 a 'private company of gentlemen' was formed. A note in the *Mining*

Journal pointed out that the mine adjoined Ecton and Dale and the area being worked was traversed by the east and west and south east veins at Ecton and the east and west lodes of Dale. 'Under Capt Niness's management', the *Journal* continued, 'success may be fairly anticipated'.

The company appears to have been mooted in the mistaken belief that by extrapolating known veins in nearby mines, if they crossed at some position away from known ore deposits, ore would be found. This remote possibility was the basis on which many mine companies were started and many examples occurred in nearby Shropshire. Even the change of name to West Ecton is not without significance, stimulating thoughts of the riches found in Ecton mine itself. A crude plan shows the extrapolation of the following so-called 'veins' at West Ecton. The shaft is shown as being on an extension of the Good Hope Lode (from Ecton) and a level is shown in the direction of a postulated intersection of the junction of the Bowler and Hamnook lodes (from Ecton Hill) together with the old Ecton east-west lode. It is known that a crosscut was actually being driven in June 1860 towards this 'junction' under Niness's direction.

The reports on the mine only occur in 1860 and although Niness stated that they were probably breaking sufficient ore in May to pay the costs of the mine. This is doubtful and the lack of reports after August 1860 is indicative that the mine had probably closed down, although William Turner, a gamekeeper on the Harpur-Crewe estate stated that he could remember the mine being worked seven or eight years previously, which would be around 1863. This fits in with a comment by John Grindon, a farmer of Warslow, that Niness worked Lime Pits 'several times since he has had the management.

Between Limepits Mine and the Dale Mine, lies Lordswood Mine of which no historical data is available. Below this, and just above the river bed is a further trial, driven along a small calcite vein and difficult to reach. The trial consists of one small, dry level.

There is an unconfirmed report of a further level close to the river to the south of Dale bridge, upstream from here, and also near to Lordswood. No traces can be found but the Leek Times of 23rd May, 1891 reported that a dog had been lost in a disused mine in Lordswood, Warslow, which may account for the entrance being blocked up.

To the north of the Dale Mine are a farther series of small mines, chiefly worked by the Dale Mine Companies. They were Asholme, White Roods and Cow Close Mines but the only known documentary evidence has already been mentioned previously in this chapter.

References
1. Derbyshire Record Office, 1952 T 7 Mining lease of 1762; Niness Collection

    Collection of plans D 934B; 2375/M No 63-65 John Harpur's Memoranda
2. Chapman S. D, *The Early Factory Masters*, 1967
3. Farey J, 1811, *Agriculture and Minerals of Derbyshire*, Vol 1, pp257, 338
4. Staffordshire Record Office, Cantrell Papers
5. Roberts J, 1900, *History of Wetton, Thors Cave and Ecton Mines*
6. Derby Ref. Library, Wyatt Coll. of letters
7. H.M. Commission on Employment of Children. Vol III, p134 and Appendix to 1st Report, pt II, p129
8. Ecton Mine Cash Book, Ferguson Collection, J. A. Robey

See also

Porter L. & Robey J. A. 1972, The Dale Mine, Manifold Valley, North Staffordshire, Part 1, Bull PDMHS. Vol 5, No 2 pp93-106 and

1973   Part 2, Bull PDMHS, Vol 5, No 3 pp161-173

1974   Part 3, Bull PDMHS, Vol 5, No 5 pp279-287

5 The Mines of the Upper Elkstones Area

Early History

Dr Robert Plot visited North Staffordshire in 1680 whilst researching his History of the County. He noted that copper existed at Upper Elkston (sic), but unlike Ecton, he did not refer to a mine specifically. With the lease of the Hill House area for mining purposes only 37 years later, one wonders if it was Hill House he had in mind. The Ecton history, (see Chapter 3.2) refers to a collection of mineral specimens put together by John Woodward which may still be seen at Cambridge. The collection was made between 1680 and 1690 and many samples are labelled 'Ekstone Mine, Staffs'.

At the time of writing, it is accepted that the documentary evidence is more compelling in favour of Ecton, but the rails in the Royledge Adit (which may have come from Hill House Mine) and an early barrow found in ancient Royledge stope workings seem to point to workings of great antiquity in the parish. Moreover, the earliest leases of both Hill House and Fleet Green nearby are dated 1717. The latter specifically refers to rights in Warslow and Fleet Green, which could indicate the presence of earlier workings at that latter farm.

Hill House Mine

In 1717, a lease was agreed for the mineral rights to the mines at Greeny Bank and at Pike Low. Pike Low and Greeny Bank relate to the Hill House area of Upper Elkstones, or Over Elkstones as it was previously known (1). A further lease was agreed for these mines in 1736. It was from Lord Chetwynd, Earl of Talbot to Messrs Mellor and Harris to delve for lead and copper on two parcels of land at Greeny Bank and Pike Low, Upper Elkstones. In June 1778, the manor of Elkstones together with 674 acres of land and various cottages were sold by John Crewe of Crewe to Richard Whillock of Ford near Grindon, John Deavill of The Green, Leek and Joseph Grindey who was the tenant of some of the land purchased. The purchase price was £3,150. The full details of the purchase is given in Appendix 1 at the end of this chapter.

Prior to this sale, a lease for ninety-nine years was agreed for the mineral rights under other, nearby land. It is possible that there was some collusion regarding these transactions with mining being the objective. This lease followed a mortgage between Moses Morris of Upper Elkstones, described as a Yeoman, and Joseph Pickford, the architect, of Derby. It is dated 18/4/1778 and Pickford advanced £1,100 to Morris secured on land at Upper Elkstones (listed in Appendix 2). At the same time, Pickford took the mineral rights at 1/8th royalty for 99 years. This lease was assigned on 26/6/1782 to Sir Herbert Mackworth and to Sir William Dolben. The consideration was 5/- (25p). The land itself was eventually sold by Morris to Emanuel Barker of Edensor, near Chatsworth.

Pickford was involved with the three Heath brothers who ran Heath's Bank in Derby. The brothers are described as being 'unscrupulous rogues' who made a living from buying up mortgaged property, foreclosing and selling it over the head of the owner. Pickford seems to have been linked with them in the sale of foreclosed property. The bank was forced into bankruptcy in 1779 (2). Saunders documents the many admirable properties which were designed by Pickford and his house in Friar Gate, Derby, is now a museum.

Mackworth and Dolben were simultaneously assembling a larger holding. It seems that they had agreed to purchase all, or some part of the land purchased by Whillock et al, for an agreement survives releasing Mackworth and Dolben from the purchase of an area of land known as the Dole, valued at £90. Presumably there was

Area Plan

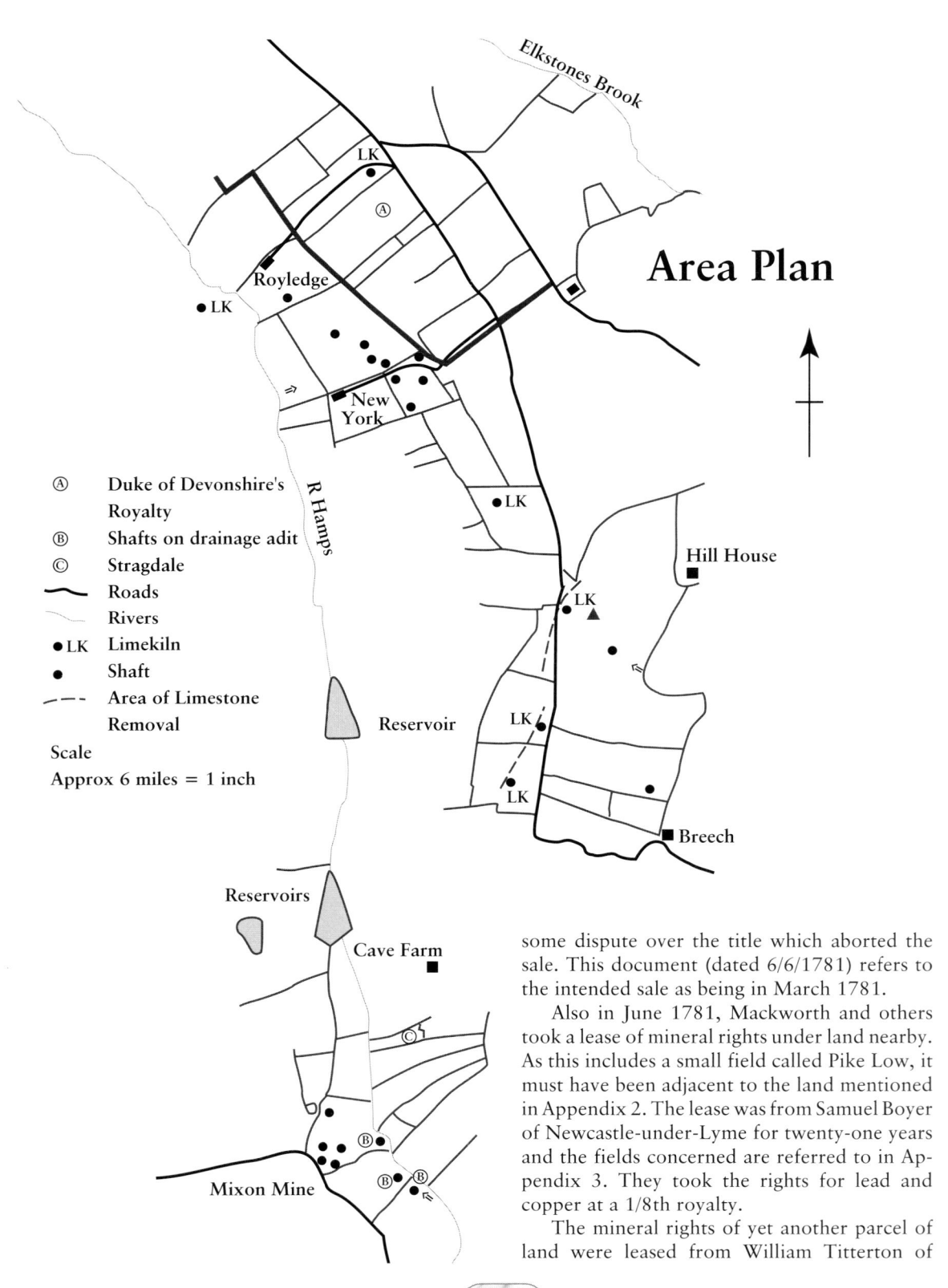

Legend:
- Ⓐ Duke of Devonshire's Royalty
- Ⓑ Shafts on drainage adit
- Ⓒ Stragdale
- —— Roads
- —— Rivers
- ●LK Limekiln
- ● Shaft
- – – – Area of Limestone Removal

Scale
Approx 6 miles = 1 inch

some dispute over the title which aborted the sale. This document (dated 6/6/1781) refers to the intended sale as being in March 1781.

Also in June 1781, Mackworth and others took a lease of mineral rights under land nearby. As this includes a small field called Pike Low, it must have been adjacent to the land mentioned in Appendix 2. The lease was from Samuel Boyer of Newcastle-under-Lyme for twenty-one years and the fields concerned are referred to in Appendix 3. They took the rights for lead and copper at a 1/8th royalty.

The mineral rights of yet another parcel of land were leased from William Titterton of

5 The Mines of the Upper Elkstones Area

Len Kirkham (left) and Tom Buxton with the Stable Field and the New York Footway Shaft behind at Royledge

Deepdale, near Grindon, for twenty-one years from 1/3/1782, again at 1/8th royalty. These rights, for copper and lead, excluded limestone. There are several lime kilns surviving in the area and the rights to work limestone for these kilns must have been leased separately. The fields covered by this lease are listed in Appendix 4.

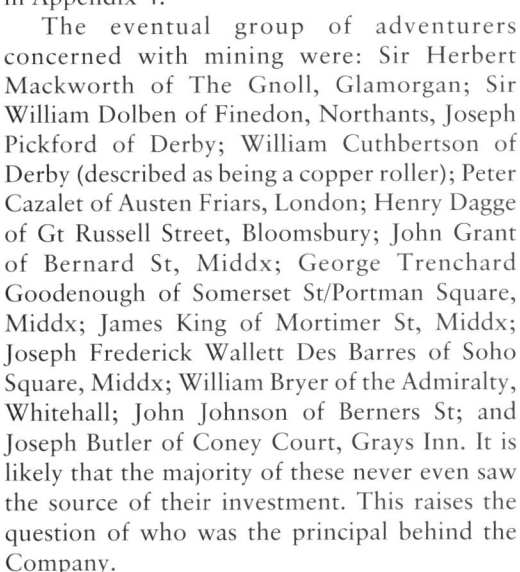

The eventual group of adventurers concerned with mining were: Sir Herbert Mackworth of The Gnoll, Glamorgan; Sir William Dolben of Finedon, Northants, Joseph Pickford of Derby; William Cuthbertson of Derby (described as being a copper roller); Peter Cazalet of Austen Friars, London; Henry Dagge of Gt Russell Street, Bloomsbury; John Grant of Bernard St, Middx; George Trenchard Goodenough of Somerset St/Portman Square, Middx; James King of Mortimer St, Middx; Joseph Frederick Wallett Des Barres of Soho Square, Middx; William Bryer of the Admiralty, Whitehall; John Johnson of Berners St; and Joseph Butler of Coney Court, Grays Inn. It is likely that the majority of these never even saw the source of their investment. This raises the question of who was the principal behind the Company.

The only 'local' investors were Joseph Pickford and William Cuthbertson and neither are known to have had other connections with mining. Perhaps the three purchasers of the Crewe lands in the area (Whillock et al) were the instigators of this mining investment following their purchase of the Elkstones estate. This may well have been as a direct result of their knowledge of the previous mining in the area and of course the success currently being enjoyed by the Duke of Devonshire at another nearby copper mine: Ecton. Additionally, mining was continuing at Mixon, a little way down the same valley, although details are obscure. In 1770, John Sneyd had bought the Onecote estate which included a farm at Mixon. A boring bar or noger, was lent by the Ecton Mine to 'Sneads Mine' in 1775 and work seems to have been active to the end of the century, with an important deposit being found in 1817. The surviving records for the last few years of the 18th Century at Mixon would seem to indicate that the rich deposit was well overdue, however.

Developments in the Early 19th Century

Nothing is known about the mining activities undertaken at Hill House at this period. A letter survives which indicates that the mine was being readied for sale by February 1800. It would seem that the mine had not been the anticipated success for the letter states 'hoping to get the best price given the money spent'. Mr Cruso, Solicitor of Leek, was instructed to offer the mining lease and the freehold for sale at the beginning of May 1800. The freehold part consisted of Big Greeny Bank Dole and a further piece of ground known as Greeny Bank, the whole totalling nearly five acres.

In March 1801, the mine had not been sold and Mr William Edge of the Acre (near Mixon)

was enquiring if he could buy the Hill House Mine timber. The earliest reference to mining at the Acre is in 1836 and it is unclear if this indicates that the timber was needed for mining there. The same letter in 1801 (again to Messrs Cruso) enquires whether Edge's son-in-law, Sampson Gould of Cheddleton, near Leek, would be interested in taking the Doles, so the land had not been sold either. The following May, Gould offered £70 for the land and the timber on the property and 'in the old level'. There seems to have been agreement to this as the lease did not prevent the removal of timber from the mine. A building on the site seemed to have fallen in and almost all the timber removed from it. This does not seem to indicate that mining had recently ceased.

Royledge Mine

The parcels of land involved in the Hill House undertaking did not include the Royledge Farm land. This is known from the sale particulars of the latter dated 1858. The particulars include the names of the fields being sold and they are different from those listed in Appendices 1 to 4. This raises the speculation that the reason for this was that the mine was being worked and therefore the mining rights were not available to the Hill House adventurers.

The accounts of Cruso's, the Leek solicitors, indicate that Edward Forbes was seeking mining leases in North Staffordshire during 1835. One of these was for the Royledge mine. Forbes was the father-in-law of Melville Attwood who worked the Ecton Mine from 1839-1844. For further details of the activities of Forbes, see Chapter 7 re Ford and other mines.

A draft lease dated September 1836 survives between Forbes and John Lomas (who owned what is now known as the Stable Field, the site of the New York Engine Shaft) and George Salt, who lived at Royledge and owned the field immediately to the north of the Stable Field which contained the workings on the Royledge Adit. This relates to the mineral rights at Royledge. It was on the same terms and conditions as the terms negotiated for the mine at Ford and additionally with Sir Augustus Henniker for his mineral rights at Grindon.

It is known that Forbes was negotiating with Henniker as early as 10th August 1835 and there are indications that agreement for the Royledge mine had been reached at that date despite the actual lease being over a year later. This is because Forbes requested that the Royledge lease be regarded as a model for the others. Although the surviving Royledge lease is only in draft form, it must have been signed for there is correspondence later relating to a breach of covenant about a requirement to keep four men at work. The lease was for twenty-one years at a yearly rent of 5/- (25p) and a royalty of 10%.

It is known that the mine was being worked while a company was being floated to raise working capital. In September 1836, the Elkstones and Ryledge (sic) Mining Company was advertising shares for sale. The capital was £20,000 in 4,000 shares of £5 each. Later papers in the Kirkham/Porter Collection would seem to indicate that this attempt was unsuccessful. It was perhaps this lack of success, plus the lack of ore at Ford which caused Forbes to backpedal on his proposed activities at Grindon, although the Ecton Mine was more successful. In fact it is possible that Forbes had already pulled out from Royledge for John Cruso wrote to a Mr J Bassett on 1/8/1836 to say that Mr Badnall, Cruso's brother-in-law, had agreed to take the Elkstone's mines from Mr Forbes.

Problems with Gunpowder

Another reference to Royledge survives which confirms that there was some mining activity at Royledge in July 1836. It also shows well the attitude to work prevailing at that time. The reference is actually to Roylatch Mine, the name which was occasionally used for Royledge and was reported in the *Mining Journal* as a result of an accident at the mine on July 21st.

The keeper of the tollgate at Butterton Moor was apparently about to retire to bed when he realised that there might be two men at the mine who wouldn't have anyone to draw them up. Upon reaching the mine (it is no short walk, especially in the dark), he found that the men were already out of the mine and the toll keeper (also a miner at Royledge) decided to sharpen his tools in the smithy, as the fire was still lit. Unfortunately he left a trail of powder between the barrel and the fire which acted as a fuse and an explosion occurred which blew off the smithy roof and badly burnt the miner. The smithy was near to the Count House.

Incredibly, a similar accident happened in 1838 at the grocers at Hartington (the building with the arches at the front). A 2cwt barrel of gunpowder was kept in a rear shed to supply local miners with black powder. The shopkeeper's 33-year old son, John Harrison and the latter's son, Dick aged ten, were playing with a servant boy, Hugh Glenn, aged nineteen. Presumably at John Harrison's suggestion, they decided to have what they termed a 'fizz' with some loose powder which was scattered on the floor. Unfortunately, there was more powder than they realised. An explosion occurred and the roof of the building rose as high as the church tower. The three were killed and 4-5 tons of hay was scattered about (*Derbyshire Chronicle*, 4/8/1838).

Activities in the 1840's

It had been the intention of the new Company (if formed) in 1836 to lease both Hill House and Royledge together. It will be noted that there are still no references to New York Mine. However it seems that Mathew Lomas of New York Farm may have worked the mine himself, or perhaps part of it, for Ralph Twigg, who was born on 1816, started work at Ecton when he was eight and 'worked at Rilidge Mine for many years and it belonged to Mathew Lomas' (Dale Mine Deposition statement) (3).

In March 1841 a draft lease was drawn up to lease the Hill House Mine (still referred to as Hill House Field and Greenway (sic) Bank; clearly a clerical error). The lessor was Sampson Gould who had bought the land and rights in 1801. His address was Leek Wharf, on the Cauldon Canal, presumably where he had a business. The lessees were Anthony Marsden of Pickwood, Leek, Thomas Kniveton a silk manufacturer of Leek, John Redfern, farmer and miller of Wetton Mill in the Manifold Valley, plus two of Marsden's family: John Marsden of Llanfairbryn, Carmarthenshire, described as a farmer and miner and Johnathan Marsden of Silian, near Lampeter, in what was Cardiganshire, described as a gentleman and banker. Redfern was probably the last miller at Wetton Mill.

His family had been there for generations. He was born around 1786 and left the Mill in 1853.

The Marsdens had other mining interests, as may be guessed by John Marsden's description. A Johnathan Marsden was working the Llanfair mine from 1807, possibly earlier, for he claimed to have been at the mine for forty years, in 1831. This mine was one of the richest in silver-lead ore in the British Isles. The value of its silver was worth more than the lead. It is situated $3\frac{1}{2}$ miles east-north-east of Lampeter. They appear to have given up there interest here by 1840. Nearby was the Rhyscog Mine. This was under the ownership of A Marsden & Co from at least 1861-75. The Rhyscog Mining Company Ltd being set up in 1860 with a capital of £15,000 in £5 shares. The Annual Mineral Statistics do not list any production, so it is unclear if the mine was in fact being worked. Maybe it was like North Staffordshire ore field, where the Statistics sometimes had little bearing on reality (4).

The lease was for twenty-one years at 1/12th royalty. Four men were to be kept at work as a minimum and there was a payment of £200 per annum to be made for land covered with spoil, which seems rather steep. An interesting provision was that the partners did not have the power to speculate in the mines. This probably means that the Company was to be on the cost book principle but that the shareholders did not have the right to withdraw from the payment of a call for more funding as and when it was required.

A New Company is Formed

The draft was drawn up into a lease the following February, 1839. The first payment was to be made on 26/3/1840. The covenant to keep four men at work was amended to take effect after three years. The draft is endorsed

> 'since the date of this lease the royalty of lead and copper has been generally reduced to 1/15th and in some localities as low as 1/20th. I have been informed that at Mixon and on the Shrewsbury estate at Ribden and Thorswood, it is 1/15th'.

For some reason, the lease was entrusted to the care of the Rev John Sneyd of Basford Hall,

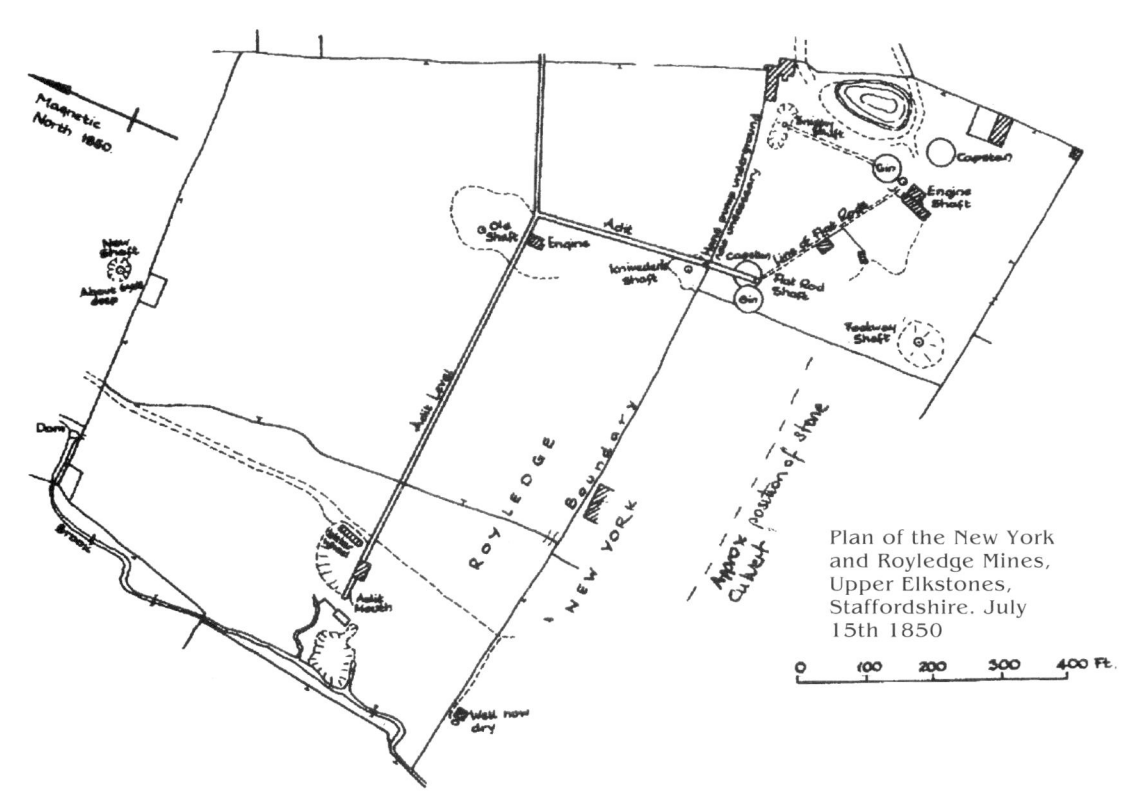

Plan of the New York and Royledge Mines, Upper Elkstones, Staffordshire. July 15th 1850

near Leek, on the undertaking that it would not be given up to either party. Sneyd was the owner of the Mixon Mine. The details of the lessors had changed from the original draft, however. They are stated as being Anthony Marsden, Kniveton, Thomas Boothman of Hardwick and Richard Gaunt of Leek, a silk manufacturer.

Boothman had considerable experience as a shareholder in mines. As early as 1824 he was working a mine under High Tor near Matlock. It was a venture described as 'brave and [equally] useless' (5). Shortly after his involvement in Royledge, he became a shareholder in the Alport and Magpie Mines and is quoted as owning the Bond Mine in Ireland (6). At the same time, he was a shareholder at Chapeldale and Hardrake, both of which failed by 1846 (7).

The latter mines were being worked by William Wyatt who had been appointed the agent at Mixon Mine in 1826. It is highly likely that it was Wyatt who introduced Boothman to the Royledge Mine. Most probably, he made little out of his association with this particular portfolio of investments.

Accounts for the Whiston smelter (8) record approximately 30 tons of ore being delivered from the Rylage (sic) Mining Co between January and June 1841 worth £260. The accounts were paid by Sneyd and Co to John Barrett and Thomas Alcock. The yield was quoted on one shipment as being $9\frac{1}{4}$% on one parcel and $6\frac{3}{8}$% on another. These are the only records noted in the Whiston accounts for the period 1831-1841.

By June 1844, Richard Gaunt had died. It is clear that he had invested in various local mines and it is likely that his interests were greater than is now known.

In 1832, he had taken shares in the Botstone Lead mine, near Wetton Mill together with a previously unrecorded mine at Bollands, Butterton. A note at the time of his death records that he had held shares in Butterton Mine and Hurst Low Mine on Grindon Moor (see Chapter 7). Bollands Hall is west of Butterton, but the mine in question is considered to be the one at Butterton Ford where a boy and three men lost their lives in 1844, but after the mine had been abandoned. The same note also records that he had held shares in Royledge and that it was 'working and Mr Gaunt owes about £100'.

Right: A barrow from the 1850s found in the upper level of Royledge Mine. On the spoil in the barrow is a 'timewaster', a tool for removing clay from boots

Below: Wind bores (air pipes) in the Royledge adit level

Some curious, indeed intriguing, correspondence also survives from this period in the hand of Thomas Boothman. It would appear that Gould, describes as 'Shylock' by Boothman, was trying to take advantage of the proprietors. He also wrote in October 1844:

> 'I ordered Kniveton to get all the rails out of the tunnel and weigh the wrought iron separate from the cast iron and take them to Ryledge (sic). There is some cast iron rails laid down at Mixon intended to be taken to Hill House, these also should be taken there. Would it not be the best to send for Kniveton and engage him to procure a cart and attend it at the loading to count and weigh the rails and lay them down at Royledge' (9).

It is believed that the rails from Hill House are still in Royledge adit.

In February 1846, John Cruso was writing to the solicitor representing Richard Gaunt's executors. George Salt of Royledge Farm was wanting to know what they were going to do about the lease of his mine Gaunt had entered into. He was clearly expecting them to honour the agreement. This would appear to concern the arrangement to keep four men at work at the mine. This was not happening and the executors were in breach of contract. There was also a comment that there was a liability to pay trespass for the time that the mine had been 'open and unworked'.

At some time probably during this period of working, a water wheel was erected for crushing purposes. It is possible that one of the two water wheels at Mixon was sold after the machinery there was advertised for sale in 1834 and that it was brought here.

Williams and the New York Venture

Some agreement must have been reached for the next lease was agreed in 1849 when the lessee was John Williams. He had come north from Lower Town, Gwennap, Cornwall and seems to have initially gone to the Ecton Mine. One wonders what sort of individual he was for the evidence points to a confrontational nature. See Chapter 3.5 for details on his time at Ecton.

Williams took out the Royledge lease, but it is clear that it was for only part of the set with the intention of trying to prove the mine at depth. The rest of the mine was still being worked by Marsden, Kniveton and others. Shortly afterwards, he sublet the lease to the New York Mining Co, being retained as manager and with Niness as the agent. The latter moved in 1850 to New York Farm and remained there until around 1854/55. (See Chapter 10 for further detail on Niness and his other activities). The farm at this period formed two separate dwellings with Mathew Lomas living in the other part.

Nearly all of the previous workings at the mine had been above river level. Two distinct lots of veins exist (near the New York Shaft and east of the Royledge Adit entrance) and these had been worked but probably separately from each other. The adit by and large ran straight into the hillside heading in an easterly direction. It clearly was not the main way in for the men or for the extraction of the ore, as has been seen by the reference to the tollkeeper thinking that the two men in the mine had to be 'drawn' out of it and the number of shafts that exist in quite a small area. The Ecton and Mixon mines were worked to quite a substantial depth and it was not unreasonable to suggest that this mine ought to be 'proved at depth'.

It was a reasonable speculation and indeed, it strikes one that it might remain so to this day. The New York Mine therefore was a section of the Royledge Mine which existed for about five or six years only. No ore returns are known although when the engine was offered for sale, a quantity of copper ore was included. It seems that the life of the venture was in the sinking of the 300ft shaft and the connection of their workings with the adit for the purposes of drainage of the New York workings. These had previously been drained by barrel haulage up the shaft(s) and then disposed. A covered launder from the mine to the brook exists to the south of New York Farm and this was possibly for this earlier drainage. See the discussion on this below regarding the possible use of mine water for the Royledge waterwheel. Williams reached agreement with the Royledge Mine proprietors in March 1849 concerning the drainage of their mine.

The New York Mining Co/ Royledge Mining Co Litigation

Shortly after subletting the mines, the New York Mining Company on March 16 1849 entered into an agreement with the adjacent Royledge Mining Company. The agreement concerned the use, by Royledge, of the New York engine, but it was very loosely worded and the short life of the New York Mining Company was noted more for its litigation than its ore output.

The relevant part of the agreement, as quoted in the *Mining Journal*, 1851, was:

> 'The said Anthony Marsden, Thomas Kniveton (a silk manufacturer from Leek) and William Tellwright, [This is the first reference to this person and other detail is unknown] do hereby for themselves and each for himself severally, agree to pay to the said John Williams half of the working cost of the engine erected by the said New York proprietors at their expense at Upper Elkstone, for the purpose of draining the said New York Mine of the water – such payment to be made every month, and to commence from the time the water begins to be drawn off from the said Rilage Mine by the said engine and to continue as long as the water is being drawn off from the said Rilage Mine by the said engine; and the said Anthony Marsden, Thomas Kniveton and William Tellwright agree to make such payments, in consideration of being allowed the use and benefit of the said engine'.

The 'said engine' referred to was a 40-inch cylinder Cornish engine, with a 9ft stroke in the cylinder and 7ft stroke in the shaft, costing £2,600, erected at New York Engine Shaft. A further shaft was sunk close to the boundary with Royledge and was fitted with pumps for draining both mines. The shaft was known as the Flat Rod Shaft and a line of flat rods extended from there to the engine. Both the shaft and engine were completed by August 1849, the Flat Rod Shaft being sunk to a total depth of 45ft below the Royledge adit level. The litigation plan shows the line of flat rods on the surface. This would seem to indicate that there was no connection between these shafts at adit level (at least initially, although one is shown on a plan of 1850) and therefore no drainage to the Royledge adit from the New York Engine Shaft, which was sunk to a depth of 200ft or so below adit.

A level was driven some 50 fathoms from the boundary, i.e. north of the Flat Rod Shaft and united with the existing Royledge adit level; water from the shaft was pumped up to this level and allowed to find its own way down the adit. The new level was probably financed by the New York Company who also paid for launders in the new level where the ground had been stoped out previously. In addition, a level was driven from the Flat Road Shaft some 7 fathoms below the adit to the boundary which effectively drained both mines to that depth. No launders were laid in the part of the adit north of the boundary, so these must have been laid below the Stable Field.

Fortunately, the litigation of 1851 focussed attention on the two mines and descriptions of both mines appeared in the *Mining Journal*. It should be appreciated however that there is no means of checking the accuracy of either report. The first report was of the Royledge Mine (*Mining Journal*, 1851, p63) and was given by a Cornish miner-cum-shareholder, one William Williams, who was visiting the area in January 1851, as part of his 'Grand Tour'.

Royledge in 1851

Williams walked up the Royledge adit level with Capt Kniveton (the mine manager may well be a different person to the mine shareholder, Thomas Kniveton. Moreover, one of the mine shafts is Knivedon's Shaft and there is a Knivedon's Lane in Leek, one wonders whether the reference to this shaft should read Kniveton's Shaft. Williams found four men at work. The adit was generally 15 fathoms below the surface and he stated that the lode was 30-40ft wide. He continued:

> 'they are now working on this lode, in which there is copper of every colour, and of high produce – all of it carbonate down to the adit under which, as far as is known, is sulphate of copper. [copper sulphide is presumably meant here, although very little has been

5 The Mines of the Upper Elkstones Area

The Count House in 1972. The water was impounded for the New York engine house boiler

found above the adit, so Williams would appear to have been right].

This mine has been worked by this company about two years, and never by more than four men at anytime underground. It appears they have sold some few hundred tons of ore in this short time, got by the four men only and from my judgement – they have now upwards of 130 tons at grass. This monstrous lode, and three others, forms a junction about the middle of their sett. At this point they commenced sinking an engine shaft more than twelve months ago, but from the quantity of water coming in they were obliged to stop.'

The shaft referred to is believed to be Kniveton's Shaft.

The Royledge Company had initially approached John Williams about a possible engine agreement and probably it was as a result of their water problems with this shaft. Presumably Marsden and Kniveton had found a new investor, Tellwright, and restarted work at Royledge. Williams said it was two years since they had started work, i.e. about 1849, when the New York had been started too.

The New York report followed shortly afterwards in April 1851 (*Mining Journal*, p159) and was written under a nom-de-plume. There were four different lodes, three of which were to the west of the engine shaft and the other to the east of the shaft. They appear to have been inclined at different angles at the engine shaft but further details regarding orientation are not given:

No.1 Lode is described as 'being upwards of 50ft wide, producing fine green and blue carbonates, red oxide and yellow sulphuret of copper, yielding large and valuable quantities at the present level. Nos 2 and 3 lodes are from 2-4ft wide of similar character.

No 4 lode, east of the engine shaft is a very strong and kindly one, but is little worked as yet – the operations being more confined to the west of the engine shaft.'

The latter was said to be 26 fathoms below the adit level and 19 fathoms below all other workings. In August 1853 the shaft was 52 fathoms deep and 34 fathoms below the adit level. (*Mining Journal*, 1853, p550).

The Litigation

The remaining histories of Royledge and New York are so intertwined around their litigation that it is convenient to treat the known history from 1849-1851 as it was made known at the Court hearings and appeared in the subsequent case reports.

The First Case

The initial cause of complaint between the two mines is not known – perhaps some petty jealousy or something similar. It appears that the main dispute, brought by New York, was in retaliation for an earlier dispute brought by Royledge (*Mining Journal*, 1851, p564). The first case alleged that in May 1850 the New York Company had 'entered the boundary of the former [Royledge] and in the face of notice, had taken ore to the value of £100' (*Mining Journal*, January 18, p33).

> 'To save expenses, the matter in dispute was referred to the arbitration of Messrs Thomas Maddock of Hanley, Staffs., mining surveyor; and Mr George Knox of Fenton, Staffs., mining agent, who appointed Mr Thomas Hall of Castleton., Derbys., mining surveyor, as umpire.'

The arbitration meetings were held on the 7th and 14th November 1850, when Royledge submitted that ore to the value of £80-£100 had been taken, the average value of copper from Royledge being £8-£18 per ton deducting therefrom return charges. In response, New York submitted that the wall on the surface did not constitute the underground as well as the surface boundary and that no trespass had been committed. They did concede that they had gone 2ft over the line of the wall on the surface which indicates how trivial the matter really was.

It was also contended by New York that the ore taken out was not worth more than £10. In support of this, New York produced witnesses who swore that

> 'none of the copper from New York was worth more than £6 p.ton out of which return charges must be deducted and one witness swore that none of the copper ... was worth more than £5 p.ton [less return charges] and when pressed as to the amount of those charges, stated them to be £5. 2s. p.ton. The evidence of this witness was strongly commented on'.

So much for the evidence of an expert witness! The case was awarded to Royledge with damages of £40 plus costs. (The *Mining Journal* of 1851, pp559 & 564 stated that damages were £80 not £40.

The Second Case

It was in retaliation for this action that New York brought the more important case of *Williams versus Marsden* and others, 1851. It will be recalled that, as outlined above, the Royledge Company had agreed to pay half the working cost of an engine to be erected at the New York Mine at the latter's expense. The payment was to commence when the water began to be drawn off from Royledge and to continue so long as it was being drawn off. The engine commenced working in August 1849 and started draining Royledge in November of that year.

The engine was worked for fifteen months until February 1851 and the working cost was £619, half of which was claimed by New York. For the latter it was submitted that the level at the bottom of the Flat Rod Shaft had effectively drained several old sumps and a stope of ore in Royledge mine (*Mining Journal*, 1851, p153).

In response, it was submitted by Royledge that the erection of the engine had been of no benefit for

> 'the drainage of the mine was sufficiently accomplished by the works which the defendants themselves had carried out' (*Staffs Advertiser*, 15/3/1851, p5).

Moreover, the Royledge miners tried to claim that as they were working above the adit, they had no need of the engine. [It is believed that they were probably working close to the surface under Royledge Meadow as an exceptionally well preserved barrow, or trundle as it was known locally, is in this area and must have been in the last area worked for it still awaits emptying].

Further, the defendants made two technical objections on legal issues: (a) that the action should have been in the names of all the shareholders and not Williams' alone, and (b) that the agreement referred to the engine as being then erected when in actual fact it wasn't. Consequently there was a variance between the statement in the agreement and that proved at the hearing. Both these objections were over-ruled with a right of appeal to the Court of Exchequer at Westminster – a right which was exercised (see below). The case was found for New York and the £309 damages were awarded. Once again the inconsistency of the several defences was commented upon rather severely – this time against Royledge witnesses!

As might be expected some of the shareholders saw the red light and one hundred Royledge shares were advertised for sale in the *Mining Journal* both in April and June 1851 by James Crofts, a sharebroker of London who had connections with Ecton and numerous other mines. Also in June 1851, 124/1,000ths shares in Royledge were advertised for sale by Mr Bell Williams land agent of Liverpool. A 15% return over the first year's outlay was guaranteed with 'a reasonable prospect of realising 30% the second year.' The shares were available at £12 each and it was stated that the lode was 20 yards wide and that one miner could cut 1-1.5 tons of copper ore per week; 130 tons of ore were supposedly lying on the bank, [presumably quoting William Williams].

The Appeal

In May 1851, the case of *Williams versus Marsden* was heard at Westminster where the Royledge Company moved that the decision be set aside upon several technical grounds, including the two mentioned above. However, the case was dismissed to the benefit of New York. The hearing had, however attracted the attention of the *Mining Journal* and was featured in an editorial comment in order to warn share holders of the dangers inherent in mine speculation (*Mining Journal*, 1851, p564). It was considered that Royledge would be liable, because the agreement had been so loosely worded, to pay one half of the engine costs as long as the New York Mine continued to be worked, even though Royledge might be abandoned. Damages and costs were stated to be at least £1,000-£2,100 plus the monthly cost of 50% of the engine costs from February 1851.

The Third Case

This was not, however, the last litigation involving New York, for in August 1851 a further case was heard at Stafford – *Unwin versus Roberts* (*Mining Journal*, 1851, p372). In this action the plaintiffs were iron and steel merchants of Sheffield and were endeavouring to recover £61 for materials supplied to the mine. The defendant held forty shares and had a position at the mine for he signed the account books. In September l849 he had also moved a resolution to order a call on shares to wipe off a deficit of £576 which had been incurred. The defendant claimed that the shareholders were not liable for goods which the manager [Williams] had obtained on his own credit, even though they were for use by the mine. As the Company had been formed on the cost book and not limited liability principle, he lost his case. Once again editorial comments appeared in the *Mining Journal* in the interests of 'honest adventurers'.

The irony of all these cases is that although Williams was a central figure he had no longer anything to do with the mine, having forfeited his shares for non-payment of a call at some unspecified time previously.

Subsequent Events

Not a great deal is known of the two mines following the period of litigation. At the end of 1851, Royledge was working primarily above the adit 'producing some good stones of copper' whilst New York was 'in full operation' and driving a deep level from the bottom of the engine shaft (*Mining Journal*, 1851, December 20th, p612).

The End Of New York

Early in 1853, New York was described as having had an end worth £20 per fathom (*Mining Journal*, p18) but that year, the plant was advertised for sale on October 3rd 1853 – see Appendix 5.

5 The Mines of the Upper Elkstones Area

The particulars of sale indicated that the Company had wound up because of a further disagreement – this time between the shareholders. The Royledge Company was still paying half the cost of the engine – amounting to £240 per annum. Presumably the plant remained unsold, for 12 months later a further advert appeared (*Mining Journal*, 1854, Sept 30th, p658) and although the site of the plant wasn't stated, the details tie in with the 1853 advert.

Around 1855, the mine lease was taken over by the proprietors of the Dale Mine and then in 1857, by the recently formed Dale Lead Mining Company Ltd, where Niness was also the agent. The original Dale proprietors bought the engine for £1,500 but only paid £500 towards this cost. After considerable dissatisfaction amongst the Dale Mining Company shareholders the engine was purchased for the outstanding £1,000 in March 1859. At a general meeting of the Company on 30th June 1860, it was agreed to surrender the New York Mine lease and the mine area resorted to agricultural use for good. The mine was pumped out for one final time prior to the removal of the pitwork to the Dale Mine (see Chapter 4 for further details on the engine while at the Dale Mine).

Royledge appears to have survived a little longer as far as mining operations are concerned. In 1855, the mine was reported to have been set to work again and to have a parcel of ores at grass. (*Mining Journal*, 1855, Dec 29th, p838). Presumably this was a small operation for in 1858 the mine was advertised to let. (*Mining Journal*, 1858, November 20th, p776). It is described as having been worked by the Royledge Mining Co but then being worked by Mr George Salt the proprietor. Salt was not the tenant of the estate which extended to 840 acres. When Royledge farm was offered for sale in 1862 on the death of George Salt, the mine appears to have become idle for the final time (*Mining Journal*,1862, June 7th p390).

In 1865, a Report was commissioned on Hill House Mine from Jacob Higson, a Mining Engineer of 94, Cross Street, Manchester. It seems to have been for a client of Challinors, Solicitors, Leek, but nothing seems to have happened as a result of it. It states that:

'trials have been made within a recent period to discover the existence of certain Metallic Lodes which had been previously worked upon by means of the old shafts...'.

He suggested the adit level be extended to the shaft on the southern boundary of the property to intersect the vein, if it existed, upon which the shaft had been sunk.

Although probably coincidence, it is known that Ecton's Salts Level was driven by two Salt brothers and it is held locally that they made sufficient out of the work to buy a farm each. Royledge and Fleet Green Farm both have a copper mine beneath them and both have been in a Salt family.

Rottenstone Bank
Just to the north of Royledge Farm is Stone Bank. Until around 1970, this dwelling was known as Rottenstone Bank. Rottenstone is a decomposed limestone used in polishing stone, because of its mildly abrasive nature. It was used at Wetton Quarry, where a highly fossiliferous crinoidal limestone was in demand. In 1858, the total British output was 270 tons. Seventy tons of this came from Derbyshire and the rest from Carmarthenshire and Breconshire (*Mining Journal*, 1858, p706). The site of the deposit in the Upper Hamps Valley is not clear, but there are surface workings to the north of Highmoor Farm, in a field known as the Pitty Field. This may be the site and it is within view of Rottenstone Bank. The house deserves to revert to the legacy of its unusual name. However Mr Tom Buxton of Royledge advises that the original dwelling with this name is now a ruin and was situated a little further to the north.

Access
It should be noted that access to Royledge mine is not available.

The Surface Features
The area around the adit entrance has been levelled using ground rock from the crusher. This has obliterated all signs of activity although a level piece of ground above the entrance probably marks the site of the wheel and the building into which the ore was received and possibly where the head of stamps worked by the wheel was located. An incline exists underground to connect the adit

with this building. This field is part of a SSSI having never been treated with artificial fertilisers.

The shafts have all been backfilled, although the tip to the most southerly shaft remains as a token reminder of previous mining activity. The shaft collar to the New York Engine Shaft has collapsed, creating a large cone, but the reservoir still survives. The Count House, has been virtually demolished. A distinct channel runs north from the Count House in a northerly direction. This has been the source of much debate about its function. It is thought to have been the source of the water supply for the wheel. It runs to the rear of Royledge farm and was probably augmented by spare domestic spring water. There appears to be some evidence that it might have been dammed. This does not answer the query of what happened after the water from the New York mines was turned down the new cross cut after 1849. The water joined another small spring at the back of the farm and then was led through a launder to the wheel. There could well have been sufficient water from the surface springs to turn the wheel without the New York Mine water.

What is clear is that the dam marked on the litigation plan did not serve the wheel, the latter was higher up the hillside to take advantage of this. The stream was probably used for buddling, i.e. separating the finely ground copper ore from the ground rock.

A lime kiln exists near to the top of the farm drive. It was built by the grandfather of Mr Tom Buxton, the current owner. Limestone was brought by horse and cart from the Ecton Mine and from Brown End Quarry at Waterhouses. When fetched from Ecton, half a load was brought to a point west of Warslow, unloaded and a further half of a load fetched. The first half was then reloaded, it being too much for the horse to pull a full load out of the valley. This practice must have had implications for the shipment of ore from the mines in the area.

Elkstones Brook

A ten fathom long trial exists by the Elkstones Brook. The same steam is known as the Warslow Brook below the village of Upper Elkstones. It is situated between Hob Hay and Herbage Barn on the north side of the stream. It is driven on a fault, with vertical beds on the left side of the passage and thin-bedded limestones cut through on the right hand side. There is no evidence of shot holes and one wonders if it was driven during the late 18th Century activity in the area. No documentary evidence for the trial has been located. However it is likely that it dates from the beginning of the 19th Century and was driven by the Dale Mine Company, for they took a lease of the mineral rights under the Harpur lands in the area. It is now known as Grindey's Hole.

Fleet Green Mine, Fawfieldhead

North east of Royledge is an area of moor which drains eastwards towards the Manifold Valley. At the southern end of the moor and to the north of the Leek-Warslow Road is an area known as Fleet Green and several workings exist here. The earliest mining reference is in 1717, when John Harpur of Warslow Hall licensed three Derbyshire miners to dig in Warslow and at Fleet Green. The term was for eleven years (an unusual length of term, was this the unexpired portion of a twenty-one year term?) and the royalty was 1/7th of the lead ore, which was not generous by local standards (10). The area of Fawfieldhead was included in the lease to the Dale Mine Company in 1800 from Sir Henry Harpur, so the mine may have been reworked shortly after then.

The only other historical data which has come to light is contained in the Whiston Smelter account books of W Sneyd and Co, In 1836, 1838, and 1839, small quantities of copper ore were purchased from John M Verga of the Fleet Green Mine Co. The total amount of ore was only 27 tons, worth £132. This is the only known reference to this person in the ore field.

The more northerly group of workings consist of two depressions, a pool of water and an adit entrance open twenty to thirty years ago and currently lost. This was used to store eggs in the entrance. They were kept for winter use in a bath of ising glass. A trial was driven underneath Upper Fleet Green Farmhouse from the river. It is about $27\frac{1}{2}$ fathoms long and was driven on an anticlinal formation, trending north on a thin lead scrin, or vein. To the south west of the farm are a series of filled in shafts which trend north-south. These are unwatered by a long sough with an entrance $\frac{1}{3}$ of a mile downstream from the farm. The sole, or floor, is below river level and was drained by an egress leat down the side of the river, thereby giving

5 The Mines of the Upper Elkstones Area

maximum drainage. The level has a bearing of north-west for 28½ fathoms to a shaft. This has been back filled, but walls were built before hand and long stone lintels laid across to keep the level open. At this point, the sough turns acutely south-west under the river.

Blacton Moor
A shaft exists a little to the east of Hoarstones, close to the old road to Warslow which ran due north from Brownlow Bridge. It has not been inspected but may be another trial put down by the Dale Mine Company, which commenced operations in 1800.

Appendix 1
The land included in the purchase of the Elkstones estate of John Crewe in 1778 was: Ryecroft Tenement (the farmhouse of Joseph Grindey), plus the parcels of land known as The Ryecroft; The Banks; The Hays; The Moor; The Further Tenement; The Nearer Tenement; The New Park; The Thowplexse; The Long Dole; The Broad Acre; The Orford Dole; The Head Dole; The two Further Doles; Plus in the possession of Joseph Grindey as tenant: The Old House Tenement plus land known as The Big Field; Broadlands; The Middle Field; The Little Broad Acre; The Harry Meadow; The Greeny Bank Dole; The Breach Acre Dole; The Orfold Dole; The Hollow Field Dole; The Calf Croft; Ditch Dole; The Calf Croft Dole; The Dirty Dole; The Big Dole in Lower Meadow; The Little Dole in Lower Meadow; The Head Dole in two parts; The Bamstyd Dole and the New Close Dole. Another undated draft document reserves to Whillock et al the right to extract up to 25 yards of limestone per annum and remove it by a road over Big Greeny Bank Dole to a limekiln. This must be at a different date, as the tenant of Ryecroft Tenement is stated to be Joseph Robins, not J Grindey as above.

Appendix 2
Land referred to in the mineral lease of 18/4/1778: The Hillhouse Field; the Grove Field; the Great Hole Peahes; the Fold Yard; the Meadows; the Pikelows; the Calf Croft; the Dole and the two Pikelow Doles.

Appendix 3
Land referred to in the lease of 1781: Bridge Field Meadow; Barn Field; Hollow Field; Long Doles; Little Field; Cricklestone; The Meadow below Wall Acre; Wall Acre; Greeny Hay Bank; Pike Low; Breach Acre; New Parks; Bean Acre. The total acreage was in excess of 68 acres. The land was tenanted by Benjamin Brindley.

Appendix 4
Land referrred to in the lease of 1782: Hillside; The Coat Close; The Old Croft; The Chappel Yard; The Salt Croft: The Back Side; The Puddle Hill; The Ash flat end; The Furlong; the New Close; and the New Intake all in the tenancy of Moses Gould.

Appendix 5
Extract from advert in the *Mining Journal*, August, 1853, p550

> 'NEW YORK COPPER MINE — TO BE SOLD, BY PUBLIC AUCTION, on the 3rd October.
>
> One 40-in. cylinder engine, 9ft stroke in the cylinder and 7ft in the shaft; a tubular boiler about 10 tons, 18 fms. of 10-in. plunger lift. Complete; 24 fms of 12-in. bottom and 14-in pumps; 10 fms of 7-in bottom and 8-in pumps; 10 fms of 5-in bottom and pumps; 7.5 fms of 9-in. bottom and 10-in pumps; 7.5 fms of 4-in. bottom and 5-in. pumps, with buckets, rods, prongs, seatings and valves, complete; 80 fms of wood rods, with plates, catches, staples, glands etc; two balance-bobs, two capstans, and two shears, complete; 100 fms of 11-in capstan rope; 10 fms of 6-in. whim rope; 50 fms of chain and two horse whims, with kibbles, shaft tackles and pullies; 50 fms of casing and dividings; 70 fms of ladders; miners tools and boxes; 40-in smiths bellows, anvil, vice, tools etc; a crusher that is worked by the engine, dressing tools and several tons of copper ore now on the floors ready for Market...'.

Although several offers were made, it was brought in for £2,500 (*Mining Journal*, 1853, November 8th, p633). The engine was later sold

The huge lintels which support the shaft debris in Fleet Green Mine Level, where the level turns south-west

to the Dale Mine for £1500. This means that either some one denied the shareholders £1,000 or the bidding was fixed. There are no known complaints about the loss of the £1,000, so perhaps one can draw one's own conclusions.

References

1. The leases from the late 18th Century up to the 1830s are held in the Kirkham /Porter Collection

2. Saunders, E, *Joseph Pickford of Derby*, 1993, p33

3. See Chapter 4; these are the statements made by miners in the Roscoe lawcase

4. Hall G. W, 1971, Metal Mines of Southern Wales, pp66 & 70

5. Warriner D, et al, *Ringing Rake and Masson Soughs etc*, 1981, Bull PDMHS, Vol 8, No 2, p93 (see also p91)

6. Willies L, *John Taylor in Derbyshire*, 1839-1851, 1977, Bull PDMHS, Vol 6, No 5, pp225, 227, 230

7. Willies L, *The Barker Family and Wyatt Lead Mining Businesses, 1730-1875*, 1983, Bull PDMHS, Vol 8, No 6, pp361, 363, 367 and *John Taylor in Derbyshire 1839-1851*, Bull PDMHS, Vol 6, No 5, p225

8. W. Sneyd & Co, 1831-1841 Accounts, C.L.M. Porter Collection

9. Kirkham /Porter Collection

10. Derbyshire Record Office D23757/7/190/2

Acknowledgements

The co-operation of Mr Tom Buxton is particularly recognised with thanks by the Royledge team, for his unstinting assistance and generous hospitality. Without his help and enthusiasm, the Royledge exploration project would never have been started. On two occasions, he even took the Wellingtons off his feet when one of the team forgot their own. Thanks too to Dave Williams for researching names on his wonderful database.

6 Mixon Mines

Near Onecote, $3\frac{1}{2}$ miles due west of the Ecton Copper Mines lies a small Carboniferous Limestone inlier which has scattered over it a number of copper and lead mines, the most important being at Mixon.

Layout of the Mixon Mine

It lies on the west bank of the upper Hamps (a tributary of the Manifold) at Mixon Mines Farm. Here exists a complex of waste tips, shafts, shaft mounds and buildings but unfortunately it is difficult to locate the position of the main features of the mine. Early in the l9th Century the mine was drained by two 40ft diameter by 4ft wide waterwheels together with a Boulton and Watt type steam engine (i.e. a low-pressure condensing engine, though unlikely to have been made by that firm, unless it was second-hand). The water supply for the wheels came from three dams, two built across the River Hamps and one across a small tributary.

The upper two dams were feeders for the main dam 1,500ft north of the mine. The supply for this dam ran along a leat, parallel to and approximately 20ft above the Hamps and then in wooden launders to the wheels. Although all the dams may still be clearly seen (one now in use for breeding fish) as can the leat, the ground at the mine was so disturbed by later mining and removal of the tips that it is impossible to locate, even approximately, the position of the waterwheels. Similarly the site of the early steam engine cannot be determined, but would probably be on the site of the later Cornish engine. Prior to the erection of these machines the mine was drained by a short, shallow adit driven in shale from a point 1,500ft downstream from the mine. The collapsed entrance to this adit can be seen issuing water as well as six shaft mounds marking its course.

Although this adit only drained the mine by about 15 fathoms it served as a pumpway for the water from the wheel pumps and the steam engine pumps, as well as from the later, large Cornish engine. The approximate position of the latter can only be judged by the quantities of ash in the tips from the boilers. In the 1850s, in addition to two engine houses and two boiler houses (one set for the Cornish engine, the other for the steam whim) there were coal yards, a capstan, saw pit, smithy, carpenters' shop, timber house, stables and cottages for the miners. None of these can now be identified, although some may have been incorporated into the present farm buildings.

The only open shaft descends to water at river level and is probably that known as South Shaft. Another shaft, close to the farm, has just a few feet of stonework or ginging visible and is possibly the Smithy Shaft. Since the only plan of the mine available is rather inaccurate the other shaft mounds and features cannot be named with certainty. The large quantities of finely crushed material on the northern part of the site mark the position of the dressing floors, but the tramway from there to the Engine Shaft cannot be traced. Garner in 1844 erroneously referred to a smelting works at Mixon, probably meaning the dressing plant, since all the evidence indicates that the ore was sent to Whiston near Froghall (SK 041472) for smelting.

A further feature of the Mixon site is a number of springs rising from the shale and sinking after a short distance. In particular a considerable stream sinks into an opening which has been explored by cavers. A low horizontal passage proceeds in a northerly direction for 100-150ft in steeply dipping beds before descending steeply to almost below the entrance. The stream disappears in a mud choke which is thought to be removable. South Shaft has been descended to water at about 100ft with two levels branching off, one being at water level which could have been the adit. (These notes were provided by Mr J S Davis).

Unfortunately the passages explored cannot be related to any parts of the mine mentioned in the documents. Also a large water filled hollow is fed by a stream which apparently rises again at the base of the mine tips near the river. Mr G W Cartledge of Mixon Mines Farm stated that the powder house was situated in the far corner of the field to the south of the mine, now known as Powder Cote Meadow.

Early History

Although Plot (1) referred to mining at Upper Elkstones in the 1660, this would not have related to Mixon; this area is not associated with that parish and it is now thought that Plot was referring to either Hill House or Royledge Mines.

The first specific reference to Mixon ocurred in 1730 when the mine was leased to Robert Bill of Farley Hall, Alton, and Thomas Gilbert of Cotton, from Ann Besvile of Eccleshall, all in Staffordshire, for twenty-one years. They were allowed the usual mining rights for sinking pits and driving soughs, for which they were to pay 1/7th of the ore raised, but the success of these operations is not known (2). The Bill family were partners in the Cheadle Copper and Brass Company and had interests in other North Staffordshire mines. Gilbert also worked other North Staffordshire mines and smelting mills. The Bill and Gilbert families were neighbours as well as being connected by business and marriage.

In 1770 John Sneyd (1734-1809) of Belmont, near Ipstones, bought the Onecote estate including a farm at Mixon which had belonged to a William Ratcliffe, Gent, of Onecote. Ratcliffe had died about this time and the property at Mixon had been bequeathed to his eldest son, also named William, who presumably sold to John Sneyd (3). The Sneyds were a very large and influential Staffordshire family, owning many collieries and works. John Sneyd was one of the instigators of the Trent and Mersey Canal; he built Belmont Hall and was noted for his treeplanting, which provided much timber for the North Staffordshire collieries and packing cases for the Potteries.

In 1775 a noger, or boring bar, weighing 33lb was lent to 'sneads Mine' from Ecton (4) and this almost certainly refers to the Mixon Mine. The references to Mixon at this time are very few, so that it is impossible to give any sort of picture of the operations there. Aitken in 1795 (5) stated that a copper mine existed at Mixon, while William Pitt writing a year later (6) said that Mixon belonged to Mr Sneyd of Belmont. It had been worked for twenty-one years, producing plenty of good copper although there was unfortunately a mixture of lead in one of the best veins.

In 1779 Robert Shore of Snitterton, Derbyshire, had owned a 5/24th share in the Mixon Mine for seven or five years with the comment 'has got nothing' (7). Shore had been the Duke of Devonshire's agent at the Ecton Mine from 1760 to 1779, when he was dismissed for the embezzlement of £5,000 after having previously made an 'error' of £1,000. In 1780 John Barker of the Derbyshire, mining and smelting concern of Barker and Wilkinson wrote to Shore, who had understandably moved out of the area, possibly to Wales where he had lead mining interests, regarding the affairs at Mixon. Apparently William Ratcliffe (obviously the son) was in charge of trials for copper at Mixon, and Barker was not satisfied that Ratcliffe (who had asked for a further £200) was spending the correct amount of money on the mine (8). It was said that large quantities of copper ore were raised during this period, but all from above the adit level (9).

In August 1797, the Cheadle Brass Wire Company made enquiries regarding a 1/16th share in the mine which was being offered for sale. They were to purchase this share if it was offered at a modest price, but there are no further details of the proposal (10).

In 1814, a Mary Billings of Butterton alleged that Thomas Marsden, miner, of Mixon was the father of her child. He had moved to Macclesfield but was served with a warrant for maintenance. There were rumours of expansion at Mixon in 1815 'which would want 200 men' by Lord Gore, Mast Beech Sneyd and Seuspir Sneyd (10a). This may have been true, for in the second decade of the 19th Century, a rich strike of copper seems to have been made at Mixon for in 1817, the Cheadle Company approved a proposal to smelt the Mixon ore.

The quantity involved was such that if the deal was approved then they would extend their Cheadle copper works by building a further smelting furnace and calciner. It seems

Mixon Copper Mine

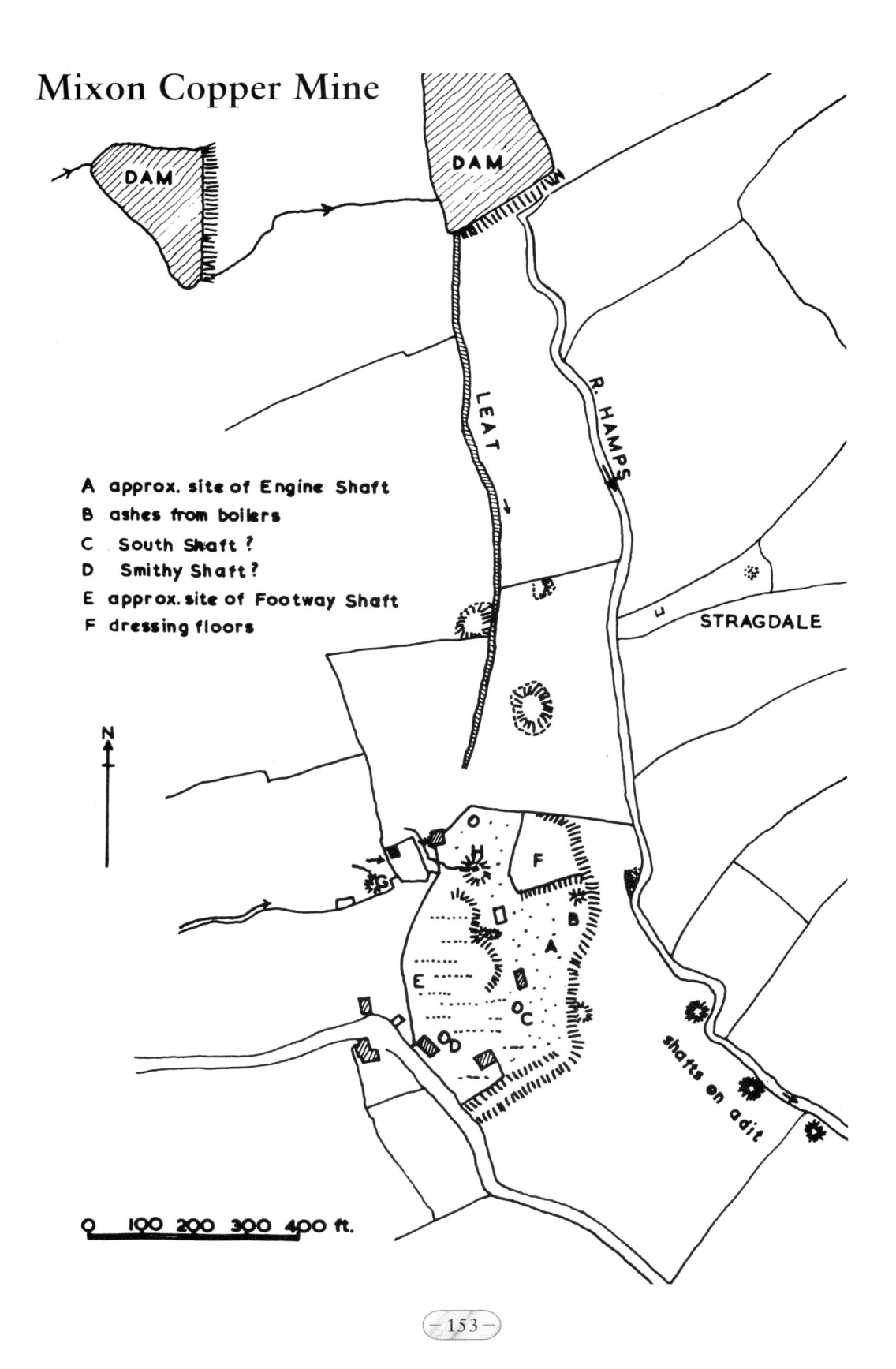

A approx. site of Engine Shaft
B ashes from boilers
C South Shaft ?
D Smithy Shaft ?
E approx. site of Footway Shaft
F dressing floors

0 100 200 300 400 ft.

unlikey that the Cheadle Company did smelt the ore for in the same year, the Sneyds bought the Whiston Smelter from the Duke of Devonshire. However, in 1817, Pitt (11) stated that part of the copper for the Cheadle works came from Mixon.

Farey (12), who visited the area in 1807, included Mixon in his list of mines. In a list of copper ores sold at Swansea from 1819-56 (the world's largest copper smelting area at that time) 359 tons of ore worth £3221 are stated to have come from Mixon Mine in 1819-20, (13). This produced 33 tons of metal equivalent to 9% copper in the ore. About this time an offer was made to the Ecton Mine manager to take over the Mixon Mine, but evidently this was not taken up. It was stated that

> 'This Mine has since increased very greatly in the richness of its works but from the way which it is managed it probably affords but little profit to the proprietors' (14).

Perhaps this is the first hint of the management problems which were to beset the mine.

Expansion by the Sneyds

In 1824 the mine was reported as closed (15), but shortly afterwards it was again being worked by three of John Sneyd's sons, William Sneyd, Clement Sneyd and Thomas Sneyd-Kynnersley. Thomas (1774-1844) seems to have played a more direct role in the Mixon Mine than his brothers, and had inherited the Loxley estate near Uttoxeter in 1815 as well as the name from his uncle, Clement Kynnersley. The Sneyd brothers were also partners in the Whiston Copper Works. The Whiston works were finally sold in 1846 to James Keys of the Cheadle Brassworks who had managed the works for the Sneyds since 1828. It is from this period in the mine's history that a fairly complete picture of the operations at Mixon can be pieced together from the papers and correspondence of William Wyatt (16 & 8).

Early in 1825 Thomas Sneyd-Kynnersley approached Benjamin Wyatt, the Derbyshire mining agent of Foolow, Derbyshire, for assistance and advice in the running of the mine for they were 'at this time rather at a loss for a little judgement how to proceed for the best'. A few months later Thomas Sneyd-Kynnersley was more optimistic and reported the discovery 'of a vein of Lead on the opposite or Western side of the Hill', where the owner was very willing for mining to take place for a fair Lord's rent. The ore was reported to be of a good sort and free from copper. They had directed one or two men to make a trial and since it was high up the hill it was thought that a level would keep it dry for a considerable depth with only a trifling expense. This was probably the Acre Mine. Lead was reported in two other places.

In the Autumn of the same year, correspondence took place with William Wyatt, requesting further assistance. The vein of lead had proved 'as miners' prospects often do, good for nothing', and they had abandoned the trial. Much greater success had been had in 'the old Copper Mine' where a good show of copper ore was found comparatively near to the surface, but it needed good management and mining experience to 'have a fair chance of getting back some of the money which has hitherto been thrown away'.

The Sneyds knew very little about mining and needed the services of an experienced manager who would be paid 'a fixed stipend which would be increased if the mine became profitable by his means'. Apart from being run by owners who knew very little of the technicalities of metal mining there was also trouble amongst the miners. Rupert Bullock, the headman, was causing considerable trouble by imposing checks and regulations on the miners, and he was opposed by Mr Twigg, the underground overlooker, who had a brother and several other relations among the men. In 1826, the Sneyds appointed William Wyatt as agent at Mixon, but his plan for the improvement of the mine was vigorously opposed by John Bennett, the leader of a company of miners, who had been appointed as underground agent. Thomas Sneyd-Kynnersley thought that the opposition had been at the instigation of Bullock.

Drainage Problems

At this time (c1826) the first indications of the drainage problems arise. The mine was heavily watered and drainage was by a steam engine and two waterwheels, all of which appear to have been installed some years previously. The engine was of 30 HP constructed on Boulton and Watt's principle with a pair of boilers and two lifts of 12-inch bucket pumps each 50 yards in length (17). It was later described as 'small and constructed on a bad principle' (1853 Prospectus), and there were certainly many complaints of its operation.

The waterwheels were each 40ft diameter and 4ft wide. One was an undershot wheel having cast iron crank and axle with wooden arms, on a cast iron pedestal, with two cast iron regulating bobs and two T-bobs with wooden slide rods working pumps. The other waterwheel had a 24ft diameter spur wheel with a treble crank and wheel for working 3 lifts of pumps. Water was supplied to the wheels via wooden launders. A new dam was built in 1825-6 at a cost of £555, but inferior materials had been used in its construction and it was thought that it would have to be partly rebuilt.

In contrast to the nearby Ecton Mine where modest pumping easily coped with the water down to nearly 1,000ft below the River Manifold, the Mixon Mine was severely handicapped by great quantities of water that quickly filled the lower workings if the pumps were not always at work. The mine was constantly hampered by too much water for the pumps to cope with, or in dry weather by insufficient water in the dams to work the wheels, while in winter the water channels to the wheels were often blocked by ice and snow. With all the dams full of water the mine could be drained, but this could take a week of continuous pumping and would leave the dams empty with nothing left in reserve. This was not helped by ice damaging the wheels in 1826, causing the water to rise in the mine. There was a great reluctance to work the steam engine, probably due to the quantity of fuel that it consumed. In the reckoning book there are payments to an engineer, a whimsey worker and 3 engine men.

In 1826 they had driven under the Ratcliffe Mine

> 'an old work which was laid dead and full of water for the last forty years',

which must be the copper trials of William Ratcliffe in 1780. This had allowed it to drain and 'a very good work' was found. They also find that:

> 'They stouped up a Gate in the New Mine which carries off all the Upper or Day Water into the Adit Level and it never comes now on to the Wheels so that the Water which stopped us when we were there last is now carried off'.

Thomas Sneyd-Kynnersley commented to William Wyatt:

> 'the ore we have been getting is of a much superior quality to any I have seen before at Mixon'.

The Appointment of Joshua Brittlebank

About 1827 Joshua Brittlebank was appointed by Wyatt as underground manager at a salary of £84 per annum. Wyatt's summary of the accounts to that date showed that there had been a loss of over £8,000 since 1824. In February 1828 Joshua Brittlebank reported to William Wyatt on the state of the mine. In the deep level they had cut the same measures that had produced ore in the shallower parts of the mine, but very little ore was found. This was thought to be due to 'the Metal Joint bearing off so fast in a North Eastwardly direction'. Brittlebank proposed driving eastwardly to cut

> 'the thick bed in hopes of drawing the water down from above as there is very little water comes in the beds we have cut'.

It was about 4ft from the bearing beds to the thick bed. They would have cut it sooner, but the men had not been above to get there due to the quantity of water that had accumulated with the watercourses being filled with snow.

The following is a typical statement of the drainage problems:

> 'We have rolled the Water this Morn but we have so little water left in the Dams that it has obligded us to apply the Engine this Forenoon but she works very bad indeed but I hope we shall be able to keep the water out of the Mine until we have a fresh supply in the Dams'.

A month later Brittlebank reported that they had driven on the east side through the thick bed, but they had found very little ore and 'the Metal increases in the Bottom Level but very slowly'. Water was still very low in the dams and if rain did not come they would have to work the engine. They had nearly 30 tons of ore ready to

PLAN of the **MIXON MINE SETT.**

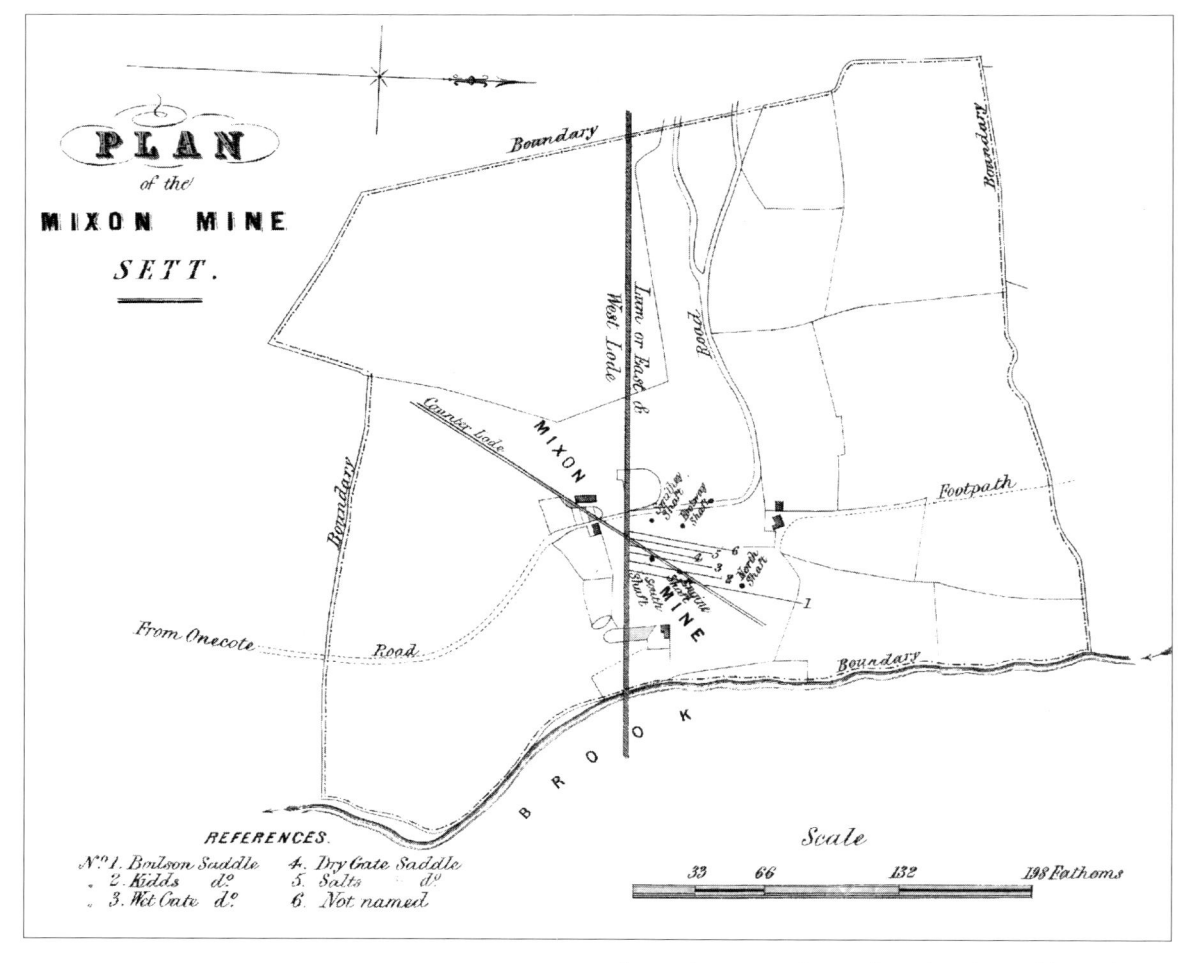

REFERENCES.
Nº 1. Boilson Saddle
2. Kidds do
3. Wet Gate do
4. Dry Gate Saddle
5. Salts do
6. Not named

Scale: 33 66 132 198 Fathoms

Above and right: Illustrations from the 1853 prospectus

take to the Whiston smelting works. Bullock was causing more trouble and Brittlebank hoped that he would be dismissed:

'I am sure there will be no peace or comfort at the place for he makes all the mischief he can when he comes over therefore I wish you would speak to Mr Sneyd's about removing him'.

In May there was heavy rain which filled the dams 'so that all the places in work were at liberty'. They were driving westwards in the Lum and although ore was always present the quantity was never very great. Some good lead ore and copper ore had been got in the 'Sun Joint' while 7 tons of 'Self Lead ore free from Copper' had been drawn to the surface, but it could not be dressed since all the water was needed to work the wheels.

Wyatt visited Mixon in August 1828 to find that the work had been static for some time and very few alterations had taken place. In the New Mine the works were poor. He proposed, and Thomas Sneyd-Kynnersley agreed, that the Bottom Level be driven southwards from the foot of the Sawney Shaft (location not known, but Sawney is a North Staffordshire word meaning a winding engine, a term that was also used in the Cheadle coalfield) (18) to crosscut the Lum. The distance being 40 or 50 yards and the cost £100 to £120.

Since the greatest part of the Mixon ore had been got from the vein and their present level was 60 or 70 yards below the Old Man (the miner's term for old workings) then assuming that the vein went downwards, a considerable quantity of copper ore was predicted. These approximate distances indicate that no survey or plan had been made of the Mixon Mine and apart from the crude diagrams in the 1853 prospectus none are known to exist today.

In late September, Brittlebank reported that the ore was not as good as it had been, but he was quite optimistic since the beds were not dipping quite so rapidly, this being indicative of a saddle. In the East gate they had found a little ore with a great quantity of water coming in through the joints. There had been no need to work the engine, but water in the dams was getting low again. They were sending a load of ore to the Whiston smelting works every day. By November 1828 'Bennetts Metal Work' was 'much as it were' and the East Forefield had become very hard again with no copper.

The beds had become nearly vertical which was also claimed to be the forerunner of a saddle. The South Crosscut was proceeding very well, being full of Spar joints. Lack of water for the wheel had drowned out the 'Bottom work', but a fortnight later they had accumulated sufficient water in the dams for the engine to be stopped. By the end of the year the South Gate had cut a joint, running in the direction of the Lum, which had cut through all the beds and the saddle, but it was barren.

Bennett's Stope was proving better than expected and there was a little ore in the North Gate. Water was coming into the workings from a strong joint. Despite the varied nature of the operations and the pessimistic tone of the reports, 1828 resulted in a profit of £820, which seems to have satisfied Sneyd-Kynnersley for a while at least:

'I wish your report had been more favourable, but we cannot get "more of a Cat than its skin", & if there are any treasures in the Bowels of Mixon Hill I

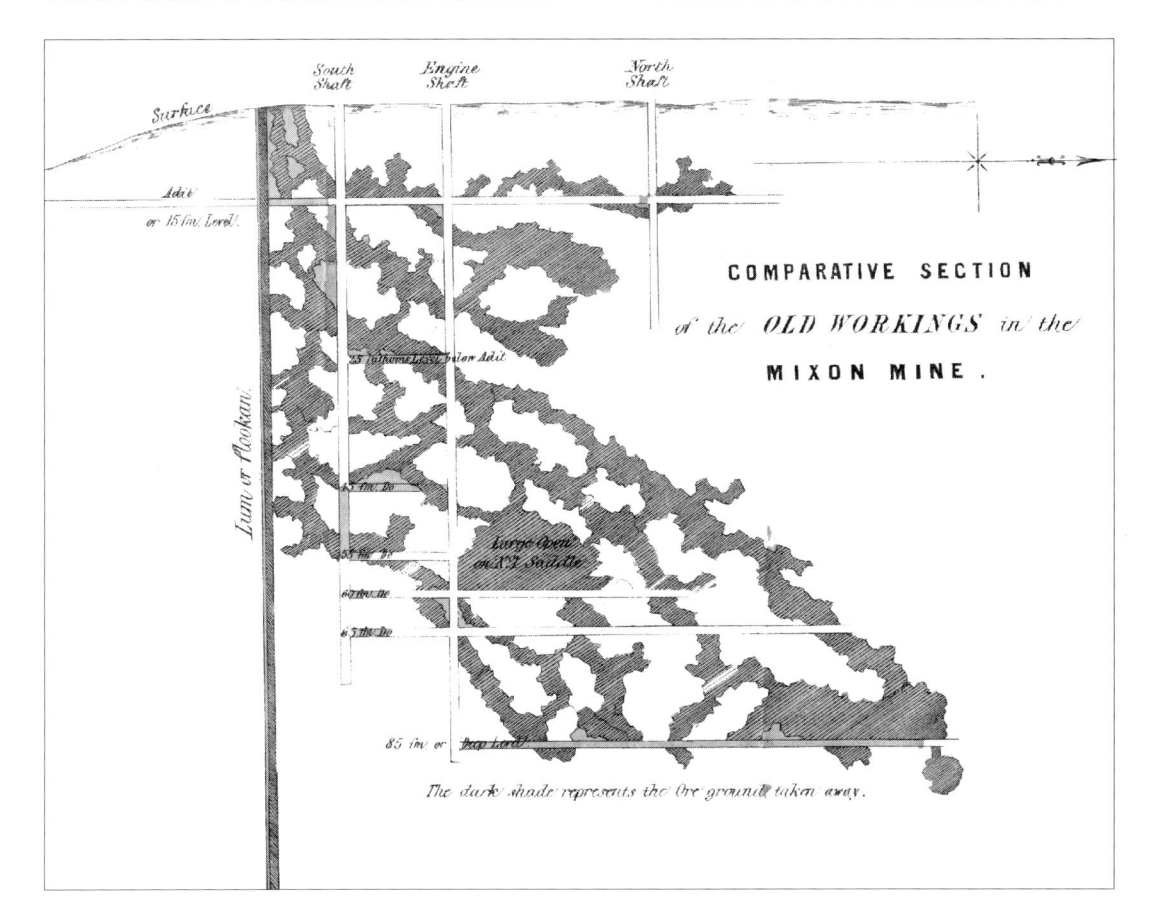

COMPARATIVE SECTION of the OLD WORKINGS in the MIXON MINE.

The dark shade represents the Ore ground taken away.

hope we shall 'ere long find some of them in the Loom when we get hither.

The dry weather has been very much against our proceeding of late… and as you have turned the Tide of Accounts for one year I hope & trust for all our sakes the change will continue'.

South of New Mixon Hay Farm, to the west of Mixon, is a level driven in an easterly direction, believed to be dated from 1828. It is likely to have been another trial made by the Sneyds.

Two Much Water, Too Little Ore

During 1829, the expected improvements did not occur and working the mine became increasingly difficult. In January the lum, for which they had been seeking in the lower workings was reached, but this only aggravated the situation by releasing a great quantity of water. The lum was found to be 3-14ft wide and full of

> 'all kinds of Minerals that generally attend Copper such as Sparr, Sulphur, Brown Hen etc but with no sign of 'Metal'.

The North forefield was producing some good copper ore but it was not increasing in quantity. The water in the dams was decreasing rapidly and even with the engine working this could not cope with the large influx of water from the lum. There was a danger that the lower parts of the mine would be completely flooded so that even with the waterwheels in operation it would take a considerable length of time to clear the water. A few weeks later there was still no copper ore in the lum, but a 'deal of Sulphur' and the wheels were troubled again by ice. By March they were still working the engine and getting some ore from the upper ground, but not enough to pay.

The fears of flooding seem to have been justified for on June 11th 1829 the Engine and Wheels had been at a stand for three weeks and the water was rising. About fifteen men had been set to work the lum but it was expected that the water would drive them out before the end of the week. A month later the mine was full of water to the level.

Fifteen or sixteen men were working in the New Mine, in the Old Mine above the water and in the Hillocks. A final blow came when a flood of water washed the puddle out of one of the channels in the lower dam, and although no damage was done to the embankment or arch, the dam was empty in a few hours.

Pessimism from the Lord of the Mine

As might be expected, Thomas Sneyd-Kynnersley was starting to feel very pessimistic on proceeding with Mixon Mine as this letter to William Wyatt shows

> 'I wish that Brittlebank's report had been better: That over supply of water underground, & the want of it above ground will oblige us 'ere long I fear to change our trade, for nothing that we can find I am afraid will enable us to bear up against the expence of the Steam Engine in dry weather'.

By the end of September the water was still in the mine as storms had caused the entry of a large quantity of day water (or rain), but the pumps were now gaining on the inflow and they hoped to drain the mine in just over a week.

By June 1830 the outlook for the mine was hardly favourable, when Sneyd-Kynnersley wrote to Wyatt:

> 'I am truly sorry all our plans have been so unfortunately frustrated hitherto by the water and by our insufficient machinery. There appears now a prospect as the water is out, of having sufficient in the Dams and Stream to give an opportunity of Proving the Gate to the Lum. If there is metal we may have a chance of doing something at the Machinery with a hope of return, if there is not and no other favourable prospects are held out, it must be hardly worth kicking against the pricks much longer'.

Very wet weather in July caused torrents of water to pour down the shaft. Since the wheels could not operate due to excessive water in the stream, the mine soon flooded again – with 54ft of water in the bottom. By November they had found no ore in the lum, but in the North Forefield the beds that had been dipping down very rapidly had started to rise again. It was hoped that in about 20 yards they would cut a saddle and there find a quantity of ore.

Later that year there was talk of leasing the mineral rights to the land on the east side of the river owned by a Mr Samuel Sutton, so that clearly all the previous workings had been to the west of the River Hamps. Wyatt was naturally rather cautious of this suggestion since there was nothing to suggest the presence of ore there. If they were fortunate ensure to meet ore in the lum, which was being proved eastwardly, then they would soon be at the end of their ground and a higher duty would be asked. Since driving the lum for another 15 yards further east would prove whether there was sufficient ore worth having or not, Wyatt suggested deferring the lease of new ground until the results of proving the lum were known.

They were raising a fair quantity of 'tolerably good' ore and if the weather remained favourable for another month they would make considerable progress in the lum. By March 1831 the Eastern Forefield of the lum was reported as being very hard and wet, but the miners said that it was quite similar to when they were 'about to get to the good works in the lum' in the shallower parts of the mine. 'Some pretty good Metal' had been got out of the Northern end of the mine, while by mid-April they had obtained a small amount of very good quality ore in driving the lum above the adit level, but

> 'as to knowing anything further of the lower part of the mine that is all over for some time I fear'.

Joshua Brittlebank Dies

By the end of 1831 they were still fighting a loosing battle against the water with their inadequate machinery, while for some unknown reason the steam engine was not being worked. Another problem was that copper prices were beginning to fall rapidly, with the result that as the miners' wages were so low most of them had left for work elsewhere and the companies had broken up.

During 1831-2, Joshua Brittlebank was very ill and he died in the latter part of 1832. It was clear that although the mine had not been fully exploited due to the great quantities of water, this could only be achieved with the expenditure of large amounts of capital which the Sneyds were not prepared to do. Thomas Sneyd-Kynnersley wrote in 1832 and 1833:

> 'I do not care how soon we shut up the Concern I only wish it had been done long ago... a tiresome, expensive and disappointing concern and I only wish we had shewn sence (sic) in being guided by your honest and friendly advice in the first instance'.

After Brittlebank's death the affairs of the mine were taken over by his son, and William Sneyd instructed Wyatt to draw all the materials out of the mine while they still had enough water to work the pumps. However the mine was still operational in April 1833 when Sneyd-Kynnersley wrote:

> 'I shall be very glad if you eventually find metal ... if not I shall most truly willing & desirous to shut up shop and get what we can out of the old materials and machinery, tho' I candidly allow Copper in large quantities would suit my temper & pocket for the best'.

The Mine is Abandoned

It is interesting to note that the working miners thought that there was much ore still to be found at Mixon, but that they had been directed at driving the wrong way. They wanted to continue working mine at their own expense, to which Sneyd-Kynnersley initially agreed, but he later changed his mind and finally suggested that Mixon Mine be abandoned at the beginning of May 1833.

All the equipment was put up for auction on July 3rd and 4th, 1834, including the steam engine, the two water wheels, all the pumps including sundry pumps of 10 to 14-inch diameter, 50 tons of cast and wrought iron, 10 tons of old ropes and all the usual carpenters', blacksmiths' and miners' tools. But the sale did not interest many buyers:

> 'Sept, 7th 1834. Customers are slack at Mixon – we have an offer of £70 p Lot for the 14 In Pumps laid down at Froghall but I shall beg my Brother to keep the offer open,'

and it is clear that a least one of the wheels remained at the mine. The other may have gone to Royledge, see Chapter 5.

The Sneyd brothers did not lose interest in mining speculations, for in 1835 Thomas Sneyd-Kynnersley bought shares in the ill-fated High

6 Mixon Mines

Above: Inside the level near New Mixon Hay, believed to date from 1828. **Opposite:** At the forefield (the far end) of the New Mixon Hay Level

Rake project, near Hucklow, Derbyshire, and previously had shown interest in the Dale Mine. In the 1840s, the Sneyds took leases of copper mines on Snowdon and near Dolgelly to ensure a supply of ore to their Whiston Works, but this was a short lived venture for they sold the works four years later.

A new Venture

In 1836, a John Pascoe took a twenty-one year lease of the mine from the Sneyds and formed the Mixon, Acre and Limekiln Copper and Lead Mining Company, with a capital of £30,000 consisting of 1,500 shares of £20 each. The prospectus to entice the shareholders told of a newly discovered mine at the Acre about 500 yards north of Mixon Mine. All the veins at Mixon were claimed to run in a direct line to Acre, while the bottom levels at Mixon had been driven 150 yards in this direction and had produced many thousands of tons of valuable copper ore.

This latter statement was untrue and only the most gullible would have believed it.

A level had been driven into the veins at Acre and copper carbonate containing 23 to 30 per cent of copper metal was claimed to have been discovered. The water that came from this level was stated to have been so impregnated with copper that a reservoir had to be built to filter it. One thousand yards south of Mixon the Limekiln Vein had been discovered being 4ft wide with 4 inches of solid lead, the rest mixed copper and lead.

Not unnaturally it was claimed that all these veins intercepted at Mixon. In one of the beds of ore there, twelve men could work abreast and there was more ore lying at the bottom of the mine than would pay the expense of setting the mine to work again, and men were still raising a considerable of ore above the water level.

During November 1836, Sneyd-Kynnersley wrote to William Wyatt to inform him of developments that were taking place at Mixon:

'A person by the name of Pascoe has taken Mixon Mine, says he has found Copper near the surface at the Acre & also lead in several places ... that is the most promising Mine at this time in England – that the late Miners have left Copper at the bottom of the value of £7,000 which sum will be all that is necessary to place a good Engine & pumps to put the Mine into work again & that all the Lum or the greater Part of it is left in by the later Miners & that it is a most rich and valuable vein of Ore that the late Coy. threw away the greater part of the Ore when they had got it by too much wasting. He is hawking a Company about 1300 shares at £20 a share – says he is getting on very well that one person has taken on 200 shares'.

In spite of the optimism, and the sale of a small quantity of ore to Whiston by John Pascoe, this apparently did not come to much, but interest in Mixon was revived 18 months later:

'What think you of some persons having been persuaded by that bright honest genius (!) Bullock to start Mixon Mine again, & that they have partly agreed to take all the remaining old machinery & have agreed with My Nephew John Sneyd to start the Mine at the Acre – & are driving a Level from that at the Old Mine at Mixon & have found some metal in their gait'.

Activities in 1838/1839

Towards the end of 1838, change was in the air. J S Smith, a 'mining agent', of Manchester, who had been working the mine on his own account since 7 June 1838, wrote to Rupert Bullock sending £50 for wages. Smith stated that

'he was promised £200 more with which I will visit the mines and pay all off up to 31st December next'

Intriguingly, he went on to say:

'A friend of mine who says he will take a large interest will be back from Cornwall in about 10 days when we are to go together. He has £10,000 free next January. Manage to the best of your abilities and write me the receipt and what ore you are getting. I have not heard from Mr Gaunt'.

The latter reference presumably is to Richard Gaunt of Leek.

Smith sent another £25 in January received from a Mr Sale and advised that more money was coming from Mr Sneyd. Bullock was told to get all ore raised up to January 1st to the Smelting House. At the end of 1838 the mine employed thirty men and boys. Smith had spent £604 on

THE
MIXON GREAT CONSOLS
COPPER MINE,

IN THE PARISH OF LEEK, NORTH STAFFORDSHIRE,

(Held under a Lease for twenty-one years, and conducted on the Cost Book principle.)

CAPITAL IN 7,500 PARTS OR SHARES.

[Deposit, Five Shillings per Share.]

Directors.
CHARLES HINKS, ESQ., DRAYTON GROVE, BROMPTON, LONDON, (Chairman.)
HENRY PARRISH, ESQ., CLIFTON PLACE, MOSELEY ROAD, BIRMINGHAM.
JOHN BRADBURY, ESQ., REGENT PLACE, BALSALL HEATH, BIRMINGHAM.

Auditors.
JOHN BARKER, ESQ., M. D., RICHMOND, SURREY.
W. C. MORGAN, ESQ., ST. ENODER, NEAR TRURO, CORNWALL.

Bankers.
MESSRS. ATTWOOD, SPOONER & Co., BIRMINGHAM.

Managing Agent.
CAPTAIN WILLIAM BISHOP, IPSTONES, NEAR CHEADLE.

Purser.
MR. THOMAS LEWIS, SHAREBROKER, ST. GEORGE'S CHAMBERS, BIRMINGHAM.

Above and opposite: Illustrations from the 1853 prospectus

the mine in the previous six months. One of Smith's backers was S H Sale (see below).

A New Company

On 15th January 1839, Smith wrote to John Attwood Beaver 'authorising and requesting' him to form the Mixon and Acre Mining Company an the following basis:

'to get a deed executed as soon as possible in the name of yourself, Mr S H Sale and Mr J A Jesse and get a working deed drawn up upon the same principle as the Tavy deed... the mine to be divided into 1,000 shares which are to be represented by 200 certificates of £5 each... It being understood that 50 such certificates or 250 shares are to be appropriated to me in full satisfaction of all my claim upon the said mine and also of the grant or sett and the materials from Mr Sneyd as per valuation amounting to £472 and I undertake to pay and

FORM OF APPLICATION FOR SHARES.

To The Directors of the Mixon Great Consols Copper Mining Company.

GENTLEMEN,

I request that you will allot me_____ Parts or Shares in your Company, and I hereby undertake to accept the same, or any less number and to pay the deposit of five shillings per Share, and Calls when due.

Name in full _____

Residence _____

Business or Profession _____

Reference _____

Dated this _____ day of _____ 185

---

satisfy W Sneyd the amount of such valuation… and to put the Company in possession of all the ores materials and machinery as the same stood on first January last and to pay off all the debts of the mine up to that date. The Company are to receive and to work the said mine and to pay the working costs and other expenses of the mines to the extent of ten pounds upon each of the remaining 750 shares before I or the holder of the 250 shares granted me above shall be required tp pay any calls, such calls being considered to be paid already in the surrender of all the mines, ores, materials and machinery to the said Company.

I further request you to appropriate such 750 shares as under viz to Mr Sale 150, to Mr JA Jesse 50 to Mr Buckley 40 to Mr Cumber 40, to yourself and friends 470….that the management shall rest with a committee to consist of myself, yourself, Joseph Ablett Jesse and Samuel Hodgson Sale'.

Smith (a Mining Agent of 71, King Street, Manchester) agreed to indemnify Beaver in the case of Mr Sneyd not agreeing to all of this. The letter is endorsed that Jesse agreed subsequently to take twenty of Cumber's shares. Smith also wrote to Bullock asking him to set bargains with the miners and to advise 'we have the lease and the Meadow Farm is included'.

Smith and Beaver had other mining and quarrying interests (see below).

Details on the Engine

On 29th January 1839, Bullock sent a report on the mine to Beaver. It shows Bullock's lack of grasp of English: the spelling mistakes are his!

'I yesterday received a letter from Mr Smith saying you was in want to no the Power of hour old Engine; the working Barrial was only 6 foot long 11 Inches Diameter which was about 24 Galln with eight blowes minuit made up 192 Galln Per Minuit; the water wheels when the Engine was stoping the working Barrial was 9 foot long 13 Inches Diameter about 6 foot 10 Inches stroke 4 to $4^{1}/_{2}$ Blowes Per

Minuit; keep the spring of the water out, the first Plan I began at the Mine was I am driving a water Level to take all the water out of the Mine above that level [he must mean the adit level] which will be at least one third which I may say will save thousands Pounds in Coal which add all used to go to the Bottom of the Mine; when it was rain we add used to have a flood af water going in to the Mine; and now we shall be able to catch it above level.

    I have six men working the for end taking the Level up which his very likely for Metal in beds that are not bearing beds but we have add both Lead and Copper Just to say by; But when thick beds come in again we may expect Metal and a good deal of it I will say in about a fortnight; I have six men Driving a Cross to the other wet Saddle which are just half way, ...'

Bullock was expecting the new Company to invest in a new engine as the water problems were interrupting the proper working of the mine. Early in February, Bullock sent to Smith the schedule of costs for January. His son James was working and he left the daily rate for Smith to set [he did so at 2/6d per day]. Bullock left it to Smith to determine his (Bullock's) remuneration, but the reply simply said 'when we are properly at work, we will see to advance yours'.

    None the less, Smith must have been happy with what Bullock was up to for he had also urged:

> 'Stick close to work, and keep as much as possible on the Mines in order that the new Company may be equally satisfied with your proceedings'.

Smith meant this metaphorically, but he might also have meant it physically had he known better, for within a week he wrote enquiring:

> 'Can you not manage without 6 men at Whiston? Surely they ought to find you assistants however do what is proper. But do not keep long away'.

    The tonnage of the Mixon ores sent to Whiston is not given, but the yield was around 11% on the Mixon No1 Crop ore and 3% on a parcel of Stamped ore. Ore sales from 31st January to 23rd February fetched £340.

Difficulties at the Mine

However for some unknown reason, the new shareholders, with the notable exception of Smith, refused to send any money to the mine. As early as March Bullock was complaining about this:

> 'as it his (sic) unpleasant to me to go on as I do and let the money be raised to discharge all the mens wages and Trademens Bills, as all his so much past due and now the summons his going on again'.

Bullock was understandably having a difficulty getting the men to continue working. He did however make a report on the state of the mine which sheds a little detail on what he was doing. It is somewhat confusing because of his writing style. It appears that the work was being concentrated on the Boilstone Saddle. He wrote (19th March 1839):

> 'When I left Mixon Mine [a few years before] the large work went Poor [presumably a reference to the large open shown on the section of the mine in the 1853 prospectus]... it [presumably the lode] went north along Boilstone Saddle... with metal more or less being a dry saddle it divided into two wet saddles'.

Bullock was exploiting both of these saddles and expected them to come together again. He was working around the clock too:

> 'the present work on the east side [i.e. the easterly of the two saddles] will employ 4 men at a time that in 24 hours will be 16 men a day'

These saddles appear to have been 10-12ft wide and yielding ore to the dressing floor. He was very optimistic, describing the joint in the saddle as being five feet wide. In other words, the ground containing the copper ore was in a vertical bed some five feet wide. However there was not much dressing going on on the surface; 'the weather his so could and frosty we have no one working on Top' (Bullock to Smith March 11th). This letter reiterated his impatience at the lack of the engine saying that he had been there eleven months and had the engine been installed, the ore would have paid for it. As it was, he felt the extraction costs would equal the ore revenues.

His work on the adit appeared to have continued too. He expected to reduce the drainage costs by a third by catching a lot of the water before it got below the adit level. He was also driving the level north hoping to cut some east-west orientated veins, including the Acre Vein.

Bullock's Earlier Days

Bullock seems to have taken the opportunity in this letter to have a swipe at his predecessor as agent, presumable prior to he dismissal some years before:

> 'The old agent worked all for self interest and not for the Co[mpany] after he had got all that I add set a liberty. He never in 5 years got 5 tons metal and I sopose he never went down under ground above 4 or 5 times per year; and did not no metal when he seed it. I believe the material [he means equipment here] was drawn out for self interest'.

Smith's Other Interests

Smith had expended nearly £400 on the mine since the beginning of his relationship with Beaver of which £250 had been spent at Mixon prior to 31st December 1838 with perhaps another £150 still to be met. The men were also involved in the Ty Mawr Slate Quarry Company, where Smith had about £150 to pay for 'sundry other incumbrances' and the North Tamar mine. This reference to the quarry may be important to it's historians, for Lindsay (19) states that it dates from about 1870. It was acquired by the famous Dorothea Slate Company in the 1930s but remained unworked. It is situated in Nantlle at SH 495529.

Smith asked Beaver for 'a few hundreds', the security being sixty shares in the Mixon and Acre Mining Company; Twenty or thirty shares in Ty Mawr, with the option of the purchase of an interest therein up to one-third, or more if obtainable, at the reduced price of £2,500 for the whole. It was Smith's intention, if this proposal was accepted, to place the superintending control in Beaver's hands and 'personally to visit and forward the works in question' (see below). Smith went on to say that he was arranging to repay a loan from Beaver of £150

> 'on account of North Tamar... and to retire the same, unless you should... prefer dividing that interest with me, or should choose to become its Purchaser'.

Reference was made by Smith (above) to a speculator with £10,000 to spend coming back from Cornwall. North Tamar Mine is four miles south-east of Launceston, near the River Tamar, in Cornwall. It may be that Beaver was interested in this proposal for having been restarted in 1836 (it was previously known as the Greystone Silver-Lead Mine), it was announced in the *Mining Journal* on 3rd August 1839 that it was to be sold to the Victoria Mining Company of Liverpool (20). However nothing became of this proposal.

We do not know why nothing became of this or indeed if Beaver was connected with the Victoria Mining Company, but Beaver was about to back away from his interest in Mixon and the two might be connected.

The shortage of funds from the investors could have stemmed from the fact that William Sneyd had still not forwarded the lease at the end of May. This was probably sent shortly afterwards but was not signed by Beaver. One reason was that they wanted William Sneyd to take shares instead of money for payment of materials taken over by the new Company. William was the son of the Rev John Sneyd and was acting on behalf of his father, for it was the latter who was owed money when Beaver was later sued. John Sneyd was habitually short of money, regularly borrowing off his friends to pay another creditor (pers comm Marion Aldis and Pam Inder).

During April 1839, Bullock had cut a very promising 'east-west joint' in the adit level. He had also been rising up to meet this point from lower down in the mine but the men were working six hours and then having to leave the working for two hours because the air was so bad. The rise was five fathoms high and the men were having to work off ladders.

The Pressures Mount

There was still no money forthcoming and Bullock was clearly under a lot of pressure:

'I wish to settle with the men first as some of them want their money to buy Cows and pay Rents etc'.

Within a couple of days, Smith sent some money, but not enough.

By the end of May, nearly £62 was due to tradesmen and £326 to the men. Some of the latter had left, refusing to work anymore until they were paid. Bullock had also laid off men to lower the expenses and reported that he only had nine miners, three labourers and three boys at work. He stated that he could set '3 sets men getting Metal when Settled with'.

On top of all this, the lower water wheel was giving way and needed new oak timbers. It was, Bullock said, the only 'dead expense': the ore was waiting to be brought out. By August, Bullock was being threatened with writs and had an exchange of 'very sharp words' with Mr Sneyd. He wrote to say that he understood that Mr Sneyd would let the mine to another party if he was at liberty.

It should be noted that not only was Mr Sneyd wanting money from the mine, he also was not getting it from his tenants, who were not being paid and were therefore unable to pay their rent. Bullock incidentally, lived at the mine, presumably at Mixon Mines Farm.

Closure of the Mine

Bullock resigned at the end of the month, presumably because of the pressure from creditors. However some of the men continued to work until 30th November 1839 when they were laid off. Smith wrote to him at the beginning of September. He gave a resume of the costs due by the Company; it amounted to £455.14.0d (£455.70p). He went on:

'I think it will appear that Mr Beaver has scarcely paid the 1/3 of his proportion of costs and as he has some few hundreds of securities of mine in hand, I think it the more unjust to throw difficulties on me in consequence of the failures of parties holding only 190 shares out of 750 – and which 190 shares have paid 5/- (25p) per share first call'.

These were the shares held by Mr Sale (150) and Mr Buckley (40). Was this George Buckley of the Ecton and Dale Mines?

Bullock had previously said that he could get £2,000 for the mine in forty-eight hours and Smith asked him to do so if that was still possible. Alternatively, he asked if he (Bullock) could assist in the forming of an additional Company, by placing the 190 shares on the basis of paying 190/750s of the working costs since 1st January 1839, less the 5/- paid on them which amount to £47.50. If half the mine could be sold, Smith could buy out the other shareholders and 'begin by myself a new Company in right earnest'. He ended by saying that if he had gone on by himself, 'the engine would have been up and then the mine would soon have been sufficiently independent of waivers'.

It was reckoned that the Company owed £593.9.5$\frac{1}{2}$d (£593.47$\frac{1}{2}$p). Bullock sued Beaver for recovery of the due amount.

Bullock versus Beaver

Beaver and Jesse, who was a solicitor in Manchester and acted for Beaver in the case, contended that all monies sent to the mine should have been applied to the new concern. Bullock had used some of the money for the payment of debts of the old Company unless he was particularly advised to use the money for a specific purpose. The case of *Bullock versus Beaver* was heard in Stafford before the Queen's Bench in 1840. Damages of £1,000 were awarded to Bullock and John Cruso of Leek was appointed arbitrator to sort out specific sums due to all of the creditors. Some of the miners had also sued in their own name. The problem for the men was that several of them were illiterate and clearly relied on the mine to be honest in what was due to them. Benjamin Goldstraw, described as a workman who had worked at the mine for fifty years, kept a record of days worked on a stick, but it didn't tell him what was due. He earned £3 a month from January 1839.

Whether the £1,000 was actually paid or was a notional amount ahead of the amount awarded by Cruso is unclear.

It is unknown also whether anyone took the mine on again before 1853. Despite the problems over money, Bullock comes across as a reasonable man and the judgement must have come as a relief and perhaps gone some way to restoring has credibility in the area. What he went on to do is not known.

The Award
The actual award was:

To Rupert Bullock	£112.7.3
To the miners	£297.8.10½
To tradesmen	£50.6.2
To costs of Bullock	£20.18.0
To the costs of the workmen	£4.14.8
To the arbitrator's costs	£32.12.4
Total	£518.7.3½

For readers interested in their family history, the names of the miners and workmen are given in the Appendix to this chapter.

The mine evidently never closed completely as copper ore was sent at least from 1831 to 1841 to Whiston. From 1836, Mixon was leased at a 1/15th royalty on the ore raised (although this was raised to 1/10th during 1839). It is said that upwards of £100,000 worth of copper been raised at Mixon, 'but that all operations had been suspended, in 1834 in consequence of family disagreements and the engine not being of sufficient power to drain the mine (1853 Prospectus). The latter is certainly true, although there is nothing to confirm the former statement.

The failure of the Mixon Mine seems to have been only one of a series of financial failures by the Sneyds, for in addition, their excursion into the copper smelting business at Whiston appears from the available accounts to have run at a loss, and they were major shareholders in the disastrous High Rake venture. Also it is said locally that the tramway which can still be traced along part of the Coombes Valley, south of Bradnop, was an unsuccessful attempt by the Sneyds to quarry limestone at Mixon Hay. It was intended to convey it by inclines and tramways to the Caldon Canal in competition with the quarries at Cauldon Low. It seems reasonable to assume that all these failures were due mainly to a lack of business acumen and foresight when embarking on costly business speculations.

Mixon Great Consols Copper Mining Company

No further information is known of the operations until 1852 and it is probable that the Company was abandoned sometime in the 1840s. In 1852, the above Company was established on the cost book principle by a Mr Lewis of Birmingham, described as being the 'purser'. He was also connected with the Dale mine. A new twenty-one year lease was agreed with a duty of 1/20th for the first two years and 1/16th afterwards. The mine was to be run with a capital of 7,500 £1 shares. The managing agent was Captain William Bishop of Ipstones. Bishop was also working iron ore in the Churnet Valley nearby and was accredited with the establishment of the iron working industry in that area.

The prospectus painted a glowing picture of vast ore deposits waiting to be removed once the drainage problems had been solved. It was proposed to erect a steam engine of at least 50-inch diameter cylinder, in addition to the 40ft diameter water wheel still in position, to drain the mine to at least twice its present depth. At that time there were 3 main shafts – South Shaft of 60 fathoms, Engine Shaft of 85 fathoms and North Shaft of 50 fathoms below adit as well as two smaller shafts, and the adit which drained the mine to a depth of 15 fathoms (1853 Prospectus).

During the previous year the High Rake Mine at Hucklow, Derbyshire, had closed down, and its machinery was offered for sale in July and August 1853 (7). This consisted of a combined cylinder compound beam pumping engine based on the Sim's principle, which had been made by Messrs. Graham & Co at the Milton Iron Works about 1843 (21). Details of the Sim's engines have been given by Barton (22). This engine had an upper cylinder of 36-inch diameter and a lower cylinder of 70-inch diameter, with 10ft stroke. It was the largest Sim's compound engine to be built outside Cornwall. It was complete with two boilers as well as 100 fathom of pitwork, 10-inch plunger pumps, balance beam, capstan and shears, There was also a 20-inch cylinder double acting steam whim of 4ft stroke with boiler, which had originally come from the Magpie Mine about 1846 (23) and two 4½-inch flat ropes 120 fathom long. This engine also worked two sets of ore crushing rollers. All this plant, as well as three horse gins, a horse crusher and a large quantity of general mining equipment were valued in March 1853 at £2,703. This equipment was sold to the Mixon Mine and work started on preparing the new site for the engines. The actual purchase price was £2,650 but £2,350 of this was paid for by the 'Lord of the Soil' – presumably the Sneyds.

At this time there were weekly reports in the Mining Journal giving the progress at

Mixon in great detail. In addition to erecting the engine house, chimney stack, two boiler houses and whim house, the adit level was cleared to the Engine shaft to let off the water that had been dammed up. The water in the level could be kept by a 6-inch box at 5 strokes per minute (presumably of the water wheel). Work started on

> 'driving towards and under the ground of our new discovery, which is about 20 fms. distant; but we will cut 3 or 4 lodes, or ore bearing measures before we drive that distance'.

Nearly all the machinery had arrived at the mine by October 1853; by the end of the year all the buildings were complete and they were ready to hang the main pump-rod. It was hoped to commence working the engine on January 5th 1854 if the rest of the castings came from the foundry.

The Usual Promising Start

During 1853, the *Mining Journal* was full of reports such as:

> 'I have never before seen a mine which is so promising an appearance and from which a considerable quantity of ore has been obtained and prepared ready for market in less than two months from the commencement of operation'.

However the reports are silent on the details of the engine from High Rake, for it is clear that it was extensively rebuilt on re-erection at Mixon. Evidently the compound engine had not proved as advantageous as originally envisaged, no doubt the more complicated valve gear, the difficulty in repacking the lower piston and the extra expense of a further storey to the engine house all contributed to this. Whatever the exact reason, the two cylinders of 70-inch and 30-inch diameters were replaced by one of 50-inch and the engine was converted to a more conventional Cornish pumping engine. The original ten feet stroke was retained, and when the engine was offered for sale a few years later, it was described as being equal to 100 HP.

Initial enthusiasm was fuelled by the discovery of a lode in the tips, 'whilst turning over the heaps of attle'. The lode was said to be yielding a considerable quantity of copper which appeared to be very rich. It seemed that more than one lode was found for in April 1853, it was intended to drive into the new lodes from an old level off the adit. Apparently these lodes, which were parallel to but separate from the six others already known, had been partly wrought but were unworked apart from a few feet from the surface. It sounded almost too good to be true and perhaps it was.

Work to Date

At a general meeting in Birmingham, held in February, 1854, William Johnson and James Pemberton, later to become important names in the development of the Dale Mine, were elected directors. The work to date was reviewed: two engine houses, boiler houses, stacks, flues smithy etc had been built. The capstan had also been fixed, shears erected over the shaft(s), and the pumping engine set to work, although the steam driven whim was still incomplete.

The engine and other shafts had been cut down (i.e. enlarged in cross-section and divided in order to separate the pump rod and winding gear from the footway, or ladders. A 15 fathoms lift of pumps had been fixed in the shaft to the adit and a second lift below this was being installed. It is of interest to note that only two levels below the adit had been met with – at 7 and 10 fathoms below the adit. Both were full of crushed rock in which had been found some good stones of lead and copper ore (*Mining Journal*, 1854, p124). Receipts (including calls on the shares) had produced an income of £3,677, but the expenditure, indicative of the pattern which followed, already showed a debit balance of £207. This figure is contrary to that stated in a later law case where it was given in evidence that the amount was £366.

Despite this, however, the management was emphatic about the prospects to such an extent that one shareholder had occasion to remark that one statement by a Capt Tregea did not appear to have been written by a miner or one who understood mining (*Mining Journal*, 1854, p382).

Throughout the summer of 1854, despite exploratory operations, no ore was raised but a change for the better occured in the Autumn and a cross-cut was driven at the bottom of the mine, in the 73 fathom level, intersecting Lewis's lode which was six feet wide and yielded copper ore which was raised and sold. The turn for the better was reflected in the shares, which were selling at 2/6d (12$^1/_2$p) above par, at £1.12.6d (£1.62$^1/_2$).

Shareholder Disatisfaction

However in September 1855 there were letters of dissatisfaction in the *Mining Journal* from Mixon shareholders, one complaining that £1,758 had been spent from January to June 1855 producing ore worth only £400-£500, another that the company chairman had held an illegal AGM.

Later in 1855 the pit work in the engine shaft had been fixed down to the 73 fathom level and twelve men were employed sinking the shaft. A review at the end of the year stated that they had 'not made such good progress this year as expected, but prospects good'; copper ore worth £710 had been sold during the year. A report dated 20th September 1856 by A Thompson and C Pascoe stated that six men were driving in the adit level to cut the western saddles and working at the 83 fathom level. There were signs of copper and lead at the end of the adit and it was thought that the ore body was near to where they were sinking in the lower parts of the mine.

A New Company

A few months later an issue of shares was made and the company was registered under the Limited Liability Act. By October 1857, the mine was in the care of Richard Niness who was also the manager at the Dale Mine. He reported that the men were making 'a trial in the shallow level, at the old mine, on the Lum, a little to the North of the fire engine shaft,' and some 'nice' ore was discovered. A railroad was built from the shaft to the dressing floors. This is the last report from the Mixon Great Consols Copper Mine, for it ceased working in 1858 and the pumping engine was taken to the Ribden Mine which had been leased by Niness three years earlier. The final depth is quoted as greater than 100 fathoms, so it is clear that the mine was never extended below the depth attained by the Sneyds (i.e. 85 fathoms below, plus 15 fathoms above adit 1evel). Presumably it was not possible to raise sufficient working capital to continue operations.

The unsettled nature of the company is indicated by the fact that the mine had at least three managers in its short life of five years. The first, William Bishop, was a Cornishman who had found a rich vein of ironstone at Consall, in the Churnet Valley, in 1852 and within the next few years half a million tons are said to have been exported from the area. By 1856, Abraham Thompson, who had been the Duke of Devonshire's agent at Ecton a few years previously, was the manager at Mixon, although he died two years later, aged forty-four, by which time Richard Niness had taken over.

More Shareholder dissatisfaction

In March 1857, a letter in the *Mining Journal* reported that calls to the total of £23,437 had been made of the shareholders, yet the ore raised had amounted to little over £2,000. It is obvious that affairs at the mine were far from good and it appears shareholders' fears that the mine management were not 'coming clean' with the true situation were not unfounded. A petition for the winding up of the Company was made by Mr G Edwards and Mr J Pemberton in August 1858.

The winding up of the Company brought to light certain discrepancies which ended with the law suit of *re Mixon Copper Mining Company – Edward's case* (24), brought by the Official Manager (Receiver) against Mr G Edwards. The report of this case coupled with material from the *Mining Journal* is indicative of how careful the mining investor had to be.

The case report indicates that because of the deficiency of nearly £2,000, it had been resolved on 20th October 1856, that the directors (of which Edwards was one) be empowered to sell the mine and wind up the affairs of the Company. This had not happened. The Company went from bad to worse and further calls for more money were made of the shareholders. On 12th January 1857, a further call of £1 was made, payable on 28th January. On the 27th, Edwards gave formal notice that he was relinquishing 200 of his 300 shares (leaving him with 100, the quantity necessary for him to be a director). Consequently, he refused to pay the call on the £200 shares.

At the directors meeting held on the 28th

January, only three directors were present (four were required for such a meeting under the Company's rules). One of these was Edwards. The meeting accepted his relinquishment of shares. To make matters worse, a similar action had been taken by the two other directors present.

A meeting of the Company on 23rd March 1859 resolved that all shares in arrears be forfeited, relieving Edwards of his obligations over the 200 shares. The case was heard in Chancery and found in favour of Edwards on account of the wording of the Company's rules. This case is not particularly important in itself, but for a letter in the Mining Journal. This concerned the meeting of March, 1857, which was chaired by Edwards. The letter states that because of the lack of information on the mine (i.e. very few reports and no accounts published 'for months') several shareholders who had heard that a rumour that the mine was to be sold had declined to pay the last call until the future was clear. It was claimed that no notice had been given of the March 1857 meeting and the writer complained that the Company refused to restore the shares on payment of the call [even when in arrears] as was the practice in other mines.

Ripping off the Shareholders

It seems clear that the Company and the shareholders had been used to the financial benefit of the directors. It should also be noted that the petition for the winding-up was also made in the name of James Pemberton who was accused of deceiving shareholders at the Dale Mine. Certainly, the directors used their inside knowledge to avoid personally paying out more money to creditors, thereby increasing the liability of the other shareholders. When the affairs were finally wound up, the shareholders had to make another, final, payment of £1.7.6d (£1.37$^1/_2$p) to clear all the debts. Hence the saving on the forfeited shares was substantial by Victorian standards.

Ore Production and Accounts for the Mixon Mine

Prior to 1819-20, when 329 tons of copper ore was sold at Swansea for £3,221 (25), nothing is known of the ore production or financial state of the mine. If there is any foundation in the improbable statement in the 1853 Prospectus that ore worth £100,000 came from Mixon then it must have been before the 1820s. From 1824-1833, there is a fairly clear picture of the financial state of the mine from Wyatt's papers. Tables

Table 1
Cash account for Mixon Mine

Period	Cost £	Total Receipts £	Ore sold	profit £	loss £	£
1819-20					3,221	
1824					2,928	
1825					1,526	
1826					1,982	
1827					2,000	est. by Wyatt
1828	1,005	1,528	1,348		523	January to April
Year ending April						
1829	2,007	3,098	2,520	91		£301 profit first half yr
						£210 loss second half
1830	1,788	1,532	1,198		256	
1831	2,319	1,695	1,305	624		
1832	1,217	675	450	542		
1833			183	657		Yr ending May
1855			710			

Table 2

Summary of copper ores* sold to Whiston Copper Works

Year	£	Tons	
1830	157	15	Part of year only
1831	686	116	
1832	333	59	
1833	169	27	
1834	98	11	
1835	256	36	
1836	216	37	
1837	108	36	
1838	30	9	
1839	95	17	
1840	7	1	* lead ore sales are not
1841	176	31	recorded

1 and 2 summarise the accounts and these show that after Wyatt took over at Mixon he was able to turn the large loss into a profit for a short time, while afterwards the losses were much smaller than previously. During this period the Sneyd brothers lost nearly £10,000 at Mixon, even though a respectable quantity of ore was raised. The total receipts include such items as powder and candles which were sold to the miners, so that this quantity is larger than the income from ore above. Very little lead ore was produced.

The quantity and value of the ore sold to the Whiston copper works from 1830 to 1841 is also summarised, although direct comparison with Table 1 is difficult due to the different accounting periods (26).

Of the financial affairs of the Mixon Great Consols Copper Mine we only know that ore worth £710 was sold during 1855. It is almost certain that this venture was a financial disaster, but nothing is known of the losses incurred.

Smaller Mines in the area

Although very little is known of the workings of the other mines in the area, there are few surface features still visible, and no mining plans are known to exist; the few facts that are known are summarised here. It would appear that they were largely trials with only small quantities of ore having been produced.

Hill House & Royledge Mines
See Chapter 5

Stragdale Mine

In 1855 the Mining Journal reported on Stragdale Mine – 'a new trial, adjoining Mixon. An adit is now being driven and it is said a lead lode may be intersected'. Mr J Wint of Manor Farm advised that Stragdale Field is on the eastern side of the River Hamps directly opposite Mixon Mine, where a small area of disturbed ground could be the site. Nothing further is known of the mine and the trial can safely presumed to have been unsuccessful.

The closure of the Mixon Mine in 1858 brought all mining activity in the area to a close and none of these small trials survived the ripple of activity and optimism of the 1850s, for by 1862 Sleigh recorded that the 'workings are now closed, the mines having proved unremunerative' (27).

Appendix

The miners and tradesmen involved in the 1849 law suit were:

Joseph Balsam; James Salt; James Bullock; William Twigg; Samuel Mycock; George Mycock; William Hill; William Millward; George Wheeldon; James Wood; Benjamin Goldstraw (his son Ben despite being owed money did not sue for it); John Brindley; Francis

Burton; George Hill; Mathew Stubbs; William Hall; Isaac Yates; John Brittlebank; May Sutton (due to her for her deceased husband); Robert Edge; Benjamin Twigg; John Salt; John Lobb; Thomas Gould and John Gould; Richard Alcock; Sampson Twigg and George Twigg; John Willshaw; Abel Cantrill; Thomas Smith; Joseph Wright; John Edge.

The tradesmen due money were:
William Grindon for powder; Williamson & Co* for powder; Goslings Executor for spades etc; William Sneyd Esq for timber; George Ball for candles; Richard Godwin for coals; James Grindey for leather; Robert Edge for Slack.

  * Williamsons also regularly supplied Ecton Mine with powder

It seems dreadful that May Sutton, left a widow, presumably with no means of support and children to bring up, had to sue for her late husband's wages.

References

1. Plot R, 1684, *Natural History of Staffordshire*
2. Staffordshire Record Office, D 240/M/K/D63
3. William Salt Library, Stafford, 132/11/4-7
4. Ferguson papers. Account books and field notes. J. Robey Collection
5. Aitken J, 1795, *Description of the Country Around Manchester*
6. Pitt W. 1796, *General View of Agriculture of Staffordshire*
7. Devonshire Collection, mining papers. Chatsworth House
8. Bagshawe Collection, Sheffield City Libraries, Nos 412, 494, 587/7, 587/76, 654
9. Mixon Great Consols Mining Company Prospectus, 1853 L. Porter Collection
10. Cheadle Copper & Brass Company Minute Book. In possession of Thomas Bolton & Sons Ltd, Froghall
10a. Thanks to Pat Bromfield for this; re Marsden, see Staffs Record Office, D5131/3/2/109-110 & re 1815, see Mycock Correspondence, Grassington Folk Museum
11. Pitt W. 1817, *Topographical History of Staffordshire*
12. Farey J, 1811, *A General View of the Agriculture and Minerals of Derbyshire*, Vol 1
13. Phillips J. A, 1884, *A Treatise on Ore Deposits* London
14. Cantrell Papers, Staffs Record Office
15. White W, 1834, *Directory of Staffordshire*, p1851
16. Wyatt Letters, Derby Library
17. Staffordshire Advertiser, 1834
18. English Dialect Dictionary
19. Lindsay J, 1974, *A History of the North Wales Slate Industry*, p332
20. Hamilton Jenkins A. K, 1976, *Mines and Miners of Cornwall*, Vol XV, pp52-53
21. Kirkham N, 1966, *Steam Engines in Derbyshire Lead Mine'*, Trans Newcomen Soc, Vol 38, p69
22. Barton D. B, 1965, *The Cornish Beam Engine*
23. Brown I. J & Ford T. D, 1967, *The Magpie Mine*, PDMHS, Special Publication No 3
24. Law Times, Vol 35, OSINS, pp399-400
25. Phillips op cit
26. Whiston Copper Co, Account Books, 1831-1834, L. Porter Collection
27. Sleigh J, 1862, History of Leek

7 Butterton & Grindon

Grindon

Although there are mines scattered across the two parishes, only one, the Botstone Mine at Wetton Mill, in Butterton parish, seems to have been worked with much capital. Many of the workings appear to little more than just shafts sunk as trials. Clearly mining for ore has been an ancient occupation, perhaps industry being too strong a word. It will be remembered from Chapter 3.2 that the Vicar or Rector of Blore, along with John and Richard Grendon of Warslow, was arrested for taking lead ore to the value of £10 from the land of Henry de Brailsford at Grindon in 1376.

Where this 14th Century mine was cannot be stated. Further, in 1608, the Quarter Session Roll of James I refers to the getting of lead ore at Grindon Low.

Today, mines may be found on Ossoms Hill with a trial running towards the shafts from the Hoo Brook, almost opposite the rear Botstone Mine entrance. However this trial did not intersect any veins and was abandoned. There are other shafts three fields to the south of Buckfurlong Farm, to the east of the village of Grindon. These yielded lead ore and a large lump of galena from this mine was in the possession of the farmer some years ago. Mines also existed at Deep Dale for they were referred to by the Children's Employment Commission in 1842, see Chapter 11). A trial also exists in the roadside quarry between the village and Weags Barn, now hidden by cotoneaster growing down the quarry face. See below for Ford Mine and the mine at Hursts Low on Grindon Moor.

There was some activity in the 18th Century however, for a lease exists, dated Christmas Day, 1742. It was between John, Lord Gower, Baron of Stittenham and Thomas Gilbert of Cotton. It related to 'all those groves, mines, rakes, pipes, veins of lead and copper ore.... and all mines and veins of rottenstone in the Lordship of Grindon.' Permission was also given to obtain stones, furze etc from the waste and Common ground to build mine buildings etc. The term was for thirty-one years at 1/9th 'clean, well washed, well dressed and merchantable ore to be 'delivered to the Bingstead and washing place'. Gilbert was to employ sufficient number of workmen and spend sufficient sums of money throughout the whole term for the getting of ore. There was a right to re-enter if the mine became disused.

In 1815, it was reported that the surveyors for General Henniker (Lord of the Manor of Grindon) had 'found lead ore plinte' (see Chapter 6, reference 10a).

Butterton

Other than the Botstone Mine, see below, there was not much mining activity in this parish. However, although hardly known beyond the village, Butterton saw an incredible act of heroism which involved a disused mine.

Heroism and Death

A chalybeate spring used to exist in the village, close to the ford across the Hoo Brook. In 1840, a mine shaft was sunk next to the spring. The latter was situated at the far side of the little croft on the right as you leave the stream and start up the road for Grindon. The spring had been bubbling to the surface since at least 1680 when it was recorded by Dr Plot for his *'History of Staffordshire'*, published six years later. At the time the shaft was sunk, it was said to be giving off the smell of bad eggs (i.e. hydrogen sulphide was present). A bed of iron pyrites, sometimes called 'fools gold', was reached, which is likely to have been the source of the gas. The miners had found a lot of pyrites and the gas given off from the water 'had a violent effect on the miners eyes'. It is known that the gas is produced from

SACRED
TO THE MEMORY
OF
JOSEPH WOOD,
ROWLAND CANTRELL,
WILLIAM HAMBLETON,
JOSEPH SHENTON.

THE THREE FIRST OF WHOM GAVE THEIR LIVES IN AN UNSUCCESSFUL BUT HEROIC ATTEMPT TO RESCUE FROM DEATH THE LAST NAMED; A YOUTH WHO HAD DESCENDED AN UN-USED SHAFT ON AUG. 30TH, 1842.

"BLESSED ARE THE DEAD WHO DIE IN THE LORD."

THIS TABLET WAS PLACED HERE BY AN EYE-WITNESS OF THIS NOBLE CHRISTIAN DEED.

In the Chancel of Butterton Church

iron sulphides in the presence of water. The gas is very toxic: only 1% of it in the air may cause death.

The mine had been closed for some time until a boy, Joseph Shenton, entered it on 30th August 1842. The ladder was still in the shaft and he descended it with his playmate. A report of the accident states that the boy reached the bottom of the ladder and said 'I am dying'. His playmate gave the alarm when, the report continued, 'three men one after the other, each attempting to rescue the preceding, met the same unfortunate fate'.

It is traditionally held that the men were working on the highway when the alarm was raised. One of the men descended the ladder and was overcome by the gas, falling off the ladder into the flooded shaft. An attempt to rescue him and the boy was then made by a second man, but he too was overcome by the gas. Despite the dangerous situation, in a gallant and selfless act, yet another man descended that lethal ladder only to meet a similar fate. A fourth man had been prepared to descend the shaft in an hapless but brave attempt to save the others but had to be restrained. He was saved from a certain death.

The mine was sealed and the bodies were never recovered. Only a plaque in the church records the names of those who died that day in an act of selfless bravery.

A Bomb in the Oven

Across the road from the mine and up the hill a little, there is a cottage on the left-hand side. Here in March 1886, a further accident happened which was also connected with a mine, if only indirectly. In the later years of the nineteenth century, traditional gunpowder was replaced in the local mines by gelatine cartridges, a form of dynamite. In the right hands the cartridges could be used for a variety of jobs – even lighting the fire at home. It was effective, but an expensive way of using firelighters. William Fearns, a miner, had taken a couple of cartridges home in order to blow up a tree for fuel. It is likely that he worked at the Ecton Mine, for it was the only one still working in the immediate district.

He placed the two cartridges in the kitchen stove to soften them and went outside for a few moments, perhaps to make a hole under the tree in which to place the cartridges and the fuse. There was a huge explosion and he ran back into the house. The kitchen was a scene of utter devastation. His mother, who had been in the room at the time was literally blown to pieces. His sister was also in the room and had an incredibly lucky escape. Although blown off the sofa, she escaped with only a few cuts. The fire grate had been blown to fragments, the pieces wrecking the furniture, whilst the windows had been completely shattered.

The day that I (LP) found this reference I had lunch with a mining engineer who was licensed to use explosives. He rented a cottage at East Ecton in the Manifold Valley. I recalled the report and he smiled a little, asking what time of year the report was dated. It appears that in all probability, Fearns had left the cartridges outside for safety, perhaps in an outbuilding or the privy. It is likely that there had been a frost that night and the cartridges were frozen, hence the desire to soften them before inserting the fuse. Placing them in the stove, he did not realise he had started a bomb ticking that had the most disastrous of consequences.

Bollands Mine

On the west side of the village may exist another mine near Bollands Hall, for Richard Gaunt (see Chapter 4) had shares in a mine at 'Bollands, Butterton' in the early 1840s. Another small trial exists between Clayton House and Swainsley, marked on early OS maps as a copper shaft. There is also a small trial by the side of the footpath from Butterton Ford to Hillsdale Hall with what appears to be a lot of water issuing from a level.

Botstone Mine

Although mentioning several local mines Farey (1811) made no mention of this mine. It is situated at Wetton Mill and the tips may still be seen just upstream from the site of the former railway station, now the car park. Whether there was any 18th Century mining here is not known. In fact very little about the mine is known.

Work seems to have been undertaken in the 1820s, for in the will of John Fynney of Compton, Leek, Staffs dated 18th August 1828, he left a quarter share of the mines known as

Botstone and Bollands at Butterton to his nephew, William Fynney Johnson, a glass manufacturer of Manchester. He died shortly afterwards and the share was sold in January 1834 to Richard Gaunt, a silk manufacturer and also of Leek for £50.

It would appear that the original share holding was between Thomas Phillips, Hugh Ford, John Fynney and Thomas Salt(? all of Leek). The latter became bankrupt and his share was purchased by William Challinor, a solicitor of Leek. The lease was from Sir George Crewe Bt of Warslow Hall and covered all the land owned by him in the parish of Butterton. A new lease was drawn up and was dated 6th September 1834, between Sir George Crewe, lessor, and Richard Gaunt, William Fynney Johnson and William Challinor, lessees, for twenty-one years. The royalty was 1/12th of all ore found, 1/5th of any coal and there was a provision in case the mine struck rich. All limestone removed from the mine, except that needed for buildings etc at the mine also belonged to the lessor. William Challinor's son, also William, and a solicitor like his father, stated in a Dale Mine Deposition statement that his father was a shareholder at Botstone around 1837. William senior's brother was a shareholder in the Burgoyne Mining Company at Ecton.

An expense account for Botstone survives from 10th September 1836 to 1st January 1837. It states that it includes building a 'Smelt House, Cope's bill for machinery etc', plus 62lbs of gunpowder. The total expenses being £558.15.10d (£558.79p).

It is unlikely that the reference to a smelt house was incorrect. It was probably drawn up by William, junior who would have been close enough to what was happening to not have mistaken this. This is the only known reference to the smelting of ore at Wetton Mill. A shaft exists under the layby at the side of the road by the Botstone tips. It is shown on a cine film of the former railway of 1932, with a circular wall around it. See also under Chapter 11.

Ford Mine

Coincidentally during 1997, this mine was reopened for the first time in perhaps a century or more. On the same day, the excavators acquired mining papers relating to the North Staffordshire ore field. These papers included the only known mining lease of land at Ford.

The lease was of land owned by James and Daniel Smith, described as being farmers 'of the Ford' in the parish of Grindon. Unfortunately, the land is not identified, but as the mine is on the only recorded vein in the area it may reasonably be assumed to be the one concerned. The lease, dated 26th October 1836 was to Edward Forbes of Douglas, Isle of Man. He was the father-in-law of Melville Attwood.

The lease was of:

'every the mines veins seams pipes groves rakes beds floats and holes of Lead and Copper Ore, caulk [barytes, barium sulphate] and Calamine [zinc carbonate] and other Metals and semi metals and Minerals whatsoever that now are or which shall or may hereinafter be found…'.

This is so generalised that no actual mine may have existed prior to the lease. The latter was for twenty-one years at a yearly rent of 5/- (25p) and a royalty of 10%.

Melville Attwood

Attwood was a young man, very much an up and coming mining entrepreneur. He was born in 1812 at Prescott Hall in Worcestershire. The above lease was not the only interest Mr Forbes had in North Staffordshire. A lease exists (Kirkham/Porter Collection) between Edward Forbes and The Revd Sir Augustus Brydges Henniker, described as a Clerk and Baronet, for the exploitation of lead and copper mines in Grindon for twenty-one years from 1st September 1838. An annual rent and royalty was agreed as at Ford.

A draft lease dated September 1836 also survives between Forbes and John Lomas and George Salt. This relates to the Royledge Mine at Upper Elkstones (See Chapter 5). It was on the same terms and conditions and there was a requirement to keep four men at work. It is known that Forbes was negotiating with Henniker as early as 10th August 1835 and there are indications that agreement for the Royledge mine had been reached at that date despite the actual lease being over a year later. Although the lease is only in draft form, it must have been signed for there is correspondence later relating to a breach of covenant about the requirement to keep four men at work. Forbes asked that the Grindon lease be on the same terms as the Royledge agreement.

Jim Rieuwerts has discovered that Attwood was working at Chrome Hill near Glutton Bridge. The Chatsworth Collection has a Hartington and the Granges Barmaster's Book with the following entry for January – June 1842 (page 45). It states

> 'put Izaac Wain (for the use of Melville Attwood Esq) into possession of twenty meers of ground in an old vein situate upon Croome Hill – beginning at the side of the River Dove near an old level and all ranging northwardly from the said river. Also three cross veins'.

This old level is at Grid Ref 071670 and is 30 fathoms long.

It must have been Forbes who introduced Melville Attwood to Ecton, although this may have been as late as 1839 when he is understood to have returned from Brazil (see Chapter 3.3). However what brought him to North Staffordshire is not clear. An Ecton account book for 1840 (1) states for January and February of that year 'Ecton copper ores sold by Messrs Forbes and Co to Sneyd'. The Whiston Account book (2) shows the same purchases although the payment was made to Melville Attwood. In fact the earliest reference to Attwood in the Whiston accounts is 14th January 1840. Prior to that, all references to the Ecton account state 'paid the Ecton Miners'.

The Whiston works seems to have taken all the local copper ore at this period and there is no reference to Ford, although there is a single reference to Grindon on 19th April 1837 when 2 tons 15cwt 1qtr of ore was purchased from 'Stoddard of Grindon at £2.2.6d per ton, 3.5 produce (3). The amount paid was £5.15.10d (£5.79). As the Forbes lease for the land held by the lord of the manor, Sir A B Henniker, is dated 1838, it seems possible that this could have related to Ford or possibly Hurst Low, (see below).

By February 1840, the Ford Mine had turned out to be a disappointment:

> 'the adjoining trial in Mr Smith's ground has turned out so very contrary to all expectations that I've no reason to expect it will be worth trying the ground of Sir Augustus' (Forbes to Messrs Cruso and Co, Solicitors, Leek).

However a year later, Forbes was contemplating the float of a Company 'for working more extensively the Ford Mines' (Forbes to Cruso). Whether this actually was successful is not known, but it seems doubtful (4).

There is no evidence to suggest that Ford Mine was reworked after the Forbes venture terminated. Clearly Attwood was more interested in Ecton, following which he went to Cumbria and then to Nenthead before emigrating to the USA with his wife(5). Whether he was actually involved is unclear but there are two intriguing references in the Ecton Cost Book 1830-1860 (6). These are:

> '20th May 1844 Sampson Sutton care of Mr Attwood's House during the arrest 7/-' and 'January-April 1845 Mathew Redfern hay for Mr Attwood's horses during the arrest £3.0.0d'.

Description of the Site

The level was first visited by Lindsey Porter in 1972. There was a sizeable tip with a lot of water issuing from the rear of it, close to a small stream. There were samples of copper ore in the tip. Some of the latter has been removed recently. It consists of shaley dark limestone and shale but no mineralisation was found.

It was not possible in the time available to find the level entrance although we were left with a feeling that it had probably collapsed, maybe deliberately. It was felt that the water was issuing from a point above the level and work was abandoned in favour of a short shaft which was sunk above and to the east of where water was issuing. The shaft was about 100ft from the pool of water which probably marks the sough tail. The point chosen was at the beginning of a long sunken trench, now partially covered by hawthorn scrub. The significance of the trench was unknown, although divining rods seemed to indicate that it was above the level.

The shaft was sunk through soil and then shale to a depth of approximately 7 or 8ft where the roof of the level was breached. The work was undertaken by Len Kirkham with various helpers. Permission to dig was given by the farmer, Mr Alcock and the diggers benefited from much advice, encouragement and even coffee provided by the adjacent land owner, Mr Dennis Middleton of Dairy House. He had been responsible for showing the level to Lindsey Porter in 1972.

A significant quantity of water was siphoned away allowing access into the level. It had originally been strengthened by wooden supports from floor to roof and a horizontal section reinforcing the roof. Since the closure of the mine, the roof has collapsed creating a significant void above the timber work. Presumably the collapse observed on the surface was associated with this. The level was penetrated approximately 200ft to a blockage. It was possible to see further along the level to another fall at a further distance of 30 to 40ft.

The part of the level explored was primarily in beds of dark grey limestone with no sign of mineralisation. The timber work was observed beyond the fall with a lot of ochre coating everything. The width of the level was initially about 4ft wide, increasing to about $5\frac{1}{2}$ft in the bedded limestone. The level had been drilled using explosives and the shot holes were approximately one inch in diameter.

The release of water from the level also allowed pent up black damp to move down towards the entrance. Further exploration was therefore abandoned and the entrance sealed. The level was photographed prior to withdrawal. **Because of the existence of this gas, the mine should not on any account be reopened.**

Exploration of the fields above the level revealed the existence of two possible shafts which could have been associated with the level. The mine is situated at the southern end of a vein marked on the Geological Survey map (7). The vein extends north to Grindon Moor where disturbed ground exists by the road to Grindon from Butterton Moor. Copper ore has been noted in the remaining tips in this area (see below).

Ford Mine was probably no more than a trial and it is not even known if it was financed by Mr Forbes himself or possibly his venture at Ecton.

Clearly much exploratory work was being undertaken at this time – there were Companies exploiting Ecton, Dale and Mixon at this date for instance – and Mr Forbes would seem to have been a serious investor beyond the three principal mines in the ore field during the 1835-1845 period.

At the northern end of the vein it passed close to Hurst Low, a tumulus. A document dated 22nd June 1844 (8) states 'Hurst Low Mine – at an end'. The inference is that a Mr Richard Gaunt of Leek (lately deceased) had been a shareholder in the mine. He was also a shareholder in the Botstone Mine near Wetton Mill, the Bourgoyne Mines at Ecton in the late 1830s as well as the Dale Mine. He may also have been a shareholder at Royledge too.

As the mines in the area began to close down, some of the miners, wishing to remain in their chosen livelihood turned to other opportunities. In 1862, a Joseph Twigg – described as a miner – of Butterton, was sinking a shaft at Blue Hills, between the Roaches and Ramshaw Rocks, north of Leek. The shaft was down $27\frac{1}{2}$ fathoms but had not reached coal (9).

References

1. Ecton Cost Book, Matlock Local Studies Library

2. C.L.M. Porter Collection

3. This probably refers to a yield of 3.5%; rich by current standards, but not by the yield from Ecton which was often much better than this. See Chapter 3.7

4. Both references from the Kirkham/Porter Collection

5. Deposition of Robert Greenhough in the Dale Mine law suit

6. Ecton Cost Book, 1830-60, Derbyshire Record Office

7. Map No 111

8. Kirkham/Porter Collection

9. A. H. Green's Field Note Book, Book C, June 1862, British Geological Survey Library

8 Wetton, Alstonfield, Ilam & Newton Grange

8.1 Bincliff Mine

The group of mines situated above the River Manifold south of Wetton and facing Throwley are near some of the most beautiful countryside in the district. The mines are generally known as the Bincliff Mines but more correctly consist of the Bincliff, Oversetts and Highfield Mines. Collectively they comprise the greatest group of lead mines in the district under discussion and there are probably more workings above river level than at Ecton.

There is not very much remaining by way of documentary evidence and no plans are known to have survived. The reason for this is probably due to the fact that the mines are chiefly shallow rake workings and although worked for a considerable period were undercapitalised and no steam engine appears to have been erected.

These mines were probably the nearest example in North Staffordshire to many of the Derbyshire lead mines, many of the latter being worked by family concerns who worked small deposits of ore until water problems necessitated a move further along the vein. The connection with Derbyshire is further strengthened by the fact that the ore was weighed in loads and dishes as was the practice in the neighbouring county although there was no system of lot and cope and the Derbyshire mining customs had no legality here.

The wave of speculative mining that gripped the area in the 1850s also came to Bincliff in 1853 when the North Staffs Consols Mining Co, was formed. The only work of any merit which differed from the previous concerns during this period was the deepening of Oversetts and Hurt's Shafts now said to be 300ft deep, and the driving of two deep levels.

Surface Features

The area is characterised by long lines of shallow workings on the rake veins, roughly north-south orientated, eight or nine of which can be discerned. Although the shafts are not deep, a number of adits were driven into the hillside from the valley. Some of these are shallow, others connecting with the rake veins, although the caver is now denied his sport in most cases because of blockages.

Perhaps the most interesting features are the 19th Century remains, because prior to this the workings were too shallow and little in the way of machinery was employed. Hurt's Shaft has a large iron wheel on top of the shaft collar. The former site of the horse whim can be clearly seen and the wheel was probably on top of the headgear which formerly surmounted the shaft carrying the rope from the whim to the shaft. Three other wheels exist at Oversetts Mine to make up a set of four – presumably two at Hurt's Shaft and two at Duke's Shaft at Oversetts Mine. Oversetts Barn gives away no convincing indications of any connection with mining operations.

Remains of several coes can be found, many of which are referred to in the survey notes. It is a pity, but to date no remains of early activity, such as buddles etc have been found – perhaps indicative of the spasmodic approach to mining in this locality. The known history of the mines relates primarily to the 19th Century and one can only roughly sketch-in the earlier details. It is possible that some of the workings are very old. Although proving nothing historically, it is worth recording that in excavations of Falcon Low Cave, on the opposite side of the valley from the mines, a small piece of lead metal was found by the Leek Field Club Archaeological Section.

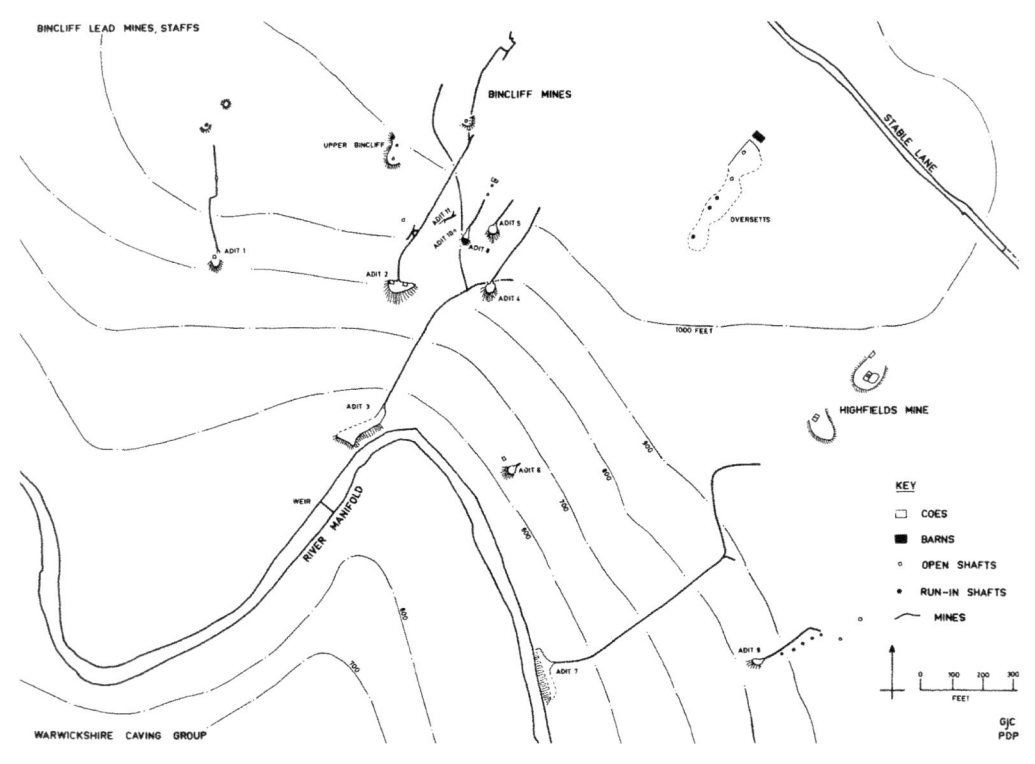

Reproduced from Bull PDMHS Vol 5, Pt5, p263 with permission

The Early History

When considering the history of the Bincliff Mines it must be understood that there was a division between the land and minerals owned by the Duke of Devonshire to the north-west and the Hurt family (of Castern Hall) to the south-east (principally Highfield Mine).

The Alstonfield Parish Registers record the baptism on July 2nd 1600 of a child of

'Margaretae F. Morgini and Agnotis Harte de Casteron, parochiae de Wetton, mynner'.

The Hurt family have owned the Castern Estate virtually continuously since the 16th Century and owned the mineral rights of the Highfield mine. It is possible that the mines were being worked in the 17th Century probably by Nicholas Hurt who was a lead miner living in 1660 (1), but unfortunately, the relationship between Agnotis Hurt and the better known Nicholas is not known. The latter became a lead merchant in the Wirksworth area and the family lived at Alderwasley Hall, having many interests in Derbyshire lead mines, a connection which continued until the late l9th Century.

Nicholas Hurt leased the rights to the lot and cope of lead ore from the Earl of Devonshire in 1626 for Wetton manor, i.e. the land adjacent to his own at Castern (See Chapter 3.2).

The Hurts' mining activities in North Staffordshire and probably Bincliff, is known from a letter from Roger Kenyon to the Chancellor of the Duchy of Lancaster dated 26th October 1630 and concerning chiefly the Thievely lead mines in Lancashire. Kenyon wrote:

'But I understand that in Staffordshire (where his Majesty hath noe lot nor cope nor other jurisdiecion in the mynes or care) there is Sir Richard Fleetwood, one Mr Hurt, and others whoe have lead mines and order and dispose the same to theire private and best benefitt, which, I heare, is in this manner: They lett the workes to Myners and reserve a part, some tyme of the oare and some tymes of the lead, to themselves, VIZT, in some places a seaventh dish in some other a sixth and where the oare is very plentifull a fifte or a foarthe dish, but that is seldome. If they reserve it in lead it is after the same rates, the charges of smeltinge reprised and this is all the gaine, and hard enough tooe, for the myners' (2).

Sir Richard Fleetwood lived at Calwich Abbey near Ellastone, south-west of Ashbourne, later building Wootton Lodge. He held a lease at the time of Kenyon's letter from the Mineral and Battery Works for the mines in North Staffordshire. The lease was granted in 1623 but shortly afterwards his operations were in difficulty and a renewal of the lease in 1640 was refused (3).

Bincliff was owned by the Duke of Devonshire from an early date and was probably acquired with his lands at Wetton and Ecton in the 16th Century. A plan of the estate, drawn by William Senior in 1617 does not indicate any mines in Bincliff. The mines are, however marked on Yates's map of Staffordshire 1775 where nine distinct 'mines' (most probably just separate shafts) are shown.

Between 1744 and 1751, the Duke's Wetton duty ore consisted of 414 loads of lead ore (approximately 110 tons of ore) which were sold to Barkers at Rowsley and Shacklow. The duty was 1/9th which gives a total tonnage of 1,000 tons (4). Whilst some of this was obviously from Ecton, some may well have come from other mines in the parish, such as Bincliff.

The Nineteenth Century History

The mines owned by the Duke of Devonshire were being worked at the beginning of the 19th Century for accounts exist from 1812. The tonnages are very low indeed the highest figure for ten years being a total of just over 18 tons raised in 1815 (5). The duty ore was 1/10th and the ore was sold to J Alsop & Co. The earliest references to a John Fallows was in 1823 which may be indicative of the age of Adit 2. The names of the mines are rather interesting: Old Morris, Old Sutton, Tar Hole, Hangworm Three Lows, Bateman, Uppersets, Goosenest, Primgap, Penny, Clay Grove, Rising Sun, Founder and Chain Shafts, Green Rake, Smiths Shaft or Hurt's Vein, Cobler, Longheath, Butcher and Friday. Both Rising Sun and Friday were the names of veins. Smelting Hill Rake existed to the south of Highfields, possibly around the lime kiln.

During the early 19th Century it is likely that many of the Duke's Ecton miners would try their hand at Bincliff, as output from Ecton was falling rapidly and many men were put out of work.

Farey (6) referred to the mine in 1811 and described it as being in 4th lime, lead. Garner writing in 1840 had little extra to add, stating simply that the galena occurred in a matrix of barytes, but was not much worked. In 1838, ore sales to Milnes & Co commenced and thereafter all the ore appears to have gone to this firm.

Throughout the 1840s, ore continued to be obtained in small quantities but it is obvious that the work was being undertaken by individual miners as distinct from a mining company. Because of this the total amounts of ore recorded are not complete, and only the ores raised in the Devonshire side of the mining area have been recorded and survive in the Barmaster's collection.

In 1853, the mines received the attention of a mining company. The particular interest of this company lies in the fact that it shows very well (perhaps better than most companies so far studied in the Staffs/Derbys orefield) how deceptive some companies could be.

Entries in the Duke's account book were signed-for by John Taylor, the Duke's mineral agent until 1844 when Stephen Eddy took responsibility. Eddy looked after the Duke's Grassington mines in Yorkshire until his death in 1861 and was also responsible for the Ecton and Bincliff mines. Judging by the amounts of output recorded it is doubtful if there was more than a handful of miners and work was probably intermittent – possibly the miners were also farmers.

The North Staffordshire Consols Mining Co

During April 1853, the Bincliff and Castern lead mines were advertised and applications for shares were invited; although not mentioned in the advert, the company was to be known as the North Staffordshire Consols. The company was to be conducted on the cost-book system and the capital was to be £21,000 in £1 shares, to be fully paid on allotment. This was somewhat unusual, for companies usually asked for a 'call' of a portion of the full value. But the same advert stated that because of 'the unlimited supply of inexpensive waterpower from the River Manifold' it is anticipated that this company will be

Above: Highfields Mine drawing shaft in 1972 with the wheel from the former head frame still on the mine **Opposite:** The Duke's Deep Level entrance in 1972

entitled to pay for the purchase of the mines, working expenses, and machinery, and make it a dividend paying mine with half the proposed capital – the use to which the remaining half of the capital was to be put was not stated.

A lease exists dated 1857, where the lessee is a Mr Tinker (see below). Presumably he was responsible for obtaining a head lease and was then successful in establishing the business.

It is possible that the reason for requiring the shares to be fully paid was to obtain as much income from shareholders before they became fully aware of the risks attached to the venture. The advert referred to the intention to erect a powerful waterwheel on the River Manifold.

'This stream will afford an unlimited and never failing supply of water powers by which the stamping and dressing of the ores can be most economically carried on the same machinery which will be wanted in order to work the mines at depths below the adit'.

There was no mention of the well-known fact that the River Manifold is usually running underground at this point for most of the year and only uses the surface bed during periods of very wet weather. A further comment was that of the entire sett (of 2,000 acres according to the advert but 6,000 acres according to the manager – *Mining Journal*, 1853, p614)

'only 4 acres have yet been proved, but within that comparatively limited space, not less than 3410 fathoms or 3 miles 7 furlongs of profitably working lodes have been distinctly traced'

– a point hardly substantiated by the amount of ore produced.

Misrepresentation

The chairman of the committee of management was the Earl of Devon and the consulting engineer and managing director was Thomas Rowlandson. The company held a lease for twenty-one years at 1/20th royalty from the Duke and 1/15th from Mr Hurt. The large expanse of the lease presumably stemmed from the fact that the land was owned by the Duke – referred to as the Earl in the advert. The boundary of the sett was 23 [?2/3] miles and Rowlandson claimed it had an average of 50 fathoms of backs above the bed of the Manifold and Dove 'with ample waterpower that no steam engine will be required'. This over-optimism, or really misrepresentation of the actual facts was followed by a further note the following week (*Mining Journal* 1853 p.634) stating that the ground could be worked to 250 fathoms below the river (despite the lack of a steam engine presumably) and that 'the number of working fathoms of paying ore ground will not be less than six million'.

Despite comments such as these the *Mining Journal* reports do give much valuable information – the only pity is that the reports were infrequent and not as prolific as those penned by Richard Niness for the mines with which he was associated a few years later, see Chapter 4 on the Dale Mine as an instance.

Several reports confirm that hitherto the workings had been shallow – an average of 30 fathoms above the River Manifold is quoted and it is probable that this figure is on the high side – and that the water had been withdrawn from the mines by means of a bucket and windlass. It is rather ironical that a letter in the *Journal* in reply to criticism of the company referred to the fact that the 'working miner' (who lacked capital and machinery) had been replaced by 'capitalists', when the work pattern remained virtually the same. However, when the first report was printed in October 1853 the shares were reported as selling at 30/- (£1.50p).

Initial Work

This consisted of clearing and securing levels and shafts. The 'Great Level' (Adit 2?) was cleared out $3\frac{1}{2}$ fathoms by mid-October. At the same date Oversetts Shaft, (probably the shaft nearest the barn) had been found to be 45 fathoms deep and was expected to cut a 'known rich lead lode' at a depth of 10 fathoms. At Highfields, the shaft was down 30 fathoms and was expected to cut a similar lode at a similar depth.

A further mine being worked was known as the Nut Bush. It is described (*Mining Journal*, 1853, p646 – as for the above) as having rock filled with small veins of lead ore and having two perfectly defined lodes going down well, within 10 fathoms of the surface. A level is also referred to, and from the brief description it is possibly Adit 9. This view is reinforced by a copy of a plan, formerly at the old Devonshire Estate Office, Buxton, but apparently now destroyed. The plan was copied by Miss Nellie Kirkham who stated that it was in a very poor condition and could not be properly copied.

Above: Hurt's Deep Adit Level entrance, 1972 **Opposite:** Another view of the Duke's Deep Adit level entrance showing how easily entrances may become lost

From the copy which was taken, the word Nut Bush appears in the locality of Adit 9 and the shafts close to it. An interesting reference is to 'work at the Wetton setts' and may refer to Wetton Hill where ore was being raised in small quantities a few years later.

Some ten months later – August 1854, at the quarterly meeting – there was a balance in favour of the mines of £577, indicating how undercapitalised the concern was. By that time, the Nut Bush Level had been driven 47 fathoms, the lode had been cut and contained ore that would be 'saving work' i.e. pay for its extraction. The men were driving on a vein in a cross-course which intersected the lode. Hurt's Deep Adit (Adit 7) had been driven 40 fathoms, requiring a further 40 fathoms before the adit would reach the various lodes to which it was being driven.

Fallow's level (Adit 2?) had been driven 190 fathoms (but probably not entirely by this company) requiring a further 40 fathoms more to intersect 'the lodes at the Copper Shaft'. The Duke's Deep Adit (Adit 3?) had been driven 15 fathoms. As far as shafts were concerned, Highfield, or Hurt's Shaft had been cleared down to 50 fathoms and there was approximately 10 fathoms further to clear. At Duke's Shaft at Oversetts a whim was being erected. At the Copper Shaft a small cross cut was being driven to cut a lode some 10 fathoms below 'where the rich lead and copper ore was obtained'.

Towards the end of 1854, Hurt's Level was over 60 fathoms long, driving a fathom per week in hard ground. High in the hillside above the level, Hurt's Shaft was down 60 fathoms yielding some good stones of ore. It was intended to sink to a depth of 65 fathoms where it was optimistically hoped to open some good ore ground. A level was being driven at a depth of 45 fathoms to communicate with the shaft and was yielding some ore – about 12 tons of lead ore per fathom. This reference is interesting for no such rich level has yet been found.

The Duke's Shaft (at Oversetts Mine) had been finally cleared and sinking commenced. It was stated (*Mining Journal*, 1854, p783) that there was only 2 fathoms to sink to get as low as the former workings. Duke's Deep Adit Level was still being driven, progress being 7ft per week. On the surface, the dressing floors had been completed and the concern was ready to dress ore 'as soon as we can get a supply of water'.

The First Sale of Ore

The following year, 1855, saw the sale of ore by the company for the first time. The accounts are incomplete, as stated above, because of a lack of information on the yield from Highfields Mine. However the *Mining Journal* gives figures which seem to indicate that the bulk of the ore came from Highfields (if one assumes the Devonshire accounts to be complete). A minimum of 35 tons is known to have been sold and as a further parcel was dressed for sale late in the year the quantity may have been 50 tons.

Wage Costs

The time book for 1855 has survived and this gives details for the first four months of the year. Less than a dozen men were employed before ore dressing commenced. and practically all work was concentrated in the Hurt Royalty. In April 1855 there were between 19-24 men employed. Wages were paid fortnightly. The ore dressers received 15/- (75p) per week and the boys (a maximum of four) received 4/- to 5/- (20–25p) per week. The day wage was 2/6d (12$^1/_2$p) per day and 1/- (5p) per day for men and boys respectively, which corresponds reasonably well with wages at Ecton during this period. The highest paid was the whim drawer who earned £1.12s (£1.60) per week but probably provided his own horse.

During October 1855, Duke's Deep Adit (Adit 3 ?) was being driven at £4 per fathom. At this time, the men at Hurt's Deep Adit were in harder ground and collectively earning 90/- (£4-50) per week. They were ordered to drive south at the beginning of October which probably indicates they had started the cross-cut at a distance of approximately 105 fathoms from the surface entrance. At Hurt's Shaft men were driving at the 60 fathom level, west of the shaft (where ore was left in the bottom of the level nearly the whole of its length – 28 fathoms 4ft. (*Mining Journal,* May 1855, p326). East of the shaft some good ore was also being produced in the 55 fathom level.

A New Discovery

The October report indicated that a new discovery had been made at the shaft, laying open 15 fathoms of backs, containing solid lead ore over one inch thick, in a lode running west from the shaft. It was anticipated that the lode would produce 14cwt of ore per fathom and stoping down the lode was let at 45/- (£2.25) per fathom. Ore from the mine at this period was fetching £11.7.6d per ton (£11.37$^1/_2$p).

Duke's Shaft was said to be dry and only 6 feet from where the lode had been cut. The men were bringing up some very large lumps of ore. During 1855, the Ecton Mountain Mining Co, was cutting its losses by selling all surplus items and the Bincliff Company purchased rails worth £50 from Ecton.

A further report occurred in the *Mining Journal* during February 1856 (p150). The various workings were still progressing and it appears that it was the intention of the agent to unite Duke's Deep Adit with Oversetts Shaft at a depth of 80 fathoms below the surface, requiring a further 30 fathoms to be sunk at the shaft.

Loose Accountancy

A general meeting was held on March 1st 1856, when there was a balance in favour of the mines of £293. Despite this, a call of 2/- per share was made. The next meeting reported a credit balance of £525 (*Mining Journal*, p464). Despite this there was a rather unfavourable report of a further meeting in July (*Mining Journal*, p500) which stated that 'accounts as these would not be tolerated in a Limited Liability Company'. The discrepancy was that the expenditure had been entered as:

Wages	£303.1.8d.
Merchants bill	£435.13. 4d.
Repayment of loan to Bank	£300.0.0
Hurt's rent and lease	£l30.10.8d.
Total	£1169.5.8d

Whilst the income was stated to be simply:

Cash received from calls and loans (February-July 10th, 1856) including proceeds from sale of ore (61 tons 13c wt) – £1,169.5.8d.

In the capital account liabilities amounted to £474.15.6d, the only assets being the buildings, whims, ladders, rails, wagons and general plant, valued at £1,000. The last two reports which have been found to date (*Mining Journal*, 1858, pp271 & 356) indicate that Duke's and Hurt's Adits were still being driven. At the former, during May, the 'forefall' (face) contained a 'fine bed joint of oxide of lead 11 inches thick with 'brown end', a local term used here for zinc and silver'. The men were driving between two perpendicular veins, 4ft apart consisting of cawk (barytes, barium sulphate) and spar, which were coming closer together. A similar situation existed at Hurt's Adit.

The reference to 'brown end' is interesting. The term 'brown-hen' has been found in reports on the nearby Mixon Mine in 1829, and at Ecton in the 1790s. In the chapter on Mixon it is suggested that brown hen probably referred to zinc blende and this point would appear to be now confirmed. The reference to silver would be purely for the benefit of shareholders, not mineralogists.

A lease survives (Dev Coll Bolton Papers) dated 9th May 1857, for the lead ore mines at Bincliff. The date suggests that it had taken some time to draw up. It was for twenty-one years, at a royalty of 1/20th and between the Duke of Devonshire and William Tinker of Alderley, Cheshire. A minimum of four miners were to be kept at work. It would appear that Tinker had ideas about building a smelting mill for once it was established, the Duke's ore would be smelted there, free of charge. The lease covered 416 acres which is a lot different from the acreage claimed in the *Mining Journal*. Presumably the Company was working upon a memorandum of agreeement in the interim.

The Bincliff and Casturn Mining Co Ltd

Between 1858 and 1860, the company appears to have been wound up, for the Bincliff and Castern mines were advertised as being to let on 22nd December 1860 (*Mining Journal*, p862). A new company appears to have been formed for there is a loose sheet in the New Ecton Mining Co book (7) which gives a summary of some accounts. The interesting point is that it refers to the Bincliff and Casturn Mining Co Ltd.

Its predecessor was established on the cost book system and was not a limited company, The time book, however, contains a few spasmodic entries from January to May 1860. Generally there were four men working in each royalty, but as they interchanged they must have been working both royalties together. The entries are chiefly for 'clearing up the old workings', and 'working at the ore', although a reference to 'getting a speck of ore' was perhaps nearer the true position.

There are no further references to the actual work done but the *Annual Mineral Statistics* for 1864 state that the mine yielded 15 tons 16cwt of lead ore producing 9 tons 5cwt of lead metal (8). The value was not stated.

The Barmaster's Book for Ecton and Bincliff (9) includes an entry on May 27th 1887 that Wm. Higton had raised 3 loads 2 dishes of ore and paid a royalty of 1/20th, amounting to

£2.13.8d. (£2.68) putting the value of the ore at approximately £54. He had also paid one shilling rent for 'the Wetton lease'.

> See Chapter 4 for a reference to a lease of the right to dig for lead and copper in the parish of Alstonfield, dated 1723.

Iron Ore Mines

The Duke of Devonshire's account book (Matlock Ref Lib) for the period 1826-61 also made several references to the raising of iron ore, and further references occur in an account book of the Duke's at the Derbyshire Record Office Matlock.

The first reference is in 1850 when royalty payments recorded for 'paint', together with a reference to 3 tons 2cwt 2qrs of brown and blue iron ore sold at £1 and 75d per ton respectively. The royalty was 9d per ton. The mine was situated 'in the parish of Wetton' and more specifically, in 1860-1861 at 'Strong Stys'. This mine is situated in a dramatic location just north of Thors Cave at Grid Ref 101555. The late Ivan Thompson of Redhurst Farm, Wetton, used to call the mine a 'paint mine'. Another ironstone mine is situated close to the Alstonfield to Gateham Road at 121569, and the Old Series Geological map (sheet 82 NE) recorded iron ore at this position.

The ore seems to have been known by several names and yellow paint, yellow ochre, yellow stone ochre are recorded. In 1850-1, about 16 tons were recorded as being raised, independently, by Wm Chadwick and Richard Sheldon. The North Staffordshire Consols Mining Co, does not appear to have taken any part in iron ore mining and the next reference is in May 1859. At this date, yellow stone was being raised at 'Strong Stys' at 30/- (£1.50) and 21/- (£1.05) per ton, the royalty being 1/20th. Small quantities were raised during 1860 and 1861 when the accounts finished (probably because of the death of the Duke's mineral agent Capt Stephen Eddy). In 1861, six tons were raised from Hope Heath, which could infer a separate deposit of ore as a further reference occurs for that year under 'Strong Stys'.

Niness stated that the Dale Mine had an interest in a mine at Hope Dale, which must have been for iron ore, but no further details are known (see Chapter 4). However it could relate to the 1861 reference above.

The accounts do not state who the ore was sold to, but nearly one ton was 'sold to Derby' in 1850. It is probable however that much of the ore was sent to the former mill at Milldale, on the River Dove, which was a colour mill about this time, worked by a Mr Alfred Leese (10). The mill was a few feet upstream of Viator Bridge, where two grinding stones can be seen. It was known locally as a 'paint mill'.

Mr Ian Else of the Chatsworth Estate Office advises that there are shafts in the fields numbered 530, 571, 600 and 630 (two shafts in this one). They are to the east of Bincliff. Some of these are marked on the White Peak 1:25 000 OS Map. Whether these were iron or lead is not known.

Plot, writing in 1686, recognised the existence of ochre in the locality and mentioned

> 'yellow and red Ochres, sometimes met with (but in small quantities) near Stanshope in the parish of Allstonfield... And I was informed of a sort of black Chalk found between the beds of Chirts, and the beds of gray Marble, sometimes a finger thick, and sometimes less, in Langley Close near Stanshope (but in the parish of Wetton) belonging to the right Honorable William Earle of Devon' (11).

In addition to iron ore, the accounts also refer to lead ore raised at the shaft on Wetton Hill, presumably the one near to Gateham. Records commence in 1850, where a Thomas Goslyne was working as a tributor, possi-

Iron ore Sales

Date	Quantity Tons cwt qrs	Value	Remarks
1850	11 13 0		Royalty 9d per ton
1851	4 13 0		
1859	10 10 0	£12.12.0.	Royalty 1/20th
1860	7 13 2	£9.14.10½	
1861	7 5 6		

Wetton Lead Ore

Date	Quantity (Tons cwt Qtr)	Value
1850	2 5 0	£6.19.11
1851	1 7 0	£4.1.9
1857	2 14 2	£32.14.0
1858	4 loads	£10.16.0
1859	1 load 3.25 dishes	£3.19.6
1860	4 loads	£12.16.0

bly working the mine on his own account. The quantities were never great and the ore was sold to Messrs Milnes, along with the Bincliff ore.

8.2 Mining at Ilam

Both Ilam and nearby Okeover were outlying estates of the Abbey of Burton on Trent, donated by the founder Wulfric Spott in his will of 1002. The Abbey was dissolved in 1539 and then reconstituted as a College in 1541, but was finally dissolved in 1545 when it was granted to the 'statesman and schemer', William Paget, one of Henry VIII's principal secretaries. There are no references to the getting of metal ores or mining in either estate in the extensive records of the Abbey throughout all those centuries.

After the dissolution, it was not long before Paget realised his investment by selling many of his acquired estates, for which process he needed a Licence to Alienate from the King. The licence for Ilam, dated 30th November 1547, allowed him to sell it to John Port/e, a member of a branch of a family of rich merchants of Chester (12). Okeover went to the sitting family who adopted the place-name for themselves.

The disposal of thousands of monastic estates was, of course, a field day for lawyers and the rather approximate identification of lands and rights in the agreements of the day, created many opportunities for long and expensive suits in the courts of equity, such as Chancery. It was not long before the Okeover and Port families were in dispute about rights on Ilam Moor, Bunster and Dovedale. In addition to the usual claims of lordship and the holding of manor courts, there was also the tangled matters of rights of common and of tithes. The final Order of the Court of Chancery, in favour of John Port, was made in November 1584, in the 25th year of the reign of Queen Elizabeth I, after the matter had been referred for decision to the Court of Queen's Bench (13).

A document in the Okeover archive, appears to be a note written by their lawyer, or his clerk, listing no less than fifty-three evidences they might produce to support their side of the case in Chancery. Two are of great interest:-

'11 ... That Raffe Okeover gave Plattes and Mylwarde lysense 16 years agoo to digge for lead ower in Ilam moar by virtue whereof they dygged thear and gott ower withoutte Interrumption'

'12 ... provethe that the plt. [Port] And his father aboute 28 years agoo wear indicted for digging of Ilam Moar for lead ower by Raffe Okeover sithene wch tyme they have not dygged thear for any ower.' (14)

The exact date of this document, and the inferred dates of the events referred to, are not clear but indicate mining for lead on Ilam Moor in the 1550s and 60s.

As was so often the case, suits in Chancery went on for many years and, meanwhile, John Port (I) had died in 1574 and his son, also John, died just as judgement was coming through in 1584. The result was that the Ports' rights were the subject of Inquisitions Post Mortem on both Johns and, since the eldest son of John (II), Robert, was a minor when his father died, the Court of Wards and Liveries.

The inquisition on John (II), in 1584, (15) lists his rights on Ilam Moor, including tithes of grain, corn and lead (plumbii). The survey or 'extent' of estates leased to Robert's remote kinsman, Sir Thomas Stanhope, to whom the wardship was awarded, refers (in English) to the 'tythes of corne hay **and lead** in Ilam and Nether Castern'. Mining was specifically referred to in a clause which – 'EXCEPTED and alwaies reserved owt of the said graunte fees, reliefs fynnes heryett **mynes of mettall**, stone and cole' (16). So, although these tithes were not mentioned in the Inquisitions, Robert could look forward to rights of mining and tithes of lead on reaching his majority – due in 1590.

The reference to mines in Nether Castern seems to indicate that they were not those later worked as Bincliffe and Highfield Mines, to the east of a disused lane from Damgate to Wetton.

8.2 Mining at Ilam

Most Nether Castern land lay to the East of Castern Hall and stretched in a band across Ilam Moor to the edge of Dovedale. But the position of these mines cannot now be determined. Over a hundred years later, when the senior branch of the Hurt family had moved to Alderwasley Hall, leaving a cadet branch as Castern, the inventory of the goods of Thomas Hurt of Castern in 1627 included – 'Half of a groove wherein lead oare is gotten xl s. [and] groove tools implements belonging to grooves xl s.' (17). The location of this groove is no more certain. The description 'groove' may indicate that the ore was obtained by excavation from the surface, rather than by shaft.

In the 18th Century, it would not be surprising if the Ports had interests in mining since, in 1731, George (Newell) Port's sister, Frances Newell, married Burslem Sparrow, described as 'Ironmaster of Wolverhampton'. Burslem and his father George Sparrow were leading players in the Staffordshire mining industry in the first half of the 18th Century and made a wider name, operating as licensed erectors of Newcomen steam engines to drain mines, which they did not only in the coal fields of Coventry and the Black Country but also in the lead mines of Derbyshire.

The first hint of mining activity at Ilam itself in the 18th Century, is very oblique. In 1777, the famous Mrs Delany, who was the aunt of Mary (Dewes) Port of Ilam, wrote about Mary's husband's affairs in a letter to her niece, 'May all his searches answer his labour, and wishes, and turn his copper into gold!' (18). If this involved mining at Ilam (which seems likely), the most probable site would be the grassy mounds and possible blocked shaft on the edge of Dovedale. In any case, it failed to rescue Port from grave financial crises, which eventually forced him to let Ilam Hall and move into cheaper accommodation in Derby.

The next mention of lead mining comes late in the century, when William Bray visited the area and published his "Sketch of a Tour Into Derbyshire and Yorkshire". The second edition of 1783, in describing Dovedale says,

> 'On a hill opposite Reynard's-hall, in an old lead mine, a few entrochi (19) are found in the stone; and in the wood beyond is a vein of ruddle, or red ochre in chinks of the rocks, which is used to mark the sheep with, and it will not easily wash out.' (20)

Looking up to the top of the Staffordshire bank of the Dove, near the famous arch of Reynard's Cave, one can see, high on the rim of the valley, the outlines of Air Cottage, built many years later by the Watts-Russell family. In a field immediately behind there are traces of excavation (SK 141523) and the Tithe Map of 1839 lists the field as 'Old Mine Close'. Mature, low spoil heaps, completely covered with meadow turf, contain calcite and traces of barite.

Mrs Sellars, an elderly lady in Ilam, told of a woman living at Air Cottage early this century, who used to keep butter fresh by lowering it in a basket down a mine shaft near the cottage, but no trace of the shaft has been found.

Further to the west is a linear plantation of beech trees, Sandbroom Wood, where there is a long wide channel in the rocks, exposing joint faces and traces of the iron oxide 'ruddle'. This channel cannot be identified as a vein – it is rather wide and there are no traces of tool marks. But it was common, as here, to plant trees along the line of an excavation and wall it off to keep cattle out. The limestone in this area is heavily dolomitised and there is an interesting dolomite pavement structure nearby.

The next period of mining activity recorded, was in the 1840s. By this time the estate was in the hands of Jesse Watts-Russell, who purchased it from the last John Port of Ilam, who could not extricate the family from the encumbrances and mortgages on the estate and sold up in 1809 (21). It was Jesse who enclosed Ilam Moor, before the 1839 Tithe Apportionment, naming several of the fields after members of the family – Max Close, Bessie Close etc. Presumably this was when Old Mine Close was named.

Whether he had useful contacts in Devon, or whether he was just avoiding using Derbyshire miners, he eventually made an agreement with a group including Devonian mining entrepreneurs. In 1849 Samuel Lewis's *Topographical Dictionary of England* reported rather belatedly – "a vein of copper, lately discovered upon this property, has been let to some Cornish [sic] miners, who are also working veins of lead-ore" (22).

In fact the Indenture of Agreement, setting up the Ilam Mining Company, was signed by

Watts Russell and the grantees on 4th August 1845 (23). The partners in the mine were listed as Richard Munt of Wood Street, Cheapside in the City of London, Straw Hat Manufacturer; James Bourdillon the elder of Great Winchester Street in the City of London, Gentleman; Christopher Robins of Landscombe near Asburton [sic – Ashburton] in the county of Devon, Gentleman; and Henry Crace of Hyren Quarry, Bickley [sic – Bickleigh] near Plymouth in the county of Devon.

Munt was in partnership with a man called Brown. Their main business is listed in London Directories as 'Munt and Brown, Straw and leghorn Hat Manufacturer. 36, Wood Street' and one of the two main shafts at Ilam seems to have been named after Brown, probably to cement their investment with flattery. By 1856, their business had diversified into 'Straw Hat[s], Milliners and Artificial Flowers' and had expanded into two other premises.

Bourdillon was a solicitor, listed in an 1850 London Directory as 'Bourdillon, James and Stafford Solrs. 2, Austin Friars Passage & 30, Gt Winchester Street'. By 1856, James was in a solicitors' practice with someone called Gunning, but still at 30, Gt Winchester Street. A Charles Bourdillon was also listed, in a firm of stockbrokers.

The other shaft, Robins, by far the greater undertaking, was named after Christopher Robins, of Ashburton (in the Lease). In the 1850 Directory of Devon, he was 'of Landscove' and listed as manager of the Penn Recca Slate Company (25). Robins was also listed as 'landowner, investor in mines, purser (secretary), eg. Avon Console (1853) and Wheal Emma (1856), both in Buckfastleigh' (25). In the 1851 census he was thirty-nine years old and described as a 'slate merchant'.

Crace is also mentioned in the MS History of the Penn Recca quarry (26). In 1861, land in Devon was conveyed to Robins and Crace together, so they were obviously well connected around the period of the Ilam Mining Company.

The only other committee member mentioned in reports, who can be identified is Charles Bischoff, another solicitor. Since Bourdillon is not mentioned again, perhaps he was Bourdillon's replacement. In 1869 a declaration was made by Charles Bischoff of 4, Great Westminster Street Buildings, in a case of bankruptcy involving the Shore family of Blore.

The Lease gives the Grantees 'full and free liberty license power and authority to dig work Mine and Search for Tin and Tin Ore Copper and Copper Ore Lead and Lead Ore and all other Metals Ores Metallic Minerals and fossils (other than Quarries of Stone)' in identified closes (27) marked on a plan. In the case of several closes it was forbidden, without express consent, 'to erect Engines, Sheds Buildings or Machinery … or 'to wash cleanse stamp spall and dress ores.' These are fields on the plateau, alongside the road from Ilam to Alstonefield and Wetton which, in addition to be prominently visible for the more intrusive aspects of the mining industry, also have a good cover of silty loam and are, therefore, of greater agricultural value.

The lease was for twenty-one years and included the usual clauses for termination, assessment of profits and arbitration of disputes. It required accurate plans to be submitted (unfortunately not surviving) and for the mine to be returned, on lapse or surrender of the lease, in a usable state. Excavated limestone was to be left for Watts-Russell's use – a valuable consideration in an area of extensive drystone walling to be constructed and maintained. There are also extensive clauses about the measurement and assaying of ore and control of mixing it with ore from other sources.

In return, Watts-Russell was to receive 'one twelfth part' of the profits – clauses being designed carefully to assess the methods of accounting for the figures. It was also agreed that if, after arbitration if necessary, it was agreed that steam pumping was needed to work the mine, Watts-Russell's share dropped to one twentieth. An interesting aspect of the assessment of sales of ore, reflecting the origins of the Devonian partners, is that ore be valued at 'the price… of the previous months at the Public Ticketing for the sale of copper ore at Truro in the County of Cornwall and as is adopted in the sale of ores raised from the Ecton Mine'. They were to account for profits annually or '… as often as they have 75 Tons' of ore.'

The grantees undertook to operate the mine 'in minerlike manner… uninterruptedly throughout the said Ilam by sufficient mechanical power… there being after the first Six Calendar Months

8.2 Mining at Ilam

not less at any time than two able bodied working miners at work in the same mine'. They also undertook to maintain all fences, make bridges for cattle over leats and fence off shafts. There were also the usual clauses giving Watts-Russell rights to distrain property if payments were late or there were other infringements of the terms of the Lease.

However, operations at the mine must have started well before the signing of the Lease, since a shaft had already led to a discovery reported in the press and, subsequently, in Llwellyn Jewitt's *Reliquary* (28).

> ... "A case in point is afforded by a very large collection of bones found in July 1845, in a copper mine near Ilam, opened in one of the hills bounding the valley of the Dove, where the shaft, when about 20 yards (29) from the surface, intersected a natural level or horizontal passage in the rock, the floor of which was thickly strewn with bones of the Fox, Wolf, Dog, Ox and Goat, some so far deprived of animal matter as to adhere closely to the tongue. They were nearly all visible to a person descending the shaft, but some were partially embedded in a thin deposit of mud, produced by the infiltration of surface water. No communication with the surface could be detected though one must have existed at some point not far distant."

The fauna seems to indicate a fairly recent period, even as late as early medieval, rather than the Pleistocene age associated with many local cave deposits. It is not quite certain which shaft was involved, though it seems Robins shaft was the first to be sunk. Bateman was accompanied on his visit to the mine by the manager, 'Captain' James Sprague. What he thought of Bateman's gustatory forensic methods is not recorded, but the discovery shows that the miners had already sunk to at least 12 fathoms (72ft) in July 1845, a month before the signing of the Mining Company lease.

Sprague seems to have been involved from an early stage, having accompanied Thomas Bateman on his visit in 1845. At a later period a Captain James Sprague was managing mines on the Tamar and in Buckfastleigh in 1851-56 (30). In an anonymous mining guide, published in the *Mining Journal* in 1853, a J Sprague, Beeralston, Cornwall, is included. It is not recorded who built the small house close to the mine for Sprague. Until recently it was mapped as 'Miner's Cottage'. In August 1847, an inventory of fixtures belonging to Jesse Watts-Russell was listed 'in the House occupied by James Sprague at The Ilam Mine' (31).

The Ilam mine did not appear in *Mining Journal* reports until 12th February 1847, when a General Meeting of the Company was held at Bourdillon's offices in Great Winchester Street. The report refers to a general meeting, when accounts for the last twelve months, amounting to £1,378 were submitted and approved. The future monthly cost was £80-£100. This, plus a repayment to the treasurer of monies advanced (about £430), meant a call of £2 per share. This would seem to indicate that there were between 750 and 1,000 shares on the register.

Of the remains of the mine, the major shaft, Robins, (SK 135528) slopes, or 'hades', at about 45° down the face of a joint in the Hopedale limestone, on a bearing of about 208°T (SSW). Brown's Shaft (SK 135526) was sunk vertically about 65 fathoms roughly along this bearing, as if to connect with Robins, though it would have had to be about 46 fathoms deep to reach vertically to the bottom of Robins. However, sinking of this shaft encountered water problems and attempts were made to dewater it. A cross cut from Robins at 45 fathoms was abandoned and another driven from the bottom of Robins at 67 fathoms (32). These measures never succeeded in lowering the water in Browns consistently and a period of melting snow and rain in April 1948 made the level rise alarmingly.

Unlike Robins shaft, this shaft has not been recently surveyed, but a cursory inspection reveals that it is also a substantial project. At surface the shaft is about 6ft x 9ft and becomes approximately 9ft square. The top 4.5ft is nicely ginged, but then it sinks in solid limestone. At just over 33 fathoms there is a level towards Robins. About 8 fathoms in there is a shaft in the floor, flooded to within 1.5 fathoms of the level. Nearby is a stows about 4ft wide and 12 inches in diameter. The level continues about 16.5 fathoms to an unfired forefield. Water level in the main shaft is at about 25 fathoms. The depth of water has not been plumbed – yet.

Another run in shaft (SK 136526), with no spoil heap, 106 yards SSW of Robins Shaft and very close to the bronze age burial mound, Ilamtops Low, may be an attempt to connect with the extensive natural caverns which seem to stretch a considerable distance west of the main shaft.

In a lime kiln quarry very close to the NE of the Low, in the deepest corner of the quarry, is an open cleft, from which cavers have felt a draught of air, which may indicate a connection with the natural cave system. This remains to be explored – requiring some excavation.

In a sparsely wooded close, the Nursery Plantation (SK 135528), about 200m north of the mine, there is a line of delvings, partly disturbed recently by the farmer. These may be ore processing remains, though one looks as if it might be a run in shaft.

On 20th March 1847, a report by the publisher, Henry English, was published in the *Mining Journal*. It stated that the shaft had been sunk 67 fathoms on the dip with a crosscut at 42 fathoms driven northwards. A new shaft, Browns Shaft, was being sunk about 40 fathoms away and was some 16 fathoms above its proposed depth. However the sinking was plagued with water.

During 1847, the main work consisted of driving north, under the sloping Robins shaft, at the 42 fathom level and driving west and east at the 67 fathom level. The west end was driving towards Browns lode, so they were clearly trying to see what the lode looked like both at the 42 and the 67 fathom levels. There were traces of copper, but none in commercial quantities. In the 42 fathom level, two men were set on to drive upwards on a copper lode which soon yielded some good lumps of copper ore. Some of the lumps weighed 4-5lbs each.

At the bottom of the mine, the 67 West was spotted with copper and mundic, whilst the 67 East consisted of prian and spar. In June, driving costs rose to over £6 per fathom, a rise of nearly £1, adding to the adventurers costs. However there were problems with poor air. A connection with Browns Shaft would resolve this but it seems to be regularly under water at the bottom. To make matters worse, there was a considerable run of attle from the upper workings. At a bimonthly meeting in July 1847 (with Charles Bischoff in the chair), it was reported that the two months costs amounted to £434.6.4d (£434.32p). A further call was made of £1. The Committee is mentioned, Messrs Morley, Courtney, Bourdillon and Crace. The first two of the names are not familiar. Towards the end of the year, they were still 25.5 fathoms from Browns Shaft, but this level may have cut Browns Lode and drained the shaft by the end of the year (it is not clear). However it is clear that the water in Browns Shaft had dropped 12 feet. It was recommended that the water be drawn out and sinking recommenced. Unfortunately, the air was so bad that it was necessary to put down air pipes and force ventilation into the mine.

By July 1847, the news was not so optimistic and the shareholders were having to get used to hearing more excuses for the poor performance of the mine. Sprague called in the famous Captain Bonsall from Ecton Mine for advice. If he was hoping to enlist Bonsall's reputation, he seems to have been disappointed – though he tried to put a gloss on it by hinting that he shared Bonsall's opinion – 'We have suspended driving 67 W towards Brown's shaft for the present, and the men are put to drive a cross cut from the bottom of Robin's shaft, in order to cut Brown's lode, as Capt Bonsall and myself do not think the lode we have been driving on is Brown's lode. J Sprague July 27th'.

By August 21st 1847, Sprague was clearly getting slightly desperate and went searching ('costeaning') further afield. By September 1st he claimed to have found three other lodes, from one of which he 'broke some very fine stones of carbonate of copper … which is near the River Dove'. These have not been identified but, at Dovedale Edge (SK 141530), there is NE/SW groove (a similar trend to that of Robins shaft). which has been excavated, throwing up conspicuous, though mature and overgrown spoil heaps. Down in the bottom of the dale, about 625 yards south of Ilam Rock and only a short distance above the river, is a trial level about 15 fathoms long bearing 295°, perhaps a test for a sough. This was found by the eagle eye of the Geological Survey's Dr Niel Aitkenhead and reveals a fault with a downthrow to the SW. The forefield of this narrow level shows only a stringer of mineralisation and certainly this could not be the site at which Sprague 'broke... stones... of copper' ore.

By October, the 67 East was not yielding much ore and there was four fathoms of water in Robins Shaft. The air at the bottom of the shaft was too poor even to draw out the water. As has been seen at the Dale Mine, the costs of removing water up an incline can be prohibitive.

The following year, the investors decided to throw in the towel and on August 17th 1848, the mine was put up for sale. The equipment shows how undercapitalised the mine was:

> 2 pairs of horse whims, with joppet heads, ropes and chains complete in good condition. Wood and iron buckets, miners dial and box, from 600-700 feet of ash and elm timber [presumably cut from Dovedale Wood], in the round in lots. Wheel barrows, gig tub, pole and sieve blacksmiths, bellows and anvil, ladders, old iron, one horse cart (nearly new), three sets of horse gearing, with sundry other effects.

The Ilam Mine was eventually defeated by the simple poverty of the lodes. The miners were probably hoping to strike similar riches to those at Ecton and other nearby mines. As it turned out, there were no economic deposits and, had they existed, the mine was not sufficiently capitalised to exploit them on the huge scale required. The reports from the mine start out with the usual exaggerated optimism and it took quite a lot of cold-eyed visits by other surveyor/visitors for the mood gradually to turn. Sprague tried his best to hype the news, but he got more desperate as the truth dawned. The excuses for lack of progress became less and less convincing and, when the end came, it was sudden and inevitable.

Another very significant mining relic on Ilam Moor (SK 136521) is a site with two shafts, spoil heaps and considerable remains of drystone walling which may represent the ruins of a 'coe'. One shaft has, for many years, been dangerously capped, with a rotten sheet of corrugated iron on the top. During 1999, this capping fell in, revealing what the farmer calls a very deep shaft. Unfortunately he tipped what must have been tons of large stones (mainly dolomitised limestone from nearby) and investigation of the shaft is now out of the question. Another nearby shaft is topped with limestone rocks, but high quality ginging can still be made out. No records of this site have come to light, but one might remember that activity on Ilam Moor had been going on for more than two years before reports started to appear in *Mining Journal*.

Other Dovedale Mines

Dr Neil Aitkenhead, whilst undertaking the geological survey of the area, discovered traces of old vein workings near Hanson Grange (SK 146544), to the east of Dovedale. The 'costeaning' straddles the old road along which Viator and Piscator approached the drop into Milldale and Viator's Bridge, in Charles Cotton's addition to Walton's *Compleat Angler*.

Dr Jim Rieuwerts states that there are other references in 17th Century documents to mining at Newton Grange, but these await further investigation.

Dr Aitkenhead also discovered a short level high on the east side of the valley at Iron Tors. The level is due west of Cold Eaton, but does not extend very far. Further mining activity is known on Wolfscote Hill too. Perhaps the most interesting feature is at the bottom of Biggin Dale where there is a small level going into the south side of the dale. It is on private land, however. This is a coffin level, with the typical coffin shape, i.e. it is wider at shoulder height and displays the sweeping pick marks characteristic of that type of construction. See also Chapter 7 on Ford Mine for a reference to a mine at Glutton, by the side of the River Dove and under Milldale Smelting Mill, Chapter 12.

8.3 Newton Grange

A little further away, there are copper shafts in the shallow Washbrook Valley (SK c 167507) between the Bluebell Inn, Tissington Gates and the Dog and Partridge, Thorpe. See page 42 for a reference to raising copper at Tissington in the 17th Century.

To the east of Dovedale at Newton Grange, a mile north west of Tissington, lead ore was mined in the 17th Century. Dr Jim Rieuwerts has kindly made available material he has uncovered at the Public Records Office relating to the case of *Robert Mowar versus John Beresford, 1686*.

Mathew Beresford of Gateham near Alstonfield recalled very ancient mines when he was fourteen years old (in 1629) in a field called Edge Close:

> 'the earth was even and the grasse grown there but saith that in their workinge when they had sunk about five fathom they found three mens skulls one whereof was of an extraordinary bignesse and some of the bones were very greate ones but the rest were but of an ordinary bignesse and saith that in the ffell or rubbish which was left in the Grooves by those persons who had anciently wrought the same there was very much lead oare and washed out from the same 20 dishes a day for two years'.

Clearly the miners had stumbled on very ancient workings. The fact that they were unknown seems clear; there was obviously no sign of the workings from the surface: 'the earth was even and the grasse grown'. Presumably the deaths had been sometime previous and not within memory either. It points to a working of potentially late medieval date. It was also rich; twenty dishes would be equal to raising approximately 4cwt of saleable ore a day for two years.

There was a further working nearby at Gorsey Close but the mines

> 'were troubled with water and the Miners there did use pumps for unwateringe thereof and laid launders or troughs in the said Gorsey Close to convey the water away and hath heard that afterwards the said Miners there did place and use an Engine wrought with horses – and pumps and Engine were placed within a quarter of a mile of Grange house'

This whim was erected about 'the beginning of the 'warrs'' although witnesses gave varying periods for its operation from half a year to two years.

Robert Ball, a miner of Biggin aged sixty-eight, recalled

> 'About thirty years since one grove in Gorsey Close was troubled with water and that the Myners thereof did place and use an Ingine wrought with horses for unwatering thereof and saith that the same engine was placed in the Gorsey Close very neare the Grange house, but cannot remember how long the same was wrought, but saith that the said Ingine did take away the spring from the well which served the said house - the Myners filled up the Swallow in the Myne when the worke was out and turned the spring to the well again - - hath knowne several coes built - in Stanlow and Edge Close - built by Calladine and Frith about 40 years since - inhabited by them and wives and children without disturbance'.

This 'engine' or horse whim was erected about 500 yards from Newton Grange House and a shaft is marked on the east side of the farm on the modern 1: 25 000 OS White Peak map.

William Blackwall of Brassington, aged seventy, stated that some of the mines were very rich. A George Wright also lived in a coe (a miner's shed built by or over a shaft) with his wife and family nearby and there was another man called Calladine who lived in a coe at Mootlow. The 'Masters of the mines' in Gorsey Close were George Byrom and John Gregson. The ore was sold to a Mr Bewley.

In 1665, a Henry Spencer freed an old vein in Gorsey Close (i.e. established his right to work it with the Barmaster) and got three loads and three dishes (nearly 6cwt) of ore. Luke Bacon, a thirty year old miner from Parwich, had taken seven meers of a vein on Mootlow in March 1686 and was mining 'Derbyshire skrin' together with a mine on Newton Moor. A scrin is a small vein a few inches wide. A mine at Mootlow was being worked fifty years previously, too, by Edward Kirke, Robert Hall, and John Sutton. They appear to have worked this along with Edge Close Mine. Mootlow was also worked in around 1672 for 'Ffrancis Robins and William Robins got ore in a new field [vein] at Mutlowe'.

Mootlow Farm is at the side of Spend Lane, south west of the New Inns Hotel.

Finally, the Court papers reveal that 'Mr Poort and his partners were possessed of mines in Newton Grange' about thirty years previous. Mr Port lived at Ilam Hall. There is also a reference to an old rake at Stanlow (sic). Standlow is situated to the east of Spend Lane and to the west of Newton Grange. South of the latter at Broad Close Farm was a mine called Hadland Top (PRO DL 4/124/7).

Another document reveals that 'About two or

three years ago (1681), John Reeds got some ore in Broad Close' and 'Great quantities were got by Phillip Lomas in Edge Close and by the Smiths – father and son – in Standlow'. This document also states that Mr Bryan (Byrom) and Mr Gregson got twenty loads a week (a little under two tons) 'with a hack' when the horse whim was working. It also sheds a little more on Standlow for it states that:

'56-57 years ago one John Mason of Ashover maintained two meers of ground that were good work in Standlow Rake'.

One mine owner was Mr Bewley of Coventry and there is a reference to a John Baker carting ore from groves in Hanson Grange (PRO DL4/123/4).

References

1. Harwood T, 1820, *A Survey of Staffs*, p357
2. France R. S, 1947, Lancs and Ches Record Soc 102, pp84-95
3. Rees W, 1968, *Industry before the Industrial Revolution*
4. Sheffield City Libraries, Bagshaw Collection, Bag 484
5. Sheffield City Libraries, Putrell Collection
6. Farey J, 1811, *Agriculture & Minerals of Derbyshire*
7. Robey J. A, Ferguson Collection
8. Hunt R, *The Mineral Statistics of Gt Britain and Ireland*, Geol Survey (Summarised by J Lawson in Memoirs of NCMRS, 2, No 3, 1973, p119)
9. Barmaster's Collection, Matlock Reference Library
10. Roberts J, 1900, *History of Wetton, Thors Cave and Ecton Mines*
11. Plot R, 1686, *Natural History of Staffordshire*, p124
12. Public Record Office [PRO] C66 Piece 792 - 30 / 11 / 1547
13. PRO C78 Piece 99 Pt. 7 25Eliz. - 09 / 11 / 1583
14. Derbyshire Record Office D231M/E417 List of Case papers re Ilam Moor c. 1579
15. PRO C142 Piece 204 Part p153 - 16 / 5 / 1584
16. Sheffield Library - Eyre Deeds Bagshaw 2535. Attached extent.
17. Lichfield Joint Record Office. Wills. HURT, Thomas of Castern. Inventory 08/09/1627
18. Llanover (Lady Augusta) 1862 *The Autobiography & Correspondence of Mary Granville, Mrs. Delany* Vol 5, p.325 Mrs Delany to Mrs Port of Ilam
19. The name used for chrinoid ossicles at the time
20. Bray, W, 1783 2nd. Ed. *A Sketch of a Tour Into Derbyshire and Yorkshire*
21. Staffordshire Record Office [SRO] D(W)1756/1/ 2 - 25 / 12 / 1809
22. Lewis, S, 1849 *A Topographical Dictionary of England*
23. Lease from the Watts-Russell collection, now in SRO - D5046/B/3/1
24. Devon County Library [DCL] 872A/PZ265; White's Directory of Devon 1850
25. Personal communication from Justin Brooke, mine historian
26. DCL op cit n.13
27. Funnily enough, Old Mine Close was not included
28. Batemen, T, *Notes on Extinct Animals of Derbyshire & Their Relation to Man* In: *The Reliquary* Vol.1 April 1861, p.226; and more fully in *Derby & Chesterfield Reporter* 18th July, 1845 p3c3
29. Reported elsewhere as 12 fathoms
30. A John T. Sprague and a Samuel Sprague were also active in Devon and Cornwall at the same time. Justin Brooke op cit
31. SRO D(W)1776/12
32. Reconciling measurements in the two shafts is complicated by the fact that Robins depths were measured down the slope, whilst those in Browns were vertical. Thus 67 fathoms in Robins was level with about 46 fathoms in Browns

See also

Boardman, P, 1982, *Robins Shaft Mine, Ilam, Derbyshire*, Derbyshire Caving Club Newsletter, 5, pp 9-12

Jones, J. A. 1982 *The Mineralogy Of Robins Shaft Mine, Ilam, Staffs* (Unpublished)

9 Mines South of the River Manifold

9.1 Mines at Blore, Calton, Swinscoe & Waterfall

Isolated shafts lie scattered across the fields to the south of the River Manifold. They include three large groups: mines at Waterfall, Ribden, near Cauldon Low and Thorswood, near Stanton. However among the scattered shafts lies one with the distinction of being the oldest in the area to which documentary evidence may be specifically used. A survey of Calton was made by William Senior in 1637. A photo of this plan has recently been published by F Cleverdon (1). The map marks two 'lead groves' which still survive on what was Calton Common. These are at SK 111497 and 114496.

Cleverdon revealed that in 1599, Edward Cockayne sold the majority of the manor of Calton to William Basset of Blore for £400. Despite giving the broad breakdown of what was conveyed, including 500 acres of furze and heath (presumably the Common), there is no mention of lead mines.

The first overlooks the village and a distinct hollow survives in the field. The other is in a field occupied by a tumulus. Up against the road (Green Lane) in the corner nearest the village is a large depression, partly infilled in modern times. This seems to be the second location. Given the age of these, an excavation of the first shaft could possibly give important information of this early mining period. Possibly these shafts are part of the workings of Sir Richard Fleetwood and Mr Hurt of Castern which pre-date 1630 (see Chapter 8). There is a further capped shaft in Green Lane near to Latham Hall at SK 116491.

Into the 18th Century

In 1707/08 a Joshua Haywood of Matlock leased the mines at Calton, Blore, Waterfall, Cauldon, Ribden and Thorswood (see also Chapter 9.2). This may have not lasted too long, for a few years later, the Gilbert family of nearby Cotton took an interest in the area.

In 1722, on 23rd January, Thomas Gilbert, Senior, leased land on Calton Moor from Thomas Rivett of Derby. The term was for twenty-one years at a royalty of every ninth dish of washed and dressed ore obtained. The land was described as being

> 'upon or within the Comon or parcell of Wast ground called Calton Moore all the Intaike or grounds heretofore inclosed therefrom...' (2)

Ten years later, in 1732, Gilbert took out a lease of mineral rights in Swinscoe from Leeke Okeover of Okeover Hall at a royalty of 1/8th of all copper and lead ore and 1/9th of all zinc ore (lapis calaminaris). The area involved was described:

> 'within all that Comon or uninclosed ground comonly called... Swinscoe moore... beginning at the Gate [the tollgate] scituate on or near the north east side of the Township of Swinscoe in the high way leading between the Towns of Leeke and Ashbourne and there proceeding northward by the ffences... to... the waterings and by the fence of the said close called the waterings to where that Close adjoyns... a certain ffarm called Musden and by the fence that divides Swinscoe moor from Musden... down to a certain poole... which divides Musden ffarm from the Lordship of Calton and from the said poole southward down the middle of a valley leading to the corner of certain lands part

9.1 Mines at Blore, Calton, Swinscoe & Waterfall

Plan of the Weaver Hills Area

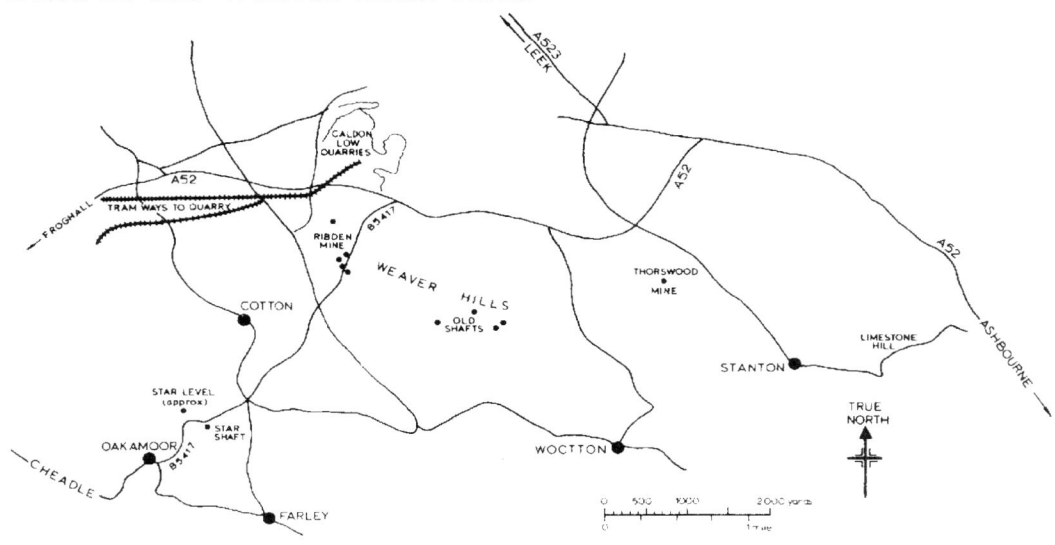

Section through Ribden Mine

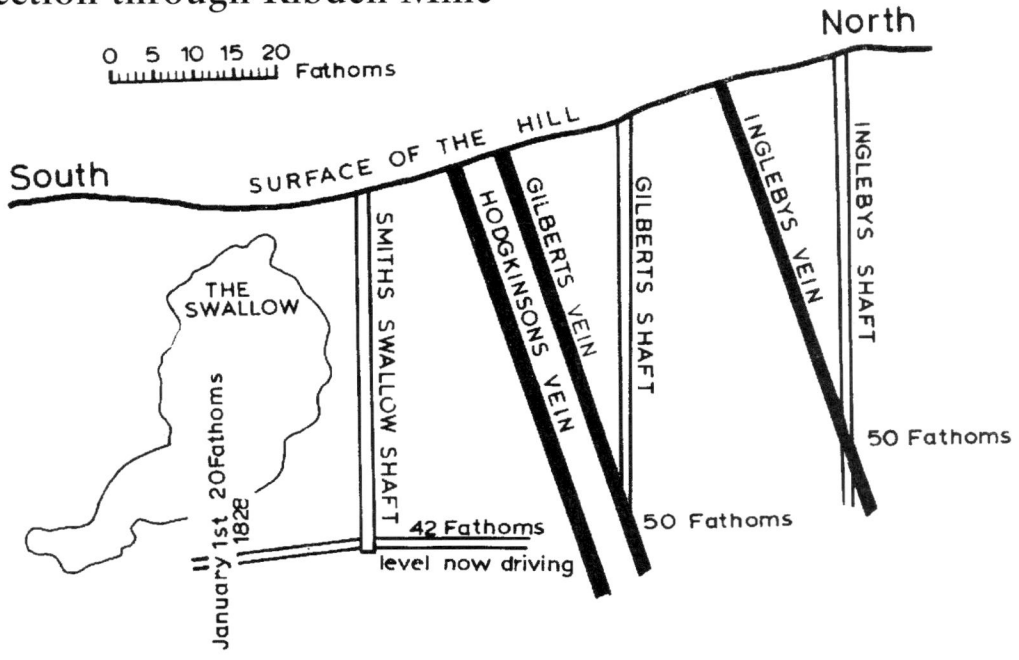

Based on DRO 934 and Bagshaw 587/40

of the mannor of Alton now in the possession of William Toplis... and then southeast [to the tollgate]'. (3)

Also in 1732, Thomas Bennit of the Clod Hall in Calton made his will shortly before his death, describing himself as a miner (4). The Cheadle Copper & Brass Co account book (extracts in the authors' possession) for 1755 refers to the payment for beer for the men at Thorswood and Clod Hall.

In nearby Blore, the Rector, Ralph Hichecock, was accused of stealing lead ore at Grindon in 1376 (see Chapter 7); a trifle desperate even if you do need a new roof. In 1643-45, John Gregson of Biggin Grange, near Hartington, was ordered to set on miners to search for and mine lead in the Lordship of Blore,

> 'being late the possessions of Wm Marqess of New-Castle and now sequestered for the use of the king and Parliament'.

John Millington of Blore also became the Barmaster, being succeeded by William Yates:

> 'It is ordered that Wm Yates of Blowre shall henceforth collect and gather the rents etc. And likewise shall oversee all the Grooves and Leadeworkes woods dears and parkes for the best advantage of the publique and shall be Barmaster for the Leadworkes within the said Lordship'.

The Derbyshire system of Barmasters fell out of use in Staffordshire probably because there was insufficient mining to warrant it and before the riches at Ecton were found (5).

North-west of Blore, there is a shaft in the landmark known as Hazleton Clump (125498).

Waterfall is to the west of Calton and to be accurate, south west of the Manifold Valley. It is, however, included here for completeness.

A group of mines exist to the north of Back-of-the-Brook. These are probably the ones referred to in a lease of mines and minerals dated 30th April 1741. The lease was between Richard Fowler of Hope, near Alstonfield and Thomas Gilbert. The land involved was eight parcels known as Waters Croft, Barn Croft otherwise Corn Croft, The Croft Leads, Little Croft, Simon Oakdens Croft, Leads Oakdens Corn Croft, Nar Croft, and Fur [?Far] Croft. These were in the occupation of Simon Oakden and Isaac Bloor. The royalty was 1/8th of all the ore and a penny cope money for every other dish (6).

The shafts are situated high on the hill above the cottages, close to what is probably an old pathway. They are sunk on the edge of a knoll of reef limestone. The shafts, some recently infilled, trend north-west to south-east on a vein of lead. There is a tradition that there is a level draining to the brook at Back-of-the-Brook. If there is, it has defied the efforts of the landowner, Mr Clive Mycock, to find it, even with the long reach of his JCB Digger. Excavation of the most promising looking shaft was given provided that 'you don't bugger up the field'. The shaft is in a reasonable condition, given its age, and the top was ginged, i.e. it has a stone lining down to the rock. There are several small workings off the shaft, but most have been backfilled with deads, or loose stone. At the bottom of the shaft, a working dips down at 45° and may communicate with the level, or sough, if it exists.

The workings in this mine suggest a large scale reworking with 1-inch diameter shot holes. However in some of the poorer parts of the vein, which have probably not been reworked, there is some evidence of potentially very old workings. It takes the form of very fine pickwork and plug and feather wedge marks. There is also evidence of possible smoke blacking and coal cinder, in an area not directly connected with the surface. This may mean the rock was broken by fire setting, and more research is expected to be done in this respect.

The excavation work here has been done by Alan Rowlinson and Daniel Hibbert.

Throwley

Near to Throwley Hall in a dramatic location overlooking the Manifold Valley, is a shaft in the south west corner of Cheshire Wood at SK 110533. There is what looks like another one nearby adjacent to the 'reservoir' at SK 108529.

Virtually nothing has been uncovered about the mines at Throwley, but a glimpse of early activity is given by Cleverdon (see above) at page 25: in 1543, Humphrey Walker had unjustly obstructed the road out of Throwley and Frances Meverell of Throwley Hall listed the difficulties this caused. He stated that he needed to 'have common highway for cart-horses and otherwise to carry lead'. Cleverdon suggests that any mining might have been short lived, but the reasons are not persuasive. If the vein was rich, as at nearby Newton Grange or across the adjacent River Manifold, the mine(s) could have been productive for years, especially as water problems are unlikely to have been too much of a problem in shallow rakes.

A document of 1565 states that there was 'hope of a plentyful mine of lead ore' in Throwley. At this time a William Delahaye was 'digging great pits' in Throwley Park to the dissatisfaction of Francis (sic) Meverell. Cleverdon has found evidence of lead mining to the west of the Hall at SK 107525 which she considers to be the workings concerned.

More startling perhaps is her reference to a mound 2.3 by 5m and consisting of lead slag covering a stone structure at SK 127507. The feature seems to be associated with charcoal burning, indicating a ore hearth on a site close to the River Manifold.

References
1. Cleverdon F, 1995, *Survey and Excavation in the Manifold Valley*, Staffs Archaeological Studies, No 5, p38
2. Staffordshire Record Office D240/M/k/d-63
3. As 2
4. Lichfield Record Office
5. Staffordshire Record Office: Staffordshire Historical Collections, 4th Series, Vol 1, pp165 &181. Thanks to David Swinscoe for advising this reference
6. As 2

9.2 Ribden & Thorswood Mines

In the region of the Weaver Hills in North Staffordshire there are a number of mines that have been worked for copper, lead, zinc and other minerals during the last three centuries. The principal mines were at Ribden and Thorswood, the former being the most important in the area. The mineral deposits are known to have been worked with varying degrees of success from before the 1680s to 1862 when the mines were abandoned. Most of the details of the workings that have survived for the 17th and 18th Centuries, consist mainly of mining leases which give the names of the mining speculators, the terms which they agreed to accept and the area to be worked, with no details of the mines themselves or the success of the venture. A few accounts and other scattered references add to the information and give a tolerably good picture of the history of the mines. The most recent venture at Ribden during 1858-1862 is characterised by verbose reports in the *Mining Journal* which compensate for the short life of the Ribden Mining Company which failed to make the mines an economic success.

Description of the Area
The Weaver Hills, rising to 1,217ft, form the most southerly part of the Pennine Chain, and from the summit there is a fine uninterrupted view of the Midland Plain. To the west of the hill lies the Ribden Mine at an altitude of about 1,100ft while the Thorswood Mine is situated on the eastern side at an altitude of 1,000ft. A number of run-in shafts are also scattered over the hill, but nothing is known of their history. Most of the shafts on the Ribden Mine lie in Farley township, although the most Northerly shaft, Ingleby's, is in Cotton township. The shafts on the Weaver Hills are in Wootton township, while the Thorswood Mine is in Stanton. All these mines are in the Lordship of Alton (or Alveton – the old name) and the mineral rights were owned by the Earl of Shrewsbury, who had a large estate at Alton and built Alton Towers in the 19th Century. The Ribden Mine lies close to the B5417 road to Oakamoor, about a mile south of the Caldon Low limestone quarries. There were at least six principal shafts on the mine.

It suffices to say that with the exception of the Swallow Shaft just to the east of the B5417, which is still open but being filled with farm refuse, the remainder of the shafts at Ribden are run in or are obscured by workings for refractory clays. Moreover, part of the site has been obliterated by the local authority using it for the tipping of domestic rubbish. Associated with the Swallow Shaft there are a number of small blind valleys and swallets in which small streams sink.

These have been investigated with the aim of entering a natural cave system (1), but extensive digging proved unrewarding.

At Ingleby's Shaft, there is an obvious funnel shaped depression marking the site of the shaft and with the aid of the engine house photographs it is not difficult to visualise what the former local landmark must have looked like. The building was demolished in the 1930s by Mellors, of Cheadle, who used the stone to construct a lime kiln close to the B5417 at Rue Hill, beyond the Caldon Quarries. Upon the first firing apparently the kiln disintegrated and the enterprise was abandoned.

There appears to be two shafts here; the main shaft adjacent to the foundation stones of the engine house and a further one on the south side marked as 'Old Shaft' on the 1889 OS Sheet. From Ingleby's Shaft there is a depression, in the form of a trench, running towards Gilbert's Shaft excavated to accommodate a line of flat rods to the latter.

Looking towards the trigpoint, there is an obvious line of surface workings running diagonally across, and up, the fields with further workings in the field to the south. This line of workings does not tie in with the only known plan of the mine made in 1826. The relative positions of the shafts as shown on this plan correspond to shafts still visible or shown on the old OS Sheet, but their orientation with respect to the north point and the directions of the veins is very difficult to correlate with the actual layout of the mine. Thus it seems reasonable to suppose that the shaft positions had been actually surveyed, but the directions of the veins and north were drawn in by guesswork. Hence the line of workings just to the south of Ingleby's Shaft is cautiously ascribed to Ingleby's Vein.

Richmond Shaft was located to the north of Ingleby's but cannot now be traced, although it could be near the rough ground in the vicinity of the Trig Point. The 1826 plan shows a shaft called Broadlow here, but the names do not appear in any of the surviving documents. Critchlow's Shaft and Lode (mentioned in 1858) have defied attempts at location.

Gilbert's Shaft can be identified, but the top, like Ingleby's, has collapsed. The site of a building adjacent to the shaft, marked on the 1826, plan has been quarried away. Much of the ground here has been worked for stone and clay and it is difficult to differentiate between mine and other waste. A few other run in shafts are visible but some must be covered by quarry waste.

On the east side of the B5417 lies Swallow Shaft and there is an unconfirmed report of a further shaft half a mile or so down the valley to the south of Swallow Shaft.

Star Wood and Level

Star Shaft (SK 061454) has been filled in with ash from the former neighbouring copper works at Oakamoor, but the level is still open by the side of the brook in Cotton Dell, at SK 059456, The level entrance is lined with gritstone and has a flat, gritstone slabbed roof. It is not a very big level if the entrance elevation is anything to go by, for it is approximately 3ft 6ins in high (1.06m) and 2ft 6 ins (0.7m) wide. There is a small flow of water from it with ochre deposits on the floor. Above the adit is a spring in disturbed ground but it could not be discerned whether this was a level or not.

Tunnel Shaft was described in the *Mining Journal* reports as being close to the tunnel on the Caldon-Froghall plateway. It is believed to be situated near to New House Farm at SK 061479 and has been filled in. Immediately to the south of this spot is a former cutting on one of the routes of the old plateway. Two levels drain from the North side of the cutting. Both of these are clearly exceedingly old and old workings nearby were referred to in the prospectus of the Oakamoor and Stanton Mining Company (see Chapter 9.2 below). Maybe these are the ones the Company had in mind.

At Limestone Hill, east of Stanton, a shaft mound exists to the west and above the brook at SK136464, though it is marked on the 1924 OS map as a lime kiln. This shaft dropped down on to an adit driven from the brook side, still clearly visible. A shaft sunk by the Oakamoor and Stanton Mining Company was above this and disturbed ground can be seen above on the knoll which is 'Limestone Hill'. There is little in the way of minerals exposed in the shaft tip or by the adit entrance, which is completely run-in, although there are large blocks of barytes (barium sulphate) on the hillside.

At the Thorswood Mine the situation is quite different, for here at least eight deep open shafts

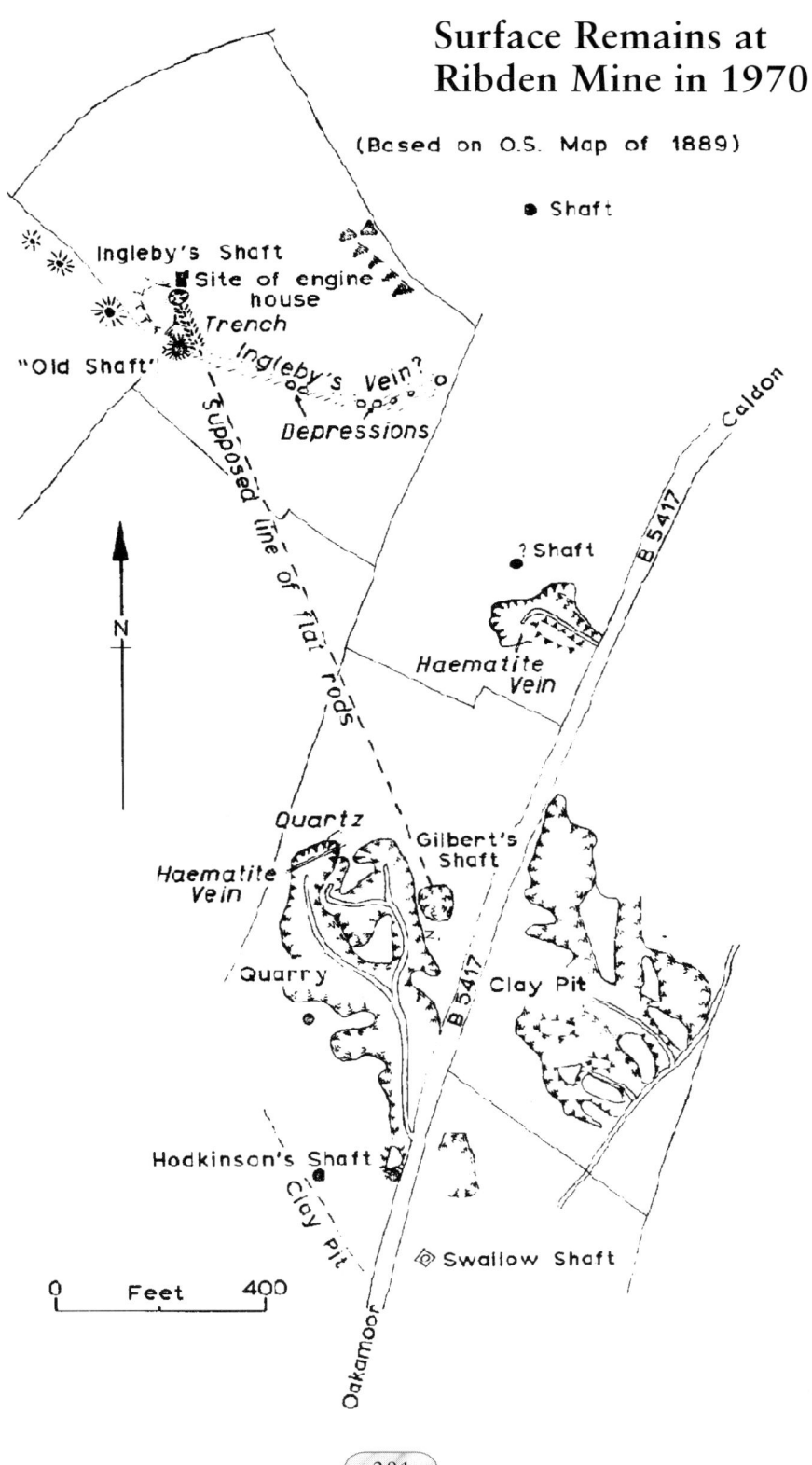

9.2 Ribden & Thorswood Mines

Surface Remains at Ribden Mine in 1970

(Based on O.S. Map of 1889)

may be found in a small plantation, and samples of calamine and galena may be found in the tips. At least one of the shafts here is known to be about 300ft deep, with a level off it at a depth of 250ft or so. The shaft at that depth is believed to be about 10ft wide too, making it one of the largest in the ore field. Unfortunately, very little of the history of this group of workings is known. Although there are outliers of limestone in the Stanton area, most of the rock here is good quality gritstone. It is also slightly peach-coloured from the barytes in the rock. The stone for Ilam Hall came from Stanton in 1821.

History of the Mines: Ribden

The earliest reference to mining in the Ribden area is given by Dr. Robert Plot in 1686, who said that lead ore had been mined there by the Earl of Shrewsbury,

> 'but none of these works were ever very considerable, nor is it likely any such should ever be found here, it being observed that wherever there is much coal, there is so much the less lead, its sulphureous spirit being too strong for the production of that Metall'.

This statement was repeated nearly word for word by Cox (2) some 44 years later.

After this early abortive attempt to work the mines, the Earl leased his rights to various adventurers who, apparently, with varying amounts of success, intermittently mined for lead and copper until the middle of the 19th Century. Although few details of the operations are known, particularly the extent of the workings or the amounts of ore raised, a series of leases exist in the Staffordshire Record Office, together with some papers in the Public Record Office, which enable the essential history of the mines to be recorded.

Seventeenth Century Leases

The leases commence in 1691 when the Earl of Shrewsbury, along with the notorious Anna Maria, Countess of Shrewsbury, and George Rodney Bridges, his mother and step father, let all the mines of copper and lead ore at Alton to William Rowley of Westminster and William Bridges of Cane Wood, Middlesex. The term was for 99 years at an annual rent of one peppercorn. The Earl was to bear 66% of the expenses of working the mines and receive 66% of the profits, while George Bridges was to contribute the remaining. This arrangement did not last long for shortly afterwards, in 1692, the Earl of Shrewsbury leased the lead mines at 'Ribden, Thorswood, Ribden Flats and Ribden Stones' to five persons who were already working the mines, for a term of twenty-one years at a royalty of 1/8th of the ore raised. The lease was specifically restricted to lead ore and if any copper was discovered it was to be delivered to the Earl of Shrewsbury.

The five people included Daniel Morley an ironmonger of Ashbourne. This confirms that a report by John Houghton FRS, in June 1693, (3), refers to mining at Ribden. The full quotation is as follows:

> 'I am further told that in the Peak in Derbyshire when they have washed the Lead Ore in a great Vat, they cast the refuse upon Heaps, which of late Years has been dug up again, and certain heavy lumps, which were not Lead Ore picktd out. These at first were sold for half a Crown the Bushel, and now are grown too double the Price, and are put in Casks and sent from the Ferry to Hull, and thence to London, &c out of which when refined very good Copper is gotten, and a Warehouse is in Derby to take it in…
>
> Upon some Queries I sent him (Thomas Mosely of Derby) concerning the Copper Oar, he answered, that he is informed by those where it was Lodged, that the Lumps dug out of the refuse Lead Oar, where not nigh so good, as those that were gotten out of the Mine by Daniel Morley of Ashbourne, at a place called Cotton, some three or four miles from that place, those being of a solid great substance as big as a Mans Fist, and some bigger, and of the colour of Ironstone; but the other would not turn to any account, being troublesome to get out of the vast Heaps of Rubbish stuff, and when got, not so good by a twentieth part, as they told me a Gentleman that came from London affirm'd; However

Mr Morley has removed it all, but has a greater quantity at Ashbourne than he well knows what to do with'.

This is largely self explanatory, although it should be noted that Morley's lease from the Earl of Shrewsbury was specifically restricted to lead ore, with any copper ore delivered to the Earl, so a separate agreement must have been made concerning the copper ore.

The Eighteenth Century Activity

In 1718 the Earl let the mines (now including both lead and copper ore) at Ribden, Thorswood, Ribden Flat and Ribden Stones to Anthony Hill of Pepperhill, Shropshire, and two lead merchants, Joshua Hayward of Matlock and Samuel Seale of Horninglow near Burton on Trent, for twenty-one years at a yearly royalty of 1/12th of the ore raised. Hayward had taken quite an interest in the Staffordshire mines, having leased the mines at Cauldon, Calton, Blore and Waterfall in 1707 and 1708 (4). The lease for Ribden and Thorswood included the rights to

> 'search Digg and Delve... and also to Sink Shafts build Coes and make Soughs in Upon and Through the Lands and Liberty to fetch and carry water to Budle and wash the sd. Copper and Lead oare there or to carry the sd. oare to the water to bee washed and to carry wood and Timber to the sd. mines and to carry away the sd. oare'.

By 1722 Anthony Hill and Samuel Seale (Joshua Hayward having apparently dropped out of the partnership) sublet the mines at Ribdens, Ribden Stones and Hallows Heath to a group of five adventurers, including Richard Halley (or Hawley) a lead merchant from Winster and William Sheldon a miner from Biggin. for the rest of the twenty-one year lease at a rent of the first dish of ore from every meer and of the ore produced thereafter, plus 4d a load cope and 4d for every meer possessed. None of the adventurers were to have more than two meers possessed together and the mines were to be worked for at least eight months in every year, while Anthony Hill and Samuel Seale were to have pre-emption of the ore produced at a reasonable price.

It may well have been Seale who prompted the Waltons of Stanshope to venture into lead mining and smelting in North Staffordshire (7) for they originally came from Egginton near Burton on Trent, less than two miles from Horninglow, and they mortgaged land at Egginton to Seale in 1721. Samuel Seale had become bankrupt by 1734.

The Gilbert Involvement

By 1727 Samuel Seale had sold his share of the lease to Thomas Gilbert of Cotton, probably due to his impending financial failure. In that year Anthony Hill and Thomas Gilbert sublet the mines again to Richard Hawley and William Sheldon, but the other three adventurers had by now lost interest in the project. The terms were similar to before, including all the mines of copper and lead in Alton with the specific exception of the Thorswood Mines, which were sublet two years later to a group of twelve miners (headed by Hall Walton) for the remaining ten years of the original lease (in 1718). Although no specific place is mentioned in the lease, the outside of the document has written on it 'A generall Article of the Mynes at Thorswood 1729'.

At Ribden the miners appear to have been no more successful than previously for in December 1732, Hill and Gilbert again sublet their rights in the Ribden Mines, this time to the Duke of Chandos who was to carry on working the mines at his sole expense. The Duke was to pay to Hill and Gilbert, one half of the ore raised from the third meer in each vein and one twenty-fourth of the ore thereafter. It was said that:

> 'there are and have been for several years past several Pits, Holes, Grooves and Shafts from which many parcels of Ore have been got and carried away'.

Since the main lease had only another seven years to run and this was insufficient for effective exploitation of the mines, Anthony Hill and Thomas Gilbert surrendered their lease in November 1733 and were immediately granted a new ore for twenty-one years. This implies that although the Duke of Chandos had only been interested in the mines for less than a year, they had become sufficiently promising for him to secure a longer period of tenure.

There was even a suggestion that the Duke had tried to bypass Hill and Gilbert and lease the mines directly from the Earl of Shrewsbury, by pretending that he had purchased Hill and Gilbert's lease, but the necessary papers could not be produced. Over a century later when interest in the Ribden Mine was reawakening (1854) there is mention of

> 'a curious series of letters, from the late Duke of Chandos, but one, who had a great deal to do with the mines and found money for their works' (5).

Their location is now unknown and little more than the bare facts of the leases are known.

History of the Mines: Thorswood

Here the activities of the twelve miners who started work there in 1729, certainly did not last more than eight years, after which time this part of the lease was worked by Thomas Gilbert and Anthony Hill themselves. During 1737-1742, a few accounts exist between Robert Bill and Thomas Gilbert which show that Gilbert owned shares in the Thorswood Mines (as well in the Burgoyne Mines at Ecton). Robert Bill of Farley Hall near Alton, was a business associate of Gilbert and a partner in the Cheadle Brass Wire Company who also acted as the bailiff for the Earl of Shrewsbury, and his accounts for the Thorswood Mine can be summarised as follows (SRO D554/55):

From the figures we can estimate that from 1737 to 1742 (although 1738 and 1741 are missing and remembering that January 1740 is 1741 by our modern calendar) about 770 tons of ore, probably mostly lead, worth nearly £2,600 were mined, over half of this in 1740 alone. When Thomas Gilbert died in 1742 he left a one twenty-fourth share in the Thorswood mine to his son John, who later became a noted mining and canal engineer.

After Thomas Gilbert's death his share of the Thorswood mine was taken over by his eldest son, also Thomas. This would be in addition to the one twenty-fourth share left to his other son John. By 1747 Anthony Hill had also died and his share was purchased by John Gilbert. It was said that as the mines were one of the best trials in England. John Gilbert had only managed to obtain Hill's share with difficulty, it being initially sold to another person

> 'who would have kept it but that Lord Shrewsbury was so Obligging as not to renew the Lease to any Body but Mr Gilbert which induced that Gentleman to Sell it to Mr Gilbert's Brother'.

Hill was described as a 'Disagreeable Partner' who was very reluctant to pay his share towards making a new trial. Soon after the Gilbert brothers obtained complete control of the mines with a new lease for

> 'all the mines and veins of Copper, Lead, Iron and Lapis Calaminaris (calamine) at Haywood and Ribden and any other lands of the Earls of Shrewsbury in Alton'

granted to them in August 1747, and they then set about forming a partnership to work the mines.

A good deal of information is given in the proposals for working the mines at Alton drawn up at this time (6). Although not quite in the over-optimistic style of the 19th Century prospectuses, it gives a rosy picture of the opportunities awaiting the adventurers. 'Great quantitys of Lead and Copper Oar' were reported to have been mined in the years 1739, 1740 and 1741, confirming to some extent the figures quoted above. The Thorswood Mine was said to have produced 'Several Thousand pounds neat Profitt', but since the 'Great vein' had been lost (reputedly by the negligence of the workmen and the difficulties with Anthony Hill), the mine had been little worked.

1737 to Xmas	duty on ore	£34.3.7
1737 to Xmas	profit at Thorswood	£11.0.4
Xmas 1738 to Xmas 1839	Duty on ore	£46.19.5$\frac{1}{2}$
1739 October	Thorswood Mine Profit	£11.5.1$\frac{3}{4}$
Xmas 1739-Jan 31st 1740	Lords duty on lead and copper ore	£142.4.0
Xmas 1741-Xmas 1742	duty on 110.14.0 tons lead ore	£33.4.6
	3. 0.0 tons copper ore	£1.10.0

9.2 Ribden & Thorswood Mines

Plan of the Ribden Mountain 1826

(Based on DRO 934)

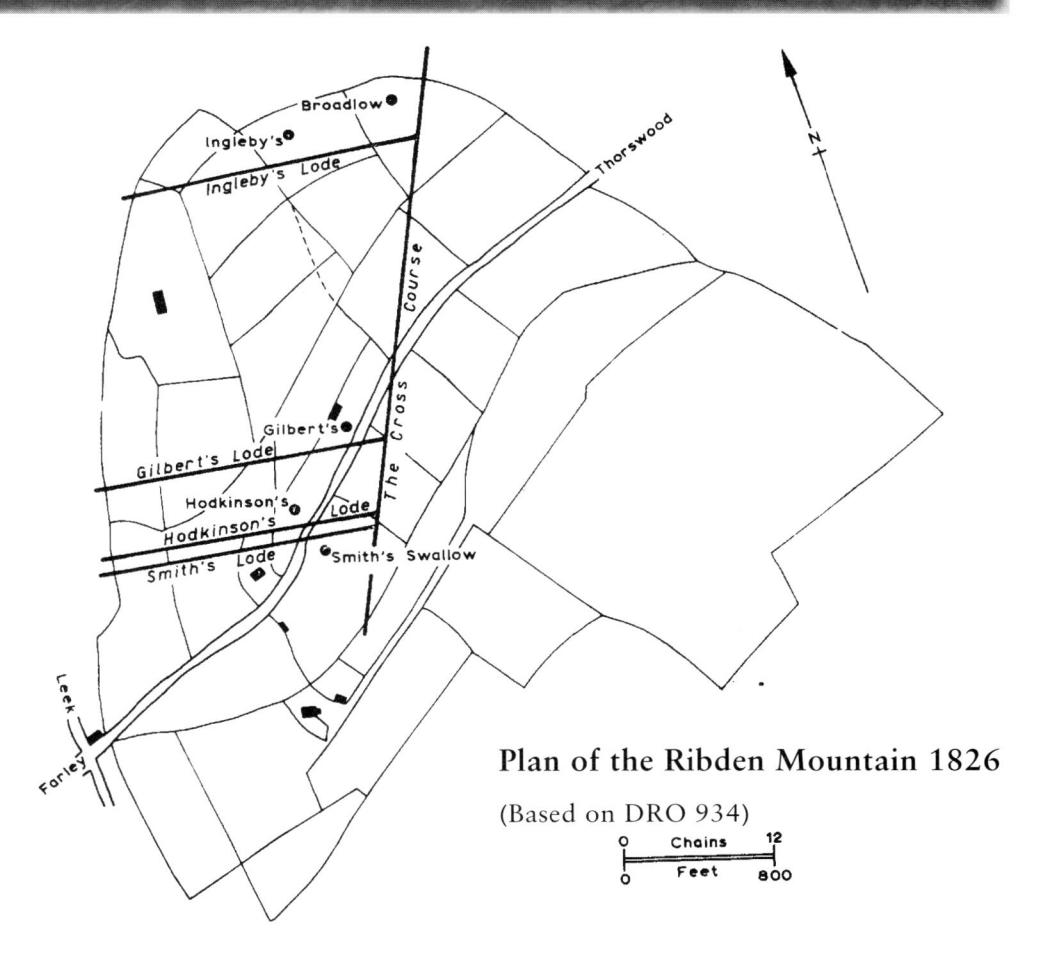

Proposals for a New Venture

It was stated that the mines were never troubled with water, that both the lead and copper ore were as good as any in England and that workmen and labourers could be employed cheaper than at most other mines. Some parts of the mines could be set to work to produce an immediate profit, but at the place where the ore was lost and at other likely places trials would be necessary. Here the engine shafts were all open with engines fixed on several of them (these would clearly be horse gins) and the workmen's tools were ready for immediate use.

The Gilbert brothers proposed to keep one half of the shares and sell the rest at 25 guineas per one twenty-fourth share,

> 'which is the price that the Gentleman who had Bought Mr Hill's share wd. have given for some parts of it but his Offer was refused'.

The partners were required to forward sums of money to get the mines operational and this amounted to £5.5.0, £10.10.0, £7.0.0, and £10.0.0 per share in 1747, 1748, 1749 and 1754 respectively. During 1748 and 1749 the cost of working the mines amounted to £461, which produced 29 tons of ore worth £402. From 1754 to 1757 the costs were £515 resulting in lead and copper ore the value of £321. The lead ore would almost certainly be sent to the Gilberts' smelt mill at Dimmingsdale, in the Churnet Valley a distance of about 3 miles (5km) This is now the house by the dam a little up the valley from the Rambler's Retreat tea room (7).

A New Lease

Little is known of the activities at the mines during the ensuing years, although the lease was surrendered in February 1763 and a new one

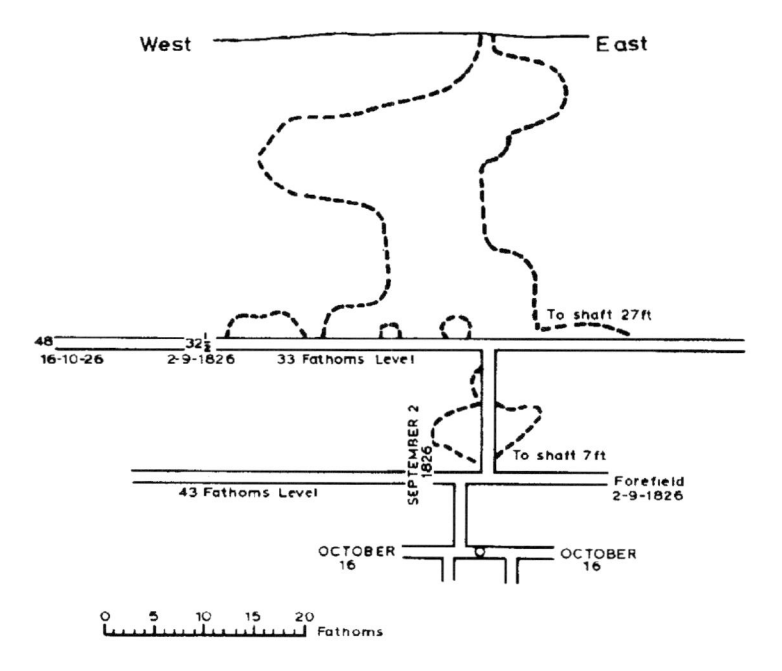

Ribden Mine: Gilbert's workings

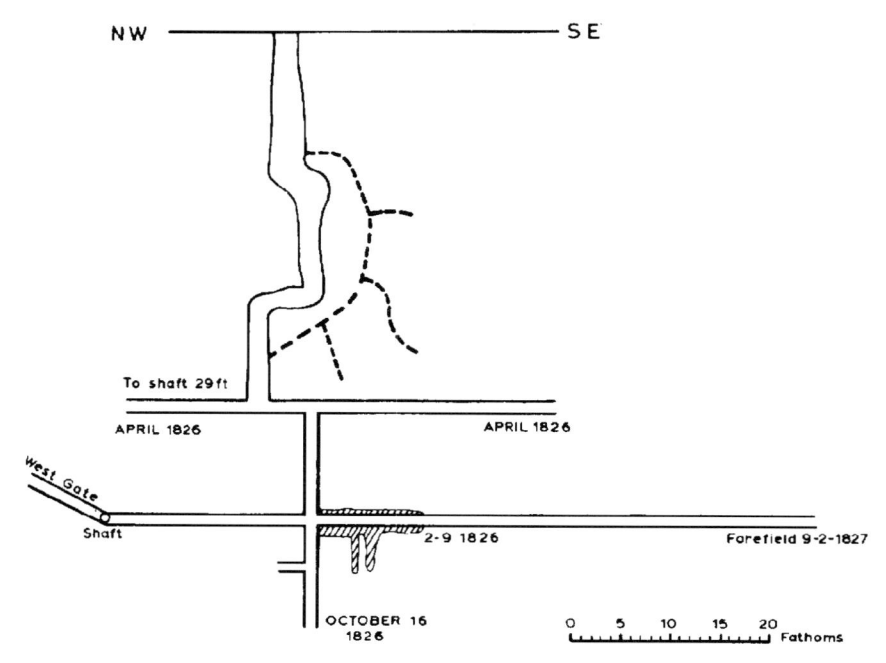

Ribden Mine: Ingleby's workings

Based on DRO 934

granted for a twenty-one year period at a one tenth duty. John and Thomas Gilbert covenanted to spend £1,000 within seven years on trials to discover fresh ore deposits. Thorswood Mine was certainly being worked during the 1760s for 63 tons of calamine was sent to the Cheadle Brass Wire Company during 1761-1765 worth £209 and just over 10 tons of copper ore worth £160 was sent there during 1769-1771 (8).

Whether this lease was renewed at the end of its term is not known, but in February 1793 the Earl of Shrewsbury granted all mines of copper, lead and calamine at Thorswood to Rupert Leigh and William Ingleby, both of Cheadle. The term was for twenty-one years at a duty of one seventh for the lead and copper ores and one eighth for calamine. Leigh and Ingleby were both partners in the Cheadle Brass Wire Company (Leigh being the treasurer until his death in 1798), and they covenanted to spend at least £50 every year on the mines. On the same day the mines at Caldon Low and Ribden were leased to John Gilbert who was now living at Worsley near Manchester for a similar twenty-one year period at the same duty, but he died on 4th August 1795.

A year later the Cheadle Company agreed to accept a share not exceeding one half in the Ribden and Cauldon Low Mines, and they decided not to adventure more than £100 (Bolton Papers). This was apparently done, for one of Gilbert's sons, John, formed a partnership in November 1796 to run the mines for the remainder of the term of the lease. The mines were to be divided into twenty-four shares, with Thomas Patten holding ten shares for the Cheadle Brass Wire Company, six more persons (including John Gilbert Jr, and two members of the Bill family) with 2 shares each and two persons with one share each. The concern was to be run on the usual cost book system, each shareholder immediately depositing £2.2.0 per share with further deposits as found necessary. The treasurer was Robert Dagley of Cheadle, a managing partner in the Cheadle Company who succeeded Rupert Leigh as treasurer to the Company in 1798.

In 1797, the Cheadle Company directed Mr Robert Dagley to make enquires regarding the present state and future prospects of the Thorswood Mine, and if appearances were not favourable then the mine was to be given up. At Thorswood the Cheadle Company is most likely to have been searching for calamine for its brass works. At the same time they recommended that the prospects of the Ribden and Cauldon Low Mines be reassessed once the £100 had been expended, but of the actual mining operations during this time we know nothing.

An account book of 1799-1800 (whose present location is unknown) indicated that the mine was being worked by eleven adventurers. During these two years, the average price of the best quality of copper ore was £51.19.7d per ton and for the second quality, £17.17s. per ton (*Mining Journal* 1859, p86). The Ribden Mine was still operating in 1802 for the Cheadle Brass Wire Company paid £12, but whether as a cash payment for copper ore, or for calls on shares, is not known.

Early 19th Century Working

A quarter of a century passed before the mines were reworked, when in 1825 a report on the prospects at Ribden was prepared for the Earl of Shrewsbury. The hydrology of the area was particularly noted, with the comment that the limestone was remarkable for the numerous joints and openings through which water passed as freely as in a bed of pebbles. It was stated that the veins had not been worked below 30 fathoms from the top of Ribden Mine Shaft where the water was always known to stand at nearly a uniform level. The report proposed that the mines be drained to a depth of 62 fathoms below the water level (i.e. 92 fathoms from the surface) by a level driven from Star Wood at Oakamoor, or to a depth of 97 fathoms below the surface by a level driven from Wootton Park.

Although Wootton Park drainage level would provide 5 fathoms greater depth of drainage and would cut the limestone sooner than from Star Wood, the latter was preferred for a number of reasons. Not only would the level intersect every vein that crossed the mining ground as well as cutting several coal seams, but the ore would be delivered at an excellent site for washing and cleaning with plenty of water available. This would be within a few hundred yards of the Uttoxeter extension of the Caldon Canal.

Perhaps the over-riding consideration was that Star Wood belonged to the Earl, while Wootton Park did not. The distance from Star

Section of Thorswood Mine

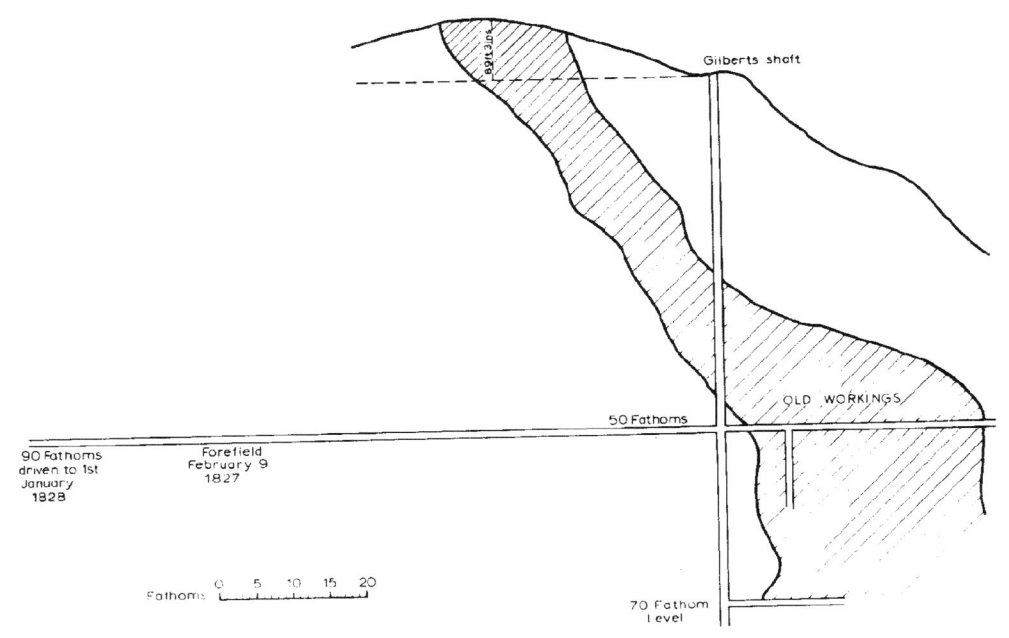

An East-West Section Showing the Dip or Underlay of the Loads in the Thors Wood Mine

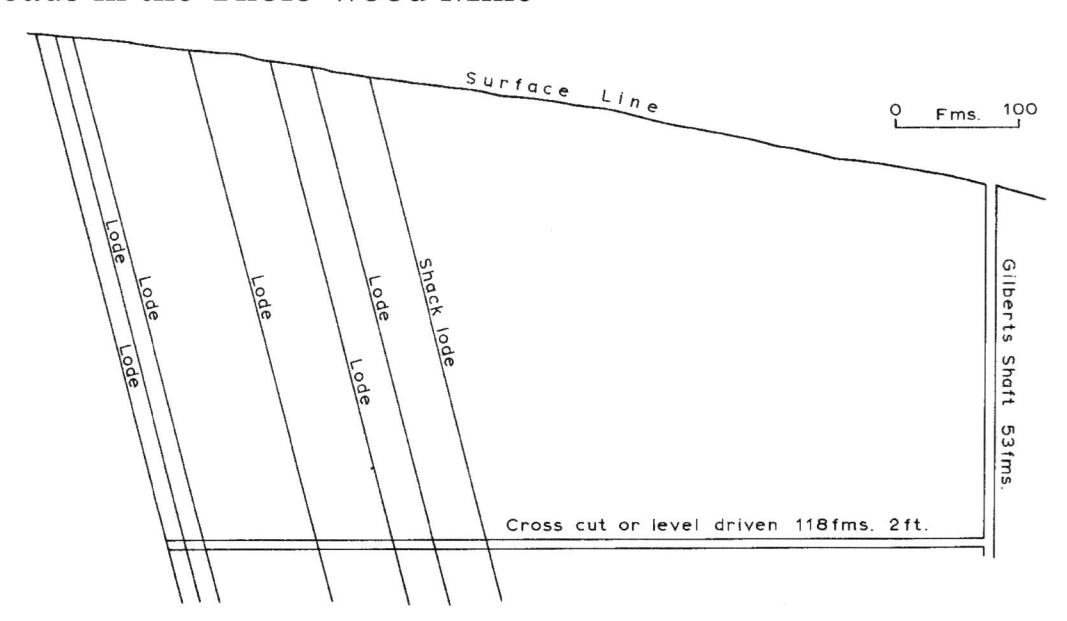

Based on DRO 934

Wood to Ribden Mine Shaft was estimated at 1,421 fathoms (1.6 miles) the first 1,000 fathoms through alternated beds of shale, grits, coal and ironstone where driving would cost £4.10.0 per fathom, with £7 a fathom through the limestone. Thus the total cost, including £700 for an air shaft, was estimated at £8,147.

Another New Company

The report strongly recommended that the Earl of Shrewsbury open the mines without delay or offer them to lessees for that purpose. Acting cautiously (and wisely) the Earl leased the mines to John Wright, Henry Lowdnes and Edmund Rundell for 99 years from 25th March 1825. The company began mining operations but were much troubled by influxes of water into the deeper workings, and to alleviate this problem a level was driven towards an under-ground swallow to take away the water. Whenever there was dry weather this level was driven day and night.

By 1828

'a Northern level from the base of the Swallow Shaft, was commenced for the purpose of flanking all the celebrated lodes called Hodkinsons, Gilberts and Inglebys in the Ribden Mountain',

so as to drain them by the swallow to a depth of over 300ft. Gilbert's Vein is clearly named after the Gilbert family, Ingleby's Vein after William Ingleby of the Cheadle Company, but the derivation of Hodkinson's Vein remains unknown.

In the annual report of 1828 (9) it was stated that they were also pursuing

'the great Thorswood level, through a hard mountain of chert and limestone, to a distance of 110 fathoms from the mouth of the shaft'.

This level was not the recommended drainage adit from either Star Wood or Wootton Park to Ribden Mine, but would appear to have been the 53 fathom level from Gilbert's Shaft at Thorswood Mine. The level had cut a number of veins, in particular one at 90 fathoms (presumably from the entrance) 'which exhibited great reasons of being the ancient lode sought for', but this proved not to be the case. The report also included a diagrammatic section through the mine, and this is reproduced opposite.

Due to a prolonged drought the previous annual report (i.e. in 1827) had been very favourable, but subsequent heavy rain from October 1827 to April 1828 had hampered progress. The swallow had been inundated and could not take the flow, thus drowning the works and halting operations in the level. The company also had coal pits in the area, to provide fuel for lime burning at Oakamoor which was a sizeable portion of their operations.

The accounts for the year ending June 1828 show that copper ore worth £1,020 had been produced, as well as lead ore worth £260, lime worth £1,022, slack coal worth £78 and bricks worth £164. Payments to the workmen amounted to £593 at Thorswood, £604 at Ribden, £892 at the colliery and £181 at the limeworks, giving a profit for the year of £174. A correspondent to the *Mining Journal* stated that in 1826 copper ore worth £2,000 was produced from Ribden and sent to Whiston for smelting.

When the company actually ceased operation is not known but it was certainly not long after this report. The drainage of the Ribden Mine by the underground swallow was a failure, they failed to find significant fresh ore deposits both there and at Thorswood, and the accounts closed with a loss of £7,000 (10).

Among the papers left by Richard Niness who was to take over the Ribden Mine several years later is a book of plans of the mines worked by the old Ribden Company. Plans on page 206 show the extent of the workings based on these old plans (11)

Following the end of operations in the 1820s, the mines lay unworked for a while. However, it is known that in May 1840, a parcel of 3 tons 13cwt of Ribden copper ore was sold to the Whiston Copper Works. This was from Melville Attwood of the Ecton Mine Company, but there is nothing to suggest that Ribden was being worked at this date, probably the ore had been left on the tips by the old company although, of course, some exploratory work may have been done in the drier and shallower levels of the mine. There is an inference that the mine was working in 1841 with Thorswood, see Chapter 5 re Royledge Mine.

To assess the prospects of the mines the Earl of Shrewsbury commissioned the Duke of Devonshire's mineral agent Stephen Eddy, to report

Two views of the Ribden Engine House after the closure of the mine

on Ribden and Thorswood. In his report, Eddy summarised the activities of the old company at Ribden, and stated that they had spent a great deal of money in driving the level from Limestone Hill in search of lead ore, particles of which
> 'may be seen in many places but I do not think that there is a probability of any discovery of importance being made in this ground nor can I suppose that the prospects were ever sufficiently encouraging to justify the trials that have been made there'.

At Thorswood he was unable to get underground as the shafts were very deep and there was no machinery on them, although lead ore and calamine could be found there. It was reported to him that large quantities of the latter had been produced. The old company had made extensive trials in the old workings but without success. Eddy thought that there was a fair chance of further discoveries. However the indications did not justify the purchase and erection of costly machinery or the driving of long and expensive levels for drainage and he recommended the Earl not to embark on any such scheme. Although it was his opinion that there was no prospect of sufficient ore being raised to make the mines profitable, there may have been sufficient return from royalties to justify letting the mine to a group of adventurers at a 1/15th duty (Talbot Papers).

Niness and Richmond from Dale Mine

Despite Stephen Eddy's discouraging report, there were people willing to risk their capital in speculative mining ventures at Ribden, and before long the lease was taken up by Richard Niness, from Warslow, and John Smith Richmond, an importer of wines and spirits, from Liverpool. The lease was from Ladyday, March 25th, 1855 but was dated the 1st September 1855 (*Mining Journal*, 1863, p14). This was particularly fortunate because under the *Earl* of *Shrewsbury Estate, Act 1843, s40*, any mining lease which was granted was 'to take effect in Possession or within Three Years after the date of such lease' and the Ribden Mining Company Ltd. was not formed until March 1858. The head lease was for twenty-one years at a duty of 1/15th of the ore raised and the lessees covenanted that no furnaces, engines or buildings were to be erected within one mile of Alton Towers, the Earl of Shrewsbury's residence.

Richmond also became a director of the Dale Mine, probably being elected in 1857 when the Dale Company was reconstituted. In addition to being a director at Ribden, he was also the Chairman of the Oakamoor and Stanton Mining Company, which sublet part of the Ribden lease in 1858, until his death in 1860. Niness was the agent of the Mixon Copper Mine at the time of the lease and had been an agent at Ecton. Whilst the agent of the Ribden Company he was also the agent of the Oakamoor and Stanton, Dale and three other, smaller companies.

The Ribden Mining Company Limited

The share notice of the Company appeared in the *Mining Journal* on April 10th 1858. The Company had a share capital of 15,000 £1 shares and the directors included James Pemberton, another director of the Dale Mine. The secretary was J D Brunton a sharebroker of London who was also the secretary of the Dale mine. The lessors were 'under agreement to assign the lease to trustees on behalf of the Company in consideration of 7,000 paid up shares to be allotted to them', which gave Niness and Richmond a stake of over 46% in the Company.

By the end of October 1858, the whole of the share capital had been allotted, chiefly to local gentry. A smithy, saw-pit and whim were erected and the dressing floors were constructed. Whilst the reports in the *Mining Journal* by Niness give a good impression of the Company's activities, they were also designed to impress the shareholders and in May 1858 he stated – 'the discovery surpasses anything I ever saw'.

In October, a 12-inch lode (30mm)
> 'was composed of the finest copper he ever saw produced from any mine in the kingdom'.

Remarks such as these had a remarkable similarity to expressions regarding the Mixon Mine a few years previous.

Initial Development

The initial development was directed at reopening Gilbert's Shaft and Ingleby's Shaft and a new shaft was also sunk on Ribden lode. The latter venture discovered copper 6 yards below the surface and the shaft was sunk where three lodes crossed. The copper was assayed 38-40% and paid the development costs. Ventilation problems, however, resulted in the men being put to work on Gilbert's Shaft in order to clear it and 'to prove its junction with Critchlow's Copper Lode on the underlie'. Critchlow's shaft was also being worked in June 1858 and yielding rich copper ore which was stockpiled for dressing, but there are no further references to it. Gilbert's lode had a bearing of 5° south of east, underlaying or dipping North at an inclination of 42°. Gilbert's Shaft was stated to have been 11 fathoms deep when it cut the lode and a large quantity of lead and copper ore had been extracted from it.

By December 1858, Gilbert's shaft had been cleared, an air machine had been erected to overcome ventilation difficulties, a whim built and a footway was being installed to the 55 fathom level at the bottom of the mine. Once the drawing shaft had been cleared, men started driving westwards and sinking on the lode, which was described as being 3ft wide and containing both lead and copper. The driving westwards was directed towards the Millstone Grit and the lode was found to increase in size with depth. The work was, however, impeded with heavy rain and the New Year saw operations being confined to cutting down the drawing shaft, to receive pitwork for a pumping engine, which took until June 1860.

Further operations were undertaken at Ingleby's Shaft, also known as the Ribden Drawing Shaft which was cleared to the bottom at 55 fathoms. The footway shaft, sunk on Ribden's lode, was also cleared and ore discovered 25 fathoms below the surface. Dr W Watson, in a report of 1859 stated that the footway was sunk on the underlay of Ingleby's lode, therefore the two lodes must have been in close proximity. At the base of the drawing shaft was a three feet lode, rich in copper carbonates and sulphide –

upon which a winze (shaft) was sunk to a depth of 60 fathoms below the surface. At that depth, two levels were driven on Ingleby's lode, yielding rich copper by December 1858.

The 50 and the 30 fathom levels were also cleared out and the latter yielded lead ore although the quantity was probably not very great. Further lead ore was obtained in a rise in the back of the 35 fathom level, which must have been on the same lode. The 50 fathom level yielded copper ore some 50 fathoms south-east of the drawing shaft. Lumps of copper ore weighing up to 1.5cwt were being broken and the lode was also explored at the 35 and 40 fathom levels.

However, development of the lode was hindered by the lack of a winding engine to wind the ore to the surface and in December 1858 it was 'resolved to purchase a steam engine to raise and crush the ore' (*Mining Journal*, 1858, p803). The ore which had been raised was assayed at an average of 30%. If this was metal in the ore, it would be very rich indeed, so it may mean the percentage of ore in the rock extracted. More likely it was meant to be the amount of metal and was an exaggeration or misprint.

A New Engine

The engine was an 18-inch steam engine of 25 HP, complete with fly-wheel and boiler and was used as a rotary winding engine. In all probability it was second-hand as it had been purchased 'on advantageous terms', but it was not the steam whim from Mixon. The close proximity of the copper and lead lodes was also indicated while the engine was being erected, for two copper ore lodes were found to be only 8ft from a lead ore lode where a winze was being sunk from the 30 to the 40 fathom levels. This lead lode also produced good lead ore and the copper lode produced ore worth £15-£20 per fathom, but strong timber was required to restore stability to the workings, as a result of the removal of ore from the two lodes.

The discovery of ore stimulated interest in the Company and in March 1859 the shares were selling at £5 per share. The wave of interest in the Ribden, Dale and the newly formed Oakamoor and Stanton Mining Company was stimulated by J Sykes of Leek, Staffs, who established himself as a sharebroker in these mines, later extending into Cornish mine shares and the secretaryship of the Blue Hills Colliery Company, on the Roaches, near Leek.

In February 1859, a new shaft known as Richmond's Shaft was sunk on a newly discovered lode North of Ingleby's Shaft. The vein was described as being large and well defined, with spots of ore, but this proved unsuccessful and was abandoned after a mere five weeks work.

Purchase of the Mixon Engine

In May 1859, the Mixon Mine pumping engine was purchased for £650. This mine which had been unworked for about twelve months was flooded and had to be drained to a depth of 100 fathoms before the pitwork could be extracted, and it took just a year to move the engine from Mixon and restart it at Ribden.

By September, over 50 tons of Mixon machinery had been moved to Ribden. During this time, both Ingleby's and Gilbert's shafts were enlarged to receive both pitwork and drawing machinery and the engine was erected on Ingleby's shaft. Despite the fact that no ore was being sold, the mine still had an available balance of over £1,000 at the end of September 1859. This state of affairs had changed little by the following summer. The engine was not started until May 1860 and work was resumed on sinking in July. Consequently the mine had been unproductive for nearly fifteen months.

This engine had started life in 1843 as a Sim's type compound engine with a small high-pressure cylinder of 36-inch on top of a 70-inch diameter low-pressure cylinder, built for the High Rake Mines in Derbyshire by the Milton Iron Works of Barnsley (see Chapter 6). It is now evident that on its sale to the Mixon Mine the engine was converted to a conventional Cornish type by replacing the combined cylinders with a single 50-inch diameter cylinder. Presumably the increased efficiency of the compound cycle was more than offset by the more complicated valve gear, the difficulty in repacking the lower piston and the extra storey needed for the engine house. It was in this modified 50-inch form when it was erected at Ribden. The original 10ft stroke (equal for cylinder and pumps) cast iron beam was retained, and at its sale a few years later it was described as 'equal to 100 HP'.

It would appear that the engine was erected on Ingleby's shaft, with the intention to pump from that shaft, together with a line of flat rods working pumps at Gilbert's Shaft some 1,400ft away and 96ft lower in altitude. After the engine had been erected, the decision to work Ingleby's shaft was postponed and all efforts concentrated on Gilbert's Shaft, which it was hoped would help to drain Ingleby's. Thus by bad planning (aggravated later by a shortage of money) the engine was encumbered by a great length of unnecessary flat rods. Richard Niness seems to have been particularly fond of flat rods, for he used them at New York and Dale Mines (and possibly at Mixon) as well as at Ribden, though they were rarely used in the rest of the Peak District. They were a means of conveying power from an engine or waterwheel across long distances to another site.

Work Recommences

After sinking had been resumed, Gilbert's Shaft was sunk to 62 fathoms below the surface and levels driven east and west, while nine men were employed in sinking the shaft still further. The lode in the shaft was up to 6-7ft wide

> 'containing a vein of gossan mixed with carbonate and sulphuret of copper six to eight inches wide without any dressing – except washing and taking out rough stones, produced 21% of fine copper',

which was sold to the Whiston Copper Works (James Keys and Son) for £26.9.2d (£26.46) per ton. Unfortunately the quantity of the ore is not known.

In the summer of 1862, some good quantities of copper and lead ore were found in the 62 fathom level west, some 18 fathoms from the engine shaft. The level had a lode 18 inches wide in the forefield (i.e. the working face) which yielded sufficient ore (probably copper) to pay for working. The level was being driven towards an intersection of cross lodes and the junction of the limestone with the millstone grit. The level was hindered by water, however, and it was decided to sink the shaft further and drive a further level at 70 fathoms deep, to unwater the 62 fathom level stopes, below the sole or floor of the level, and prove the ground at the lower depth. Just before the 62 fathom level work was discontinued, a north-south rake lode crossed the level and the end produced

> 'malachites, black and brown and sulphurets of copper, with a good flookan (clay matrix) and friable quartz with well defined walls'.

Further stones of copper were obtained from an outcropping vein in a quarry near the engine shaft.

The 70 fathom level, which was driven east and west on the course of the lode enabled the level to be reworked and copper was found in sufficient quantities to sell of a parcel of rich ore to Messrs Thomas Bolton and Sons of Oakamoor.

Running at a Loss

From the above it will be clear that there was little income to match the expenditure. At the Annual General Meeting in 1860, the mine cost (chiefly wages) for the twelve months ending June 30th 1860, were £3,730 or an average of £310 per month, which were remarkably consistent with the Dale mine cost for the same period. The only income was from the calls made on the shareholders and clearly such an unsatisfactory situation could only have one ultimate conclusion. The value of the shares dropped considerably with Sykes offering them at 4/9d (24p) to 5/- (25p) through much of 1861, whereas for comparison Dale shares were from 15/- (75p) to £1 (both £1 shares).

Matters were hardly improved by the resignation of Brunton, the Company Secretary, in September 1860. Although the exact reasons for his departure are not known, it appears that his managerial ability was suspect, and he also lost a lot of money in the Shropshire lead mines. Brunton was replaced by Mr J B Reynolds, also of London, but in 1862, the office was moved to Derby and Mr W C Watson was appointed secretary.

The exploratory work in the 52 and the 70 fathom levels at Gilbert's Shaft, and the shortage of working capital set the scene for a dispute which ultimately led to the dissolution of the Company. Evidently, Niness saw the future of the Company in exploiting the lode in these two levels, but others did not. Ingleby's Shaft remained unworked with the bottom under water. No pumping had been undertaken here for it was hoped that the pumps in Gilbert's Shaft would drain the former. A report by W Hanmer in 1861 reiterated some of Niness's views more enthusiastically and recommended that the lode be developed further and the engine shaft be sunk a further 30 fathoms to prove the lode at a much greater depth.

A Showdown at Uttoxeter

Hanmer's report was also reiterated, in April 1862, in a report by Capt Richards of West Snailbeach Mine who stated that 'many hundreds of tons may be taken here' (i.e. at the 70 fathom level). He also recommended stoping in the sole or floor of the 62 fathom level further west than the existing stopes and Hanmer agreed with him. This report obviously contradicted Niness's view, for if hundreds of tons were ready to be exploited he was obviously being incompetent in not raising the ore. Discontented shareholders were soon writing to the *Mining Journal* and one of them wondered whether the mine was being worked with an ulterior view for he had heard that if the Company was wound up there was another party ready to take over the mines.

At a shareholders' meeting held at Uttoxeter in May 1862, Niness, Richards and the shareholders came face to face. Niness said that the hundreds of tons of ore did not exist and resigned from his agency of the mine, insisting that Richards and Hanmer come and bear out their reports by getting the ore which they said was there. As Niness was one of the largest shareholders, he said that he would be only too pleased to participate in the profits to be had! Richards was asked to take over and offered to do so at 12 guineas a month and 'the usual prerequisites' for two years. This was not accepted and then Richards asked for seven guineas a month. An offer to work the ore on tribute at £1 in the £1 of ore less the extraction costs and royalty was also refused, Richards claiming that agents did not work tribute bargains. This was basically an offer to take all the profit.

Niness was asked to reconsider his resignation, which he did. Richards, however, maintained the courage of his conviction in a letter to the *Mining Journal,* shortly afterwards. In addition he quoted a shareholder at the meeting saying that there was no money to pay the men at the end of the month and that it was useless to go on working.

Liquidation

The shortage of capital had resulted in the company issuing 5,000 £1 preference shares (to bear a minimum dividend of 10%) in late 1861. The shares were only partially taken up. At the meeting of June 1862 it was stated that as the shares were intended to provide the necessary working capital for future developments, the Company had no alternative to voluntary liquidation, with the hope that a new company could be formed at once to see the realisation of ultimate success.

However no new company was immediately formed; the plant and machinery were put up for sale in September 1862. In addition to the two engines, a 12-inch capstan rope 140 fathoms long and unused, plus a 60 fathom 12-inch capstan rope, used but in good condition, were offered for sale indicating that the steam whim could have been little used. Thus the cost of its purchase and the cost of cutting down and casing Ingleby's Shaft for pumpwork which was never installed (not forgetting that the huge engine house was to all intents and purposes built on the 'wrong' shaft) was all wasted capital.

In addition, the pumping engine was also hardly used, although if the expected ore deposits in the 62 and 70 fathom levels of Gilbert's Shaft had been found and the preference shares taken up, a different picture may have resulted. It is said that the Cornish pumping engine was sold to a North Staffordshire colliery. With the benefit of hind sight, it is clear the Ribden was a good example of a typical mid-19th Century limited liability company – it was under-capitalised, spent far too much on unnecessary machinery instead of exploration (to attract shareholders' interest) and was wound up when the capital was spent, after four years of unprofitable working.

In conclusion, it is interesting to mention a further reference to the mine which occurred in late June 1864. The reference is in the diary of A S Bolton, of Moor Court near to the Oakamoor Copper and Brass Works (Thomas Bolton and Sons) where he was the principal partner. Bolton was a very astute man, quick to appreciate the role of copper in the new and developing industry of telegraphy. Bolton sampled copper ores from a very wide area – hence the parcel of ore which he bought in 1862, from Ribden.

The reference simply states that he 'went to Ribden to meet Mr Walker and look over the mines'. Whether the thoughts of a high quality ore on his doorstep attracted him cannot be said with certainty but after a close examination of his diaries, this is probable. In any event, the issue was evidently dropped for Ribden is not mentioned again. Whether he was the 'interested party' ready to take over the mine – mentioned above – unfortunately cannot be proved but may well be likely.

References

1. Gill D. I, 1966. Eldon Pothole Club Journal, 7, No 1, p68
2. Cox T, 1730, *History of Staffordshire*, p108
3. Houghton J, 1703, *A Collection for Improvement of Husbandry Trade*, Vol 2, No 45, June 9, 1693
4. Sheffield City Libraries, Arundel Castle Mss, WD316, WD 795
5. Staffordshire Record Office:
   D 240/A/I/52 Will of Thomas Gilbert 1741/2
   D 240/E/III/52 Mining Leases 1722, 1727, 1733, 1763
   D 240/M/E/III/40 & 50 Mining Lease 1793
   D240/M/K/d. Mining leases 1692, 1693, 1718, 1729, 1732, 1735
   D554/55 Accounts between Thos. Gilbert and Robert Bill
   D554/142 Agreement 1796
6. Public Record Office, Chancery Masters Exhibits, C107/179
7. Robey J. A, 1970, Bull PDMHS, Vol 4, Pt 1, pp217-221
8. Bolton Papers Minute Book and Account Books of the Cheadle Brass Wire Company. In possession of Thomas Bolton and Sons, Froghall (also on microfilm in Staffordshire Record Office, No 58)
9. Derbyshire Record Office. Bagshawe Colln, 587/40
10. Talbot Papers, Arundel Castle, No 232, Photocopies in SRO No 1146
11. Derbyshire Record Office, 934 Niness Colln of mining plans

9.3 The Oakamoor and Stanton Mining Company Ltd

In March 1859, a share notice appeared in the *Mining Journal* announcing the formation of the above Company, following the assignment of part of the head-lease to Niness and Richmond from the Earl of Shrewsbury. The rent paid to the Earl was a minimum amount of £10 per annum, and a royalty of 6d per ton upon ironstone and coal and 1/15th upon copper and lead ores. The capital was £50,000 in £1 shares, of which only 40,000 shares were issued. In consideration of the assignment Richmond and Niness were to receive £2,000 in cash, payable in four instalments over 15 months and an allotment of 3,000 fully paid up shares which were not transferable for two years without consent. They also agreed to take 800 shares and to pay the four calls on them. The area of land held by the Company was considerable, being 2,000 acres in Cotton parish and 1,250 acres in Stanton parish.

Before the end of March 1859, all the 40,000 shares had been allotted, including 400 to A S Bolton (see under Ribden & Thorswood). The first call of 5/- (25p) gave the company a working capital of £10,000. The interest shown in the Company during its first few months was unusually great, probably because the shareholders thought that it would be a second 'Ribden'. The latter was receiving considerable attention during this period and was considered to be a good speculation. In May 1859, the shares were selling at 27/6d (£1.37$^{1}/_{2}$) but this soon dropped to around 7/6d (37$^{1}/_{2}$p) which was more reasonable. Even so, the shares were still selling above par.

Also, during May a Board of Directors was appointed which included Richmond and Bolton. Amongst their colleagues were several local landowners and industrialists, whilst two were also provisional directors of the recently formed (and short lived) West Snailbeach Mining Co, of Rorrington in Shropshire. One of these two, Major Henry Fitzgerald, was later the chairman of both Ribden and West Snailbeach. The secretary was Brunton, the secretary of Ribden as well as Dale and West Snailbeach mines.

The initial operations were directed at three distinct localities – Stanton, Star Wood in Oakamoor parish, and at Tunnel Shaft in Cotton parish. Later, explorations were made at the old Thorswood lead mine near Stanton, but operations were concluded here before exploration was finished, with the winding up of the Company.

Limestone Hill, Stanton

Operations commenced here in March 1859 on the outcrop of a large vein, which was visible at the surface. The rock for many yards either side of the vein is described as being 'charged with rich spots of lead of various sizes'. A new shaft was sunk to a depth of 20 fathoms, which, at a depth of about 10 fathoms passed through a natural cavern, 'with which large deposits of ore are often met'. The main part of the lode was, however, to the east of the shaft and a cross-cut was driven at 20 fathoms depth to cut the lode.

The lode, when it was cut, yielded good stones of lead ore so it was decided to open up an old level driven from the brook into the hillside. This was the adit originally driven by the old Ribden Company in the 1820s at Limestone Hill to the east of Stanton. The level was cleared out for its total length of 90 fathoms as well as a shaft eight fathoms deep, which cut the level some 20 fathoms from the entrance. These old workings were situated about 10 fathoms below the new shaft and cross-cut and sinking was resumed in order to communicate the two sets of workings. However the reports suddenly end in September 1859 and it is not known what further activity took place or whether the communication occurred.

Thorswood

The work done here was confined to exploring shafts and clearing out debris. The main shaft was secured to the bottom and found to be 53 fathoms deep.

The plan on page 208 also shows a further level at 70 fathoms depth, but the *Mining Journal* reports do not mention any levels below the 53 fathom level and consequently the shaft could not have been cleared below this depth. During this period (1859-1860) an adjacent footway shaft was cleared and a footway installed to the bottom, which appears to have connected with the main shaft – Gilbert's Shaft – at the 41 fathom level. This level appears to have been cut through some of the Old Man's workings and the ground was described as being crushed, making the work tedious. A further shaft to the west of the above was also cleared and the final report on this shaft was that 35 fathoms had been cleared without reaching any levels. Unfortunately, the Company was wound up before explorations were effectively carried out.

Star Wood

Operations commenced here in May 1859 in opening up an old adit level driven towards Star Shaft sunk near to the top of Star Wood at Oakamoor. Work was confined to clearing the level which took until September. The greater part of the first 40 fathoms was through a seam of coal 18 inches thick. The work was, however, hindered by the collapsed nature of the level and poor ventilation. The level when cleared was found to be 105 fathoms long. However the air was so bad that the work was suspended and the men moved to Thorswood. At the end of the year, an 'air machine' was installed and the forefield (working face) was extended to communicate with the shaft, which was completed in February 1860. At the shaft itself, a horse whim was erected to clear the shaft in May 1859, and it was hoped to raise coal here. The shaft is stated in the *Mining Journal* to have been at least 30 fathoms deep. The level and shaft were probably sunk in the 1820s for a plan of 1826 shows the level and two proposed shafts 'at the site of Star Shaft' (1).

Tunnel Shaft

At the northern end of the mine sett, a further shaft was sunk near to New Hayes Farm on the now disused tramway from the Cauldon Low Quarry to Froghall Wharf, on the Caldon Canal. The shaft was sunk in search of ironstone to a depth of 20 fathoms. In June 1859, a Creswell's portable steam engine was purchased and erected at the shaft in order to relieve the mine of

9.3 The Oakamoor and Stanton Mining Company Limited

water. It was started on July 23rd 1859, and was probably the only steam engine in the Company's possession. A capstan and shears for winding was also erected and larger pitwork was installed only a month after the engine was started, indicating trouble with the water.

Cresswell's engine is illustrated in an advertisement in the *Mining Journal* of 1859 (p527). The shaft had two levels – a shallow level of little importance – and the 20 fathom level, which cut a vein of ironstone 63ft from the shaft in December 1859. The discovery was highlighted in the *Mining Journal*, although the location is given incorrectly as Star Wood. The ironstone was known locally as 'Froghall Stone', but it quickly split into small branches, possibly because of a fault traversing the workings.

In March 1860 the ironstone workings were put in the hands of a Mr J G Binns who appears to have made money and a name for himself in the locality through the working of iron ore in the Churnet Valley, near Belmont, a few miles to the north-west. His report was very unfavourable and left no doubt that there was no workable ironstone anywhere on the Company's property. The Chairman of the Company, Mr R J Butler of Alton Towers, saw Richmond and Niness who agreed to release the Company from its obligation to pay the remainder of the purchase money (£1,500) if the Company reassigned the lease back to them.

Butler suggested that the Company be wound up to save the £1,500 and the remaining working capital. The Bankers held bills for £4,000 and had a further claim of £200 against the Company, but it was hoped that the sale of the machinery would discharge the debts and leave £4,000 to divide between the shareholders, indicating that the Company had made a loss of some £6,000.

Liquidation

Several shareholders wanted the Company to continue its operations at Thorswood and Stanton, but the Company was wound up in August 1860. No new company is known to have been formed and the mines appear to have been unworked ever since. What is rather strange is that the Company had sufficient capital to finance further work at the lead mines and this was not incompatible with the objects of the Company, but with such poor management the shareholders were better off recovering as much as possible of their money.

The company had no clear directives and wasted much money. They held the rights to a large tract of land which had little mineral potential. Thus instead of obtaining the advise of a reputable agent, such as Stephen Eddy, and acting on his recommendations they opened levels and shafts anywhere there was a hint of mineralisation, ironstone or coal. The ironstone and coal on their property was not worth extracting and this should have been clear to them very early. The most promising site was at Thorswood, but this was not pursued. Perhaps they thought that here only calamine could be produced, and the calamine method of brass making had been replaced by then by direct alloying methods.

References

1. Derbyshire Record Office, 934, Niness Collection of mining plans

10 Richard Niness of Warslow

Richard Niness was a mine manager, or agent and came from near Camborne in Cornwall (? from Chasewater). It is now known that he came to the Manifold Valley in 1847 or earlier, working initially at Ecton where he was a director with the Company, which was established in 1846. In 1847, he also became the agent at the Dale Mine. Thereafter, he became involved with quite a few local mines and gained a not inconsiderable reputation. This chapter looks at what is known about the man and his activities. Further details on him are to be found in Chapter 11, which discusses the Court Case brought against the Dale Mine and him for causing river pollution.

His family bible records that he married Kate Hunt at St Edwards Parish Church, Leek, Staffs on 29th July 1849 (her actual name was Katherine de Vere Hunt and she was Irish). After her marriage, she called herself Kate Hunt Niness. Many of the letters sent from Richard Niness to his solicitor (Challinors of Leek) were written by her and signed KHN, although other letters survive in his handwriting (see pages 230/231). The Dale Mine proprietors took a lease of the New York Mine at Upper Elkstones and he went to live there. He was certainly there in January 1850 and the first four of his nine children were born at 'Elkstones' according to the family bible. It is likely that he lived in part of New York Farm, which was two dwellings at that time. The first, also called Richard, was born on 16th July 1850 and the fourth on 4th February 1854. Presumably he moved back to Warslow when operations ended at New York in 1855 and work started at the Dale Mine ahead of the Dale Mining Co Ltd being registered on the 29th October 1857. Three of his sons, William, Bertram and (?) John, emigrated to South Africa to work for Cecil Rhodes. Was William the author of the quotation on page 2 of this book?

At the Dale Mine he joined the three directors, James Pemberton and Thomas Lewis, both of Birmingham and and a Mr Johnson and this confirms a remark in the *Mining Journal* of 1858 that the mine was worked 'by three gentlemen up to June lst 1857'. In June of that year, probably because fresh capital was required, the Dale Company sold its assets to a new company, the Dale Mining Company Ltd and Pemberton Lewis and Johnson were elected onto the board of directors.

Niness was appointed the agent of the 1855 partnership and he continued in this capacity for the Dale Mining Company Ltd. His association with the above-named directors is of interest, particularly in the case of Pemberton, for they both had interests in several other mines including Ribden and Mixon. Pemberton had joined the board of the Mixon Great Consols Copper Mining Company, possibly in 1855, when he joined the new Dale Mine venture with Lewis, who was the purser [secretary] at Mixon.

In January 1857, the Mixon Company was wound up and a new Company, the Mixon Copper Mining Company Ltd, was registered to carry on the work at the mine without the shackles of the large debt which its predecessor had built up. Niness was appointed the agent, probably because of his links with the Mixon/Dale directors. The company was short lived however and the mine closed before Niness was able to put it on to a financially viable footing, for his last report was in October 1857. In August 1858, Pemberton presented a petition to the Lord Chancellor for the winding up of the company (*Mining Journal*, p519) and the machinery was sold to the Ribden Mine where Niness was also the agent and Pemberton a director. During that year, Pemberton severed his connections with the Dale Mine and concentrated his capital in Ribden, a move which he must have regretted when the company was wound up in 1862.

Richard Niness

In addition to Niness's activities at Mixon, he had other interests at Upper Elkstones. He was the agent at New York mine which neighbours Royledge, as mentioned above, and is situated a mile or so North of Mixon.

New York had a 40-inch steam engine on the mine in 1851 and worked under Niness's direction.

The lease of New York Mine passed to the Dale Company partnership and the engine was sold, after considerable dissatisfaction among the shareholders, to the Dale Mining Company Ltd for £1,000 in March 1859 although it was valued at £1,500. At a general meeting of the latter on 30th June 1860, it was agreed that the New York lease should be surrendered and his links with New York ended.

The Limited Company shareholders (or at least some of them) felt that the original partners, which included Niness were 'ripping them off'.

Despite Niness's association with the smaller mine of New York, with the closure of Mixon the majority of his time would be confined to working the Dale Mine, but the formation of a new company in April 1858 to work the Ribden Mine at Cauldon Low widened his activities once more.

Niness was appointed the agent of the Oakamoor and Stanton Mining Company which took an assignment of part of the Ribden lease in 1858 to work iron ore, coal, lead and copper ores from small veins surrounding the more complex Ribden ore deposit. In the same year, he took over an old small mine known as West Ecton or Limepits Mine for a private partnership of which few details are known.

Niness, however, had a further ace up his sleeve in ensuring he gained the agency of Ribden and the Oakamoor and Stanton Companies, and the ace was in the person of J S Richmond a wine merchant of Liverpool. Richmond became a director of the Dale Mining Company, probably from June 1857 when the new company was formed, and therefore was well acquainted with Niness. In addition he was also the chairman of the Ribden Mining Company a position he held from the company's formation until he death in August 1860; Richmond Shaft at Ribden mine being named after him. Both Niness and Richmond were the joint mesne landlords of the Ribden Mining Company and held 46% of the shares between them.

Further, Richmond was also a director of the Oakamoor and Stanton Company by virtue of his large shareholding and consequently, with the additional influence through Pemberton (mentioned above), Niness was able to secure the agencies of both the companies.

Following the liquidation of the Oakamoor and Stanton Company in 1860 and the Ribden Company in 1862, Niness's activities were chiefly confined to the Dale Mine although he appears to have been retained to produce reports on other mines on occasions (eg. West Snailbeach Lead Mining Company in 1859). With the completion of the New Dale Engine Shaft in 1863, the Dale Mine started producing lead ore and blende in quantities which may be regarded as substantial compared with Derbyshire lead mines, where only Eyam and Mill Dam were producing any ore in significant quantities. However the closure of the Dale mine in 1873 brought to an end his activities in North Staffordshire after some twenty-five years.

An Appraisal of Niness's Activities

Niness was probably responsible for the formation with others of the Companies where he was employed, with the exception of Ecton and possibly Mixon. He initially obtained a lease from the mineral owner to rework old mines and then aroused interest amongst investors who formed a limited company to work the mine concerned. Niness was paid for the assignment of the lease in mine shares and was retained as the agent or 'resident engineer'.

It seems certain that he did not sell out his shares, however. This may have been due (to a certain extent) to the fact that Niness was unable to sell his shares, for at the Oakamoor and Stanton Company he could not sell them two years after the date of registration of the company which did not last this long). His financial gains were, therefore commensurate with his position as a mine agent, for his share capital was of paper value only, until dividends were realised which did not happen at any of the mines with which he was connected.

Consequently, it is reasonable to say that his operations were fair practice and it only remains to consider whether he deserved the reputation he gained in the late 1850's as an agent of not inconsiderable experience. This is not easy, for the bulk of the evidence of his activities is from reports of his own hand. At Mixon, the mine was practically finished when he took over the reins and cannot be considered.

Operations at Oakamoor and Stanton finished because it was discovered that there were no deposits of iron or coal of commercial value worth working. The consulting engineer's Report (by J T Woodhouse, of Woodhouse and Jeffcock, Derby) spoke favourably of ironstone and was based, partially at least, upon Niness's advice and experience. Niness (jointly with Richmond) was not only the mesne landlord, but the two held £2,000 cash, 3,000 paid up shares and 800 unpaid shares from the Company in consideration of the assignment of the lease and consequently the Report was possibly tainted by Niness's financial interests.

At the Ribden mine, Niness came close to forfeiting his lease, in which he had covenanted to commence working the mine within three years. The Ribden Mining Co took over the mine only a few months before the time limit expired and consequently one can only assume that Niness had experienced difficulty in floating a company. Shortly after the Company was floated 'great quantities' of lead ore were found at the Dale, probably to boost the sale of shares at both of the mines, for the Ribden reports were carefully prepared to ensure that Niness's connection with the Dale was not overlooked by prospective shareholders.

Furthermore, very soon after work commenced at Ribden, Niness was painting a very rosy picture of the mine's prospects. There can be no doubt that Niness tried very hard to do this which would be chiefly to his own advantage, for along with Richmond, he was the joint owner of 46% of the shares. Yet despite this, it is probably fair to say that the prospects and risks were an acceptable speculation.

However, the share capital was spent in purchasing machinery and development. A great deal of money must have been spent in cutting down Ingleby's and Gilbert's shafts and in the purchase of a steam whim for Ingleby's Shaft and the Sim's engine from Mixon, both of which could hardly have been used. Despite this expenditure, against which there was little ore raised to offset it, Niness considered the mine a good speculation for a further Company and he was probably right.

If the Ribden Mine was a good speculation, the Dale Mine was even better. Niness was, however, severely hindered by uneconomical working conditions, but he raised sufficient ore to meet working expenses until a new shaft sunk in 1863 reduced ore-extraction costs and put the mine on a profit making basis. Even so, the reports of his own hand in the *Mining Journal* sometimes create the impression, albeit over a century later, that although he was a successful agent at the Dale Mine, his reputation during the days of the Dale, Ribden, Oakamoor and Stanton Companies was overstated. Especially if gauged in terms of the profitability of the Companies with which he was connected. One cannot help remembering that under his management, the No 2 Engine Shaft at Dale – a shaft some 105 fathoms in depth – is 39ft out of plumb at the bottom. How on earth did he allow that to happen?

After the closure of the Dale Mine, Niness was later connected with the Peak Forest Mining Company in Derbyshire and he died at Chapel-en-le-Frith on 8th October, 1894 aged seventy-one years as recorded on the family grave at Warslow. It is a large one situated to the right of the south porch of the church.

In addition to the links created by Niness between the mines, there was one further link that deserves a mention. The Secretary of the Dale, Ribden and Oakamoor and Stanton Companies was J Dickinson Brunton. He seems to have been a poor choice and was removed from his position at the Dale Mine after complaints from the shareholders.

Niness's wife Kate survived him and died on June 1st, 1902, aged 77 years.

11 Ore Dressing in the Manifold Valley

Ore Dressing at Ecton after 1764

During the 1760s ore smelting was started at Ecton on a limited scale and this continued to be the case well into the next century, even though the large Whiston works were in operation during most of this period. It appears that only the copper ore unfit for general sale was smelted into coarse copper at Ecton, while after the building of the Whiston works waste ores were smelted to reduce their bulk for transport to Whiston. All the lead ore was smelted at Ecton and naturally all the ores were dressed at the mine where there was ample water for the purpose from the River Manifold.

The earliest description of the ore dressing comes from Efford in 1769 (1), who gave a very clear indication of the processes, all of which were done manually.

'The Ore, when conveyed out by the boys is thrown together in a heap, and two men with large hammers, or sledges are employed to break it into small pieces. This done, it is carried in small hand-barrows by little boys, to a place under a shed, erected on purpose to be picked and sorted, and is then laid by in different parcels, best, second, and worst, this operation is performed by little girls from eight to twelve years of age, who are surprisingly quick at the work, separating the various kinds with astonishing dexterity. From this place, the Ore is carried to another large and convenient shed, where about fifty women sit back to back, on benches, to buck or beat it with flat hammers, still keeping every particular sort separate, from each other. The Ore, now reduced to a small sand, is again removed to the huddles, for washing, where an old experienced Cornishman has the superintendency of it, as a great deal of the finest ore would be lost, if this operation is not properly performed. Here then it is curiously washed and cleansed, and afterwards exposed for sale in the open air, in various heaps, ticketed according to the different qualities and quantities'.

Pat Bromfield has discovered from the Chatsworth wage accounts that the old Cornishman was Philip Tangye, who lived in Warslow.

When John Byng visited Ecton in 1789 he remarked on

'the many children employed in the laborious pounding of the stone, by which hand work they may gain 6d. per day. The women wash the ore' (2).

In 1772 there were 90 ore dressers, while 116 workers were dressing copper ore and a similar number dressing lead ore in 1784.

The term 'ore' used by the old miners has quite a different meaning from that in modern mines. The old miners extracted the mineral bearing rocks and discarded the obviously barren stones, thus providing an initial sorting. At the surface the ore dressers manually removed waste stone, followed by crushing and washing (or 'buddling') in water to remove more waste materials. The resultant 'ore' was sent for smelting. Today mechanised extraction removes minerals and waste alike and this mixture is now known as ore, while the product sent for smelting is termed 'concentrate'.

11 Ore Dressing in the Manifold Valley

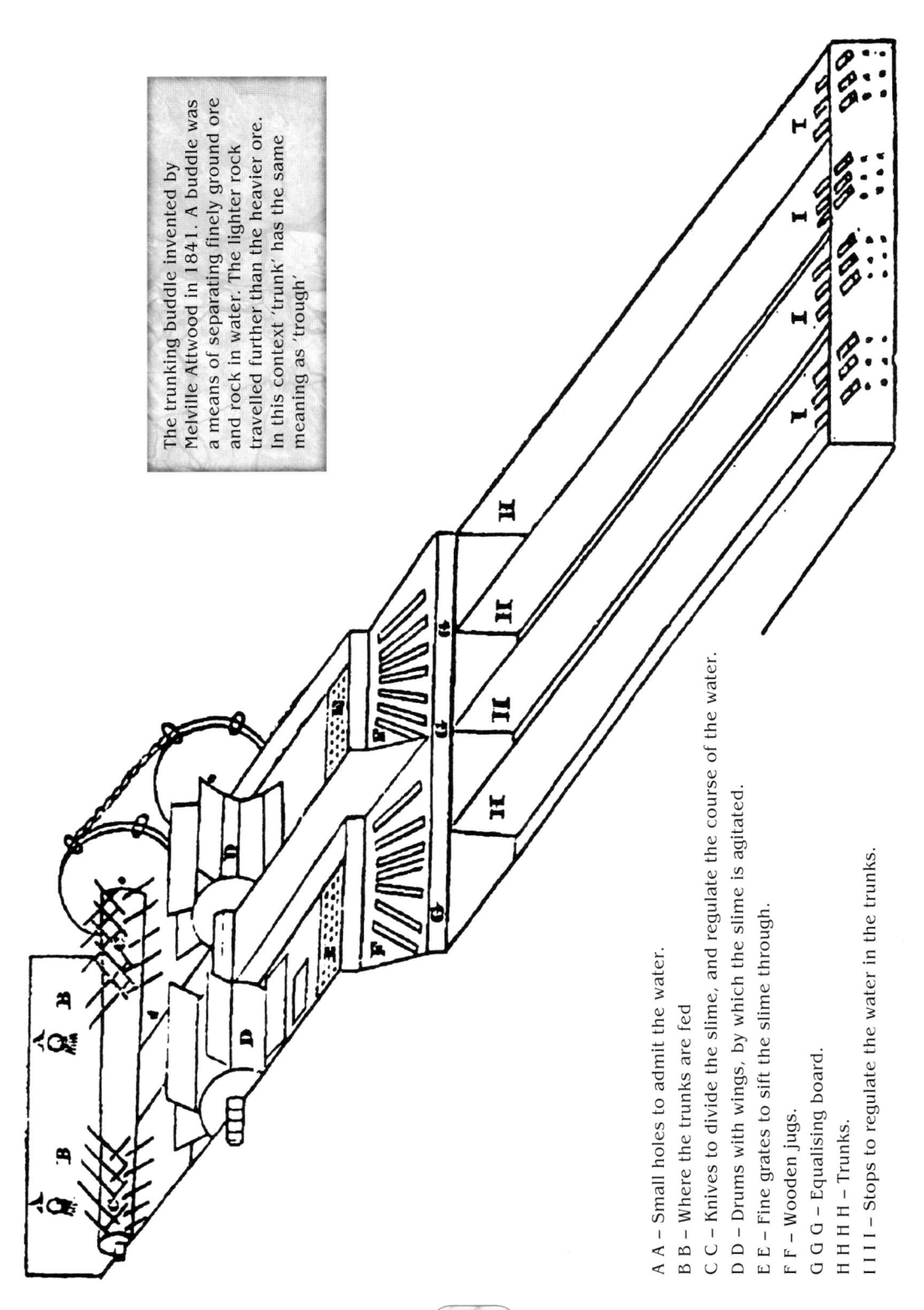

The trunking buddle invented by Melville Attwood in 1841. A buddle was a means of separating finely ground ore and rock in water. The lighter rock travelled further than the heavier ore. In this context 'trunk' has the same meaning as 'trough'

A A – Small holes to admit the water.
B B – Where the trunks are fed
C C – Knives to divide the slime, and regulate the course of the water.
D D – Drums with wings, by which the slime is agitated.
E E – Fine grates to sift the slime through.
F F – Wooden jugs.
G G – Equalising board.
H H H H – Trunks.
I I I I – Stops to regulate the water in the trunks.

Stamps Yard Swainsley

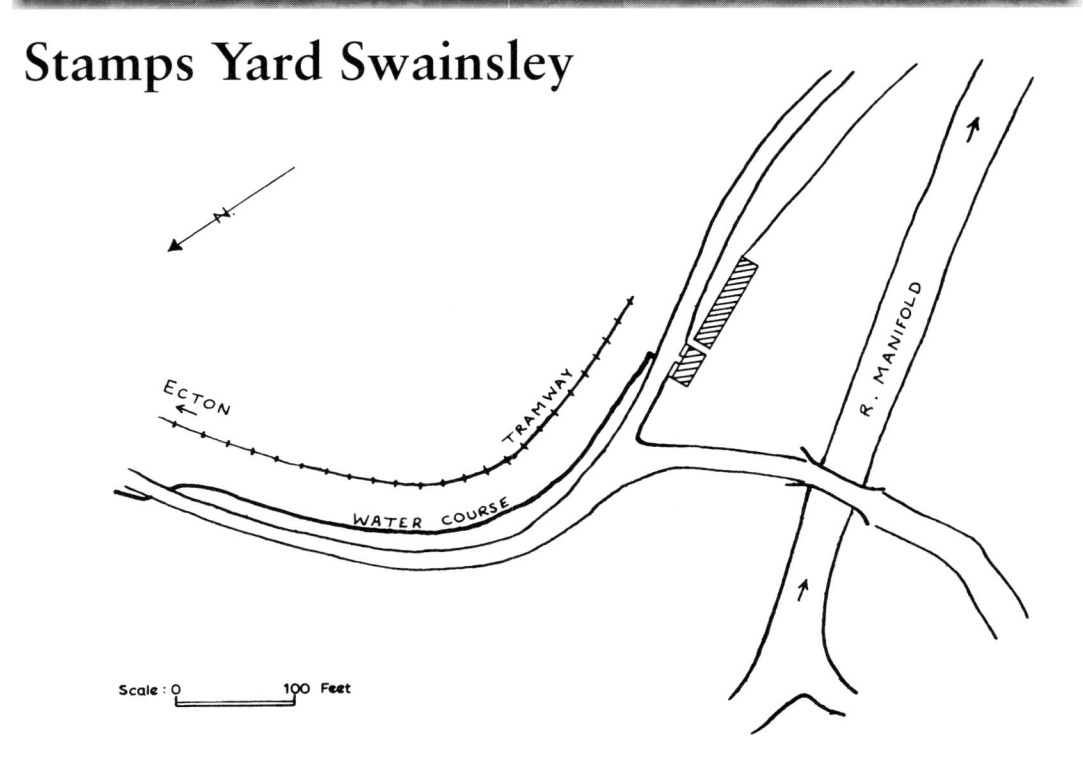

Ecton and the Burgoyne Mines, Ecton

These two mines were worked separately until 1851, when the Ecton Mountain Mining Company took out a lease of the two royalties on Ecton Hill for the first time since the Duke of Devonshire finished operations in the Clayton Mine in 1822. Until 1804, the Ecton ore was dressed at the side of the river and thereafter on the hillside after the newly driven Salt's Level communicated with the Ecton drawing shaft.

Water was supplied from the Fish Pond via a gritstone launder, or water channel, which had been used since 1784 to provide power for the Ecton slag mill, situated in front of Birch's Level at the road side near to the Clayton Mine entrance. This seems to have closed in 1826 and thereafter, the water was used on the dressing floor (and by four cottages at East Ecton). The water was collected chiefly from Chadwick Mine, flowing directly from the sough tail into the reservoir. Ore was raised up the Ecton drawing shaft and wagoned out along Salt's Level onto the hillside and along to the dressing floor.

This site did not remain the sole dressing floor, for a Stamps Yard was built at Swainsley shortly after the appointment of John Taylor as the Duke's Mining Agent in 1818.

The Burgoyne ore had a separate dressing floor, on the flat ground between Clayton and Birch's Levels. It was the practice to throw the finely ground waste material into the river and turn the waste water into the river too. William Mellor, the occupier of Wetton Mill Farm related that there were times when the river water was too cloudy to drink and supplies had to be obtained from the adjacent Hoo Brook! He had lived at the Mill since 1865. See Chapter 5 for details of John Redfern, whose family had lived at the Mill for generations and Chapter 3.2 for other details on the Mill.

The Stamps Yard was situated by Stamps Bridge at Swainsley and consisted of two heads of stamps worked by a waterwheel. Water was brought through a covered launder or leat. A weir was built across the river opposite the Clayton adit entrance to provide sufficient head of water. The start of the launder may still be seen in the river bank, although it has been blocked by stone. It is likely that the wastes would be dumped into the river below this weir from the Burgoyne dressing floor, especially as the volume was significant at times.

Benjamin Yates in a Deposition re the Dale Mine case (see below) stated

> 'I worked for about seven years on the [Ecton] dressing floors which were then very extensive, one part of them adjoined the river and all the thick muddy water ran into the river and all refuse, eg. waste sand and mud was thrown direct into the river'. He also stated 'I also remember the Ecton Stamps being erected about fifty years ago and I was one of the first employed there, I remember tenting the stamps during the night in my turn, for the Stamps were worked night and day for several years. All the waste was thrown into the river'.

Yates has started work at the mine when about twelve years old (i.e. in 1811). Many of the Deposition papers (referred below as DP) emphasise the river dumping and it should be borne in mind that they had been called on behalf of the Dale Mine defence.

A Tunnel in the Tips

Intriguingly, he goes on to state that:

> 'at R Niness's request, I went to show him where an arched tunnel ran through the Ecton Mine hillocks and which was quite buried. I particularly well remembered it through having passed through it hundreds of times in my youth and when working on the Ecton dressing floors. Richard Niness was then Agent at both Ecton and Dale Mines'.

This tunnel was found during the excavation of the tips and ran in a north – south direction along the extent of the tips (pers. comm. the late John Bonsall of Apes Tor Cottage, Ecton). What on earth was it constructed for? It seems reasonable to suppose that it connected the mine manager's house at the road side with the dressing floor. Such extravagance seems unlikely when the mines were being worked by the cost book companies. It is also unlikely to have been built before the construction of the hillside dressing floor in 1804. As the Stamps Yard was built in 1818, presumably the tunnel was built between these dates.

It seems possible that it was built to protect a supply of water to the house from the Fish Pond launder or to provide a covered way for the manager to reach the dressing floor from the house. Yet a further use could have been to keep men at work when the mine was failing and there was insufficient work for the large numbers of contractors working at the mine. The tips eventually hid the tunnel completely and it became forgotten until found during the removal of the waste. A photograph of the mine tips being removed has recently been published (3). There is a distinct line running up through the tips towards the dressing floor. Was this the tunnel or the site of it following its removal?

Evidence that the Ecton dressing floor was retained after construction of the Stamps Yard comes from Andrew Barker (DP) who worked at the Dale Mine from 1847. However prior to that he had worked at Ecton, principally between 1832 and 1847 'sometimes at the Old Ecton Mine floor and sometimes at the Ecton Stamps'. James Barker stated (DP) that ores dressed or cleaned at the Stamps were all buddled or washed at Ecton Mine old floors previous to it being wagoned or carted to the Stamps. Water from the Ecton old dressing floor ran direct into the river'. It therefore seems reasonable to suppose that the old hillside dressing floor retained this function during the life of the Stamps Yard. A railed tramway was constructed to convey ore to Swainsley. It is shown on Staley's plan of the hillside dated 1820 and kept at Chatsworth. The tramway ran down the side of the road, past Ecton Lea. Hence the above reference to 'wagons' as well as carts.

Ore from the River

John Taylor brought John Goldsworthy to Ecton and he supervised the erection of the Stamps and the reclamation of ore from the tips. He continued to work at Ecton after the Duke ceased work and his son told John Millward of Longnor (described (DP) as being a Surveyor and aged eight-one years), that the Captain had cleared £10,000 out of the working the Ecton mine tips over a ten year period. He had even recovered copper and lead slimes from the bed of the river. Mr Samuel Fynney described (DP) as being eighty-five years of age and a 'farmer and landed proprietor', stated that 'during the time Mr Goldsworthy worked the Ecton Stamps, I have seen such quantities of refuse wheeled into the river that you could walk across the river on the refuse'.

Ore From the River Eclipsed by the Sun

A graphic account of Goldsworthy's activity in reclamation is provided by Benjamin Yates. He states (DP) that

'I remember two men (Richard Rowe and John Simmonds) about 56 or 57 years ago, getting a large quantity of copper out of the river (his date is incorrect, see below). I was one who assisted to weigh one of the parcels of copper which they had got from the bed of the river and which weighed about 30 tons and they dressed it in the field at the riverside [just upriver from Ecton Lea]. They dressed more than one parcel which they got out of the river but I helped to weigh only one parcel. It had all washed down to where it had been retrieved from the Ecton and Clayton Mine dressing floors. On the same day as we were weighing this copper ore, there was an eclipse of the sun and it went dark'.

There was no total eclipse of the sun in this country between 1724 and 1927 but there was an annular eclipse on the 15th May 1836. It covered the area between Whitehaven to Darlington and northwards to Perth. Its effect at Ecton would have produced at least a 90% eclipse and possibly slightly more (pers comm Dr David Harper, Royal Greenwich Observatory, Cambridge). It would have turned daylight to almost night time, as was correctly reported by Ben Yates. There was no previous 19th Century eclipse like this. Presumably it went as dark as it did here on August 11th 1999.

The accounts of the Whiston Smelter record no purchase of Ecton copper ore between May and September, 1836 when 42 tons of 'stamp ore' valued at £255.15.11d (£255.80p) was purchased along with 8 tons of 'crop ore'. Clearly a total of 42 tons was extracted from the river during the summer of 1836. It is not recorded whether any lead slimes were also recovered, but this is likely.

Shortly after the copper slimes were recovered from the river, Melville Attwood and his father-in-law, Edward Forbes, took a lease of the Ecton Mine. The Ecton Chapter (3.5) indicates that Attwood did not return from Brazil until 1839 but Forbes was negotiating leases earlier than this (See Chapter 7, re Ford mine). During this time, James Barker was the Ecton surface manager, living at Ecton Lea. There are two semi-detached cottages there and he lived in the one farthest away from the river.

The Stamps Yard in the 1840s

Barker let all the surface bargains or contracts and his son, also called James, took the management of the Stamps Yard for about seven years in partnership with William Stubbs of Butterton (i.e. for the whole of the time of the Forbes/Attwood period. Among the men they employed were William Harrison, Charles Brindley, John Cantrell, Thomas Ferns, James Adams, John Adams, Isaac Gould, Robert Brindley, Thomas Stubbs, James Gould, Elias Mather, Isaac Yates and others – many surnames which survive in the area to this day.

At the Stamps Yard there were fifteen heads of stamps, nine on one side of the water wheel and six on the other. James Barker Jnr stated (DP) that other machinery at the Stamps Yard included a grinder with two pairs of rollers, six hutches or jig tubs, six trunking buddles, three patching buddles, two tie buddles, two washing up buddles, and one tossing machine. The dirty water from all the machinery was turned into the mill race which ran from the wheel to the River Manifold. This culvert or race was stated to be 'four score yards in length' confirming Staley's plan of 1820 which shows the race running parallel to the road to the end of the field.

An advert was placed in the *Mining Journal*, April 1841 (p117), for the Ecton trunking buddle. A description with it was signed 'A', (for Attwood). It consisted of an elongated trough in which the slimes were agitated by a rotary motion from the waterwheel. After being placed in the upper end of the trough, the shovel-fulls of slimes were broken up by knives protruding from an axle. They were then flushed by water down to baffles, described as being 'wings on a drum'. The water then ran into four channels or trunks where the slimes settled in typical fashion of a buddle, i.e. the heavier ore dropped to the bottom near the top of the trunk with the lighter gangue material, which was unwanted, travelling further down. Wooden plugs were used to control the height of the water in the trunks. The names of some of the buddles mentioned above are previously unknown but the tossing machine may be another name for a dolly tub where the water was agitated in a barrel after fine slimes had been added.

Stopping the Waterwheel for the Manager's Tea

All the refuse was wheeled into the river, such that you could walk across quite easily. It was left for the winter floods to wash it away. Interestingly, James Barker added that if Melville Attwood

> 'wanted a dish of trout he frequently stopped the water from going over the wheel which worked all the machinery at the said Stamps dressing floors and out of the culvert or water course I have seen considerable quantities of fish taken'.

The Stamps Yard was included in the sale of the lease of plant and machinery in 1866. It is unknown when it was last used, but Mather's early work (in 1866) was at Waterbank Mine and he erected dressing plant on the mine, using water from a surface reservoir, probably using mine water pumped up the engine shaft above the adit level, similar to the system used at the Dale Mine. The erection of Swainsley Hall in 1867 by Mr Roscoe surely would not have taken place if the activity outlined above was still happening, even if it was on a reduced scale.

Despite the battle he was prepared to have with the Dale Mine, Roscoe seemed reluctant to do the same with the Duke of Devonshire. Even so, one cannot imagine him putting up with the dumping of refuse in the river opposite his house or listening to the clank of the machinery all day and potentially all night when he was on holiday (he lived and worked in London). He wouldn't have built his house there.

Between the Wars, an article appeared in the Leek newspaper stating that a Leek chemist, Mr Cope, had descended the swallet at Wetton Mill (presumably the solution cavity filled with domestic rubbish in the 1960's at the end of the field adjacent to Wetton Mill Farm). He had found a lake big enough to take a boat. It contained blind fish and had a sandy beach. This latter feature seemed hard to explain until one remembers the crushed refuse carried away by the River Manifold.

The *Childrens' Employment Commission Report* of 1842 refers to the mines at Ecton and Dale. There were no children employed in the mines, only in dressing. Evidence, taken by Samuel Scriven from one of the boys, Melville Attwood and George Buckley of the Dale Mine is given in full:

'James Twigg, aged 16, Examined March 5:

"I am a dresser of copper and lead; that I sift it and clean it with water. There are seventeen of us doing the same sort of work; the mill at which we work is a quarter of a mile from the mine; none of us ever work in the mine; there is no boy under eighteen there; they have men. James Barker, the mill man or master, looks after the waterwheel: we do not interfere with it. We all come to work at seven in the morning and go home at six; we are allowed half an hour for breakfast, and take it in the smithy; we go to dinner in the smithy at twelve o'clock, and take an hour; we go home to supper; I can read a letter, and write; I go to school; I used to go the school; there was a school at the mine once, but there is not now because there is a better (sic) at Warslow. We all work by the day, and get 6s. a-week. We have no night work. After March we get our wages raised to 7s. The work agrees with us all very well. I would rather be a miner than a farmer. I have been a miner or dresser six years about."

At the stamping-mill I examined eleven of these boys, and found them all able to read fluently, having learnt at the Methodist sunday-school; their employment was similar in kind and degree.

11 Ore Dressing in the Manifold Valley

Melville Attwood, aged 25, Examined March 5:

"I rent the mine which you have explored with me of his Grace the Duke of Devonshire. I have not more than fifty or sixty hands now at work, including the boys which you have examined at the stamping-mill; these boys, with some few men, work by day wage, the rest are tributors, who work by the ton, or rather so much in the pound. The hours of work are light, from seven to six; the meals will take them an hour and a half. We have no mines of any consequence in the immediate neighbourhood. All the boys can read, some can write; they received their education in the dissenting schools in the parish; we have no church school nearer Whetton (sic). Upon the whole I look upon them as lads of very good character. I have had no occasion to question their honesty or soberiety; there is nothing in the nature of their employment detrimental to their health, as they all work above ground. I have two steam engines, and one water-mill outside, and one large waterwheel in the mine; none of the boys are allowed to work at them or near them. I never hear any complaints from the boys as to the work; indeed they all appear to strive which should do best, as I give to the best bridler every now and then a book (the *Young Man's Companion*, or something else,) as a reward; and also the same prize to the best vanner. I regret the want of church accommodation and a resident minister for this parish of upwards of six hundred persons, and think that if the fact was represented to his Grace he would be sure to have one."

Signed M Attwood

Mr George Buckley, aged 60, Examined March 17:

"I have been the agent of the North Staffordshire Mining Company four years and a half; we have 18 men employed below and on the bank; there are only two boys under 18 years of age engaged, and these are dressers of ore; neither of them can read or write; one has no parents, the other only a mother; there wages are 8d per day; they are occasional labourers. There are no other mines in this neighbourhood now in work, except Mr Attwood's, the Ecton Mine; there are no coal mines either, or any other description of work in which children are engaged in any numbers nearer than Cheadle or Leek."

Signed George Buckley'

There is an appendix to the report which contains additional comments as follows:

'The only lead or copper mines to be found of any consequence in this part of the county are those of Ecton, belonging to his Grace, the Duke of Devon (sic); of the North Staffs Mining Co, close by; and at Deep Dale, near Grindon. To the first of these, I was accompanied by the Rev. C Westlake, of Leek, which I descended. Its enormous magnitude and depth (1500 ft) rendered it a formidable undertaking; however it was accomplished with some effort, but save the satisfaction it gave me, to no purpose, as no young persons were to be found. On returning to the surface, I visited the stamping mill and there examined about 20 lads whose respective ages varied from 10-18, who with two exceptions could read and write; all attended when the weather would permit, the Sunday schools of one or other of the immediate parishes, there being no church, chapel or school nearer than Butterton or Wetton (2 miles). All these boys were healthy, happy and contented; their hours of work (which is that of sifting and cleansing the metallic ore) were regular, from six to six*; the time for meals 2 hours, which they always had and their wages paid by the week, amounting to 7s, they never work overtime or are employed at night.

11 Ore Dressing in the Manifold Valley

In the North Staffs Co's works there are only 20 men and no boys. In the Deep Dale only four old men and no boys' (4).

*This evidence conflicts with that of James Twigg, which seems more reliable. James Roland, a mine surveyor of Warslow, stated (DP) that the Dale Mine dressing floor also started work at 7am.

The mines were clearly following the trend and had stopped employing women in the dressing process. There was also a move to reduce the number of boys so employed (5). Mechanisation was helping this but the water-powered equipment of the Stamps Yard was an exception in the Peak District ore field. It tended to be more primitive elsewhere on the whole, including being out of doors. It has been noted above that as early as in 1769, the Ecton women who dressed the ore did so in a 'shed'.

The Years of Colin Mather

Although a new dressing floor was being prepared at Ecton in 1862, no other details of this are known nor any other significant further detail on dressing at Ecton prior to the involvement of Colin Mather in 1866. He was known as 'Cast-Iron Colin' and was a well known innovative engineer. He brought fresh capital and new ideas with Waterbank Mine being central to his activities. The mine lease was advertised for sale in June 1866. The cost book for September 1866 states:

'Waterbank steam engine was brought from Manchester and delivered at Waterbank on Tuesday 25th Sept 1866. The boiler seated – Engine and all its appendages was erected – and was started to work on the Tuesday following, the 2nd Oct., by Colin Mather Esq of the Salford Iron Works and at his sole expense'.

In October, men were employed in constructing the engine reservoir at Waterbank including carting clay to seal it.

A New Kind of Buddle

Among the equipment erected at the mine was Mather's patent revolving buddle, which was powered by the engine referred to. The purchase by the mine of a stone crusher (£80) and a spiral cylinder (£25) was also made. There was a large ore crusher (no doubt the one just mentioned) and Marsden's Patent Ore Breaker. Presumably the large lumps were reduced to fit the ore breaker and the buddle used for separating the fine ore particles or slimes as they were known. Mather's patent was issued in 1867 (No 2568) – for a 'machine for washing ores, grain, wool, and other mineral, vegetable and animal substances'. The illustration attached to it is clearly shown as being sited at Waterbank, although it does not say so.

The machine consisted of a hollow cylinder open at both ends and placed in a slanting position. The interior consisted of a worm and buckets or lifters. The ore was fed in at the bottom end of the cylinder and was worked upwards by the means of a circulatory screw. The screw and buckets agitated the ore and it was washed by water, which was fed in at the top end. The top of the cylinder was perforated which was used to separate the smaller pieces of ore from the larger lumps which would be repassed through the crusher.

In 1868, a note appeared in the *Mining Journal* (p386), regarding Mather's patent washing-up buddle which presumably was the same machine. Written by 'RN' – probably Richard Niness of the Dale Mine – he stated that the machine was 8ft long and 4ft in diameter and would effect a saving in washing alone of 60%. Mather claimed that the invention used less water which would be an important factor on Ecton Hill where all the water for dressing had to be pumped up the engine shaft. Presumably the buddle and the ore breaker would have remained at the mine until work finished in 1874.

Marsden's Ore Breaker

Marsden's Patent Ore Breakers (more correctly Blake's, manufactured by Marsden, who sold them under his own name) well known in the mining and quarrying industry. Two are preserved on the edge of the Peak District – at Cheddleton Flint Mill near Leek and at Teggs Nose Country Park near Macclesfield Forest (in an old gritstone quarry). The patent registered by E W Blake was in America, for no patent was registered in this couintry either in Blake's or Marsden's name. Henry Marsden spent some time in New York and then went to the adjoining state of Connecticut, where Blake lived, in 1850.

Marsden introduced the machine to the UK market in 1855 (6). Over 10,000 were manufactured at the Soho Foundry, Meadow Lane, Leeds and many were exported. It won countless gold and silver medals at various exhibitions. Coincidentally, one of the testimonials used by Marsden in his advertisements was from Thos Goldsworthy and Sons of the Ecton Emery Works in Manchester. In December 1871, R B Goldsworthy stated (DP) that he worked at the Ecton Emery Works and that he was the 'grandson of the late John Goldsworthy of the Ecton Mine'.

The Science Museum has a half scale model of the ore breaker and the description attached to it states that it was 'introduced by E W Blake of Newhaven, Connecticut in 1858' (not 1855). The machine was capable of running at 250 rev per minute and according to size, break from 4 to 13 tons of rock to a size of a 2-inch cube.

Dressing in the 1880s

The Ecton Co Ltd commenced operations in 1883, following the closure of the previous company's activities in 1874. It was 1885 before the Company started breaking ore and the need for a dressing floor was required. The equipment was second-hand and came from Cornwall. It was delivered by train to Hartington Station, taking nine railway wagons in transit. A skipway was installed in the Clayton Mine shaft so that the ore waggons could be brought up the shaft and then wheeled out of the adit, a distance of some 1,600ft.

The tubs were pushed by boys, who had also to contend with the water flowing down the adit and out of the mine. An incline was built with timber up the hillside over the Duke's gravel pit to reach the dressing floor on the same horizon as the launder from the Fish Pond at Back Ecton. A two-storey engine house was erected containing the hauling engine with the reception area for the wagons on the upper floor. A further incline was built on the north side of the building so that the wagons could be taken down to the dressing floor.

On the latter, an open fronted shed was erected for the jig tubs in front of the launder. It would appear that there were three jig tubs situated in front of the holes still to be seen in the remaining back wall of the building. There were

Above and opposite: two letters from the Dale Mine to the Company's solicitors at Leek. Many letters were written in Mrs Niness's hand and signed by her husband, but he could write, as the letter above shows. The letter opposite followed threats by Richard Naylor to Niness who was then fearful for his life

also two circular buddles. Ground ore was shovelled onto the cone shaped area in the middle of the buddle and water poured over it. The lighter gangue travelled furthest from the middle, eventually collecting in the trough at the outer edge where it was shovelled out and thrown away.

The heaviest ore was concentrated at the top of the slope. The material in the middle of the cone was rebuddled to avoid being lost. Brushes were suspended from rotating arms to keep the surface smooth. After the mine closed, the wooden boards which covered the base were removed and used to build a hen cote at Lanehouse Farm, Butterton. This survived until the 1960s. It was most unusual for the boards were broadly triangular shaped.

The crusher was hand operated. It had a hopper on the top and the ore was fed through this onto rollers. It remained on the dressing floor until about the time of the Great War. Most of the machinery, however, was sold to Mill Close Mine when the mine closed (pers comm the late J Bonsall of Apes Tor, Ecton). The site of the buddles can just about be made out, but the trees planted in about 1960 are growing across the site. For a description of the surviving features on the hillside, see Porter, 1969.

The Dale Mine

The Dale Mine is situated opposite the Ecton Mine, on the Warslow side of the valley. The royalty was owned by the Harpur-Crewe family who owned the nearby Warslow Hall and at one time had a significant estate in the Staffordshire Moorlands. The mine worked lead ore from an inclined pipe-working. It also had an adit nearly a mile long. It stretches to Warslow Hall and is marked as such on the plan on page 11. It is held locally that the adit finally reached a position below the gates of Warslow Hall and this is confirmed on the plan.

The tradition that the mine closed because of pollution problems has persisted down to this day despite a lack of evidence to support this. Mrs Vera Barber and her brother, John Greenhough, the grandchildren of Capt Richard Niness of Warslow, advised that their mother had said that the case had made her father (i.e. Capt Niness) a ruined man, although he seems to have gone on to run the Peak Forest Mining Company after the Dale Mine closed. (pers comm to L Porter, June 1971).

This situation changed in mid-1997 when a substantial quantity of legal documents was obtained. A large quantity of them concerned the case of *Roscoe versus The New Dale Mine Ltd and Richard Niness*. They give a good insight into the mine and also to ore dressing in the valley. They also put flesh on the bones of historical facts, for the personalities of the litigants and the many miners who made depositions on behalf of the mine show through. Many aspects of life in the valley are brought out once more, often details of the kind that would otherwise have been lost for ever. Detail from the Depositions are referred to below by the reference (DP). All are dated from the period October 1871-January 1872. Details of Richard Niness can be found in Chapter 10.

Richard Roscoe was a London solicitor, of 23 Regents Park Road, married to Honora, a grand daughter of John Taylor, the Duke of Devonshire's mineral agent. She had been coming to Ecton to stay at the cottage her grandfather used as a residence on his occasional visits to Ecton. She could remember ore being dressed at Ecton in 1851.

The Building of Swainsley Hall

Roscoe had purchased the Swainsley land on 26th March 1866. It consisted of Swainsley Cottage and 29 acres of land. His house was built in one of the fields called Upper Sun Dole. Swainsley was only used in the summer and Roscoe had taken fishing rights from the Duke of

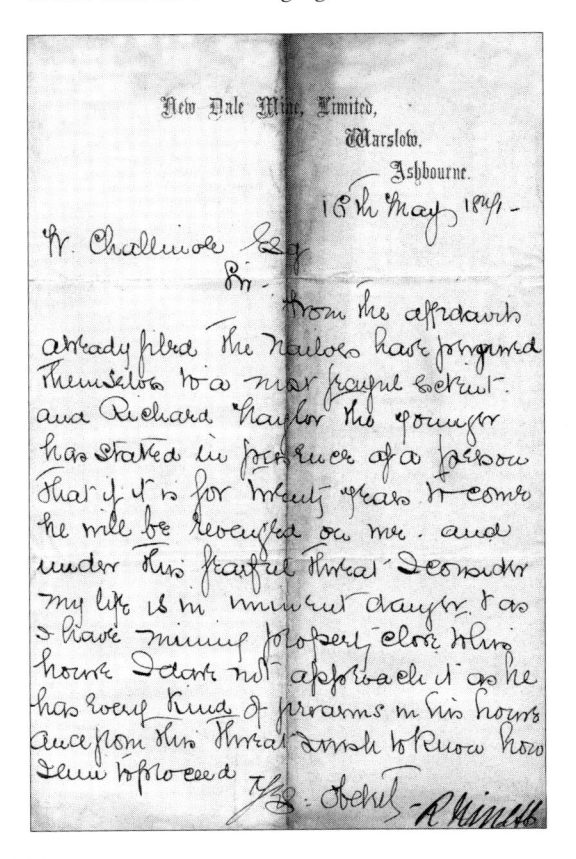

Devonshire in 1868. This had been on the east bank of the river only. Despite this, Roscoe had erected weirs across the river upstream from Swainsley without the permission of Sir John Harpur-Crewe, who owned the west bank and its fishing rights.

William Turner, gamekeeper to Sir John, stated (DP) that fish in the river had been 'scanty' since a big flood in the autumn of 1868 which had killed 'an awful lot of fish'. The crux of Roscoe's case was that the River Manifold was a valuable fishing river, which was being polluted by the waste water running from the Dale Mine dressing floor.

The latter was a 'workshop' under the *Workshop Regulation Act, 1867*. It had therefore been inspected regularly since 1869 by Robert Farrow, a sanitary inspector from Leek. He stated (DP) that the pumping engine lifted the mine water to the adit (at a rate of 84,852 gallons every twelve hours) and an additional 30,267 gallons to the dressing floor over the same period of time, giving a total of 115,119 gallons per half day flowing over the gauges (presumably installed under the Act) and reaching the river either via the adit or the dressing floor. Mr Farrow reported that the water, after use on the dressing floor, flowed 33ft through a catchpit 16ft long, 1'4' wide and from there to a second catchpit and then onto a third both being 28ft long and 7'6' wide.

Other water from another part of the dressing floor went through the second and third catchpits before all water left the floor for the culvert which flowed into the ditch which ran down the south side of the road to reach the river by Dale Bridge. This road, incidentally, was turnpiked which must have been to the annoyance of the Ecton Miners, who would be charged to use it. Although there are no trace of any properties at Dale Bridge, there are records of at least two houses existing near to it. In fact James Roland's deposition states that he lived 'in the office near to the Dale Bridge and close to the riverside'.

Prior to the dressing floor being moved to its final position at the Top of the Dale, ore was dressed close to the No 1 Engine Shaft. A culvert was made in about 1854 from the old floor, according to Niness. It was made from stone and was about nine inches square, being required to take water from a 5-inch lift, or pumping pipe. This floor closed in 1863 when the new floor opened, the old Cornish-style engine house being brought down by explosives to provide stone for the new engine house. The catchpits mentioned above were installed at that time. They are probably the first to have been used in the valley to try and effectively cleanse the water, although a 'small wooden box' acted as a catchpit on the old floor.

The 'old' floor had certainly been in existence in 1847, when Niness arrived at the Dale Mine, with water being pumped to the surface for this purpose. Prior to 1847, water was brought to the mine by a leat from the stream, which feeds the ponds at Warslow Hall. The water was used both by the dressing floor and for a hydraulic pumping engine (letter from Niness dated January 13th 1872).

A set of stone built 'filter beds' can be seen clearly on the hillside at the site of the old floor. If water was cleansed by the small box mentioned above, was this part of the buddling system?

A New Shaft and Dressing Floor

The new dressing floor came into operation in November 1863. There was a crushing house which contained a 'double rolled crusher' worked by a rotary engine. In 1872 the head dresser was James Barker. In 1863 he had assisted in the erection of the new floor, in making the hutches or jig tubs, buddles or catchpits 'for the precipitation of the light minerals of both lead and [zinc] blende ore'. The first sampling of ore had taken place in March 1864 and the lot of 68 tons was purchased by Messrs Wass and Sons.

A nice point was that Mr Wass was so impressed by the way the ore had been cleaned, he gave James Barker a sovereign to treat himself and the other ore dressers. Barker stated (DP) that for five or six years, they broke 40-60 tons of lead ore and from 40-50 tons of zinc blende per month. The lead ore had gone to Wass and Co and possibly the blende too. Although this yield had been achieved in 1864-65, the statistics prepared for the Court case defence show a different story.

Supporting the Plaintiff was Richard Naylor, who lived at the cottage closest to the river at Ecton Lea. What had turned him against the Dale Mine and Niness isn't known. He seems to have been an unlikely accomplice for Roscoe; he was well known as a fish poacher and had been arrested by the Warslow Constable for Sunday poaching of conies (rabbits) and fined £5 for it. He poached the River Manifold with Ben Twigge, a saddler and farmer of Ecton.

He probably lived at East Ecton where the Twigges are known to have had a saddlery in the outbuilding of the right hand cottage close to the East Ecton shaft. Naylor married two of Twigge's sisters – Mary Anne and later, as a widower, Maria. Apparently one of the places to poach the best fish was just below where the Dale Mine water reached the river, i.e. just below Dale Bridge. Naylor had been a Constable in Manchester, but the appointment had only lasted 17 days!

The defence case rested on the mine being able to prove continuous use for over twenty years. The case was heard in 1871 and went in favour of the mine, but Roscoe appealed. His barrister, incidentally, was his brother-in-law. One would have thought that it would have been an open and shut case. Refuse had for years been thrown into the river not only by the two Ecton Mine dressing floors, but also from the Botstone Mine at Wetton Mill, let alone the water from the Dale Mine and the dirty water from Ecton and the Swainsley Stamps. Even if not continually, one would have thought that the legal right had been established beyond reasonable doubt. Even Naylor allowed his farm animals to walk into the river from his farmyard. All the effluent from the yard drained into the river and this section of it was where Roscoe fished!

The Mine Capitulates

However while preparing for the appeal, the defence Counsel realised that despite the miners' depositions, it could not be proved that the Dale Mine had used the river had been used for a continual period of twenty years. Five witnesses claimed this in affidavits, but three of them admitted under cross-examination that in fact this was not the case. In fact it appeared that between 1847 and 1854, the mine had not been used below adit.

Moreover if George Buckley's operations in the 1840's had drained water to the river, the mine could not prove that he had a right to do it. The amount of water being discharged had increased to about 170 gallons a minute, with some 60 gallons being pumped to the dressing floor and Counsel did not believe that they could convince the Court to believe that there was no fouling of the river. Roscoe's action stated that the pollution was injurious to his fish and cattle.

Under the circumstances, the defence Counsel was of the opinion that they would fail. Consequently, he consented to Roscoe taking an injunction on his (Roscoe) giving the mine two months (until 1st April 1873) to construct catchpits to cleanse the water adequately and paying his taxed costs in two halves: 50% when taxed and the other on 1st April 1873. The catch pits were duly made but they were not finished until September 1873. However a further document indicates that a case was down for hearing in Chancery on 2nd December 1873,

> 'that R Niness may stand committed to Stafford Jail for breach of the injunction granted on the 14th December 1872 to restrain the defendants, the New Dale Mine Ltd from discharging sludge or refuse or foul water into the River Manifold'.

The fouling took place on several occasions in the first two weeks of November 1873.

However, no report of the case has been found, so presumably the threat of jail caused some other course of action.

It is difficult to appreciate the contempt Roscoe must have been held in as a result of his actions. On a tenuous case, despite the Counsel's Opinion, – for the same result against the Ecton Mine seems far from assured – he had put perhaps as many as fifty hands out of work. Although the mine was not doing well at the time of the action, the stress and work involved must have had a consequence upon Niness's management. Feelings towards Roscoe, who had only been in the district but a short time, and only then in the summer, must have rightly been palpable.

Mrs Vera Barber and her brother indicated that 'Dick Naylor told my grandfather on his (Naylor's) deathbed that he had stirred up the Dale water' (pers comm 17th June, 1971). This was twenty-six years before Naylor's involvement was discovered. It would appear that the fouling of the river in November 1873 was Naylor's doing. It certainly seems to have coincided with the closure of the mine for the final time although there is a story that the mine closed after men were brought out following an explosion. This has yet to be substantiated. It will be noted that Naylor wasted no time following the completion of the catchpits.

In fact it is more than likely that the story is true. A plan deposited at the Derbyshire Record Office by Vera Barber and belonging to Richard Niness shows the new catchpits together with a filter bed. The plan is dated 4th January 1873 and described as being 'John Wheatcroft's plan'. It is reasonable to assume that this new arrangement was implemented. It would be difficult to imagine dirty water reaching the river on several dates within two weeks if this arrangement was operating. However if Naylor was going up the adit to stir up the water, then the pollution could have happened despite the best intentions of the mine.

Whether Niness went to jail isn't clear. A further case was heard in February, 1874, when some of the miners brought an action in the County Court against the mine – presumably over unpaid wages. It seems likely therefore that the mine closed at the end of 1873 – possibly with the manager in jail. If so, it would have been a sad conclusion to the mine.

What also isn't clear is the anger created by the loss of jobs at the Dale Mine. There had been an altercation at Naylor's house before the appeal when a group of miners went to see him to express their concern at the prospect of losing their job. Niness also had written to his solicitor to say that he was concerned at the threats Naylor was making. The latter kept firearms at Ecton Lea and Niness was clearly concerned for his life at one point.

Roscoe continued to spend his summers at Swainsley. It was sold around 1890 to Sir Thomas Wardle of Leek (pers comm Mr Stuart Worthington, a descendant). It was Sir Thomas who extended the house in the 1890's on the west side. It was later extended to the east in around 1910.

Finally, Vera Barber said that she remembered her mother saying that the women on the Dale Mine dressing floor used to sing 'Green grow the rushes oh' as they worked. It brings a human touch to an inherently 'dry' subject! The Dale Mine tips are now nearly none existent. They were removed to provide the foundation of the 'new' road from Warslow Brook to Warslow village. The 'new' engine shaft is situated in a small croft near to the house at Dale Farm. It should be avoided at all costs. The shaft is about nine feet in diameter and 600ft deep. Its precise location can only be indicated in general terms and the nature of the covering is unknown.

Botstone Mine, Wetton Mill

Little is known about this mine, but it was working in the 1830's and in the following decade. The mine closed around 1850 and the equipment advertised for sale. This included a waterwheel operated by the River Manifold. Presumably it powered the dressing floor machinery situated on the top of the tips close to the river, where the latter may still be seen. The drive would presumably have been worked via a vertical spindle, similar to the one illustrating Willies' 1975 article (op cit) and formerly working at Eyam. The main shaft was still open when the Light Railway closed in 1934. It was surrounded by a circular wall and may be seen on the cine film made of the railway just before it closed. This shaft was subsequently filled in and was situated beneath the lay-by which may be seen opposite the tips.

There is evidence of the intention to build a smelter here in the 1830s. See Chapter 7.

Bincliff Mine Near Castern

These mines are situated downstream from Beeston Tor. There are a considerable number of shafts and levels and some are probably quite old. All are situated on the Wetton side of the valley.

Very little is known about this group of mines in general, let alone the dressing which took place there. The biggest problem was the shortage of water. Even river water was scarce other than in winter owing to the river flowing underground at Wetton Mill. A report in the *Mining Journal* in November 1854 stated that 'as soon as we can get water we shall attend to the dressing'. The same source in April 1853 stated that the only means to get water out of the mine was by bucket and windlass. Therefore all the water for dressing had to be drawn out of the mine. This wasn't so bad if it was being removed for drain-

The incline rising above Royledge Adit Level was made to haul wagons out of the mine directly onto the dressing floor adjacent to the waterwheel driven crusher

age purposes anyway, but it wasn't much use if you were breaking ore in the middle of a dry period.

Prospective shareholders in this venture had already suffered at the attempts of the proprietors to dupe them over water. In April 1853, the Company, known as the North Staffordshire Consols, placed an advert in the *Mining Journal* stating that 'because of the unlimited supply of inexpensive waterpower' [from the River Manifold], considerable financial benefits would be likely to accrue.

The advert also referred to the intention to erect a 'powerful waterwheel on the River Manifold. This stream will afford an unlimited and never failing supply of waterpower by which the stamping and dressing of the ores can be most economically carried on'. The river must be dry at Bincliff for more than half of the year and this misrepresentation was disgraceful.

Details of wages at this time are given in Chapter 8. The ore dressers in April 1855 received 15/- (75p) per week and the boys (a maximum of four) received 4/- to 5/- (20p to 25p per week). This was similar to payments for boys at the Dale Mine in 1842 but behind what was being paid by Melville Attwood at the Ecton Stamps. The payments to the men was comparable to payments at Ecton.

Lower down river, there would appear to be evidence of an early lead smelting site close to the river. See Chapter 9, page 199.

References

1. Efford W, 1769, *The Gentleman's Magazine*, Reprinted in Bull PDMHS, 1961, Vol 1, No 5, pp37-40

2. Andrews C. B, 1954, *The Torrington Diaries, 1781-1794*, p187

3. Porter L, 1997, *Bygone Days in Dovedale and the Manifold Valley*, p60

4. Anon, 1842, *H.M. Commission on Children's Employment: Mines*, Vol 3, p134, plus Appendix to 1st Report of Commissioners, Mines, Pt 2, p129

5. Willies L, 1975, *The Washing of Lead ore in Derbyshire during the Nineteenth Century*, Bull PDMHS, Vol 6, No 2, pp53-594.

6. Anon, 1888, *Industries of Yorkshire*, Pt 1, p167

12 Smelting

12.1 Smelting of Ecton Ore Prior to 1764

When Ecton was being worked in the mid-17th Century the techniques of copper smelting at that time involved wood, peat and coal as a fuel in an ore hearth blown by bellows driven by a water-wheel (1). The use of coal to fire a reverbatory copper smelting furnace was not evolved until the 1680s. To meet these needs the Ecton ore was smelted at Ellastone, some 10 miles from the mine but much nearer the fuel supplies, where the River Dove would provide all the waterpower needed.

The Ellastone smelting mill was built, or at least modified from an existing building, in 1660-1. Leather bellows were used, so this was presumably prior to the introduction of the all wooden bellows quoted by Plot in 1686 (2). The annual rent for the copper mill was £25, probably paid to Sir Richard Fleetwood the owner of Ellastone, who was also a co-partner with the Duke of Devonshire in the Ecton Mines. Fleetwood lived at Calwich Abbey nearby, later building Wootton Lodge to the north-west. In August, 1665 the mine and mill were let to Mr Mumma who paid £150 for the mill, and it seems that they were still operating in 1668, but by 1686 when Plot reported his visit (of 1660) the mine and mill had been closed some time. The site of this mill is still known as 'Copper Mill Yard' (see below).

The next smelting operations that we know of were in the period when Ecton Mine was controlled by John Gilbert-Cooper, the copper ore being smelted at Denby, 8 miles north of Derby, where Cooper had an estate including a number of high quality coal mines. In 1746 all his Derbyshire estates were sold, but he continued to operate by leasing the land containing his copper works from the new owner. His partner in the Denby copper works was John Rotton of Duffield, Derbyshire; the company evidently also worked the copper mines at Middleton Tyas in Yorkshire and a copper rolling mill in Derby, as well as possibly being concerned in a brassworks at Birmingham and a copper works at Swansea.

The date of commencement of the Denby works is not known, and, like the Ecton activities of the same period, very little is known of the operations there. It is possible that some the ore from the Ecton Mine was sent to Denby for smelting from 1739 to 1760. However the Duke's ore, paid as a royalty, went to Patten and Co at Warrington between 1752 and 1759 and it seems likely that it would have been sent with the rest of the Ecton ore shipments, indicating that the latter might well have gone to Warrington too.

After John Gilbert-Cooper's lease expired in 1760 the ore from the Duke's mine was sold by the system of ticketing to Cooper and Rotton at Denby, Thomas Patten at Cheadle, and Charles Roe at Macclesfield. The Cheadle and Macclesfield copper works are outside the scope of this book, but fortunately they are documented elsewhere (3). Ticketing involved the sending of samples of the parcels of ore to the smelting works who analysed the content and bid accordingly.

In 1768 there was a proposal to let the Denby smelt and this gives a general account of the works. There were furnaces for calcining, smelting, reducing the regulus, running the regulus into coarse copper, as well as roasting and refining it into fine copper. Eight furnaces were in use with two more in repair, although another para-

Behind the lorry is the Clock House smelter being used by the Creamery. Beyond it used to be a calciner built like a potter's bottle kiln

graph in the same document quotes six calcining, five smelting and two refining furnaces, each furnace operated by two men. The smelting furnaces cost £70 each to build and the calcining furnaces £50. Each ton of ore required three tons of coal, at 3s 8d ($18^1/_2$p) per ton, to produce fine copper and it was thought that 2 tons of Denby coal would do the same as $2^1/_2$ tons of Cheadle coal.

The carriage of ore from Ecton to Denby cost 19s (95p) per ton, while the carriage of the finished copper by road to Derby cost 6s (30p) per ton, a further 8s (40p) to Gainsborough along the river Trent and a further 10s (50p) by sea to London. There was also a battery mill, which was 'like an Iron furnace'. The works needed a capital of £3,000. The Denby smelt finally closed some time shortly after Cooper's death in 1769, while today the site, still known as 'Copper Yards', is marked only by waste copper slag and a few ruined cottages.

Copper smelting at Ecton commenced with the budding of a calcining furnace in 1764 and by 1767 a smelting furnace had been erected, while a report written in 1772 stated that there were four smelters at Ecton, with 'for the most part two Furneses in work at a time at Ecton one Calcining Ore the other Smelting'. These were all reverberatory furnaces or cupolas, except for the blast furnace for slag smelting erected later. They initially only smelted a very small fraction of their total output with only 34 tons of coarse copper metal sold from 1765 to 1769; this is equivalent to about 3% of their production, assuming an average produce of 15% copper from the ore concentrates.

12.2 The Whiston Copper Works

After 1770 when the Duke smelted all his own ore, the number of men employed on this task at Ecton rose considerably, with twenty-four smelters in 1779, thirty in 1780 and thirty-nine (including eight lead smelters) in 1784, Surprisingly enough, the number dropped to only twenty copper smelters and four lead smelters in 1786 during the period of peak production. Lead smelting at Ecton is first mentioned in 1783, and this may signify the disuse of the Lode Mill (Greenlow Field) smelting mill. Two years later work started on the construction of a water course from a dam near the Chadwick Sough at the back of the hill to the mine.

12 Smelting

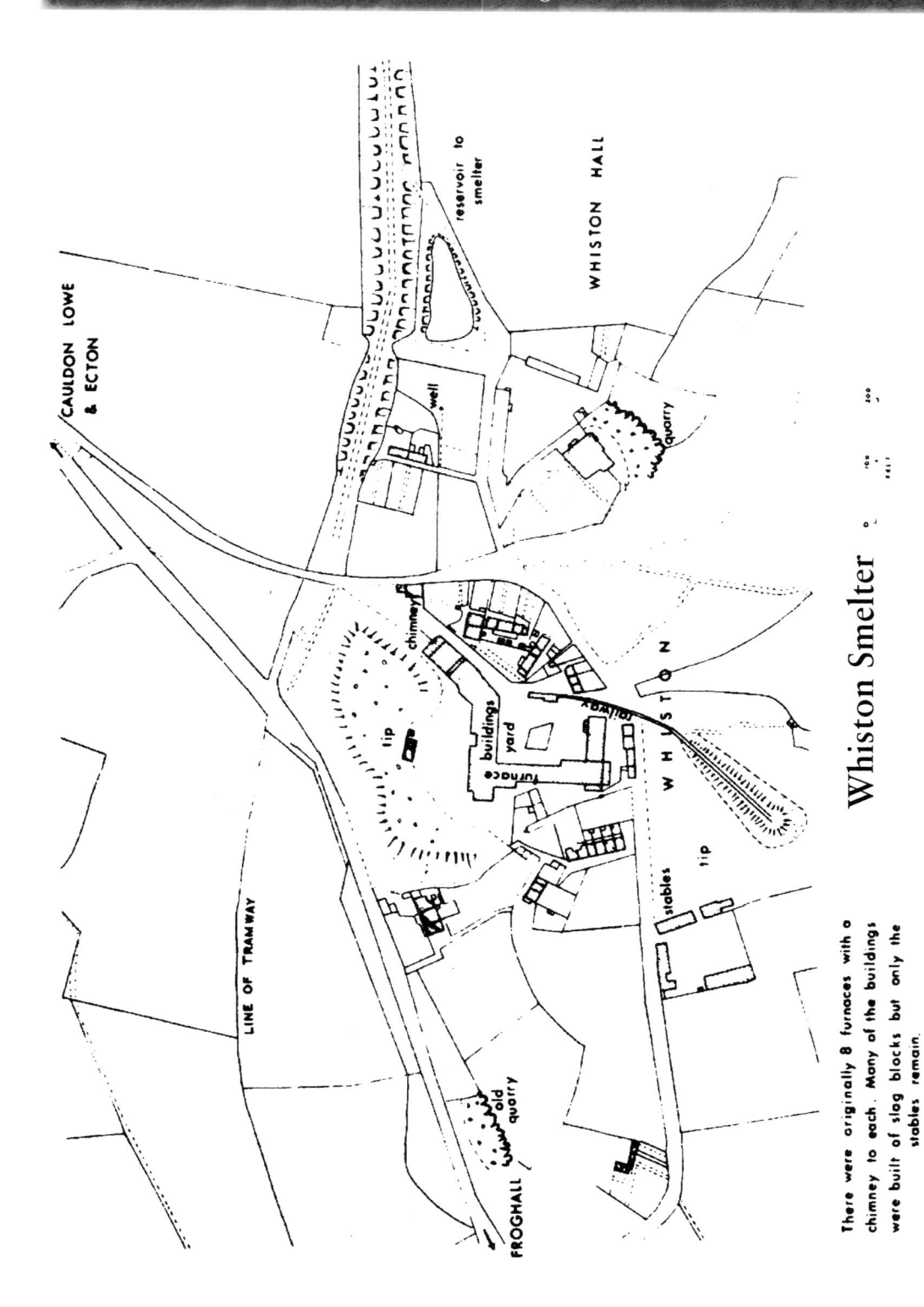

Whiston Smelter

There were originally 8 furnaces with a chimney to each. Many of the buildings were built of slag blocks but only the stables remain.

12.2 The Whiston Copper Works

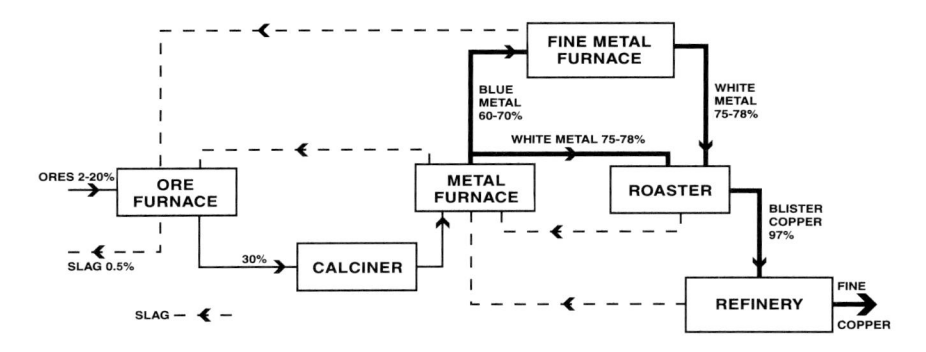

Flowsheet of the Welsh process of smelting copper ores

The dam was made in 1786, but the water course, covered with stone slabs was not finished until two years later. This channel was to supply water to the waterwheel that powered two pairs of bellows at a blast furnace for slag smelting constructed in 1787-8 at the southern end of the mine buildings (see page 76). The reservoir later became known as the fish pond and a small valve house was erected. The channel can still be traced for much of its length along the 800ft OD contour. The slag mill was used to extract lead from the lead slag and for 'Extracting Copper from the Black Slagg'.

By 1798 when ore output had dropped considerably there were only two copper smelters and two black slag smelters at Ecton, with two copper calciners, four lead smelters and two black slag smelters three years later. Dr Hatchett, describing Ecton in 1796, said

> 'at this Mine they roast the copper ore but do not smelt it. The galena is not now smelted here but it is carried to near Cheadle, but the lead slag is here worked over again in what is called a Slag Hearth worked with Bellows. The second slag contains copper and is again smelted for it'.

This statement is not strictly correct for lead was smelted here at this time, not at Cheadle, nevertheless the accounts do confirm that there was much lead and copper being reclaimed from the slags at Ecton at the end of the century.

Fluorspar was used as a flux for both copper and lead smelting, and was supplied by Henry Knowles (and later by William Knowles) at Masson in Derbyshire, with the cost of the carriage at 12s (60p) per ton costing nearly five times the value of the spar at 2s 6d (12 $\frac{1}{2}$p) per ton! An interesting item appears in 1797-9 when they were pounding sulphur for use as a flux, as well as purchasing mundic (iron pyrites) from the Blithe Mine Proprietors at Alport in Derbyshire. Smelting and calcining at Ecton ceased during 1823, and afterwards when the private companies worked the mines, they sold the dressed ores directly to smelting companies few of whom had any direct connections with the mines.

In 1770 the future of the Ecton Mine was sufficiently optimistic for a self-contained unit for the production of copper metal to be set up. This consisted of copper mines, smelting works and collieries to supply fuel, all under the control of the Duke of Devonshire's agent. It is a very early example of a vertically integrated business.

To put this plan into effect, Robert Shore made come calculations to decide the most suitable site for the smelting works. There were four possibilities – ore smelted at Denby, ore smelted at Ecton with either Kingsley coal or the superior Denby coal, or smelting at Kingsley. Shore's calculations showed that Ecton was the cheapest, with carriage of the copper ore to Denby as the most expensive. However Shore grossly underestimated the quantity of coal required (4), and this could have been done deliberately to put the Denby works at a disadvantage. If the calculations are made on a more realistic basis then smelting at Kingsley becomes the most economical, with Denby a close second.

The Move to Whiston

The final choice was to erect a copper smelting works at Whiston near Kingsley, close to the Duke's collieries at Foxtwood and Hazlecross, both part of the Cheadle coalfield (Fig 1).

The Whiston smelter

Whiston was an excellent choice of site, being on the edge of the coalfield and close to supplies of high quality furnace stone and fireclay, both essential for the construction of the furnaces. The site was to prove even more fortunate a few years later when the Trent and Mersey Canal was finally opened and the Caldon branch taken to Froghall, less than one mile away. Also, the tramway from the Cauldon Low Limestone Quarry to Froghall Wharf built in 1777, passed near the copper works, being only the second line in the country to be authorised by Parliament. The last line between the Wharf and the quarry only closed in 1920. The canal was to be a major supply line for much of the heavy machinery and other goods for the Ecton Mines and Whiston Works.

In the Ecton Mine accounts for 1769 we find the entry 'Messrs Cowper & Rottons bill for sundry goods £328.10.10d', which probably refers to equipment sold from the Denby smelting works when it closed down and intended for the Duke's new Whiston smelter. In the early months of 1770, £250 was paid for land at Whiston, the roads leading from Ecton to Wetton Mill and Hillsdale were widened to cope with the extra traffic and the roads around Whiston were also improved. A pen was built on Grindon Moor to act as a store and depot for ore and coal.

The Early Years

A report dated the 18th October, 1772 gives a good picture of the early years at the Whiston works, where there were eight furnaces, six for reducing the ores and two for refining. Although it is not stated, they would certainly be of the reverberatory type. Five of the ore furnaces were usually at work at any one time (the other one being rebuilt), three of which were for smelting ore and slag and two for calcining ore and regulus. The smelting furnaces each took a charge of 3cwt of ore and 1cwt of slag, and each could handle thirty charges per week, while the calcining furnaces took eleven charges every week with 10cwt of ore or regulus to a charge.

The refinery had either one or two furnaces in work depending upon the quantity of coarse copper sent from the smelting furnaces. Coal cost 9s (45p) a ton, including carriage to Whiston; the smelting furnaces usually consumed six tons each per week and those calcining ore or regulus took 3 tons each per week. A cheaper coal at 6s 6d ($32^1/_2$p) a ton had been tried but was found to be unsuitable. At this time Whiston employed 12 smelters, 4 labourers and 7 carriers.

The Production Process
The production of copper metal from the sulphide ores is a complicated process, but the procedure at Whiston in 1772 was as follows -
1. The ore was calcined for twelve hours.
2. 3cwt of calcined ore and 1cwt of slag was smelted for four hours to give a black regulus.
3. This regulus was calcined for twelve hours, melted for three hours and tapped off, still as a regulus.
4. After forty hours smelting the regulus produced coarse copper.
5. The coarse copper was calcined for twelve hours and ladled into iron pots. This was repeated two or three times.
6. After calcining in the refining furnace for twelve hours the fine copper was toughened and cast into cakes, tiles or bowls.

Such was the high quality of the 'botham ores' from Ecton that they were usually mixed with coarse ores, to enable more copper to be extracted and to act as a flux for the high quality ores.

The pyritic ores as produced from Ecton were complex copper-iron sulphides $CuFeS_2$, CuS and $CusFeS_4$. The initial process of calcining (or roasting) drove off excess sulphur, while heating the resulting regulus (nowadays termed 'matte' – a partly smelted mixture of copper and iron sulphides) in the presence of air converted the iron to oxides which combined with sand to form a slag.

The resulting 'white metal' was virtually pure Cu_2S and further roasting in the presence of air converted this to coarse copper, which was further refined to produce the pure metal. A simplified flowsheet (see page 239) shows that as the percentage of copper increased the waste slag (which still contained a small quantity of copper) was returned to an earlier stage so that eventually the slag contained less than 0.5% copper and was discarded (5).

Extension of the Works
To be able to deal with the rapidly increasing quantity of ore raised at the mine, which by 1780 had increased to over four times that raised ten years earlier, the Whiston smelting works were enlarged in 1780-1. Several entries in the accounts referring to 'the new Smelt House' and 'the New Buildings', while two years later they purchased 'A Miln to Break down topper Metal' weighing 5 tons from Thomas Patten's Warrington Copper Works.

By 1779 there were 60 men employed at Whiston and this number appears to have been approximately constant up to the years of peak production. Afterwards there was a dramatic reduction to 22 men in 1798 comprising of 5 smelters, 2 calciners, 1 furnace builder, 12 carriers and a superintendent, with only 4 roastmen, 2 smelters and 2 regulus grinders three years later. In 1805 they obtained estimates for the purchase of a blowing machine to be worked by a cast iron waterwheel, but this project never came to fruition, although a crushing machine was purchased for Whiston at the same time for £68.

As the period of the Duke's operations drew to a close and the output from the Ecton Mines decreased, the Whiston works contracted correspondingly and there was no attempt to purchase ore from other mines to keep the smelter working at full capacity. In spite of this the Duke's smelters at Whiston were certain not backward in improving their techniques, for in 1812 and 1814 Mr. William Sheffield, who was the superintendent of the works as well as acting as the agent for Montague Burgoyne's and Col Bulkeley's interests in the mines, patented improved methods of extracting copper and other metals from their ores. Later these improvements were to be used widely in the copper works in the Swansea area.

Into the 19th Century
In 1844 Garner (6) described the production of zinc at Whiston, where 'we noticed six of these crucibles of clay arranged in a circular oven, of a similar form to those used by the potter. Callamine is here more particularly used for the manufacture of brass'. The production of zinc and brass seems to have been a mid-19th Century venture for earlier only copper was made here. Garner gives a particularly clear picture of the various operations necessary to produce fine copper.

'The small ore is first calcined in a furnace, being frequently stirred to prevent fusion: this rids it of a portion of its sulphur, arsenic, &c, and it is then melted in a second furnace, where part of the slag, iron, &c, is got rid of: the melted ore is then run out into water, when it puts on the form of coarse shot, of a dark colour: the ore may now contain one third metal. It is again several times recalcined, and remelted, being each time granulated, or else formed into large pigs. It is next roasted, previous to the processes of refining and toughening.

In the operation of toughening, the brittle, crystalline, purplish-red metal is covered, in the melted state, with charcoal; and then a pole of wood (birch or larch) is inserted into the melted metal, which is attended with an ebullition, owing to the escape of carbonic acid gas, and the copper, on cooling, obtains the desired properties of malleability, &c.

This process of poling requires care, and if overdone, produces effects different from those desired; in which case an opposite course must be pursued, the air being freely admitted. After poling, the metal at Whiston is formed into large cakes, small ingots, or shot; the last being obtained by letting the melted copper fall into a well of water'.

Despite technological advances in smelting, poling is still carried out in the final stages of copper refining.

In 1818 the Whiston copper works were closed down and by 1821 had been sold to William Sneyd, Clement Sneyd and Thomas Sneyd-Kynnersley, three brothers from one of the largest and most influential North Staffordshire families who owned and worked the Mixon Copper Mine, later to become a supplier of ore to the smelter (7). In 1828 a partnership for twenty-one years was formed between the Sneyd brothers and James Keys who owned the Cheadle Brassworks, who paid £437 and became entitled to 1/8th of the profits. The Whiston works were to be called William Sneyd & Co, with James Keys as manager who was to get £2 per week in addition to his share of the profits. The company was eventually dissolved in 1846 and the works were sold to James Keys for £3,300 who carried on the business with his son John, under the title of James Keys and Son.

The works continued for many years afterwards smelting the copper ore from the smaller Staffordshire mines, as well as the small amount still being raised at Ecton. However, increasing quantities of ore from out of the county, particularly from Coniston and North Wales as well as much foreign ore, were purchased to keep the smelt in operation. The Whiston works finally closed about 1890, and just after the turn of the century the buildings were demolished to provide building stone for a new church at Whiston.

We can get a good idea of the state of the works as they looked in the latter part of the 19th Century (see pages 237/238). Today all that remain are a few cottages (many of them partly built with slag blocks). The vague outlines of the buildings visible a few years ago have now been grassed over along with most of the tips of waste slag, although much of this has been removed for road making. The use of copper slag for road making commenced at the turn of the 19th Century and continued until this century, being highly suitable for this purpose.

12.3 Greenlowfield Smelting Mill, Alstonfield

The location of this mill has been uncertain, but it is now thought to be Lode Mill, just north of Mill Dale (the name may well be a corruption of Lead Mill), as a nearby field (although on the Derbyshire side of the river) is known as Greenlow.

Although in the l8th Century all the galena mined in Staffordshire was sent to Derbyshire for smelting; at least two smelting mills were operating in the region at that time. These are in addition to the lead cupola built at Ecton prior to 1783 to process the galena from the Duke of Devonshire's mines and a lead slag mill built at the same place in 1787-8; these probably ceased working in 1826 when the Duke of Devonshire gave up his operations at the Ecton mines.

Another smelting mill existed at Alton, which is beyond the scope of this book. The reader is referred to that for completeness (8). Although

12.3 Greenlowfield Smelting Mill, Alstonfield

Above: Lode Mill at the end of the 19th Century. It was originally the Greenlowfield Smelter
Below: The only known photo of Mill Dale Mill (other than one of the gable end), probably taken at the same time as the one above

12 Smelting

not much is known of the history, particularly the quantities of ore processed and its source, sufficient documents are available to enable some record of the operations to be given.

The earliest Staffordshire lead smelting mill known was at Greenlowfield or 'Reigis end' in the parish of Alstonfield, the details of which are recorded in two leases in the Staffordshire Record Office (9).

Work on building the mill commenced some time before October 1739 by William Hall Walton, a yeoman of Stanshope one mile south of Alstonfield, but by this time it had not been completed. Walton's son, Hall Walton (described as a gentleman), was among a number of adventurers who took subleases on the mines at Ribden and Thorswood in 1722 and 1729, but these were very short lived ventures, while an attempt to lease copper and lead mines at Grindon in 1736 may not have been executed, unless the lease is in draft (D 593/I/3/22).

In addition, Hall Walton was one of the adventurers who commenced the Ecton Sough in 1723 (10), but this venture is supposed to have cost £13,000 with no return (see Chapter 3). The fact that Walton was not included in the second lease for the sough in 1739 indicates that heavy losses in this venture had necessitated his father's withdrawal from the lead smelting business.

On October 2nd 1739, William Walton agreed to finish the mill with its dam, floodgates and watercourses before the 11th November, and then to convey all his rights in the mill to Paul Nightingale, a grocer from Derby, for £100. The author (JAR) has not found any other connections between this Nightingale and the lead trade, so the reason for his interest in the Alstonfield mill remains obscure, unless it was thought that this was a lucrative market for investment.

The mill was not finished on time and the conveyance never took place, so that on the 10th May 1740, it was agreed in order that the mill could be completed for the 'smelting and running of lead ore' that Paul Nightingale should employ a workman to finish the building, the expences to be deducted from the £100 payable to Walton. This was apparently done by July 1741 at a cost of £90, when the mill was leased to Paul Nightingale for a term of 99 years for a nominal sum, plus the £10 necessary to complete the transaction. In addition Nightingale made a loan of £500 to William Walton and his son, confirming that financial pressures could have been the reason for Walton giving up the smelting mill. All the tools and implements were also sold to Nightingale.

Thomas Gilbert Takes Over

Nightingale's interest in the mill was not to last long for 6 months later, on 16th January 1741 (1742 by the modern calendar) the mill was assigned to Thomas Gilbert of the Inner Temple, London for the remainder of the 99 year term for the sum of £200. Thomas Gilbert came from Cotton in North Staffordshire and was brother to John Gilbert the noted canal and mining engineer. The smelting mill was described as having two hearths, with 'Mill Pools, dams, floodgates, Wheels, Bellows and other Utensils and Implyments' so clearly it was a lead ore hearth of the type illustrated by Clough (11).

Apparently Paul Nightingale relinquished his rights to the mill due to financial reasons so as to raise £200, for the lease states that the agreement could be made void if he paid back the £200 back to Gilbert, plus $4^1/_2$% interest, by July 16th 1742. Gilbert may well have had interests in the smelting mill before he formally acquired it for his father's will (also Thomas Gilbert) dated two weeks before the assignment from Nightingale includes the statement 'my son Thomases share of the smelting mill at Greenlow ffields' (12).

It would seem likely that the source of supply of ore for this mill would come from the mines on Ecton Hill for the Burgoyne royalty was being worked at this time by Thomas Gilbert, Robert Bill and others. (The Bills came from Farley, and as well as being neighbours of the Gilberts they were business partners and related by marriage). The only documentary evidence for the Ecton Mines being the source of the ore is contained in an account between Thomas Gilbert and Robert Bill in 1741 (13):

'Cash paid Mr Nightingale for Mr Bill £100, rec'd. in part from Mr Bill at Ecton £2.12s so remains £87.8.0.'

Of the smelting mill's subsequent history nothing is known, apart from £1.9.6. paid for bricks 'to the Smelting Mill' on 27th October 1743 in the same accounts, which could refer to either the Greenlowfield or Alton mills. It seems likely that the mill became disused about 1760 when the Alton Smelting Mill was taken over by the partnership who were working the Burgoyne mines at Ecton.

12.4 Mill Dale Calamine Mill

The only references to this mill appear in a ledger of the Cheadle Brass and Copper Company. This ledger is in private hands in Cheadle, but the author (JAR) has a copy of the notes made from it by the late Herbert Chester. It covers the period 1730-64, and seems primarily to be accounts for calamine.

As zinc metal was so difficult to extract from its ores, the early methods of making brass (a copper and zinc alloy) involved heating copper metal with calamine (Smithsonite or zinc carbonate) and charcoal in a crucible. The charcoal reduced the calamine to zinc which immediately alloyed with the copper granules. This was also known as the cementation process.

Before use the calamine had to be cleaned, ground to a powder (usually with a vertical edge-crushing millstone) and roasted for about six hours. This converted the zinc carbonate to zinc oxide and removed excess moisture. This reduced its weight by 35% or up to 50% if the ore was wet, so it also eased transport costs. After roasting the calamine became lumpy and had to be ground again before being sent in sacks to the brass works. It was these initial processes of roasting and grinding that were done at Mill Dale, so it was not strictly a smelting mill (even though it is referred to as such in one instance), rather it was a roasting and grinding mill. Although horse power was often used to crush the ore, presumably at Mill Dale waterpower was used to turn the grinding stones.

The earliest reference to Mill Dale is in 1750, when almost 13 tons of coal was delivered to the 'Cally House at Milldale'. There were also 'Ex[penses] pd for building the Calcining Furnace, Materials £11.18.2, which presumably refers to Mill Dale. By the end of the year calamine was being sent to the mill from Croom (? Chrome Hill) and Parkhouse Hill near Longnor in Upper Dovedale, Biggin and from further afield in the Peak District, such as Sheldon near Bakewell.

By early 1751 there were expenses at 'building Calcining Furnace at Milldale' and for 'the Mason at Alstonfield… for his building the Cally Furnace'. The latter reference confirms that it was the Mill Dale in the Dove Valley and not any other dale with a similar name (such as Millers Dale near Tideswell, which was called Miln Dale in the 18th Century).

The roasted calamine was sent from the Mill Dale furnaces to the Cheadle Company's brass works at Old Spout and New Spout (now known as Brookhouses) near Cheadle.

Soon the Thorswood Mine on the Weaver Hills became a major source of raw calamine, with ore being sent from there in 1751-2, 1759-60 and 1764 (see Chapter 9). Calamine also came from mines at Tideswell, Monyash, Youlgreave, and Castleton. There was even a 'Journey to Llanymynech in Shropshire to see about Callamine there'.

In 1752 12cwt of calamine 'for Druggists' was produced. This was, presumably, purer than the usual grade and ground finer to make into calamine lotion.

The latest date at which the Mill Dale furnaces are specifically mentioned is 1759, after which time it is not known if the mill continued working. It is likely that after a promising start the output from the Thorswood Mine did not live up to expectations, and so there were no local sources of ore of any consequence. The Cheadle Company are likely to have concentrated their efforts at their Bonsall calamine mill, which operated from the 1750s to about 1830 and was closer to the mines of the Matlock/Cromford/Winster area where calamine was also an important mineral in addition to the galena usually produced.

By the 19th Century the site was used for grinding colours for paint (calamine could also be used to make a whitish zinc-based paint) using locally mined iron ores. Today there is just a small building which houses a National Trust information office, together with a later millstone in the remains of the wheelrace. A photograph survives which shows a mill building. It was situated on the river at the end of the

Plot's engraving of the Ellastone Bellows

Hall and Wootton Lodge. He had a long interest in lead and copper mines, and although there are only a few scattered references he worked the Burgoyne royalty at Ecton in the Manifold Valley (i.e. the Clayton Mine, not the main Ecton Copper Mine which was owned by the Dukes of Devonshire).

In 1665 the Ellastone mill was let to a Mr Mumma; this is almost certainly Jacob Mumma, a 'Dutchman' who had a brass wire mill at Esher in Surrey. He was an important, although enigmatic, figure in the copper and brass industry at that time.

In 1660 £8 7s (£8.35p) was paid for 'Leather and hides for bellows', but when Dr Robert Plot visited the area 20 years later he reported that the copper from Ecton had been:

'Smelted at Ellastone not far off [it is actually 9 miles away in a direct line, and much longer by road], where they had mills, etc., for the purpose; but all was out of order before I came thither, and the famous wooden bellows that had no leather about them carried away to Snelston in Derbyshire'.

Plot includes an engraving of these bellows, described as 'Designe of a foreigne Engine'. As the original bellows did use leather (see above) this innovative design had probably been introduced by Jacob Mumma when he took over in 1665.

Ellastone was not an obvious choice of site for copper smelting if the main source of the ore was from Ecton. It was close to supplies of wood for fuel and it was, of course, close to Fleetwood's estate, but if ore from Snelston only 2 miles away was smelted there, or if Fleetwood had a financial interest in the Snelston mines, then this would have made the siting of the mill more understandable. There was a small copper mine near Fleetwood's Wootton Lodge so ore may also have come from there.

The location of the mill can now be pinpointed from a map of the Calwich estate from the 1730s (Staffordshire Record Office D3730/1). This shows the 'Copper Mills' with buildings

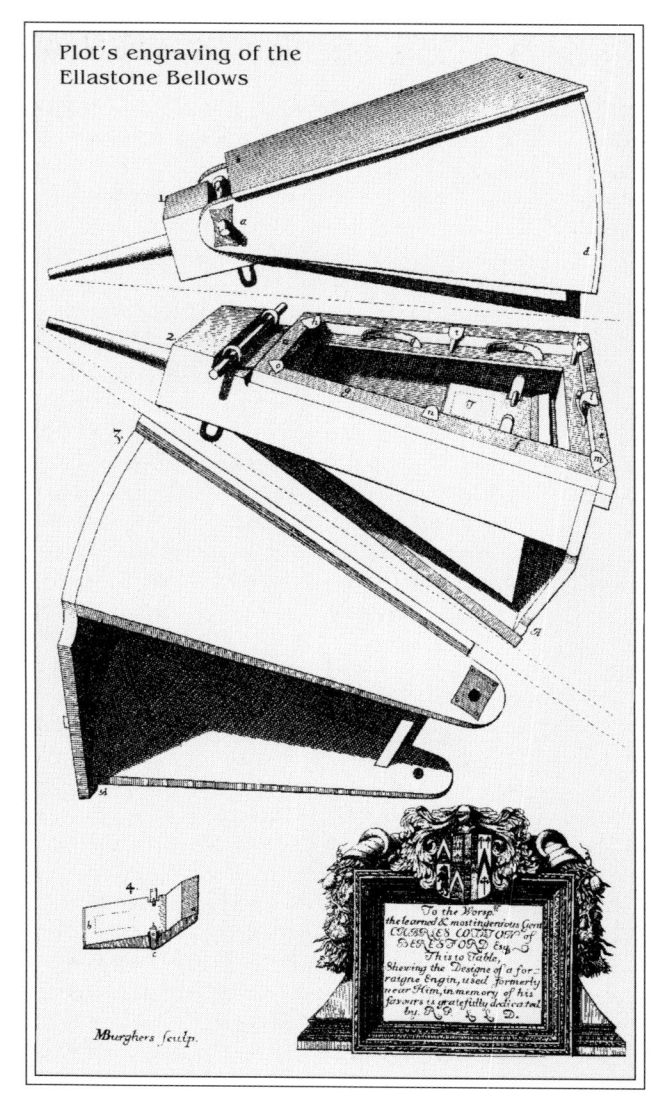

lane from Hope Dale, on the Staffordshire side, like Lode Mill (see Chapter 8 for later references to this mill when it was used for grinding iron ore for paint and Chapter 14 under **Paint**).

12.5 Ellastone

There was a copper smelting mill at Ellastone in the late 17th Century, and although the reader is referred to an earlier article for fuller details (Robey, 1969), a map of the nearby Calwich Estate has recently come to light which shows the exact location.

The mill was built, or modified from an existing building, in 1660-1 and was owned by Sir Richard Fleetwood, who owned Calwich and a waterwheel, approximately halfway between the corn mill on Dove Street (both fed by a stream flowing into the Dove) and the bridge over the river leading to Norbury, where there was another corn mill. A neighbouring small field is shown on the map as 'The roasting-house piece'. See also Chapter 13.

12.6 Packhorse Routes to Whiston (14)

Relating to the Manifold Valley and referring to Dr Garner, in 1879 the latter wrote: '50 years ago [the valley] was scarcely known and rarely traversed except by strings of mules carrying bells and bags of lead and copper ore'.

1. From Ecton

The copper mines at Ecton in the Manifold Valley, were worked from the 17th Century until 1889. In the very early days the ore was carried by packhorse to be smelted at Ellastone, then later at Denby, about 3 miles east of Belper; the route to Denby was via Newhaven. However, from 1770 onwards the ore was smelted at Whiston (SK 041473), above the Churnet Valley. The Duke of Devonshire, who owned the Ecton mines, had chosen Whiston for his smelting works as being near to his coalpits at Foxt Wood and Hazlescross, both on the Cheadle coalfield. Trains of up to seventy packhorses (Farey states that they were mules) were at first used to carry the ore and the route that they followed is known from a map of 1769 and from local tradition.

The map shows two routes: the first from Ecton via Warslow, Onecote, Ipstones and Froghall to Whiston; the second from Ecton via Wetton Mill, Hillsdale, Winkhill Bridge, Bellyband Grange and Windyway Cross to Whiston. As the Whiston works was not built until the year following the date of this map, the two routes were evidently in the nature of preliminary plans and it is fairly certain that it was the second route that was actually followed; it would soon be realised that the alternative route was 3 miles longer and involved a quite unnecessary descent into the Churnet Valley at Froghall with a correspondingly steep climb out again to Whiston. It is possible, of course, that after the packhorses had unloaded their ore at Whiston, they would go down to Froghall so that their panniers could be filled with coal from the Duke's pits for their return journey; no packhorse travelled with empty panniers if this could be avoided. The average cost of carrying ore in the early 19th Century was 1s per ton per mile.

Following the route from Ecton in more detail, the way as far as Wetton Mill (SK 095561) is sufficiently obvious. An estate map of 1617 shows no bridge at Wetton Mill although Darfur Bridge, half a mile downstream is marked. By 1770, however, when the packhorse trains began to come this way, there would have been a bridge at Wetton Mill. It is recorded that a bridge there was swept away by floods and was re-built in 1807, by the Duke of Devonshire at a cost of £184. The road from Ecton to Wetton Mill had been maintained at the Duke's expense since 1770.

Having crossed the Manifold, the packhorses turned along the north side of the Hoo Brook; the route is now a footpath. About a mile up this side valley, the old bridleway that links Grindon and Warslow in a straight line is crossed, and at the same point the Hoo Brook is left, another little valley leading forward and upward to Hillsdale Hall (SK 079554), which bears the date 1620. The packhorse route came between walls to enter the farmyard of the Hall from the north. Continuing from Hillsdale Hall a hollow-way can be seen in a field north of the lane leading to Grindonmoor Gate, near which is The Pen, once a stockyard for ore and coal. From Grindonmoor Gate the packhorse way has become a metalled road and this can be followed past Felthouse to Waterfall Cross (SK 069516), which was once a local landmark; the farmhouse there was formerly an inn. The packhorses then went due south down Benty Grange Lane. On the east of this lane, just before it joins the A523, is a narrow strip of land – a slang – walled off from the remainder of the field; this was a grazing area for the packhorses.

From the other side of the main road, the packhorse way led to a ford (now a bridge) across the River Hamps, beyond which the line is followed, roughly, by a footpath leading over the railway in the direction of Ballamont Grange (SK 059496); this is the 'Bellyband Grange' of the Ecton to Whiston Map of 1769 – evidently the map was drawn by someone more familiar with the harness of packhorses than with Norman French! About 300 yards up the road from Ballamont Grange the packhorse way is marked by a field wall and can be followed by footpath to Windyway Cross (SK 059490); this 'cross' is a tall stone placed on the sky-line as a marker when these hills were unenclosed. From the markstone, the packhorse way is established by a straight field wall with a footpath on its north side. The line aims directly at the site of the Whiston copper works, and for the final mile coincides with the A52.

The Duke of Devonshire ceased to maintain the road from Ecton to Wetton Mill in 1826. The old packhorse route from Wetton Mill to Grindon Moor was too steep for a cart-way and the later route left the Manifold at Swainsley, where a Stamps Yard had by this time been established for crushing the ore, and followed the lane to Butterton. From there the Duke of Devonshire had to improve the rough track marked on Yates's Map of Staffordshire (1775) leading towards Grindon-moor Gate and the road became known as the Duke's New Road; it's now called Pothooks Lane. Another modification was necessary beyond the River Hamps, an easier way was made and soon acquired the name of Duke's Lane from the fact that the Duke of Devonshire's copper ore was carried that way. Duke's Lane climbs south from the modern bridge (SK 068506) over the Hamps, crosses the railway and joins the old Cauldon to Whiston road at Park View Farm (SK 066487); local people say that one object of this route was to avoid paying tolls at Windy Harbour tollgate (SK 062488).

2. From Mixon

Copper mines at Mixon (SK 046573) were worked intermittently from about 1730 until 1858. At first the ore was probably carried by packhorse to the Cheadle Copper Works, but after the 1820s the ore was taken to the copper works at Whiston. For information on the route followed by the packhorse trains we are indebted to Mr S Fern of Onecote.

From Mixon to Onecote, the way followed the line of the present farm road above the River Hamps, but then turned south-west; about midway between Onecote New Hall and the turn down to Onecote Grange, a pair of stone gateposts in the wall on the west side of the road indicate the start of the climb over Morridge. The way between the gateposts is now built up but clearly led into a broad hollow-way lined with beech trees; it is shown on Yates's map of 1775. The way ahead led between Hopping Head Farm and the ruins of Willow Meadow Farm; there is no footpath but, with permission, some lengths of packhorse hollow-way may be traced if care is taken to discount several deep natural watercourses that have also cut into the hillside.

Arrived on Morridge the way descended to the Leek-Ashbourne road and from there probably continued through Lower Lady Meadows (SK 026530) before climbing to Ipstones Edge, which could be followed to join the copper route from Ecton at Windyway Cross.

References

1. The furnaces used would be similar to the lead ore hearths, illustrated in R. T. Clough, *Lead Smelting Mills of the Yorkshire Dales*, 1962
2. Robey, 1969, op cit
3. Robey J. A, 1971, Bull PDMHS, 4, No 5, pp348-356
4. Raistrick A, 1967, op cit
5. He quotes 10 tons of ore ('which holds two Tuns in Twenty' i.e. 10%) needing 4 tons of Denby coal; the true figure would be nearer 40 tons
6. Hopkins D .W, 1970, Bull, Hist Met Group, 5, No 1, pp6-8
7. Garner R, op cit
8. Morton J, 1983, Thomas Bolton & Sons Ltd, 1783-1983
9. Robey J. A, 1970, *Two Lead Smelting Mills in North Staffordshire*, Bull PDMHS, Vol 4, Pt 3, pp217-221
10. Devonshire Collection, mining papers at Chatsworth House
11. Clough R.T, 1962, *op cit*
12. Staffordshire Record Office, D240/A/1/52
13. Ditto, D554/55
14. Dodd, A.E & E. M, 1974, *Peakland Roads and Trackways*
15. Burne, S.A.H, 1915, *Arch. Papers with Special Ref to N. Staffs*

13 The Ellastone Smelter Survey

Historical Background

The area was managed in the monastic period by the Augustinian Order at Calwich Abbey, located two-thirds of a mile north-east of the survey area. The Augustinians are presumed to have constructed a fishpond between the Abbey and the River Dove. A leat, known locally as 'Hammer Ditch', runs west from the pond to join a small mill pond in Ellastone village. A stream runs south from this mill pond and forms the eastern boundary of the survey area.

The Ellastone copper smelting mill was built or possibly modified from an existing building in 1660/01 (see Chapter 12). The Ecton Copper Company paid an annual rent of £25 for the copper mill, which was probably paid to Sir Richard Fleetwood. Together with the Duke of Devonshire, Fleetwood was an investor in the Ecton Mines. Both mine and mill were operating in 1665. But by 1686 a survey of the area by Plot reported that both had closed. The site of the mill is shown on a plan as 'Copper Mill Yard', SK 119425.

It is noted that two brooks feed the mill pond of the corn mill just upstream from the smelter site. These are the Hammer Ditch and the Tit Brook. Iron slag has been found in the stream bed. This slag begs the question 'was there an iron forge here, perhaps operated by the Abbey'? It is suggested that, with the use of a tilt hammer in such a forge, the derivation of the original names of the streams, Tilt and Hammer, can be explained. However persuasive this may be however, in a mainly agricultural area, another name for a horse is a 'tit', so this may be the derivation.

A survey of the Calwich Abbey Estate c1740 in the Lichfield Record shows the 'Copper Mill' on the west side of the stream that runs southward from Ellastone to the River Dove. On the east side of the stream the land is identified as the 'Copper Roasting Piece'. The 1847 Tithe Map of the same area shows a leat running through the area of the Copper Mill. The leat can still be identified in the field south of the survey area as a linear ditch. The first edition 25 inch map published in 1880 makes no reference to either the leat or the 'Copper Mill'. One feature common to all three maps is a building that lies on the north side of the field against the road. This building doesn't exist now, its position is roughly on the line of the farm track that forms the northern boundary of the survey area.

The Site Now

The surveyed field is used for rough grazing and is still known as 'Copper Mill Field'. It is bordered on the north and south side by iron fencing. The western boundary with Dove Street is partly hedge and wall. The stream that flows southward to the River Dove from the Ellastone village reservoir forms the eastern boundary of the site. An electricity pole stands in the western side of the field.

Much of the field is hummocky with occasional shallow gulleys generally trending towards the stream. An obvious shallow terrace runs parallel with the stream.

Mole activity has revealed the underlying soil. Dark grey soil occurs in a distinct area on the north-west side of the field with occasional fragments of slag and pieces of coal. One large fragment of black glassy slag with green-blue copper staining was found. Several pieces of tap slag were also found in the stream. The soil adjacent to the stream was light brown in colour.

At the time of the survey, water levels were low enough to permit a detailed examination of the stream banks. Large masonry blocks and other walling were noted in the west bank in the southern part of the survey area.

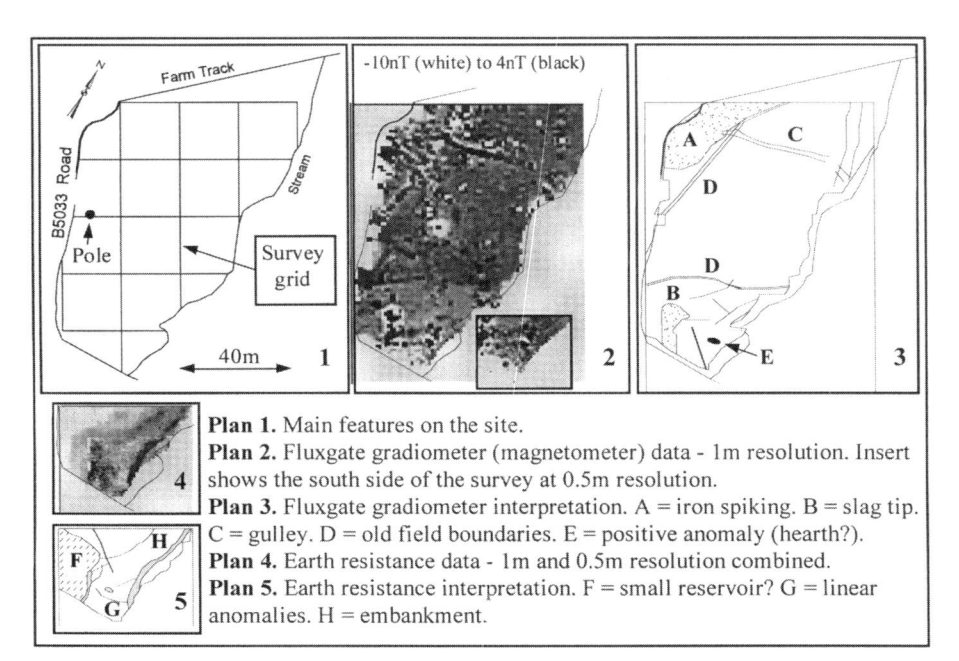

Plan 1. Main features on the site.
Plan 2. Fluxgate gradiometer (magnetometer) data - 1m resolution. Insert shows the south side of the survey at 0.5m resolution.
Plan 3. Fluxgate gradiometer interpretation. A = iron spiking. B = slag tip. C = gulley. D = old field boundaries. E = positive anomaly (hearth?).
Plan 4. Earth resistance data - 1m and 0.5m resolution combined.
Plan 5. Earth resistance interpretation. F = small reservoir? G = linear anomalies. H = embankment.

Slags

Further samples of slag were found during the survey. They will undergo further study in the Department of Archaeological Sciences at Bradford University.

Discussion

The geophysical surveys have added much to the interpretation. By comparing the geophysical data with early maps it has been possible to draw some conclusions on the layout of the site.

The initial physical examination of the field provided some evidence for both iron and copper slags being present in the field. The iron is predominantly in the north and copper to the south. This has been borne out by fluxgate gradiometer data. It showed a strong spread of iron spiking and much noisier data in the north west corner which could not be linked to a feature on the ground. In the southern part of the field an area of positive data with a lower range of values to those in the north, could be related precisely to a low mound.

Evidence from the 18th Century Tithe Map shows that the copper smelter was located in the southern part of the field, whilst in the northern part a small building was located on the bend in the road. It is now presumed that much of the northern slag and higher values are associated with the use of this building.

Most of the 'spikey' data was located on the north side of a linear feature interpreted as a probable field boundary and may correspond to one shown on the Tithe map. The presence of coal in the top soil in this area may complement the presence of iron rich material. It would be of interest to know what the building was used for. For example, was it a blacksmith's shop?

In the southern half of the field, a distinct change is noted on the fluxgate gradiometer data. It is possible that the northern part of the field was farmed, whilst the southern portion remained unfarmed. This could have been due to structural remains or copper contamination, although neither are evident now. There are a number of linear features which converge on the southern area with a distinct grouping around another positive anomaly.

It is tentatively suggested that this anomaly could represent the site of a smelting hearth or furnace. The uniformity and clustering of the positive data would suggest that the data represents a structure. Unfortunately very little is known about 17th Century copper smelters for a firm conclusion to be drawn. The earth resistance data (low resistance) suggests that a small reservoir could have been located to the west of the slag tip. The remains of a leat noted in the field to the south of the survey area would have channelled water to the River Dove.

Linear features located south of the slag dump and running approximately north west – south east could represent a channel which took the water from the reservoir directly to the

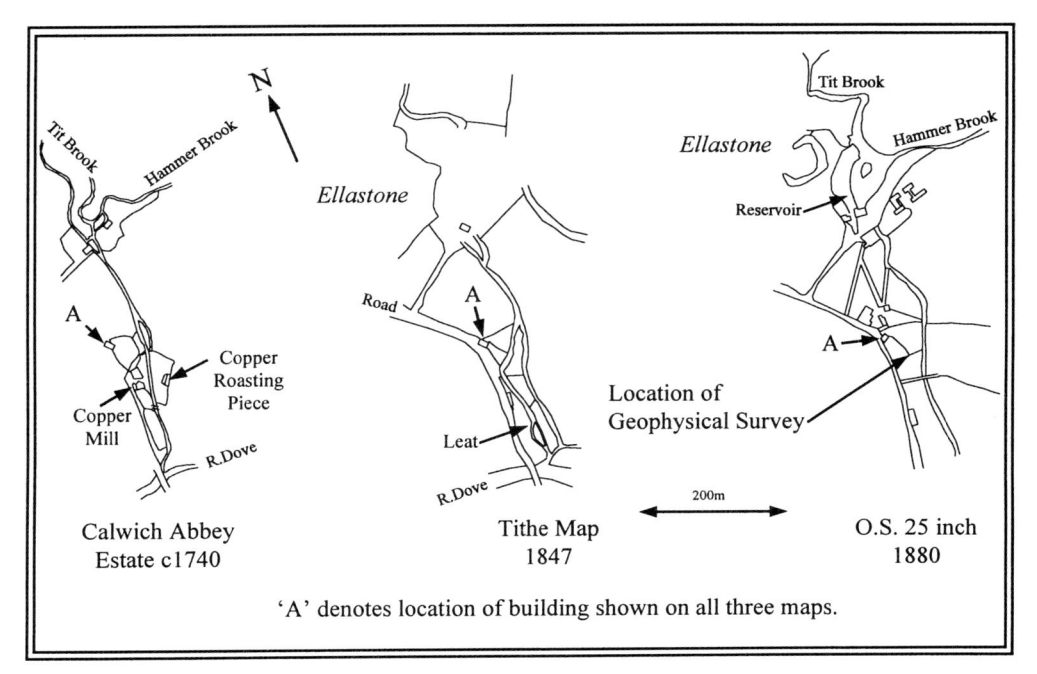

'A' denotes location of building shown on all three maps.

stream. Strong linearities seen on both the earth resistance and fluxgate gradiometer data indicate that some form of embankment was present to control the route of the stream. Masonry in the bank of the stream suggest it may have had a stone core. Other masonry protrudes from the field into the bank of the stream at a location which lies close to these geophysical anomalies.

Unfortunately only a broad interpretation can be made of this site. It is only possible to say that the key components associated with smelting operations are present. These include waterpower represented by a stream, reservoir and leats and a probable smelting area with associated slag dump. No known copper smelting sites of a similar age have been excavated for any direct comparison or further interpretation to be made.

Conclusion

As with any survey work of this type there are no straightforward conclusions that can be drawn from the survey data. The survey has however pointed the way to several features worthy of further investigation.

Having identified the main components of the site it is vital that further information is drawn from the site. Further geophysical work would provide very little additional information on the site layout. However a small 5m by 5m grid survey across the anomaly thought to be the smelting hearth may provide further information on the dimensions of this feature. It would also be useful to survey the area east of the stream, identified on the 18th Century Tithe Map as the 'Roasting Hearth Piece'.

A further survey in the field to the south would also determine if any activity associated with the smelting extended into this area.

In view of the lack of understanding as to how this and other similar sites functioned, it would be advantageous carry out a partial excavation of the site. This would enable key features to be identified and be tied in with the geophysical responses, and also provide an understanding as to how such a site functioned.

Acknowledgements

I would like to thank: The landowner, Henry, and Bill Stretton, for their interest, and allowing the survey to go ahead, Lindsey Porter and Wes Taylor for initiating the survey and Margaret Vernon for assistance with the fieldwork. I am also grateful to Drs Gerry McDonnell and Armin Schmidt, Department of Archaeological Science, University of Bradford, for allowing use of the equipment.

Reference

Vernon R W, 1998, *Second Interim Report on Geophysical Surveys at the Ellastone Copper Smelt Mill Site, Staffordshire*, Dept of Archeological Science, University of Bradford

14 North Staffordshire Copper and Lead Mining Terms

The recent publication of the most comprehensive listing of Derbyshire's lead mining terms (*Glossary of Derbyshire Lead Mining Terms* by J H Rieuwerts) is recommended – not only because of the terms it includes but because of additional historical detail supplied by the author. At the time of publication, I was able to add a few North Staffordshire words to Jim Rieuwerts creditable achievement. Following publication, a more thorough search, more out of curiosity than anything else, resulted in a more substantial list of words.

Many of these seem to be peculiar to North Staffordshire, especially the word 'saddle' and the words associated with that particular geological feature. Other words seem to have been adopted to a slightly new meaning, such as 'fang'. It is likely that many words located by Jim Rieuwerts were used in North Staffordshire but have not been recorded. It is only by chance that several words have survived – in a single inventory of the Dale and neighbouring mines. It is in fact the only inventory to survive relating to the mines in this orefield.

Clearly the volume of records on the orefield is significantly less than for the much larger one in Derbyshire. Moreover, Jim Rieuwerts work is the result of a lifetime's study. None the less, sufficient words associated with North Staffordshire have been found to merit this listing.

> References to MJ means *Mining Journal*

Adit
A drainage level, see also sough. The word was inter-changeable, so that the Ecton Sough was later known as the Ecton Deep Adit (often now called Deep Ecton Adit)

Attle
Waste containing little or no ore (MJ 1847, p68)

Beaters
A local term for a bucker. New stails for beaters were bought in 1865 at Ecton. They were used to break up lumps or ore prior to separating the rock and spar from it

Bob stand
At the Dale Mine they had 'cleared foundations for two bob stands or loadings' (MJ 1863, p90)

Bonsall's Trials
The 19th Century shafts sunk on the back of Ecton Hill by Capt Samuel Bonsall. All on Burgoyne Royalty and most in the vicinity of Bowler, Goodhope and Clay mines

Bote Gate
In 1767 the Ecton miners were driving a bote gate. This became the underground canal at the 34 fathom level used for ore removal to Apes Tor Shaft

Bradder
A photograph of the miners outside Clayton Adit, probably taken in 1883, shows them wearing a Bradder or hard hat made from papier-mâché. They were manufactured in Bradwell, hence the nickname. One of the Ecton bradders is preserved at the Mining Museum at Matlock Bath

Branch
Used in the same context as a branch line on a railway. 'Driving a cross-branch' to Good Hope Mine, Ecton (MJ 1852, p185)

Brown Hen
Described by Rieuwerts as inferior lead ore, often contaminated with limonite, a brown earthy oxide of iron. In the Ecton Mine in the 1790s, they were working Brown Hen and there are refer-

ences to 'driving through ye Brown Hen or Mineral' and 'dressing the Brown Hen ore'. The Mixon agent in 1829 reported a vein with 'the minerals that usually attend copper, such as Spar, Sulphur and Brown Hen'. See Joint below for a further reference

Bucker
These were large flat iron-made hammers used to break down the ore. They were in use at Ecton in 1769 when Efford visited the mine

Buddles
There were six buddles at the Stamps Yard when it opened. Various types were used at the Ecton Stamps Yard in the 1840s. These included patching, trunking, tie and washing-up buddles. A running buddle is mentioned as being at White Road Mine in 1823. An advert for the Ecton Stamps Yard trunking buddle appeared in the *Mining Journal* in 1841 (see Chapter 11)

Bunches
A concentration of the ore deposit. There is a reference in the MJ 1847, p512 relating to Ecton

Bunding
A platform in a shaft, 1767/70 (J Harpur's Jottings, DRO 2375/M No 63/65)

Byelift
A second set of pumping pipes installed in case of failure of the main lift. The Dale Mine installed one when they were worried about being inundated by water (MJ 1860, p401)

Captain
The mine manager. The most celebrated at Ecton was Capt Bonsall. He was captain for 33 years until his death in 1870 and was the nephew of Sir Thomas Bonsall. He lived at the roadside house at Ecton which must have been part of his emolument for after his death his successor, Capt Beresford, lived there

Carriage
A local term for a deposit of ore. At the Dale Mine, the men were driving in the pipe vein near the carriage. There was a 18ft high stope which included a quantity of iron pyrites (MJ 1861, p115)

Cased and divided
The division of a shaft by timber to separate the footway from the part housing the winding and/or the pumping equipment. There is a reference to 'casing a shaft' at East Ecton in February 1862, when eight men were paid 2/6d (12.5p) per day. In June 1867, men were casing pumps at Ecton according to the Cost Book. This was a Cornish word and only appears after the arrival of Richard Niness. At the New York Mine sale of equipment in 1854, there was included 'casings and dividings'

Caunter Lode
See Counter Lode

Clevics or Clevise
At White Road Mine in 1823 there was 'a pair of Engine ropes with large iron clivics at the end of each rope'. In the same inventory but at the Dale Mine there was listed 'one pair of engine ropes, chains, caps and clevics and turntree, stowe, forks, turn ropes, and clevises'

Coe
Mine buildings usually situated by, or surrounding a shaft

Collar
The top of a shaft

Cope
Payment to the owner of the mineral rights to permit ore to be sold to the buyer of the mines choice

Counter Lode
Noted at the Ilam Mine and at the Burgoyne Mine, Ecton (considered to be Clayton) (MJ 1847 p72). The term was also used at Mixon where it is clear that it ran contrary to the other veins at the mine.

Crop Ore
Reference to Ecton ore in the Whiston Smelter Accounts for the 1830's and 1840's. It relates to high quality ore delivered to the smelter. This was not ground up small and consisting of fine particles. This type of ore, known as slime, resulted from the various washing operations of the buddling process which was concerned with its separation from rock and spar or gangue

Cross Course
A vein cutting the one being worked. In 1852, men were working on a fault on a cross course at Clay Mine, Ecton (MJ 1852, p185). In the drawing level of Salt's Level at Ecton, there is the 'Ida Alley Cross Course'

Above: The *footway* shaft at Waterbank Mine, Ecton. The remains of the ladder may be seen protruding from the water **Opposite:** *Coes* at Waterbank Mine, Ecton, one still with the roof on. The *collar* of the Engine Shaft is in the foreground. The photograph was taken in 1924

Cross Gate
Mentioned by Rupert Bullock at Mixon in 1839. Another name for a cross-cut

Dampt
Killed by gas. Mentioned in the Alstonfield Parish Register in 1642 'dampt in a groane at Eckton'. See further reference to this in Chapter 3.3

Dead rent
A lump sum paid per annum instead of a royalty for access. In the 1880's, the miners paid £100 dead rent for access across Devonshire land in Clayton Adit to reach the Clayton pipe working

Delve
To search for ore. Referred to in a 1736 lease for Hill House Mine, Elkstones, 'to delve for lead and copper on two parcels of land'

Derrick
Regarding the new shaft at Narrowdale Mine, 'we shall have to erect a horse whim or derrick' (MJ 1871, p66)

Draftage
Referred to in the 1860 accounts for Ecton. An allowance of $24^1/_2$lb per ton was made on ore sales. Perhaps it was to allow for loss of weight as wet ore dried out (following the dressing process which involved separation in water)

Drawing
A term used in association with a level or a shaft along which, or up in the case of a shaft, ore was removed from the mine

Drifts
Included in the Gould to Marsden lease of 1839 at Royledge. A drift is more usually associated with the coal mines of North Staffordshire than metal mines. It refers to a horizontal working going into the side of a hill, for instance

Fang
A clay sealed stone culvert made in the floor of a level for the purposes of ventilation (Rieuwerts). In 1765, the Duke of Devonshire's account book for Ecton refers to 'fanging and railing at the deep

level'. As the water left the mine beneath floorboards laid in the adit, it is probable that this reference relates to this

Floats
Included in the Gould to Marsden lease of 1839 at Royledge. It is a description of a type of deposit. Rieuwerts describes it as being ore either at or near the surface including ore retrieved from the remains of old dressing floors

Flookan
A reference to the clay found in a vein. It was often used by Richard Niness and was a term he brought with him from Cornwall. The clay found on the upper surface of a bed of ore associated with a saddle (i.e. a wing) was known as whey. Richard Niness refers to whey flookan at the Dale Mine 75 fathom level (MJ 1871, p1159) but this is confusing. 'A soft, clayey substance, which is generally found to accompany the cross-courses and sides, and occasionally the lodes themselves; but when applied to a vein, it means a cross vein or course composed of clay, some of which are several fathoms in width' (Orchard, 1991). See also under Lum

Forebreast or forefield
The part of a level being drilled by the miners. Dale Mine (MJ 1861, p4)

Fork
'The success in forking the surface water was better than expected' at the Dale Mine in 1858. It relates to the removal of water from within an area of the mine

Footway
The ladderway in a shaft. At Ribden there was a footway at Ingleby's Shaft (MJ 1859, p87). Men were working on a footway at Bag Mine, Ecton in 1867. Just beyond the Clayton engines shaft at the adit level may be seen the Clayton footway shaft

Gate
A level, mentioned in 1832 re Mixon Mine in a letter to William Wyatt from Thomas Sneyd-Kynnersley. Also, East Gate Level at Ecton Mine

Gin

See whim. Gin was a Derbyshire term not often used in North Staffordshire

Gossan

Richmond Shaft at Ribden Mine had a vein with 'a fine gossan and a good flookan' (MJ 1860, p540). Orchard (1991) states that this refers to 'peroxide of iron and quartz, generally occurring on the backs of lodes'. Backs means the surface side of a lode or vein. It is unclear whether Niness meant quartz in this context, although a sample of it was found by the author in the quarry now backfilled by domestic waste at Ribden

Groane

Old name for a mine. Mentioned in the Alstonfield Parish Register, 1642

Grove Clock

To 'James Brown for repareing grove clock £1.16.6d'. Ecton Day Book 12/5/1770. Pat Bromfield's thesis argues that the clock was necessary, as a shift system operated, especially for the watermen working the pumps

Grove Clothes

Rieuwerts (1998) refers to clothes being purchased for the mine manager or sometimes for the miners. There is a reference to grove clothes in the 1823 Dale Mine inventory. Efford (1769) stated that the Ecton miners worked naked except for coarse canvas drawers, as skin renewed itself but cloth did not. Apparently the mine water was slightly acidic and it eventually rotted clothing

Groves

Referred to by William Senior on his map of Calton, 1637, referring to lead groves or mines. The area of Ecton Hill which includes the Bowler, Clay, Good Hope mines is referred to on an old map as Groves Closes

Halvans

Lead ore 'from the Halvans' 1861, Ecton. This is a Cornish word and the equivalent to slime ore. It is suspected that the term in this context may have been to denote the recovery of ore from waste material

Hearth Fleakes

Two large ones were recorded in the 1823 Dale Mine inventory. Rieuwerts (1998) records the word 'Fleakes' in Derbyshire as a screen of intertwined brushwood used as a weather protection around washing floors, gin circles etc. Presumably this reference at the Dale mine relates to something similar around a hearth. The latter is probably a blacksmith's hearth as no ore hearth is recorded here

Hitches

During the sinking of the new engine shaft at the Dale mine, a cistern plat and bearer hitches were cut at the 66 fathom level. The report goes on to mention 'hitches for catches for the main rod and also hitches for stays for the same' (MJ 1863, p90)

House paper

Probably wall paper for the mine office. Ecton Cost Book, December 1866

Joint

A vertical fissure in the rock. Often could be clay filled and non productive but could be good ore bearing ground along the axis of a saddle: 'cut the wet saddle with a very strong joint about five feet wide' Rupert Bullock to JS Smith, March 1939 re Mixon.

Huckle Joint: the joint associated with a anticlinal saddle and a Trough Joint: the joint associated with a synclinal saddle, see also Trough (Watson, 1860).

In December 1864, three men were paid 2/2d (11p) per day for 22 days on contract work for 'driving west after the lum joint', probably in Good Hope Mine, Ecton.

'A fine bed joint of oxide of lead 1.5 inches thick with brown end* – a local term for zinc and silver' at the Dukes's Adit, Bincliff (MJ 1858 p356. *Probably a typographical error for 'hen'

Kibble

The container used to haul ore to the surface at a shaft. One of the iron kibbles from Ecton is preserved at the Peak District Lead Mining Museum at Matlock Bath. It is unknown from which mine it was recovered, although it was stored for years in the barn at the first cottage on the right as one goes up the lane to Back Ecton from Apes Tor. Maybe it was used at nearby East Ecton Shaft, but this is speculation only

Knock Bark

Rieuwerts (1998) states that this was the ore prior to beating after the obvious solid pieces of ore had been extracted. A knock bark riddle is mentioned in the 1823 Dale Mine inventory as being at Hayesbrook Gate Mine

Knocker
A person employed to beat or buck the ore. The Chatsworth reckoning accounts for Ecton refers to a knocker in February 1761

Launder
A wooden water course. In 1858 men were 'laying launders to take the water' in the Dale Mine Adit level where it was crossed by the Lum. A collar launder was being prepared at Ribden (MJ 1861, p435). This was a means of removing the water pumped up the shaft to a cistern or drain, if the water was not required for dressing or the mine boiler. The 1823 Dale Mine asset inventory records that there was 70 yards of laundering. Launders were laid in 1851 in the Royledge Adit on the boundary between Royledge and New York Mines. This was to stop the water draining along the adit from sinking down into lower workings where the ground had been worked, or stoped, out and then backfilled. In 1973, the author (LP) heard the term 'laundering' used in the context of guttering around a house in Hartington

Leat
A water course. See also launder

Lime
'Slacking and cauking lime for building at Dutchman, 18 days at 2/6d (12.5p) per day'. Preparation of lime mortar for one of the buildings at the entrance to Dutchman level, July 1860

Loss of Tools
In 1868, this appears in the Ecton Tributors' account. It seems to be a hire charge for tools and was levied at 1/- (5p) per month

Lot
Duty paid to the mine owner for free access to the mine and also access to wood and water

Lum, or lumb
An east-west orientated fissure found in the Dale, Ecton, Mixon and Royledge Mines. At the Dale Mine, the lum was described as being a cross lode, 70 fathoms in width. They were similar to a cross course, but differed 'both in mineral content and in their effects on the veins with which they are associated and cut across'. A lum vein was 'usually of great magnitude, and are commonly entirely filled with marl and decomposed limestone, although in the immediate neighbourhood of the pipe-veins some ore proceeding from the saddles is mostly found attached to the cheeks of the vein' (Watson, 1860). The clay seems to have been referred to as 'flookan' by the Cornish miners such as Niness and differed from the clay found above ore in the wings of a saddle and known as 'whey'

Metal
Ore; 'Driving in metal', R Bullock to J S Smith, Mixon 1839. At the Dale Mine, they were 'putting in timber over the old workings from the new shaft to the metal winze'. The vein in the metal winze was described as being 21ft wide (MJ July 1870, p574). A little later, the vein was composed of spar, chert, whey, flookan and stones of lead and zinc (MJ 1871, p154)

Mine shoes
There is a reference to this in the Ecton Cost book for 1854. Maybe the mine bought shoes for the manager. See also under Groove Clothes

Noger
A drill or boring bar. One was lent to Mixon Mine in 1775 by Ecton Mine. This is particularly interesting as it must have been something special; perhaps made from harder iron or with a differently shaped bit on the end

Offle
There are several references to this, eg. 1 ton 1cwt sold at £4.10s per ton. It must relate to one of the types of fine ore in the separating process for the Ecton Cost Book refers to 'offle budlings' in the tribute account for 1855

Ore
A Chatsworth reckoning book of 1764 records the following kinds of Ecton ore: Handaway, Slime, Old Hillock, Stamped. The latter is interesting for it denotes the possibility of a stamps machine although Efford in 1769 stated that all the ore was broken manually by women

Paint
A local reference to iron ore. There is a reference in the 1851 to 'royalty on paint' and in 1861, to yellow paint from Strong Stys. This is a mine near to Thor's Cave, above the Manifold Valley. It was also obtained at a mine called Hope Heath, thought to be between Wetton and Alstonfield. A further entry in 1859 refers to 10.5 tons of yellow stone from Strong Stys being sold for £12.12s.0d (Duke of Devonshire's Wetton Account book, DRO). The watermill at Mill Dale was used to

grind the ore to powder and it was then mixed with lime wash to colour the latter yellow or red. The mill was known as a paint mill

Plat

A working area to pile ore or deads prior to removal from the mine according to Orchard (1991). See MJ 1854, p783, re Bincliff Mine

Rider

'Men are driving between two perpendicular veins 4ft apart (cawk and spar). These form a rider and coming nearer together when ore should be found', re Bincliff, (MJ 1858, p356)

Run Ground

A collapse in a working. In 1856, Ecton miners were paid 2/6d (12.5p) per day for 'opening old run ground'

Sawney Shaft

'Wheel houses' according to the English Dialect Dictionary (EDD sb2). Probably an engine shaft. The reference has only been found once, in a reference to Mixon in 1828. However Sawney is a North Staffordshire word meaning a winding engine. See Chapter 6

Saddles (see also Joint)

Wet saddle mentioned by Rupert Bullock at Mixon in 1839. Clearly one that was issuing a lot of water, which the miners regarded as a good sign of ore. Bullock also refers to a dry saddle, presumably the opposite to the above. Watson (1860) describes the saddles, which seemed to be particularly common in the North Staffordshire orefield, and gives the names attributable to particular features. Saddles were highly contorted ground within a short distance, i.e. it was very much a localised occurrence, often associated with minor faulting and vertical fissures known as joints together with some horizontal strata similar to flatwork, but again only occurring over a short distance.

A synclinal saddle was known as a trough saddle and its apex was a trough. Conversely, the top of an anticline was a huckle and the formation was known as a huckle saddle. Ore was often found either side of the apex and the ore-bearing beds were known as wings. A clay band was associated with the top of the wings and was known as whey or wheyboards. The clay in Royledge Mine is sometimes milky in colour, although often stained light brown by iron, presumably from the overlying shale beds. The term 'whey' is possibly derived from its colour. See also Joint.

In the Dale Mine 43 fathom level, a huckle and a trough saddle were located in the same level (MJ 1857, p745)

Sample

When the larger mines were ready to sell ore, they sent a sample of the different lots to interested smelters so that they could test it to judge it's metal content. One of the Ecton copper samples wrapped in brown paper and addressed to J Keys at the Whiston Smelter is preserved at the Peak District Mining Museum

Sett

Used to describe the area of land being worked by the mine. There is an Oversetts Mine at Bincliff

Silex

Chert. A single bed of silex over 4ft thick was found at a depth of 56 fathoms in the New Dale Mine's Engine Shaft No 2 (MJ 1862, p4 and p366)

Skipway

A framework which enabled the hauling of a loaded wagon up the shaft so that it may then be removed down the adit to the surface. One was introduced into Clayton Mine in 1884

Slapdashing

Presumably painting with lime wash and the origin of the well known term for poor quality work. In March 1868, John Bland was paid for slapdashing the house; 8 days at 3/- per day (15p)

Slimes

Finely ground ore. The Whiston Accounts for 1831 mention slime ores and it was a common reference thereafter at various mines

Sough

A drainage level

Stamps Yard

The water-driven crushing mill erected at Swainsley in 1818. In the period 1837-1844 it worked day and night crushing and separating the ore. It closed in 1866

Stenting

This term was used concerning tributors at the Dale Mine: 'I could not think of stenting them any longer time than cutting the ore in the back of the 54 fathom cross cut' (MJ 1871, p66)

Stentwork
In a reference to the Dale Mine 75 fathom level being driven south, Niness said that he had been 'obliged to remove some men from here to do stentwork, as some of the men have left the mine through, as they say, not getting sufficient wages' (MJ 1871, p654)

Stull
In 1871, the Dale Mine was 'putting in a stull to hold the stone to keep open the ground'. This is another word brought from Cornwall by Richard Niness. The Dale Mine required considerable amounts of timbering but of course all of it is now under water and cannot be seen. The more common term is stemple (MJ 1871, p106)

The O'm
This is a field name and relates to the field due south of the Ecton engine house in which many old shafts may be seen sunk on a north south vein. It probably gets its name from someone seeing a reference to OM on a plan of the area. **The Old Man** is a local term used both here and in Derbyshire to mean old mens' workings

Ton
Copper ore was weighed at 21cwt to the ton. Part of the reason for this seems to be to compensate for the weight of the water in the copper when it was weighed after the dressing process

Tossing Machine
Used at the Ecton Stamps Yard in the 1840s. Probably refers to a dolly tub. The latter incorporated blades to agitate the water and help separate the heavier pieces of very finely ground ore from the gangue (spar or other minerals accompanying the ore) which was lighter and therefore remained in suspension longer

Tram Level
There are many references to paying for contract work on the driving of the Good Hope tram level in 1864. It relates to the long extension of the Dutchman Level at Ecton. In 1884, the Ecton lads employed at pushing the mine tubs through the mine were referred to as trammers. There is also a reference to a tram road in the Ecton Cost Book for 1851

Trespass
Payment for a right of way – referred to at Royledge in 1846. See also dead rent

Tribute
A system whereby men would take a contract to work ore for a percentage of the value. They usually purchased their own powder and candles and employed all the labour necessary to complete the work. Unusually, the word was used in the context of a royalty in a letter to Jesse Watts Russell of Ilam Hall by Thomas Sneyd Kynnersley of Loxley Hall re the Mixon Mine in December, 1832

Trindles or Trundles
An iron wheeled barrow. Mentioned in the Dale Mine asset list of 1823. One survives in the six fathom level above adit at the Royledge Mine. It is probably an error for the word 'trundle'. In the same inventory there is a reference to 'five old cast iron wheel barrow trundles' at the Hayesbrook Mine. The author's (LP's) wife, Stella, uses the word 'trundle' to mean a young child's toy pram etc, but the principle of an object which is pushed along is clear

Turntrees
The lease of 1839 from Gould to Marsden gave free use of the ropes and turntrees. A turntree was another name for a stowes or capstan for moving a bucket or kibble up or down a shaft. Rieuwerts (1998) states that in Derbyshire, a turntree was more correctly the barrel of the stowes around which the rope was wound. The 1823 Dale Mine inventory refers to 'turn roping from Dale Shaft'. The last surviving stowes in the North Staffordshire orefield was found in East Ecton Adit when the author (LP) reopened the mine in 1972. Unfortunately the barrel was missing and it has since collapsed, but a photograph of it may be seen in Robey and Porter *The Copper & Lead Mines of Ecton Hill, Staffs* (1972), illustration 22

Tut Work
It seems to be a form of contract work where the men were paid by the fathom. Ecton Cost Book, 1866

Underlie
The hade (or dip) of the vein or pipe. Referring to the workings in the Dale Mine at the 37 fathom level, Niness reported that 'the pipe definitely has a different underlie than between the 26 and the 37' (MJ 1860, p401)

Vault
The caverns in Ecton Mine. J Harpur's diary of 1767/70, called Jottings (DRO op cit)

14 Mining Terms

A bradder and a kibble photographed at East Ecton Farm in the 1960s. They are now in the Peak District Mining Museum

Water Carriage

A level for the removal of water. Mentioned by J Harpur, 1767/70, at Ecton. In this instance the reference was to the 34 fathom level which was also the underground canal (DRO op cit)

Watercut

At Ribden Mine they were 'now very busy opening watercuts to keep water out of the mine' (MJ 1858, p681)

Whim

A means of drawing up a shaft. 'It referred to a horse-operated winding apparatus. The horse walked on a circular track set outside the shaft collar. A massive pivoting wooden column located in the centre of the horse track supported a horizontal drum, around the circumference of which was wound the winding rope. The rope passed over one or two pulley wheels set in a frame at the shaft head. Attached to the rope was the kibble' (Rieuwerts). The term gin was not common in the North Staffordshire orefield. Whim was used instead. A gin was mentioned in the 1823 list of assets of the Dale Mine and others were listed at Hayesbrook and White Road Mines. It is likely that the list was compiled by George Cantrell who came from Derbyshire where the term gin was common. Gins are marked on the litigation plan concerning Royledge and New York Mining Companies, 1851

Windboar
Mentioned in the Valuation of the Dale Mine/Hayesbrook Mine assets in 1823. Likely to be the same as wind trees – hollow timbers used for pipeing pumped air. Two wind boars about five feet in length survive in the Royledge mine adit

Windlass
'pumps and windlasses with two handles which draw ye water up into troughs'. Ecton (J Harpur's diary, 1767/70, DRO op cit)

Wings
The ore bearing beds either side of a saddle (Watson, 1860)

Winze brace
At the beginning of May 1858, work 'commenced cutting ground for a winze brace' at the Dale Mine. A reference to a 'wing brace' at Ribden (MJ 1861, p435) could be an error unless a winze was being sunk in the wing of a saddle, as both reports were written by Richard Niness. Alternatively, it could relate to the wing or the side of a saddle. In 1866 the Dale Mine was 'cutting a winze brace in the old mine to put up a windlass' (MJ 1866, p426). A winze was a shaft sunk between two levels

References
1. Orchard, W.G, 1991, *A Glossary of Mining Terms*

2. Watson J. J. W, 1860, *Notes on the metalliferous saddles of Derbyshire and Staffordshire*, The Geologist, No 3, pp357-369

15 Bibliography of papers on North Staffordshire Mines

Ecton

Barnatt, J & Thomas, G   1998, *Prehistoric Mining at Ecton, Staffordshire: A Dated Antler Tool and its Context*, Mining History, Vol 13, No 5, pp72-78

Barnatt, J Rieuwerts, J et al   1997, *The early use of gunpowder in the Peak District: Recent exploration and re-evaluation of the workings at Stone Quarry Mine and Dutchman Level, Ecton*, Mining History, Vol 13, No 4, pp24-43

Critchley, M. F   1979, *A Geological Outline of the Ecton Copper Mines, Staffordshire*, Bull. PDMHS, Vol 7, No 4, pp177-191

Guilbert, G   1994, *Hammer-stones from the copper-mining site at Ecton Staffordshire*, Bull. PDMHS, Vol 12, No 3, pp26-27

Guilbert, G   1994, *More on the Ecton Hammer-stones*, Bull. PDMHS, Vol 12, No 4 p14

Porter, L   1969, *Ecton Hill – A Study of the Surface Features*, Bull. PDMHS, Vol 4, Pt 2, pp156-169

Porter, L   1970, *Ecton Hill – Part II - Underground*, Bull. PDMHS, Vol 4, No 3, pp195-216

Porter, L   1997, *Bygone Days in Dovedale and the Manifold Valley*, Ashbourne Editions. This book has several photos of the Ecton mine buildings etc

Porter, L   2001, *The Ecton Mine, Staffordshire, 1883-1891*, Mining History (in press)

Porter, L & Kirkham, L   1998, *Ore Dressing in the Manifold Valley*, Mining History, Vol 13, No 6, pp40-48.

Rieuwerts, J. H,   1960, *Ecton Mines and some problems of preservation*, Bull. PDMHS, Vol 1, No 2, pp20-21.

Robey, J. A   1969, *The Ecton Copper Mines in the Seventeenth Century*, Bull. PDMHS, Vol 4, No 2, pp145-155

Robey, J. A   1975, *The Burgoyne Mines at Ecton in the Seventeenth Century*, Bull. PDMHS, Vol 6, No 2, pp71-72

Bincliff Mines, Manifold Valley

Porter, L & Robey, J. A   1974, *A History of the Bincliff Lead Mines, Wetton, Staffs*, Bull. PDMHS, Vol 5, No 5, pp271-278

Dale Mine, Warslow

Porter, L & Robey, J. A — *The Dale Mine, Manifold Valley, North Staffordshire*

1972 Part 1, Bull. PDMHS, Vol 5, No 2 pp93-106

1973 Part 2, Bull. PDMHS, Vol 5, No 3, pp161-173

1974 Part 3, Bull. PDMHS, Vol 5, No 5, pp279-287

Ford Mine, near Onecote

Porter, L & Kirkham, L — 1998 *Ford Mine, near Grindon, North Staffordshire,* Mining History, Vol 13, No 6, pp21-22

Mixon Mine, near Onecote

Robey, J. A, & Porter, L — 1970, *The Copper and Lead Mines of the Mixon Area,* Bull. PDMHS, Vol 4, No 4, pp256-280

Robey, J. A, — 1970, *Drainage of Mixon Copper Mine, Onecote.* Journal Staffs. Ind. Arch. Soc, 1, No. 1, pp1-7

Ribden Mine, Cauldon Low

Robey, J. A & Porter, L — 1971, *The Metalliferous Mines of the Weaver Hills, Staffs, Part 1* Bull. PDMHS, Vol 4, No 6, pp417-428

Porter, L & Robey, J. A — 1972, *Ditto Part 2,* Bull. PDMHS, Vol 5, No 1, pp14-30 Geological Notes by T D Ford

Royledge & New York, Elkstones

Porter, L and Robey, J. A — 1972, *The Royledge and New York Copper Mines, Upper Elkstones, near Leek, Staffs,* Bull. PDMHS, Vol 5, No 1, pp1-9

See also:

Porter, L — 1971, *Richard Niness, Mineral Agent of Warslow in Staffordshire,* Bull. PDMHS. Vol 4, No 5, pp362-369

Robey, J. A — 1970, *Two Lead Smelting Mills in North Staffordshire,* Bull. PDMHS, Vol 4, No 3, pp217-221

Robey, J. A — 1994, *The Upper Dove Smelting Mills,* Bull. PDMHS, Vol 12, No 4, pp12-14

Jackman, P. S — 1996, *The History, Productivity and Mineralogy of Snelston Mine, Ashbourne, Derbys,* MH, Vol 13, No 1, pp19-30

Subscribers List

RG Adams, Brierley Hill, West Midlands
Dr CI Adderley, Hulland Ward, Derbys
Neil Aitkenhead, Keyworth, Notts
Stephen Alcock, Cheddleton, Staffs
Arkwright Society, Cromford, Derbys

Roger Bade, Morden, Surrey
Colin Bagshaw, Burton Upon Trent, Staffs
Peter Bailey, Tissington, Nr Ashbourne
W Bailey, Summertown, Oxford
AH Ball FRGS, Mossley, Lancs
Stuart Band, Ashover, Derbys
Dr John Barnatt, Buxton, Derbys
Thomas Barr, Mitcham, Surrey
David G Barras, New Mills, Derbys
Peter & Valerie Bateman, Ecton
Richard A Belson, Norwich, Norfolk
John S Bennett, Warrington, Cheshire
MC Black, Esq., Ware, Herts
Bob Bell, Bromborough, Wirral
Michael Billington, Alstonefield
Peter Billson, Derby
Paul Billups, Crewe, Cheshire
Alan Bolton, Royston, Barnsley
Bookthrift, Ashbourne
Don Borthwick
Anthony Botham, Hanley, Stoke-on-Trent
Colin Bowden, Bishop's Stortford, Herts
Tony Brewis, Epsom, Surrey
Ron Bridger, Luton, Beds
T & S Bridges, Ovington, Northumberland
CR Bridgwood
SJ Brooks, Ashbourne, Derbys
Dr Ivor J Brown, Wakefield
Anthony Browne, Cheadle, Cheshire
David J Burford, Ashbourne
Nigel R Burns, Bristol
Thomas J Bury, Butterton, Staffs
Bruce Buswell, Warminster
Tom Buxton, Royledge, Elkstones

Ian P Cameron, Moira, Swadlincote, Derbys
Roger Cannon & Jane Powell, Hulme End
Dr Mike Carter, Cheddleton, Staffs
Peter James Challis, Moreton, Wirral
Michael G Chambers, Alvaston, Derbys

Christine Chester
Robert J Clark, Leek, Staffs
John A Coddington, Newcastle upon Tyne
Ray and Carolyn Cork
John W Cooper, Nottingham
Rosalie Courage, Ellisfield, Hampshire
Peter R Cousins, Lichfield, Staffs
Geoff & Elizabeth Cox, Ecton, Staffs
Paul T Craddock, British Museum
John F Craig, Sevenoaks, Kent
RJ Critchlow, Grindon
Pat Cronin
David Crowther, Derby
John & Alison Crowther, Whaley Bridge
Stephen JA Curr, Allestree, Derby

Dr D Dalrymple-Smith
Maurice Deakin, C.Eng, FIMinE, Matlock
Paul Deakin, Trentham, Stoke-on-Trent
Derby City Library
Derby Museum and Art Gallery
Derbyshire Archaeological Society
Sir Oscar De Ville, CBE, PhD, Sonning, Berks
Nigel J Dibben, Hatherton, Cheshire
Evelyn M Dixon, Belper, Derbyshire
Clive J Downhill, Buxton, Derbyshire

Tim Eades, Alstonefield
Embsay Steam Railway, nr Skipton

Mr SC Faulkner, Elkstones, Derbyshire
Dr Trevor Ford, Oadby, Leicester
James R Freeman, Derby
Tony Fretwell, Bishop Auckland
Peter J Frost, Ecton
Ted Furnival, Dales Cottage, Alstonefield

Kitty, Rebbeca, Garlick
Geology, Oxford Brookes University
Michael C Gill, Sutton, Yorks
Mr RW Gilman, Consall, Staffordshire
Pam & Philip Goodwin, Ipstones
Gillian & Duncan Gorham, Stanton-by-Bridge, Derbys
Roger Gosling, Alveston, Gloucestershire
David Gough, Newthorpe, Notts

Robert Gratton, Dronfield, Derbys
Peter Greaves, Bonsall, Derbys
Ernest Gregory
Gary J Griffiths, Alstonefield, Ashbourne
Kath Gunson, Sheffield
Dr Peter Gutteridge, Nottingham

Philip Harburn, Peterborough
Lorraine & Brian Hawkins, Alstonefield, Derbys
Roger J Hawkins
Hawkridge Books, Castleton
John Henner, Oxford
Adrian Henstock, Nottingham
John B Hicklin, Belper
Mike Higgins, Doncaster, South Yorkshire
Mark Higginson, West Hallam, Derbys
John S Higton, Draycott, Derbys
HL Holliday, Royton, Oldham, Lancs
Stewart C. Holt, Newark, Notts
Roy Hudson, Lowdham, Notts
Mr William Hughes, Waterhouses
Charles & Susannah Hurt, Casterne Hall, Ilam
EL Hurt, Bulwell, Nottingham
Rod J Ireland, Leyland, Lancs

Dr DMD James, Cwmystwyth, Wales
Marcus Jecock, York
Dr Barry Job, Newcastle-under Lyme, Staffs
John A Jones, Kegworth, Derby
MH Jones, Taunton, Somerset

John Keeley, Mousehole, Cornwall
Richard & Christine King, Dunbrook, Derbyshire
Mike Langham, Buxton, Derbys
TJ Larimore, Chaddesden, Derby
Dr David Kiernan, Barnsley
Len Kirkham, Knypersley, Stoke-on-Trent
Dr JA Knight, Shirland, Derbyshire
Jon Knowles, Clayton West
JM Kyle, Wandsworth, Birmingham

Jon Lane, Alstonefield
Colin C Lansdell, Norwich, Norfolk
W Gordon Lee, Ambergate, Derbys
Peter M Lewis, West Bridgford, Nottingham
Local Studies Library, Matlock
MJ Luff, Ravenstone

Graham A Makepeace, Llangenny, Powys
K Makin, Todmorden, Lancs
Damian J McCurdy, Golborne, Lancs
DC McKee, Nottingham

Colin Mills, East View, Ecton
John N Mills, Ipstones, Staffs
Steve Mills, Chelford, Cheshire
Mole, Royal Forest of Dean
Mrs C Moyes, Brooklyn, Waterfall
Alan E Mottram, Derby
Phil Mottram, London

National Trust
Lord PJ Naylor, Cromford, Derbys
David R Neal, Dolgellau, Gwynedd
David Noble, Stanton, nr Ashbourne

Hedley Oldfield, Esq, Sheffield
Nicholas O'Reilly, MSc DIC, Wootton, Derbys
Mr & Mrs Geoffrey Orme, Mapperley, Nottingham
Orpheus Caving Club, Derbyshire

WJD Parkhouse, Coleford, Glos
A. Partington, Marple
Roy Paulson, Lea, Matlock
Douglas Paling, Exmouth, Devon
Peak District Mining Museum
Peak District National Park Authority, Bakewell
Augustus R Pegg, Ticknall, Derbys
John Pickin, Leswalt, Wigtownshire
The Picture Book, Ashbourne
Ray Poole, Leek
Boyd & Jenny Potts, Hulland Ward, Derbyshire
Michael Potts, Nottingham
Mr Poulsom, Burntwood, Staffs
John L Preston, Talke, Stoke-on-Trent
Rosalind Prince, The Old Nick, Warslow

Christine & Michael Rayner, Cressage, Shropshire
Susan Reiblein & Andy Symons, Manor House,
    Back of Ecton
William G. Rhodes, Alstonefield
Brian Rich, Leek, Staffs
R Allan Richardson, Longridge, Lancs
Dr JH Rieuwerts, Sheffield
Mr Brian Rowbotham, Ye Olde Royal Oak, Wetton
Neil Rowley, York
Derek Rushton, Leek, Staffs

D Sargent, Norwich
Prof William AS Sarjeant, Dept of Geological
    Sciences,
 Univ. of Saskatchewan, Saskatoon, Canada
John Saul, Queensbury, York
Ron Scholes, Leek, Staffs
J Scothon, Butterton, Leek

A flooded winze in Joan Vein, a level in Clayton Mine, Ecton. Its depth is unknown

Alan Scragg
Phillip Shaw, Glossop, Derbys
Richard Shaw, Aylestone, Leics
Mark Sissons, Market Bosworth, Leics
Dr W Slatcher, Rochdale
John F Smith, Alstonefield, Ashbourne
Tony V. Smith, Little Hayfield, Derbys
Paul W Sowan, Croydon
Jim Spencer, Didsbury, Manchester
Jane Steer, Allestree, Derby
Derek Stephenson, Blackfordby
Anthony N Stubbins, Chesterfield
E Swindells, Elkstones, Derbys
WT Swindells, Onecote, Leek, Staffs

Wes Taylor, Walton on Trent
David B Thompson, Betley, Crewe
Paul Thompson, Winster, Derbys
A Jonathan Toyn, Uttoxeter, Staffs

University Of Nottingham, Hallward Library

Rob Vernon, Walton, Wakefield
Antony Vetta, Peppard Common, Oxfordshire

David Wagstaff, Anglesey
Michael J Walsh

David Walters, Oakamoor, Staffs
Cathryn Walton, Leek, Staffs
Dr G Warrington, Nottingham
Edward A Watkin, Betley, Staffs
Roy T Weaver, Paddock House Farm
David Webb, Woodthorpe, Nottingham
Dr John D Wilcock, Stafford
Barrie Wilkinson, Butterton, Leek
Robert V Willan, Natland, Cumbria
Dr Lynn Willies, Matlock Bath
William Salt Library, Stafford
Colin Williams, Norfolk
David Williams, Tideswell, Derbyshire
John Wilmot, Matlock Bath, Derbyshire
David C Winnard, Warslow, Derbyshire
John Wolff, Nottingham
Prof. F Wolverson Cope, DSc, CEng, FIMM, FGS
Stuart Wood, Clifton, Ashbourne
Graham Woods, Calton, Staffs
Dr Andrew R Worthington, West Runton, Norfolk
S G Worthington, The Old Rectory, Blore, Ashbourne
Terry Wraxton, Longton, Staffs
Mrs M Wright, Hucknall, Nottingham
Ray & Jonathan Wright, Clearwell Caves, Glos

Index

A

Absenteeism	103
Acre	137
Alport Mine	82
Alton Smelting Mill	245
Antler tool	38
Attwood, John Beaver	162

B

Back-of-the-Brook	198
Barker and Wilkinson	68, 108
Bassett, Walter	60, 63
Biggin Dale	193
Bill, Robert	204, 215
Bincliff and Casturn Mining Co Ltd	186
Blacton Moor	149
Blithe Mine	239
Blore	196, 198
Blue Hills	178
Blue Hills Colliery Company	212
Bollands Hall	175
Bonsall calamine mill	245
Bonsall, Samuel	78-9, 80, 83, 84, 86, 101
Boothman, Thomas	140, 142
Botstone Mine	175
Boulton & Watt Engine	58, 64, 81, 82, 83, 87
Brittlebank, Joshua	116, 155, 159
Brown's Shaft	191
Brunton & Co	125
Brunton, William	70
Buckfurlong Farm	173
Buddles	226
Burgoyne Mining Company	71, 74, 79, 80, 176
Butterley Company	70, 71

C

Cantrell, George	70-2, 79, 101
Castern	188
Cattle plague	103
Cauldon Low Mines	207
Chalybeate spring	173
Chandos, Duke of	203
Chatsworth Open	71, 93
Cheadle brass works	34
Cheadle Copper and Brass Co	152
Chrome Hill	75, 177
Clayton Sough	44, 51, 68
Cleaver & Co	75
Clockhouse Smelter	88-9
Clod Hall	198
Cockfighting	103
Coffin Level	81, 193
Cold Eaton	193
Cotton Dell	200
Cotton mill	114, 115
Cow Close Mine	119, 134
Curr, John	70

D

Deepdale	137, 173
Denby copper works	236
Dimmingsdale	205
Double spiral balancing drum	58, 60
Dovedale	192
Dressing floors	34, 52, 63, 64, 93, 99, 129, 151, 169, 184, 211, 225, 226, 227, 233

E

Eclipse of the sun	226
Ecton, Clayton and Waterbank Mining Co	87
Ecton Co Ltd	88, 97, 230
Ecton Consolidated Mining Co	31, 83
Ecton Copper Company	74, 75
Ecton Copper Mine Co	77, 78
Ecton Mine Company	75, 109, 209
Ecton Mountain Mining Co	80
Efford, W	50
Elkstones Brook	148
Employment of Children	104, 134
English Crown Smelter Co	94
Eyam Mining Company	9

F

Falcon Low Cave	179
Flat rods	111, 122, 127, 143, 200, 213
Fleet Green	114, 135, 147, 148, 150
Flint, Cornelius	52, 54, 58, 60, 62, 70, 71, 72, 100, 101, 102
Forbes, Edward	75, 138, 176, 226
Ford Mine	176
Foxtwood	239

G

Gateham	187
Gilbert, John	51, 52, 58, 68, 204, 207
Gilbert, Thomas	51, 67-8, 196, 198, 203, 204, 207, 215
Gilbert-Cooper, John	47, 50, 51, 104, 105
Goldsitch Colliery Co	82
Goldsworthy, John	72, 74
Gould, Richard	115
Gradbach Mill	114
Greenlowfield Smelting Mill, Alstonfield	242
Grimshaw and Co	62
Gunpowder	40, 41-3, 44, 46, 48, 50, 101, 103, 175, 176

H

Hadland Top	194
Hammer stones	38
Hanson Grange	193
Hartington	41, 47, 54, 74, 92, 108, 109, 115, 177, 198, 230
Hayesbrook	110-16

Index

The bottom of an ore-chute in Bag Level, Clayton Mine, Ecton

Hazelbarrow	120	Hope Heath	187	Iron Ore Mines	187
Hazlecross	239	Hurst Low	178		
Hazleton Clump	198	Hydraulic pumping engine	117	**L**	
High Rake Mine	167				
Hill House Mine 135, 138, 139, 147		**I**		Latham Hall	196
				Level, Boat	51, 52, 53, 54
Hollybank Mine	131, 133	Ilam Mining Company	189	Limepits Mine	119, 133, 134, 220
Hope Dale	119, 187	Ilam Moor	188		

Index

Limestone Hill 200, 216
Llanfair mine 139
Lode Mill 67, 242
Lum 71

M

Magpie Mine 167
Marsden's Ore Breaker 229
Masson 239
Mather & Platt Ltd 86
Mather, Colin 31, 86, 87, 98, 101, 229
Mather's patent revolving buddle 229
Medieval History 38
Mill Dale Calamine Mill 245
Mill Dam Mine 9
Mineral and Battery Works 40
Minerals 20
Mines Royal 40
Mold Foundry 90
Mootlow 194
Mumma, Jacob 43

N

Narrowdale 133
New Ecton Mining Co 31, 83, 84, 86, 186
New Mixon Hay 158, 160
New York Mine 111, 118-25, 139, 142-48, 218, 220
Newcomen 115, 116, 117, 172, 189
Newton Grange 193
Nightingale, Paul 67
North Staffordshire Consols Mining Co 181
North Tamar mine 165

O

Okeover 188
Onecote ore pen 64
Ore hearth 199
Ore Production 41, 57, 75, 104-7, 109, 170
Ossoms Hill 173

P

Packhorse Routes 247
Paint mill 187
Paint mine 187
Parkhouse Hill 245
Patten, Thomas 236
Peak Forest Mining Company 231
Peak United mine 9
Penn Recca quarry 190
Pensions 102
Pickford, Joseph 137

R

Rhyscog Mine 139
Ribden & Thorswood Mines 199
Ribden Mining Co 211
Richard, Sir Fleetwood 40, 41, 44, 46, 196
Roades, Jeremiah 41
Robins shaft 191
Ropes for Hauling 60
Roscoe, Richard 231
Rottenstone 147
Royledge Mine 118-125, 142-8

S

Sandycroft Foundry 90
Shore, Robert 50, 52, 53, 58, 101
Sim's engines 167
Smacker's Open 71
Smith J, S 161
Snelston 246
Sneyd, Rev John 139
Social Conditions 98-101, 103
Stamps Yard 34, 36, 72, 84, 224-27, 229
Standlow 195
Star Wood 200, 216
Stragdale Mine 171
Strong Stys 187
Swainsley Hall 231
Swainsley Mine 75, 76

T

Taylor, John 43, 72, 75, 77, 100, 103, 104, 107
Thievely lead mines 180
Thompson Abraham 77, 78, 80, 118, 169
Throwley 198
Tissington 41
Transport Costs 101
Tunnel Shaft 200, 216
Ty Mawr Slate Quarry 165

V

Ventilation 57, 211, 216

W

Wages 41, 60, 95, 99-103, 159, 161, 164, 172, 185-6, 213, 227-8, 234-5
Walton, Hall 203
Warslow Mill 114
Warslow Mineral Co 115, 116
Wass & Sons 130
Water blast 131
Water Engine 54-8, 62, 74, 99, 102
Waterwheel 34, 55, 57, 58, 67, 72-5, 84, 120-1, 133, 142, 151, 154-5, 158, 182, 213, 224, 226-8, 234-5
West Ecton Mine 133
West side 175
West Snailbeach Mining Co 215
Wetton Hill 64
Wetton Mill 41, 64, 89, 224, 227, 233, 234
Wheal Concord Mining Co 76
Wheal Walter 76
Whiston Copper Works 237
Williams, John 76, 118, 119, 121, 142-4
Williams, Thomas 30
Wyatt, Benjamin 154
Wyatt, William 140

LANDMARK COLLECTOR'S LIBRARY

LATHKILL DALE
Derbyshire, its Mines and Miners

J. H. Rieuwerts

246x174mm; hardback; matt art paper; 112pp £13.95

A revised 2nd edition of the original book published in 1974. It incorporates considerable changes as a result of further research, plus more photographs.

The book covers:
1. The Mining Area – veins and surface features, geology and mineralisation
2. Early History – the Bristol Company and early court cases
3. The late 18th Century – including the era of the London Lead Company; the Hillcarr Sough Company
4. The Mandale Company – 1797-1820
5. Power to drain the mines – Lathkill Dale Mine, 1825-1842; Mandale Mine 1825-1851; Lathkill Dale Mine and vein after 1851: Gank Hole and Lathkill Dale level
6. Features visible today
7. Chronology; glossary; bibliography; references; index

LEAD MINING IN THE PEAK DISTRICT

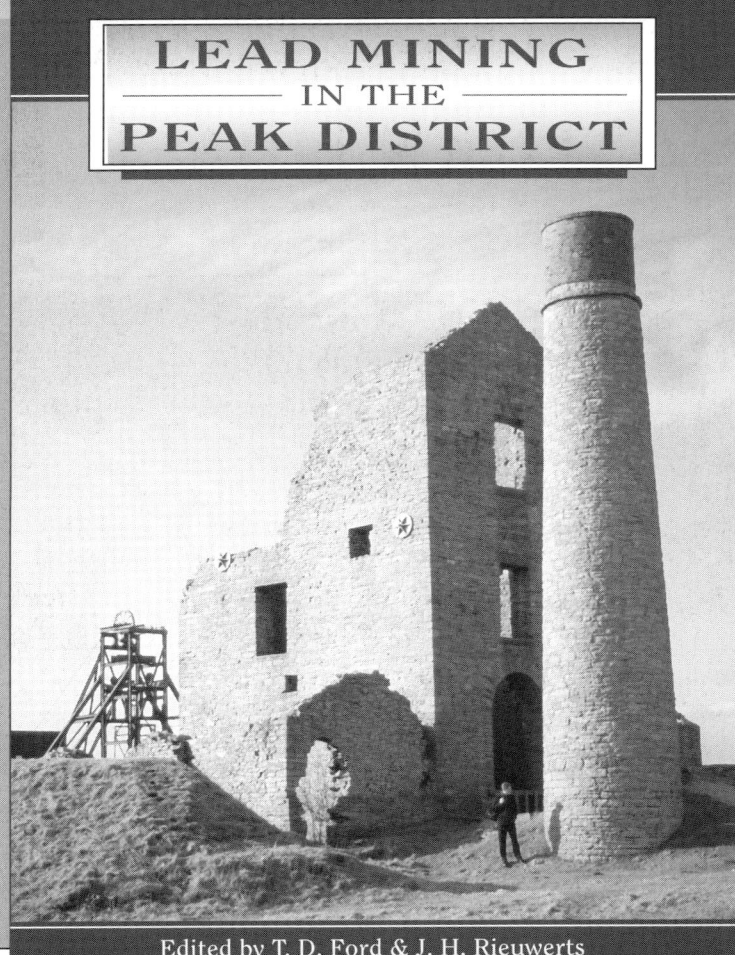

Edited by T. D. Ford & J. H. Rieuwerts

A5, paperback, matt art paper, 208pp £9.95

The 4th edition of this popular book. It describes the history of the main mining areas of the Peak and includes an itinerary for visiting 18 separate areas. The book has been updated to take into account new research; includes Peak Forest and the Ecton Mine and also incorporates colour photography for the first time.

Some of the photographs of underground scenes are stunning and from the collection of Paul Deakin, F.R.P.S.

The chapters cover: Introduction — Geology; History; Castleton; Peak Forest; Hucklow, Eyam & Stoney Middleton; Sheldon & Magpie Mine; Ashford Black Marble Mines & Mill; Lathkill Dale Mines; Hillocks & Knotlow Mines, Monyash; The Alport Mines; the lead mining village of Winster; Wensley-Darley area & Mill Close Mine; Matlock area; Cromford & Bole Hill; Good Luck Mine; Wirksworth; Carsington Pasture & Brassington; Crich; Stonedge Cupola; Ecton Copper Mines; Glossary & Further Reading; Index.

For our full ordering address, see page 272

Eighteenth Century Life in the Staffordshire Moorlands

The Impact of the Ecton Copper Mines on a Rural Community

Based upon Pat Bromfield's thesis, this impressive book is for those interested in mining and social history in the Staffordshire Moorlands or in family history. Packed solid with facts based upon original research, it centres around the workers at Ecton Mines from 1769-1825, when the mine was worked by the Duke of Devonshire.

The type of work they did, its effect upon the family and the local community is considered in detail plus the effect of employment at the mine on the Moorland's parishes.

Contents

Part 1: The Labour Process at Ecton Mine

1. Male working patterns at Ecton, 1768-1779

2. Women and children at Ecton Mine

3. Ecton and the family economy

Part 2

4. Ecton workers in a peasant society

5. Moorland women: their economic contribution

6. Bastardy among Ecton workers and others, 1760-1830

7. Population growth and migration, 1750-1812

8. Conclusion

Landmark will publish this impressive work subject to sufficient demand. It is approximately 130-140,000 words in length. The price will depend on the quantity printed, but will be about £19.95

246x174mm, approx 256pp, hardback

If you are interested please contact Landmark Collector's Library by phone (01335) 347349, Fax (01335) 347303 or e-mail landmark@clara.net
We will send you further details and an order form in due course.

Landmark Collector's Library, 12 Compton, Ashbourne, Derbyshire DE6 1DA, UK